Privatisation: sell off or sell out?

Dr Bob Walker is a Professor of Accounting at the University of Sydney, and is well known for his contributions to reform of accountability arrangements in both the private and public sectors. He is a third generation chartered accountant. He has served as chairman of the Australian Shareholders' Association, and from 1995–1999 was chairman of the NSW Council on the Cost of Government, a standing audit commission on NSW finances. He is currently chairman of a state-owned corporation.

Betty Con Walker is an economist, with experience in both the private and public sectors. She worked for some years at CSR Ltd and served on various government advisory agencies before joining the NSW Premier's Department, followed by NSW Treasury. She has worked with various governments, including four years as a financial adviser and spokeswoman for a former NSW Premier and Treasurer.

Bob Walker & Betty Con Walker

PRIVATISATION
Sell off or sell out?

The Australian experience

ABC BOOKS

Published by ABC Books for the
AUSTRALIAN BROADCASTING CORPORATION
GPO Box 9994 Sydney NSW 2001

Copyright © Bob Walker and Betty Con Walker 2000

First published 2000
Reprinted July 2006

All rights reserved. No part of this publication may be reproduced, stored in a retrieval system or transmitted in any form or by any means, electronic, mechanical, photocopying, recording or otherwise, without the prior written permission of the Australian Broadcasting Corporation.

National Library of Australia
Cataloguing-in-Publication entry

Walker, R. G. (Robert Graham)
Privatisation: sell off or sell out?
Bibliography.
Includes index.
ISBN 0 7333 0797 3
I. Privatisation—Australia—Evaluation. 2. Government ownership—Australia. 3. Australia—Economic policy—1990- . I. Con Walker, Betty. II. Australian Broadcasting Corporation. III. Title.
338.9250994

Designed and set in 11/13 Sabon by
Midland Typesetters, Maryborough, Victoria
Printed and bound in Australia by Griffin Press, Adelaide

2 4 5 3

To our parents

We owe them everything

Contents

1 **Introduction** 1
Politicians have let us down 4
Public servants have let us down 6
Failure of parliamentary oversight 7
Consequences 8
Alternative approaches: A better way 13

2 **Sale of the Decade** 17
Privatisation by level of government 18
Privatisation by sector 18
Privatisation by value 19
Privatisation by type of sale 19
Privatisations completed 20
Privatisations announced but not completed 23
Transfer of wealth 24
What's next? 25
Potential sales of government trading enterprises 26
Emphasis may shift from 'sales' to 'outsourcing' or 'franchising' 31
Privatisation in stages? 34

3 **Touting Privatisation** 37
Crisis in government finances 39
Claims:
'The proceeds of privatisation could reduce the budget deficit' 42
'The proceeds of privatisation could reduce government debt' 48
'The proceeds of privatisation could reduce the burden of interest costs as a result of a reduction in debt' 58
'The proceeds of privatisation by reducing debt will maintain (or improve) our credit rating and keep interest costs down' 59

Investing in other things   63
Claims:
    'The proceeds of privatisation could be used by governments to do things sooner'   63
    'The proceeds of privatisation could be spent on alternative ventures'   67
Reducing risk   70
Claim:
    'The sale of government trading enterprises would avoid involvement in risky business'   70
Increasing efficiency/Reducing costs   75
Claim:
    'Privatisation is necessary because government trading enterprises are inefficient and more efficient private sector firms can provide the same services at lower cost'   75
Selling like the rest   77
Claims:
    'The sale of a government trading enterprise is necessary because part of it has already been sold'   77
    'The sale of a government trading enterprise is necessary because the industry is privatised in other countries'   78
Selling before the price falls   80
Claim:
    'The sale of a government trading enterprise is necessary because if it isn't sold now, its price will fall'   80
Summary   82

4   Government Trading Enterprises Have Been Undervalued   84
Assessing the case for privatisation   86
How 'GTE accounting' differs from private sector accounting   87
How efficient are Australia's GTEs?   91
Initial analyses of Steering Committee on National Performance Monitoring of Government Trading Enterprises   95
Efforts to standardise GTE accounting   96
Impact of accounting methods on reported profits of GTEs   97
Profitability of GTEs—using private sector accounting   104

Understatement of GTE profits 109
How can the performance of GTEs be assessed? 112
Effect of capital structure on reported profits of GTEs 116
Profits versus dividends 117
Postscript 118

5 **To Sell or not to Sell: Financial Implications** 121
Analysis of cash flows 122
'Modelling' the privatisation decision 128
Retention value 129
Proceeds of sale 129
Implications of analysis 136
Estimating retention values—in practice 140
Critical assumptions about 'the cost of capital' 143

6 **Contracting Out/Outsourcing** 144
Governments can't do everything, and nor should they try 144
Times (and markets) change—but sometimes, the public sector doesn't 145
The rhetoric of outsourcing 148
Steering not rowing 150
The hit-or-miss way some governments have gone about outsourcing 153
Misinformation about the benefits of outsourcing 157
Shortcomings in public sector management information systems don't help 161
Financial analysis and accounting distortions 165
Application to the public sector 165
The outsourcing decision—financial considerations 169
Flaws in some government-issued guidelines on outsourcing 172
Non-financial considerations 176
Public service pensions and outsourcing 180
What lies ahead? 182

7 **Private Sector Infrastructure Development** 189
Private sector use of 'financial engineering' 189
The role of the Loan Council 190
Finding ways around the global limits 191
How the Loan Council gave the game away 195
Further erosion of accountability 199

Privatisation through off-budget financing of
  infrastructure projects   202
BOOT schemes can be highly expensive   203
The period of BOOT schemes is getting longer and
  longer   208
Off-balance sheet financing arrangements affect urban
  planning   212
The extent of off budget financing arrangements   212
Back-door financing avoids accountability to parliament
  and the public   213
Disclosure of contract summaries?   218
Reforms needed to restore accountability   221

8   **Australia's Worst Privatisations   224**
    Loss of value to the public sector   224
        CSL Ltd   224
        Telstra   225
    Loss of services to the community   229
        Commonwealth Bank   229
        Housing Loans Insurance Corporation   230
    Loss of commercial and social opportunities   233
        Telstra   234
        CSL Ltd   234
    Badly handled privatisations   240
        Intimidation to prevent public debate: HLIC   240
        Undermining value: ANL   242
        High transaction costs: GIO   247
        Eroding investor protections: GIO   251
        Poorly designed sale arrangements: Pipeline
          Authority   257
        Sale at any price: State Bank of New South
          Wales   265
    Wooden spoon award: Australia's worst
      privatisation   274

9   **A Better Way**   276
       Debate about the role of government   276
       More careful and skilful analysis   282
       Improved accountability for the use of public resources   285
       Fostering the values of public service   292
       Better-qualified people   295
       Separating players from score keepers   298
       Final comment   299

Appendix to Chapter 5

A note on the concept of 'cost of capital'   300

References   322

Index   331

1

Introduction

DURING THE 1980s and 1990s, the Australian public sector went through unprecedented turmoil. The last two decades have seen major changes in the way government operates—largely through the impact of privatisation in its various forms—yet there has been minimal public debate about the rationale for these changes, and the likely effect on the role of the public sector in contemporary society.

There have been some spirited arguments about the case for selling or retaining the latest candidate for privatisation. We've seen debates about whether governments should sell off banks, insurance companies, airports, gaming, electricity generators and distributors, water businesses, and lately, telephony. Some years ago, there were arguments about the merits of outsourcing hospital and school cleaning, road maintenance, data processing, and the management of jails. Some have questioned the rationale for having the private sector build and manage core business activities—like main roads, hospitals, or water treatment plants.

But public debates about the privatisation of one or other business or activity have inevitably focused on the immediate impact of that sale and have usually overlooked larger issues, such as:

What businesses should governments be in?
or
What sort of things do we want our governments to do?
or
How do we want our governments to operate?

Within narrowly focused debates about the merits of privatisation, three major themes have been evident. In one sense, all suggest major issues—except that they all are presented as self-evident answers. Perhaps they should be restated as 'claims'. Those three themes (or claims) are:

Claim 1: that the public sector should be smaller;

Claim 2: that governments should get out of activities which are 'properly' the domain of the private sector.

Claim 3: that privatisation is needed to reduce public sector debt.

This book examines these claims in some detail. But one point must be made at once. Many of the arguments of the style that 'public sector is bad' and 'private sector is good'—and vice versa—are founded on ideology rather than evidence and analysis.

Take the claim that there is a 'need' for smaller, leaner government. That claim has often been associated with a subtext that 'the public sector is inefficient' while 'the private sector is efficient'. It is easy to make such claims on the basis of ideological predispositions. It is also easy to suggest reasons why this might be so: for example, it may be claimed that individuals in the private sector face incentives to perform more efficiently than public servants. But it is harder to assemble evidence to demonstrate that the private sector is more efficient than the public sector, and in the few instances that such a task has been attempted, the findings were case-specific. Certainly there is little evidence to explain why the private sector may be more efficient than the public sector in some situations, but not in others.

Many who claim that 'the public sector is inefficient' are often generalising from casual (and thoughtless) observations. A common example concerns sightings of a group of labourers, most of whom are leaning on shovels rather than vigorously digging trenches to repair gas or water mains. Experience suggests that even the young and fit find it hard to dig trenches for more than a few hours at a stretch, even when working in teams, one using a pick, the other a shovel. Middle-aged labourers might find it harder. Yet the chance observation is interpreted as shirking and as evidence that the private sector could do better. Maybe it could, but private sector employers usually employ apprentices to dig ditches, and few have to hand-dig trenches day after day. The critics don't stop to think about the circumstances under which the community comes to employ middle-aged labourers to do hard and dirty work. They certainly don't reflect on the circumstances in which those men, many of migrant origin, found themselves in such jobs. And they certainly don't speculate about how they would go, themselves, at the business end of a shovel.

Conversely, some of the defenders of the public sector are just as guilty of ideological reactions. Some even convey the simplistic notion that any attack on the performance of the public sector, or

Introduction

any change in the role of the public sector, is inevitably 'bad'. If a welfare agency decides to stop providing a particular service and to fund a non-government organisation to engage in that work on its behalf, the response of public zealots may well be that this is 'bad', simply because it diminishes the role of the public sector. To our way of thinking, a better test would be to ask: what does this mean for the clients? Will they get better service at the same (or reduced) cost?

The fact is that there have been very few efforts to explore these issues in a systematic and rigorous fashion.

Even so, in the face of claims about the need to have a smaller government, or a differently focused public sector, we ask: What are the facts? Where is the supporting evidence?

Sadly, it seems that political debate—like fashions in clothing—often echoes overseas experiences. There have been successful political campaigns in other developed Western countries, based on slogans about 'smaller government', or 'public sector inefficiency', or the 'need to reduce debt', and some of these campaign ideas have been shamelessly recycled in Australia.

The idea that governments should be 'smaller' was articulated (if not scripted) by former US President Ronald Reagan. The idea that governments should get out of certain activities was promoted by former British Prime Minister Margaret Thatcher, who was in a better position than Reagan to promote the idea that privatisation would enable reduction in public sector debt. The Reagan-Bush administrations presided over the most massive blow-out in government debt in the history of the USA. When ideas about smaller government, public sector inefficiency and debt reduction were echoed by Australian politicians, few commentators paused to consider whether these claims were actually relevant to Australian conditions—or made good financial sense.

Let us note (with resigned understanding rather than criticism) that many of the advocates of privatisation are from the ranks of individuals within the financial services industry. Arguably these people had knowledge and expertise to comment on these matters. As such, they also (directly and indirectly) stand to gain if governments pursue privatisation. The advocates are often merchant bankers, lawyers, accountants, stockbrokers and a collection of 'consultants' and lobbyists—all of whom might expect to benefit from advisory work, in 'preparing' agencies for corporatisation, in drafting plans for privatisation, in compiling prospectuses or offer documents for trade sales, and from commissions on public offerings and the subsequent trade in newly-listed securities. Some businesses stand to profit if governments allow them to build, own and operate newly-constructed tollroads or hospitals.

It could be argued that these involvements by advocates of privatisation involve a conflict of interest—maybe so. In light of recent experience, probably yes. But expertise should not disqualify anyone from participating in public debate. And, let's face it, the political process largely involves individuals promoting self-interest. However, some of these 'experts' have engaged in advocacy of outsourcing or privatisation that has ranged from shoddy to downright dishonest. Arguably, the effect of their actions was to damage the national interest.

In wartime, actions which damage the national interest are labelled 'treason'. What term shall we use to describe selfish advocacy of actions which may financially privilege some while damaging the economic interests of the community as a whole? If 'economic treason' is too strong a term to use about the pursuit of self-interest in this context—after all, some may truly believe in what they are doing—how about 'economic vandalism'?

Politicians have let us down

Australia's political leadership has failed to articulate a clear rationale about the role of government. If the role of government is to be reduced, why is that so? What should be left? Is there a case for expanding the role of government in areas where the private sector has failed to deliver services, ensure equal access to information so that markets can work, or control damage to the natural environment?

A more challenging question: what criteria should governments use to determine what activities should be ruled in or ruled out as part of the role of the public sector?

None of these questions have been debated or made explicit. The closest most politicians have come to any form of intellectual engagement about these issues has been to argue for and against privatisation of the latest target—or to criticise the activities of predecessors. Governments have 'done' (or debated) banks, airports, gaming, data processing, toll roads; and the management of jails; the debate has got particularly sticky when it came to telecommunications and electricity generation or distribution and gas in Victoria; and the debate has just started about control of water and waste water systems. The aftermath of the losses or failures of enterprises like the state-owned banks in New South Wales, South Australia or Victoria, not to mention the activities of WA Inc, seemed to be a consensus that the role of government was not trying to 'pick winners'. Yet almost a debate later, those lessons seem to be forgotten as governments subsidise or invest in projects in the name of 'economic development'.

In short, the Australian community has yet to be presented with

Introduction

a clear rationale for determining what sorts of things governments should do, and what they should avoid.

The community has inherited a set of arrangements whereby governments provide a range of services and subsidies—not all of which can be easily justified. Governments have also established agencies which are mainly funded through charges for services—the so-called 'government trading enterprises' (GTEs).[1] Many of these GTEs (notably in the areas of banking, insurance, and electricity generation and distribution) have been prime targets for privatisation, and many are already in private ownership. Yet while some governments have downsized departments or sold-off GTEs, political leaders have failed to present an overall vision for government in the second millennium.

Moreover, politicians have failed to demand, or present, a reasoned analysis of sustainable financial policies (e.g. what will happen if the proceeds of sale of profitable government trading enterprises are spent on short-term projects or non-revenue earning infrastructure?). Politicians have failed to present systematic arguments and opportunities for debate on the merits of reducing public sector activity. They have blindly accepted the advocacy of a loose alliance of far right economists, business interests, consultants, lobbyists—all united by self-interest.

However, some politicians who have played a crucial role in promoting privatisation are less deserving of criticism. Why? Because few politicians have training in accounting, economics or finance. Those who do are rarely given responsibility for economic portfolios. Perhaps it is because they know too much to sound convincing. Perhaps they are unable to simplify issues in the way that the politics demands.

This lack of economic expertise in the ranks of politicians may be a source of concern given the magnitude of the decisions they may be taking—decisions which can affect the lives of thousands of employees and involve the sale of great enterprises worth billions of dollars. It is rather chastening to reflect on the comments of one

---

1 The term 'government trading enterprises' (or 'GTEs') is used throughout this book. International statistical standards refer to 'public trading enterprises', and establish tests for identifying PTEs. Data published by the Australian Bureau of Statistics follows these conventions. For most purposes, the terms 'GTE' and 'PTE' may be taken as synonyms. However, many governments refer to agencies as GTEs (or even 'government *business* enterprises') on the basis that these agencies have been directed to charge for services and act in a commercial manner. Since some of these GTEs (such as internal audit bureaus, or departments of 'public works' or 'administrative services') derive the bulk of their revenues from other government departments, which in turn are primarily funded by allocations of revenues derived from tax revenues, they would not be classified as PTEs for statistical purposes.

senior Coalition politician. When he was a state Premier and Treasurer, he would avoid answering financial questions by replying 'I know my limitations'. Now he is overseeing the privatisation of some of the country's largest enterprises, and oversighting the process of deciding which brokers and advisers might earn tens, or even hundreds, of millions of dollars from handling the sale of GTE shares to the public.

Politicians are largely dependent on advice from the public service. At the same time, some politicians may well want to be surrounded by those who give them the kind of advice they like to hear. (Again, that comment is offered in a spirit of tolerance and understanding. We admire some politicians, especially those consumed with the desire to make the world a better place.)

With rare exceptions, the political process has also been at fault. Parliaments have failed to demand a full analysis of the pros and cons of privatisation (though in one rare example where they did, media pressure seems to have compelled independent politicians to fall into line before they had really studied the report). Merchant bankers and lawyers have persuaded politicians that contracts for the outsourcing of infrastructure construction contained 'intellectual property' that deserved to be protected—even though the material was hardly novel, and much was already in the public domain. This enabled governments to protect these contracts from parliamentary scrutiny (and helped big legal firms to charge multi-million dollar fees for new contracts by adapting text already on their word processors). One parliament (Victoria) has even passed legislation exempting these arrangements from Freedom of Information legislation.

Public servants have let us down

The public service—the 'system' (and those responsible for maintaining the standards of public service)—has also let us down.

There are a lot of myths about the public service. Some nostalgia buffs have promoted the 'ideal' of the Westminster tradition, and promoted the myth that senior public servants used to give the government of the day independent advice without fear or favour. Maybe some did (and still survived). Even so, it is likely that, in decades past, the open and critical expression of views within bureaucracies was hardly encouraged.

Leaving history aside, arguably the current decade has seen the worst politicisation of the public service. There has been a culture change, of sorts. It is most clearly evident in the way that incoming governments make new appointments of favoured candidates to senior positions. It is also reflected in the subtle resistance of some past appointees to the initiatives of incoming governments, or failure (in seemingly innocent omissions) to take initiatives in anticipation of potential problems. For the most part, many in the public service are intent on 'survival' at all costs. Public servants are wary of both ministers and chief executive officers. Any advice that may be unpopular is often suppressed, or buried within documents so that the authors can always say 'we did bring this to your attention'.

Those public servants who work hard and think about what they are doing and take initiatives are also taking risks. If you don't do anything, you don't make mistakes. Indeed, as we came to the end of the 1990s, the culture of 'survival' seemed to be the dominant shared value of senior administrators.

In that setting, outspoken opposition from public servants to privatisation or contracting out has been an extremely high-risk activity. One cannot know what has been said between chief executive officers and ministers, but public documents reflect the way that the public service in some jurisdictions has fallen into line. Guidelines on how to assess the merits of privatisation (or 'contracting out') have been muddled and technically flawed. Some sets of guidelines include sensible analyses on one page, but offer ideological statements or political slogans on another.

The muddled thinking reflected in some government publications—or even tender documents for proposed asset sales—also suggests another explanation for past behaviour. The public service is not really equipped to analyse the financial implications of privatisation or contracting out. Recruitment practices have tended to encourage promotion within the system—regardless of whether favoured applicants have experience, relevant training or skills. In some measure, this reflects the insecurities of those senior financial officers who lack the qualifications and skills required of their private sector counterparts. The end result has been that the public service does not always recruit the best and the brightest in the areas of financial administration.

Failure of parliamentary oversight

The traditional 'Westminster' system of parliamentary oversight of public sector expenditure evolved at a time when governments only spent money from taxes. The whole apparatus of 'budgets', budget speeches, budget debates, and appropriation bills was developed at a time when the British parliament had seized control of the public purse from the monarchy, and was concerned to ensure that the taxes raised from the populace were only spent on those matters approved by the parliament.

In the mid nineteenth century, governments didn't run

businesses, and didn't raise revenue from those businesses. The great parliamentarians of the time did not consider how parliament might oversight the spending of moneys raised by government trading enterprises. Yet the Westminster system of parliamentary accountability remains today—even though government 'budgets' can be significantly affected (if not distorted) by transactions involving GTEs. Some of those transactions involve the payment of dividends from profits, or 'interest' on 'loans'. Other transactions involve dividends in the form of returns of capital. Others involve sale of assets to GTEs, with the proceeds of sale being recorded in cash-based budgets as 'revenues'. The extreme case sees government cash-based budgets being sweetened by the proceeds of sale of GTEs to private businesses or private shareholders.

Consequences

Privatisation through the sale of Australian government businesses since 1990 has generated proceeds of over $95 billion—equivalent to over $13,500 per household. This figure only refers to the full or partial sale of government businesses. It does not include the sale of individual assets such as land and buildings; nor does it include the value of private sector involvement in public infrastructure, nor the value of services outsourced.

While the extent of privatisation through sale of businesses is easy to identify, the extent of the involvement of private sector firms in infrastructure projects is harder to quantify after changes in Loan Council reporting requirements. Likewise, while some governments have token reporting requirements relating to sums paid to *consultants*, these do not cover sums paid to *contractors*.

Key elements of the advocacy of privatisation have been crude appeals to flawed notions of financial management. The community has been subjected to a series of simple, repeated messages:

Debt is bad.
Debt imposes costs on future generations.
Governments should reduce debt.
Privatisation will reduce debt.
The public sector is too big.
The public sector is inefficient.
The private sector is more efficient than the public sector.
Privatisation will reduce the size of the public sector.
Privatisation will lead to increases in efficiency.

It must be recognised that privatisation has drastically changed the social and political landscape in Australia. It has:

Introduction

- **produced massive wealth transfers within the community**—shifting wealth from the community as a whole ('government') to those within the community who can afford to hold shares in listed companies, or (often more significantly) engaging in little publicised deals with other companies in which members of the public cannot invest;
- **conferred privileges on insiders**—ex-politicians or ex-public servants who had privileged access to commercial information—who were able to exploit their knowledge, contacts and experience to make super-profits from buying businesses or contracting to supply services to government;
- **often led to loss of services to the community**—services which had been delivered by government-owned businesses after the 'market' had failed to provide those services;
- **led to loss of jobs in government**—jobs which were not necessarily replaced by similar jobs in the private sector. While privatisation is not the only source of downsizing, it seems noteworthy that in the federal government, more than 100,000 jobs have been lost (equivalent to around one in three public servants) since the Coalition came to office in 1996;
- **led to spurious claims about savings to the taxpayer**—the apparent savings from downsizing have been substantially offset by retrenchment payments and by the fact that some former employees were re-hired as 'consultants' at much higher fees. Added costs have been incurred as a result of the loss of 'corporate memory'. Stories abound of consultants wasting months to discover facts which would have been obvious to longterm employees;
- **risked the marginalisation of rural communities**—through a reduction in services such as the closure of government offices in regional centres, or loss of access to rail freight, or entire rail services. Plainly, governments were not alone in undertaking these cost-cutting endeavours. Some differential treatment of city and country was probably inevitable, given the pace of change in technology. However, the social impact of the closure or downsizing of a branch office is more strongly felt in small communities than in large cities, and can have a multiplier effect on local economies;
- **seen the dismantling of some government-owned state-based monopolies**—in the provision of services (such as electricity);
- **contributed to the formation of more powerful, national oligopolies**—as newly privatised firms seek economies of scale through amalgamations, or the integration of services providing energy in different forms (electricity and gas);
- **arguably, contributed to environmental damage**—as newly-privatised agencies seek to expand their market share by

reducing prices and hence increasing consumption of electricity from coal-fired generators;
- **put a brake on (or even reversed) a trend towards more open and accountable government**—as private commercial interests have argued for exemptions from public scrutiny of documentation regarding 'build own operate transfer' (BOOT) schemes, and similar arrangements, and some governments have formally exempted these documents from the purview of Freedom of Information legislation;
- **eroded institutional arrangements for public sector accountability**—as an increasing proportion of public sector financing activities is not subject to parliamentary scrutiny through the formal Budget process, while an increasing proportion of service delivery is left in the hands of private contractors whose work may not be reviewable by public sector auditors. Moreover, in some jurisdictions, public trading enterprises have been permitted to outsource their audit function; in others, the Auditor-General's office has been required to compete with private audit firms for the provision of audit services. Either way, such steps both diminish the role of the office of Auditor-General, and compel a reduced standard of public sector auditing (which traditionally has involved reporting of findings about waste and inefficiency or weaknesses in internal controls—matters which private sector auditors do not view as issues to be investigated in a financial statement audit, or as matters to be referred to in their formal, published reports);
- **subverted the planning process**—by promoting infrastructure projects (such as tollways) which could be readily-packaged as BOOT schemes, ahead of other projects (such as investment in education or public transport) which might produce a higher ratio of community benefits to costs;
- **significantly eroded regulatory protections for investors in the Australian securities market**—as governments were allowed to engage in pre-prospectus advertising, to undertake public offerings without making prospectus information readily available to potential subscribers, and to stampede first-time investors into subscribing to new issues without even the opportunity to review documents explaining the potential risks of such investments. Government activities in promoting public offerings of shares have re-shaped industry practice, for the worse.

Privatisation might also be seen as having changed society in positive ways, through

- **an extension of share ownership**—the securities market is a major vehicle for marshalling savings for new investment, and greater

Introduction

depth in the securities market is a positive development for the Australian economy. Australia's large privatisation program in the 1990s has led to an increase in the number of people directly holding shares. According to the Australian Stock Exchange, the proportion of adults directly owning shares has risen from 10 per cent in 1991 to almost 32 per cent in 1998 (ASX, *Share Ownership Survey for 1994*, and *1998 Update*).

If individuals who hold shares indirectly through insurance and superannuation funds are included, then the proportion of adults owning shares has risen from 15.5 per cent in 1991 to over 40 per cent in 1998—though the latter development has been affected by the introduction of compulsory contributions by employers to employee superannuation schemes. These figures would be higher following the sale of the second tranche of Telstra shares in October 1999.

Not everyone sees this growth in numbers of shareholders as a great benefit. The fact that millions of Australians now own at least a few shares in a formerly government-owned business (and have made a few dollars in the process) does not mean that privatisation has produced equitable outcomes, let alone that it has cured social ills. As one contributor to the letters page of the *Sydney Morning Herald* wrote:

> At birth in May 1957, I held a stake in the State Bank, GIO, Qantas, Australian Airways, Telstra, and the Commonwealth Bank, but in 40 years my birthright has been frittered away by various governments, and my pension and future medical bills may not be paid.
>
> Prudent MPs maintained these institutions through wars and depression, but their successors squandered them for the 'Budget bottom line'. They diminish the commonwealth, and concentrate riches in privileged hands (*SMH*, 24/5/97).

- **the reduction of governments' costs in some areas**—in some instances, private sector providers may have genuinely done the same (or better) job, for less money. There is a concern that the use of contractors has enabled government to cut levels of service, without being held responsible for these post-privatisation outcomes. However, these monetary savings have not (as yet) led to significant reductions in either taxes, or the costs incurred by the community when purchasing services from government-owned businesses.

The promotion of privatisation has created a climate in which few governments are prepared to seriously contemplate new public sector initiatives, even where there is evidence of market failure.

Governments have become very cautious, and have found it safer to rely on the 'market' to allocate resources and deliver services—sometimes in areas where government intervention, properly managed, might have led to more equitable or more efficient outcomes.

For example: governments have tended to allow private operators to provide bus transport services to newly-developed suburbs on the outskirts of major cities. On the face of it, the government is leaving the provision of these bus services to the private sector. Yet, in substance, these services are largely dependent on the subsidies paid for transporting children to schools. One suspects that reliance on private operators, and a system of backdoor subsidies, insulates governments from community demands for higher standards of transport services in these areas. A notable exception was the November 1999 announcement that the NSW government was acquiring the business of a western suburbs bus operator to provide concessional fares, and upgrade service standards to the level provided in the other regions of Sydney by government-operated buses.

It is of course virtually impossible to assess the extent to which changing views about the role of the public sector have led government to avoid new ventures.

Probably some initiatives were well left alone. Few would suggest that any government should repeat the disastrous forays of the Cain government in Victoria, which set out to promote economic development throughout the state, but ended up funding high-risk ventures in metropolitan Melbourne. The NSW government invested in the Eastern Creek Raceway and the Hungarian TAB. Given the experience of the South Australian, Victorian and NSW governments in owning regional banks, few would commend that form of investment—at least while banks are poorly managed and poorly oversighted by state Treasuries.

But, at the end of the day, it seems that history will regard the 1990s in particular as a sorry period in Australia's social and economic development.

It was a period in which many academic commentators referred to the 'new public sector management', when old-style approaches to public administration (in Australia and elsewhere) were supplanted by 'economic rationalism' and 'managerialism'. In truth, some of the changes occurring within the public service were merely catching up with management practices which had been standard in the private sector for decades. There is merit in:

- articulating the objectives of an organisation, and seeking to monitor performance in achieving those objectives;

Introduction

- reviewing specific activities to see whether they are delivering what was promised;
- spelling out the responsibilities of those filling different positions within organisations; and
- holding individuals (particularly senior managers) accountable for their performance.

In practice, a group of advisers and consultants managed to capture the imagination of a group of senior public servants and politicians to create upheaval in the management of the Australian public sector and the wider economy. And they all let us down.

The 1990s was a period in which any form of change in the management of the public sector was called a 'reform' even though the evidence quickly accumulated that pursuing the latest management fad usually did not work. Throughout the period, there was a lack of attention to some of the basic elements of financial management. Rather, the self-styled reformers relied on crude instruments to drive efficiencies—such as unrealistic rate of return targets, or the separation of 'funders' and 'providers', or requirements for activities to be outsourced.

It was a period in which a generation which had enjoyed the benefit of free health services, free public education, and free care for the aged, suddenly decided that 'the user should pay'.

It was a period which saw a major change in the employment practices of government agencies. There was a time when the availability of jobs 'on the railways' or 'with the water board' (or 'the council') was a form of social safety net.

Government bodies employed large numbers of manual or clerical workers, sometimes not very productively. The management of large workforces may have left a lot to be desired. However, even with better management, over-manning arrangements were not sustainable, since the tasks performed by clerks or ticket sellers could be undertaken at far lower cost by fewer staff, using established and well-tried technology. The work of draftsmen could be undertaken at lower cost using computer-aided design.

It does not necessarily follow that it is fair or equitable for governments to undertake wholesale retrenchments without exploring other options. These can include giving some long-term employees a 'soft landing', by allowing them to work until retirement (with their positions being eliminated at that time); or establishing formal programs for the retraining and re-deployment of redundant staff. Many employees have been happy to 'take redundancy', and start a new career. The hardest hit have been those in their late 40s or 50s, without readily-marketable skills. A 'whole of government' approach could involve a proactive search for alternative avenues of probationary employment for displaced staff in other agencies, as an alternative to retrenchment.

Ironically, while governments have slashed staff numbers in public trading enterprises through a combination of downsizing and privatisation, numbers of staff in general government agencies have actually increased in recent years. Between 1990–99, 'general government' employment increased by 12 per cent in NSW, 16 per cent in Western Australia and 23 per cent in Queensland. Victorian 'general government' employment fell by 7 per cent over the decade, but actually increased 4 per cent in the last three years of the Kennett government. The biggest job cuts were in the Commonwealth public sector, which shed 25 per cent of its 'general government' staff since 1990, with most of the cuts occurring since the Coalition government came to office in 1996 (*Data purchased from Australian Bureau of Statistics*, 1/12/99).

The public sector should not act as a sheltered workshop. But the fact remains that the last two decades have seen the public sector's role as an avenue of last-resort employment removed. Today many school leavers are likely to have trouble finding *any* job. After trying, and failing, many just find it easier to take the dole. Arguably, both the taxpayer and the community at large are better served by the creation of more opportunities for productive employment.

In some areas of Australia, we are starting to see second-generation unemployment. The social problems which flow from this, and the disenchantment of others (who see themselves as working hard and hence subsidising those who do not) are coming to the surface. Many would argue that the need to do something to reduce unemployment is a pressing responsibility, and priority, for government.

Yet to some politicians and bureaucrats, public sector budget results are not a means but an end. They argue that government spending (whatever it may be as a proportion of Gross Domestic Product) has to be reduced. They point to the consequences of budget deficits on government debt.

Privatisation offered the promise of reducing the interest costs borne by current generations, by reducing government debt. It mattered little that the sale of government assets meant that fewer services would be available for the next generation, or that the next generation might have to pay for services which had previously been either cheap or free.

There has been an alarmingly selfish streak in the arguments of some who promote smaller government and believe that privatisation is one way to achieve this end. They also have little patience with the needs of the aged or the infirm or the disabled, and want to dismantle arrangements for social welfare. They have promoted or supported the sell-off of government businesses in order to reduce debt, and hence the finance costs currently payable on that debt.

In the latter respect, the socially selfish may have erred since the sale of profitable businesses means a loss of revenues. It may take a decade or more before the impact of those lost revenues is discernible in the finances of Australian governments—probably at a time when newly-acquired infrastructure, partly bought with the proceeds of privatisation, is in need of upgrading or repair. Because all governments have indulged in privatisations to some extent, the overall impact may be difficult to discern. But Victoria, which has sold the most of any state, is likely to experience the greatest burdens.

The momentum for privatisation is such that one can only expect that control of more basic public utilities will fall into the hands of multi-national players, acting unashamedly in the interests of their majority (possibly foreign) shareholders. Tollroads will be controlled by local and foreign enterprises, which may have so expanded their network that motorists will have to pay several tolls to travel any significant distance. Different standards of health services will be available to those who can afford them, and those who cannot. The provision of education services may be further opened up to private entrepreneurs, with the consequence that access to higher education in particular will be open to two distinct groups: those who can afford to pay, and a much smaller cohort of students who are there on the basis of merit.

This is a sad but avoidable scenario, at least in part. There has to be a better way.

Alternative approaches: A better way

There is a need to rethink the case for government involvement in a range of activities. In fact, there is a need for governments to regularly reassess whether to sell assets in order to fund new capital projects, reduce debt, and meet the cash flow requirements of emergencies or unforeseen disasters. Governments should proactively seek to use contractual arrangements to secure the expertise of private firms.

There is a need to reassess whether the public sector really has the financial skills to analyse some complex financial transactions—and if not, how it can rapidly acquire those skills (through recruitment, training or contracting).

There is a need to rethink the role of parliament in scrutinising commercial transactions—some involving billions of dollars.

Some deals have often been handled by executive government, in private, with details of contracts involving taxpayers' money—our money—claimed to be 'commercially confidential'.

There is a need to reconsider the values which underpin public administration.

One manifestation of privatisation is contracting out. Another is the bringing in of the private sector to undertake major infrastructure development for the government (for example, freeway construction) under contracts where, in effect, the private sector may benefit from the government's coercive power of resumption of land/easements, plus establishment of regional monopolies (e.g. in transport). Finally, there is the manifestation preferred by these groups—that is, the sale of government trading enterprises.

As noted above, if one has some understanding of the incentives facing different stakeholders, one may have a better understanding of why they advocate certain things. Having made that point, then in the interests of full disclosure, it is as well to give some brief indication of the incentives facing the authors in writing this essay.

Not money. There's little reward in putting together a non-fiction book of this type.

Not ideology (at least of a compartmentalised party-political kind). The authors have nothing against private enterprise—far from it. One is a third generation chartered accountant, and former chairman of the Australian Shareholders' Association. He has devoted a fair amount of time trying to promote systems of regulation which work in the interests of individual investors. The other is an economist, who worked for more than a decade with a major corporation before a stint in the public sector, and lately works as a consultant to business. The authors are both self-confessed 'economic rationalists', who are appalled at how so much of the political debate about selling public assets and downsizing the public sector has been based on rhetoric, sloganeering and irrational, flawed financial analysis. They have been horrified at the way misleading descriptions of benefits of privatisation (e.g. reduction of debt, reduction of interest costs, preservation of credit ratings) have been repeated uncritically by the consultants, the public servants, the politicians and the financial press.

2

Sale of the Decade

THE SHEER SCALE of the sale of public assets demonstrates the enthusiasm with which governments in Australia pursued privatisation in the 1990s.

The sales data presented in this Chapter are confined to 'privatisations' in the sense of full or partial transfer of ownership of Commonwealth and state public assets to the private sector. This process refers to the sale of enterprises which are 'going concerns', and excludes the sale of individual assets, such as land and buildings. For example, it excludes the unprecedented level of property sales during the NSW Coalition's period in office from 1988 to 1995. In that period, the NSW Coalition government obtained over $4 billion from the sale of 'surplus' government properties.[1]

In brief:

- The 1990s have seen an increasing amount of privatisation in Australia. A similar trend is evident overseas. However, Australia has had one of the larger programs among Organisation for Economic Co-operation and Development (OECD) countries.
- In dollar terms, Australia's privatisations have been second only to the UK.
- As a percentage of Gross Domestic Product, Australia's privatisations have been second only to New Zealand.
- State and Commonwealth government privatisations in the 1990s have raised over $95 billion from sales.

---

1 To June 1991 the sale of 'surplus' government properties generated $2.2 billion (*1991–92 NSW Budget Paper No. 2*, p. 524). Comparable figures were not disclosed in later years' Budget Papers, but the NSW Public Sector Consolidated Statements reveal that sales of property, plant and equipment generated an additional $1.9 billion between July 1992 and June 1994.

- During the first half of 1999, Australia was the worldwide leader in both announced and completed privatisations. Australia led the world with 15.4 per cent of the worldwide market share (*Thomson Financial Securities Data*, 19/7/99).
- Privatisation has occurred in three main sectors—financial services, electricity and gas, and transport and communications.
- Assets have been mainly sold by public floats or through trade sales.

Privatisation by level of government

The first major Australian privatisation was the 1991 sale of the first tranche of shares in the Commonwealth Bank.

In the case of many government trading enterprises (GTEs), privatisation had been preceded by a phase of corporatisation under which they were required to:

- achieve certain commercial benchmarks;
- pay tax;
- borrow funds without a government guarantee;
- have any regulatory advantages removed.

Since 1990, sales of GTEs and other agencies owned by the Commonwealth totalled over $48 billion. Equivalent sales by state governments were nearly $47 billion.

Victoria, by far, dominated the states with sales valued at over $31 billion.

Privatisation by sector

Most Australian privatisations have been in public services such as electricity, communications, transport and financial services. Gambling agencies have also been sold by some states.

Privatisations of financial services agencies have included the Commonwealth Bank and three state banks in NSW, WA, and SA. The sale of the State Bank of Victoria is not included as a privatisation since it was sold to the Commonwealth Bank while it was in public hands. The Commonwealth Bank funded this purchase by its first share issue in 1991. Financial services privatisations have also included the sale of six state insurance offices.

In transport, privatisations have included Qantas, airports across Australia and the sale of the business units of Australian National Railways Corporation (except interstate track).

The communications sector was dominated by the part-sale of Telstra.

Sale of the Decade

Victoria sold its electricity generators and distributors and its gas distribution industry. South Australia has, in substance, sold the major part of its electricity industry (though the deal was structured as a 200 year lease).

Privatisation by value

The largest privatisations were the sale of 49.9 per cent of Telstra in two tranches for over $30 billion, followed by the sale of the Victorian electricity generators and distributors at $22.5 billion (this includes cash proceeds at the time of sale but does not include additional revenues from licensing and franchise fees—except for Loy Yang B). Next ranked were: sale of the Commonwealth Bank at $8.1 billion, Victoria's gas distributors at almost $6.3 billion, the state banks at $4.5 billion, airports at $4.1 billion, the distribution and retail arms of South Australia's electricity industry at $3.5 billion (through a 200 year lease), state insurance offices at $3.1 billion, West Australia's Dampier-Bunbury natural gas pipeline at $2.3 billion, and Qantas at $2.1 billion.

Privatisation by type of sale

Most sales of government agencies in Australia have been undertaken through:

- trade sales; and/or
- public floats or the public issue of equity.

Exceptions were a few small Commonwealth businesses which were employee/management buyouts.

Of the over $95 billion estimate of sales since 1990, trade sales raised $50 billion, while public floats raised over $45 billion.

The largest examples of trade sales were the Victorian and South Australian electricity companies, which went mainly to overseas companies.

The Reserve Bank has estimated that foreign interests were successful in a little over half (by value) of all trade sales.

The largest example of a public float was the sale in two stages of Telstra, which included sale of equity to individuals and to institutional investors, both domestic and foreign.

Qantas was privatised through a combination of trade sale and public float: a stake of 25 per cent was sold to British Airways, with the remainder offered later to individual investors.

Privatisations completed

A list of privatisations completed in Australia in the 1990s is shown below.

Table 2.1
PRIVATISATIONS IN AUSTRALIA (a)

	Proceeds $ million	Type of Sale	Year of Sale
COMMONWEALTH			
ADI	347	Trade	99/00
Aerospace Technologies of Australia	40	Trade	94/95
Airports:			
Adelaide and Parafield	362	Trade	97/98
Archerfield	3	Trade	97/98
Avalon Airport Geelong Limited	1.5	Trade	96/97
Brisbane	1 387	Trade	97/98
Canberra	66	Trade	97/98
Coolangatta	105	Trade	97/98
Darwin, Alice Springs, Tennant Creek	110	Trade	97/98
Hobart	36	Trade	97/98
Jandakot	7	Trade	97/98
Launceston	17	Trade	97/98
Melbourne	1 307	Trade	97/98
Moorabin	8	Trade	97/98
Mt Isa and Townsville	16	Trade	97/98
Perth	643	Trade	97/98
Auscript	1	Staff buyout	97/98
Aussat	504	Trade	91/92
Australian Airlines	400	Trade	92/93
Australian Industry Development Corporation	25	Float	89/90
Australian Industry Development Corporation	200	Trade	97/98
Australian Multimedia Enterprises Ltd	29	Trade	97/98
Australian National Railways Corporation	95	Trade	97/98
Commonwealth Serum Laboratories (CSL)	299	Float	93/94
Commonwealth Bank	1 311	Float	91/92
Commonwealth Bank	1 686	Float	93/94
Commonwealth Bank	3 390	Float	96/97
Commonwealth Bank	1 770	Float	97/98
Commonwealth Funds Management	63	Trade	96/97
DAS Business Units:			
Asset Services	19	Trade	97/98
Australian Operational Support Services	2	Trade	97/98
Australian Property Group	3	Trade	97/98
Centre for Environmental Management	0.01	Staff buyout	97/98
DAS Distribution	1	Staff buyout /trade	97/98
Dasfleet	408	Trade	97/98
Interiors Australia	0.1	Staff buyout	97/98
Works Australia	4	Trade	97/98

Sale of the Decade

	Proceeds $ million	Type of Sale	Year of Sale
Housing Loans Insurance Corporation	108	Trade	97/98
Moomba-Sydney Pipeline System	534	Trade	93/94
National Transmission Network (NTN)	650	Trade	98/99
Qantas	665	Trade	92/93
Qantas	1 450	Float	95/96
Shipping Businesses	21	Trade	98/99
Snowy Mountains Engineering Corporation	1	Staff buyout	93/94
Snowy Mountains Engineering Corporation	0.3	Staff buyout	94/95
Snowy Mountains Engineering Corporation	0.3	Staff buyout	95/96
Telstra	14 330	Float	97/98
Telstra	16 000	Float	99/00 00/01
Total Commonwealth	**48 426.31**		

NEW SOUTH WALES

Axiom Funds Management	240	Trade	96/97
Government Insurance Office	1 260	Float	92/93
NSW Grain Corporation	96	Trade	93/94
NSW Investment Corporation	60	Trade	89/90
Tab Ltd	937	Float	97/98
State Bank of NSW	527	Trade	94/95
Total New South Wales	**3 120**		

VICTORIA

Electricity Industry:

Citipower	1 575	Trade	95/96
Eastern Energy	2 080	Trade	95/96
Hazelwood/Energy Brix	2 400	Trade	96/97
Hume	8	Trade	98/99
Loy Yang A	4 746	Trade	96/97
Loy Yang B	544	Trade	92/93
Loy Yang B	1 150	Trade	97/98
Powercor	2 150	Trade	95/96
PowerNet	2 555	Trade	97/98
Solaris	950	Trade	95/96
Southern Hydro	391	Trade	97/98
United Energy	1 553	Trade	95/96
Victorian Electricity Metering	8	Trade	97/98
Victorian Network Switching Centre	8	Trade	98/99
Yallourn Energy	2 428	Trade	95/96

Gas (distribution) industry:

Westar/Kinetic	1 617	Trade	98/99
Multinet/Ikon	1 970	Trade	98/99
Stratus/Energy 21	1 670	Trade	98/99
Transmission Pipelines Australia	1 020	Trade	98/99

Other:

Aluvic	502	Trade	98/99
Bass (Ticket sales)	3	Trade	94/95

Privatisation

	Proceeds $ million	Type of Sale	Year of Sale
GFE (Gas & Fuel Exploration) Resources	56	Trade	95/96
Grain Elevators Board	52	Trade	94/95
Heatane Division of Gas & Fuel Corporation	130	Trade	92/93
Port of Geelong	51	Trade	95/96
Port of Portland	30	Trade	95/96
Portland Smelter Unit Trust	171	Trade	92/93
State Insurance Office	125	Trade	92/93
Tabcorp	609	Float	94/95
Victorian Plantations Corporation	550	Trade	98/99
V/Line Freight Corporation	163	Trade	98/99 95/96
Total Victoria	**31 265**		
QUEENSLAND			
Bank of Queensland (40%)	129	Float	99/00
Gladstone Power Station	750	Trade	93/94
State Gas Pipeline	163	Trade	96/97
Suncorp/Qld Industry Development Corp	698	Trade	96/97
Suncorp-Metway Ltd	610	Float	97/98
Suncorp-Metway Ltd	1 011	Float	98/99
TabQ	267	Float	99/00
Total Queensland	**3 628**		
SOUTH AUSTRALIA			
Austrust Trustees	44	Trade	94/95
Enterprise Investments	38	Trade	94/95
Etsa Power and Power Utilities	3 500	Trade (200 yr lease)	99/00
Forwood Products (Timber)	123	Trade	95/96
Island Seaway	2	Trade	94/95
Pipeline Authority of SA	304	Trade	94/95
Port Bulk Handling Facilities	18	Trade	97/98
Radio 5AA	8	Trade	96/97
SA Financing Trust	5	Trade	93/94
Sagasco	29	Trade	92/93
Sagasco	417	Trade	93/94
Samcor (Meatworks)	5	Trade	96/97
Sign Services	0.2	Trade	95/96
State Government Insurance Commission	175	Trade	95/96
State Bank of SA	10	Trade	94/95
State Bank of SA	720	Trade	95/96
State Chemistry Laboratories	0.3	Trade	95/96
State Clothing Corporation	1.4	Trade	95/96
Total South Australia	**5 399.9**		
WESTERN AUSTRALIA			
BankWest	900	Trade	95/96
Dampier-Bunbury Natural Gas Pipeline	2 303	Trade	97/98

Sale of the Decade

	Proceeds $ million	Type of Sale	Year of Sale
Healthcare Linen	9	Trade	96/97
State Government Insurance Office	165	Float	93/94
Total Western Australia	**3 377**		
TASMANIA			
State Insurance Office	42	Trade	93/94
Total Tasmania	**42**		
TOTAL STATE GOVERNMENTS	**46 832**		
TOTAL ALL GOVERNMENTS	**95 258**		

(a) 'Privatisation' in this table refers to the sale of government trading enterprises or business units, and does not include the sale of assets such as buildings, plant or equipment.

Sources: Reserve Bank of Australia, *Privatisations in Australia*, December 1997, and Reserve Bank of Australia, *Demutualisation in Australia*, January 1999; documents published on the internet by the Commonwealth Office of Asset Sales and IT Outsourcing; newpaper reports and journal articles. Where there are inconsistencies in data published by the Reserve Bank and other sources, the former have been preferred. Note that the Reserve Bank's data appear to reflect net proceeds in an individual year, without adjustment for vendors' subsequent outgoings as a consequence of guarantees or other contractual arrangements.

Privatisations announced but not completed

The sale figures outlined above will increase significantly when a number of transactions announced in 1999 are completed. These sales are expected to take the total figure for Australia to over $100 billion. Some of these are listed below.

Table 2.2
PRIVATISATIONS ANNOUNCED BUT NOT COMPLETED

	Estimated Proceeds $ million	Type of Sale	Year of Sale
COMMONWEALTH			
Removals Australia	n.a.	Trade	99/00
Sydney Airports Corp (Kingsford Smith, Bankstown, Hoxton Park, Camden Airports)	3 000	To be determined	To be determined
STATES			
South Australia			
Optima Energy	800	Trade	99/00
11 Ports	n.a.	Trade	99/00-00/01

Privatisation

	Estimated Proceeds $ million	Type of Sale	Year of Sale
Western Australia			
AlintaGas	1 000	Float 51%	99/00
		Trade 49%	00/01
Northern Territory			
Tab	10-20	Trade	99/00

n.a. – not available.

Transfer of wealth

Any sale which produces a massive profit to those with funds available for investment is effectively a transaction which is producing a loss to the broader community. Or, in the dry language preferred by financial economists, such transactions involve 'wealth transfers'.

An analysis of a *selection* of the country's privatisations in the last decade which resulted in the issue of shares suggests that post-issue profits to shareholders have to date amounted to over $48 billion. (There are some short-cuts in the calculations, since no allowance is made for inflation or general movements in the values of publicly traded securities since these sales, but the data are indicative.)

Table 2.3
TRANSFER OF WEALTH

Company	Seller	Price paid to Govt (a)	Value at 31/12/99	Profit to private sector
Telstra (b)	Commonwealth	$30.3b	$53.2b	$22.9b
CBA	Commonwealth	$ 8.2b	$23.7b	$15.5b
Qantas	Commonwealth	$ 2.1b	$ 4.6b	$ 2.5b
CSL	Commonwealth	$ 0.3b	$ 2.9b	$ 2.6b
Tabcorp	Victoria	$ 0.6b	$ 3.8b	$ 3.2b
Tab	NSW	$ 0.9b	$ 1.4b	$ 0.5b
BankWest	Western Australia	$ 0.9b	$ 2.0b	$ 1.1b
TOTAL		**$43.3b**	**$91.6b**	**$48.3b**

(a) Price paid for Telstra includes the instalment due in November 2000.
(b) Note that the value for Telstra is only for the 49.9% of issued shares—not all of Telstra. Telstra reached an all time high of $9.16 on 30 November 1999. At this price, the 49.9% listed shares would be valued at almost $59 billion resulting in profit to the private sector of over $28 billion.

Staunch advocates of privatisation might choose to interpret this increase in the value of former government enterprises as showing how businesses perform better when in private ownership. But this simple argument is hard to sustain when it is recognised that many of the corporations in the above list retained the same senior managers *after* privatisation.

It is widely accepted that initial privatisation offers are generally priced low because they have to succeed politically. Many buyers of shares are voters, and ministers will want them to succeed as shareholders so that they have goodwill towards the government.

There is no objective guide to value until the securities of privatised companies are traded on the sharemarket. However, recent research revealed that investors in private floats on average lose half their money after three years. In contrast, those who have invested in government floats have been big winners. Findings of the study (as released to the media) were that:

- government floats had outperformed the market by about 23 per cent over three years;
- private floats lost money over three years—an analysis of the performance of more than 250 private floats found they were 'the equivalent of throwing money down the well'. Private floats earned negative returns over each of the three years after listing, 'with a mean three-year average return of minus 51.6 per cent' (*Sunday Telegraph*, 27/6/99).

This confirms that sale of government businesses through public floats were generally at low prices. This in turn means that the sales involved 'wealth transfers' from the community as a whole to those elements of the community with the capacity to invest in the securities market.

There are no reasons to believe that the pricing of trade sales was any less generous to purchasers of those businesses.

What's next?

Residents of Sydney used to joke about salesmen who could sell you the Harbour Bridge. After the experience of the 1990s, that doesn't seem so funny. The sheer scale of the sales of public assets to date might suggest that there is little left to sell. Indeed, even before the 1999 Victorian election, major legal firms in Victoria were reported to be wondering how they might replace the income they had generated from Victoria's $31 billion privatisation program. One senior partner is reported to have lamented:

Privatisation

There's nothing obvious to replace it. Maybe Asia is the answer ... perhaps it will come from a range of areas, but nobody really knows (*Australian Financial Review—AFR—20/5/99*).

Yet many advocates of privatisation are unlikely to stop promoting the (supposed) merits of reducing the size of government, so long as there are fees to be earned. Indeed, to some, the privatisation process has barely started. The editor of the *Institute of Public Affairs Review*, Michael Warby, saw boundless opportunities for privatisation, explaining that

we haven't worked out a limit yet (*The Australian*, 27/4/98).

Yet since 1998 the political climate in Australia has changed, as political leaders have ruled out the privatisation of specific agencies. No Australian political leader has suggested a total ban on privatisations in all its forms—nor would that be sensible. On the other hand, no political leader has clearly articulated their vision as to the boundaries of the public sector—what governments should do, and what they should avoid (or divest).

Potential sales of government trading enterprises

It seems likely that, with some notable exceptions, privatisation through the *outright sale* of government trading enterprises may be less significant than other activities.

If the first round of privatisations in different jurisdictions involved some relatively uncontentious sales—notably banks, insurance companies and other businesses in the financial services industry—then the remaining candidates for sale include agencies whose sale might have been unthinkable, a decade ago. Most of the current potential targets are government trading enterprises directly engaged in providing basic essential services to the community.

Telecommunications

High on the list is the potential sale of the remaining 51 per cent of Telstra. Forget reassuring comments that the initial sale was not a problem because the Federal government would be retaining a majority interest. The government's determination to proceed to a full sale was confirmed in its 1999–2000 Budget. On 22 June 1999, one day after the Senate passed the sale of the second, 16.6 per cent tranche of Telstra shares, Prime Minister Howard announced:

We will keep trying because we think getting the rest sold will help retire debt. It will be hard but we will keep trying (*The Australian*, 23/6/99).

And on the day that the second tranche was floated Finance Minister Fahey stated:

Today marks the day the Government sets its sights on T3 because the benefits are clear (*The Australian*, 19/10/99).

This plan to sell the remainder of Telstra will not be without its difficulties, given the changed composition of the Senate in July 1999, and the strengthening reservations of the Prime Minister's Coalition partners from the National Party. However, some of the arguments for sale deserve close attention.

One argument, advanced by Treasurer Peter Costello and Communications Minister Richard Alston, claims that other comparable countries have transferred ownership of telecommunications completely into private hands. The facts do not support this claim. More on this in the next Chapter.

Another argument is that privatisation will produce better services. One example of this argument was provided by Prime Minister Howard who on 22 June 1999 asserted that voting against the privatisation of Telstra would prevent Alice Springs receiving SBS television programs. This was probably just a mistake. Warren Snowdon, the Labor member for the Northern Territory, was quick to point out that Alice Springs already gets SBS.

The 'better services' argument may also be contested by phone users, particularly in regional Australia, who have been complaining that cost-cutting by Telstra has resulted in fewer technicians available to fix faults. Indeed, on 27 September 1999, the Australian Communications Authority (ACA) announced an investigation into Telstra's service performance after the company had failed to meet minimum customer service guarantees. According to the ACA, the most significant performance result in relation to the fixed network was the continued degradation of service responsiveness by Telstra to customers seeking new connections in urban and major rural areas without infrastructure (*SMH*, 28/9/99). With full privatisation, many in country regions are afraid that they would face higher charges and poorer services as Telstra strives to boost profits and dividends for its private shareholders.

It seems remarkable that the Commonwealth government would be planning to sell-off its majority interest in telecommunications at the same time that the international securities market is bidding up telecommunications stocks to record levels—in recognition of the strategic significance of this industry in the 'information economy'. Provided majority government ownership is retained, Telstra is well placed to protect and advance the interests of the Australian community in this arena. Even so, more work needs to be done to establish service standards for consumers.

Water

Arguably the prime target of privatisation advocates is the water industry. To quote a business magazine:

> In Australia, investment bankers are salivating at the prospect of water privatisations. Many have hired specialists from the public sector to prepare them for when the lobbying intensifies ... (*BRW*, 20/4/98)

Why? Water is basic to life. Domestic demand for water services is largely inelastic—it is unaffected by changes in price. Water services can be very profitable—as evidenced from overseas experience. Much of Western Europe's water and sewerage has been privatised and the companies involved are making fat profits. The British lobby group Water Watch has claimed that shareholder dividends account for between 12 per cent and 42 per cent of water bills for ordinary customers (*BRW*, 20/4/98).

Some states have already privatised elements of their water businesses, or have commissioned reports to evaluate the impact of privatisation, or have taken steps to restructure water agencies in a manner which might be seen as a prelude to privatisation in future years.

South Australia has outsourced management and operations of water and sewerage for 15 years to the United Water consortium. A report leaked to the State Opposition back in 1998 canvassed options for the privatisation of SA Water (estimated to be worth about $8 billion), including a share float.

In Victoria, Melbourne Water has been split into one wholesale business and three retail businesses, all are corporatised state enterprises. Each has outsourced field maintenance services. The over 80 water authorities, which previously supplied Victoria's provincial towns have been amalgamated into 15 state-owned businesses.

The former Kennett government involved private-sector interests in water-treatment projects, and proposed the involvement of private firms in the provision of wastewater treatment facilities and services for the towns of Echuca and Rochester (*1999–2000 Victorian Budget Paper No. 2*).

In New South Wales, water boards have been corporatised. Water and sewerage businesses are estimated to be saleable for around $20 billion. Early in the 1990s, NSW involved the private sector in the construction and operation of water-treatment plants valued at a total of more than $500 million.

The former Queensland Borbidge Liberal-National government was considering privatising three water pipelines in the centre of the state. The Queensland Commission of Audit, a body set up by the Borbidge government in 1997, had recommended an end to public ownership of water assets, and the government appointed Deutsche Morgan Grenfell to advise it on the sale of this infrastructure.

Arguably, the outright sale of water 'businesses' can be expected to create great political difficulties. Even the Kennett government in Victoria was reduced to an incremental approach of 'privatising' elements of water services. But the stakes are high—reportedly some $70 billion which could be raised from the sale of water assets (*BRW*, 20/4/98). Some are confident that further privatisation business is just around the corner. According to Allan Griffiths, a director of Deloitte Consulting, a 'second wave' of water reforms is expected in Australia in the next three years (*AFR*, 18/5/99).

This 'second wave' may not involve the sale of entire water businesses. But other approaches—such as leasing existing assets, outsourcing management, or the use of 'build own operate transfer' schemes for the construction of new infrastructure—may have the same effect of transferring control of the water industry to the private sector.

Electricity

While Victoria has privatised its electricity industry, and South Australia has just about done so, the prospect of such sales remains a contentious issue in NSW.

The Carr Labor government, through its Treasurer Michael Egan, floated plans to privatise electricity in May 1997. The response was fierce and sustained. Members from both the left and right wing factions combined to defeat the proposal at the October 1997 Annual State Labor Party Conference. By August 1998, the NSW Treasurer was telling Melbourne business people that the privatisation plan was 'overwhelmingly opposed' by voters and 'you can't just thrust things down people's throats' (*SMH*, 22/8/98). And on 28 August 1998, it was reported that the Carr government had scrapped plans to go to the State election next March advocating the sale of the $25 billion NSW electricity industry. The Premier said:

> That means my party will go to the people in the next election with its existing policy there in its platform which says no electricity privatisation. I think the other focus will be on whether we've simply sold too

much of the public sector and left ourselves exposed to a higher level of foreign ownership (*SMH*, 28/8/98).

By the 1999 NSW election campaign, the Carr Labor government made it even clearer that the sale of the power industry was totally off its agenda. In contrast the Opposition outlined a plan to sell the industry. Labor was returned with an increased majority.

A rural commentator, Peter Austin, later observed:

> The trouncing that the Coalition received at the recent State election had a lot to do with its central policy plank of privatising electricity, and little wonder (*The Land*, 8/4/99).

There is a belief in some quarters that advocates of the privatisation of the NSW electricity industry have not given up, but are simply waiting until the next opportunity presents itself. Some have noted that, despite the NSW government's announcement before the last state election that the industry would not be sold, after the 1999 election the NSW Treasury continued to operate a 'Structural Reform Directorate' which included an 'electricity ownership branch' an 'electricity projects branch' and an 'electricity project coordination & legal advice branch'. Even the 1998 annual report of the NSW Auditor-General, published in March 1999, referred to the 'possible sale of the electricity industry' as a factor potentially affecting the activities of the audit office. The NSW Treasurer, eight months after the NSW elections, also made clear he still held the view that electricity privatisation was an appropriate policy (*SMH*, 20/11/99).

Transport

Private sector involvement in road construction through readily-packaged toll way schemes can be expected to continue—but arguably the largest proposals will involve further access of private operators to government-owned heavy rail networks.

In part this is driven by national competition policy, whereby governments are expected to allow others to use their heavy rail systems. Government actions to split up rail authorities into a series of businesses—running urban or country trains, any remaining freight businesses, with a separate business charged with managing the infrastructure—can be seen as a way of converting unwieldy, overmanned, inefficient organisations into leaner and more manageable businesses. It can also be seen as a radical and risky step, given that the resultant tensions may not all be creative.

Of particular concern are government expectations about the performance and capital requirements of the agencies charged with maintaining and upgrading rail infrastructure, and the extent to which different organisations involved in running these operating and maintenance businesses can coordinate their efforts (voluntarily or otherwise) to minimise risks.

Health services

Different Commonwealth governments have tried to encourage the public to take out health insurance, in different ways. The current Coalition government has actively sought to encourage more members of the community to take out private health cover. In this context, the continued retention by the Commonwealth of Medibank Private is likely to be questioned.

The possible sale of Medibank Private was canvassed during debate of the Coalition's privatisation policies in the late 1980s and early 1990s. Of twelve agencies then identified as likely candidates, eleven have subsequently been sold (although the sales were undertaken by the Labor government, not the Coalition). The only agency unsold from that list is Medibank Private. In late 1999, a spokesman for the Federal Minister for Health advised that there were 'no immediate plans' for its sale, but that discussions about the prospect had been held with the Minister for Finance 'several months ago' (*SMH*, 23/12/99).

Emphasis may shift from 'sales' to 'outsourcing' or 'franchising'

It seems likely that the next wave of privatisations will involve greater emphasis on outsourcing or franchising than on sales.

In many respects outsourcing is less politically sensitive than the outright sale of a government trading enterprise. Many outsourcing arrangements promise cost savings, and can be undertaken without publicity.

The Victorian government has already extensively contracted out services. According to its 1999–2000 Budget Papers, excluding the service agreements of the Department of Human Services, the total annual expenditure on contracting by all departments is currently estimated to be close to $1 billion, up from $840 million in 1996–97 and $650 million in 1995–96. The expenditure on contracting is evenly split between contracts for direct services to the community and contracts for services provided to departments and agencies. Over 90 per cent of these contracts, by value, are with private sector providers.

Outsourcing arrangements—even for larger, high profile

agencies—can also be seen as a way of softening up the community, preparatory to sale, particularly if they can be presented as a way of introducing 'competition'.

Take Australia Post. In July 1998, the Minister for Communications Senator Richard Alston outlined plans to introduce reform legislation later that year to reform Australia's $4 billion postal market. The reform package involved the deregulation of international mail and the introduction of competition from July 2000 for items weighing more than 50 grams.

These reforms will mean that around 90 per cent of Australia Post's business would be open to competition from private firms. Meantime the government promised to freeze the standard letter rate at 45 cents until 2003. (The latter might have been intended to defuse community hostility yet it also could be seen as acknowledging the efficiency of an organisation which would thereby have managed to hold the price of a standard letter at 45 cents for more than a decade.)

Outsourcing the responsibility for constructing and managing new infrastructure—a matter examined in more detail in a later chapter—is also attractive for governments seeking to maximise their impact through a capital works program. According to the 1999–2000 NSW Budget Papers, New South Wales has already contracted nearly $5 billion in 'build own operate transfer' projects providing transport, electricity, water and sewerage infrastructure (*1999–2000 NSW Budget Paper No. 2*). Before the 1999 election, the Kennett government in Victoria declared its plans to build on its experience with 'build own operate' (BOO) and 'build own operate transfer' (BOOT) arrangements by extending these to a wider range of activities. These were: private provision of hospital services in Mildura and Berwick; waste water treatment services in Castlemaine and surrounding areas; water treatment services in the Coliban, Central Highlands and Grampians regions; traffic camera services; and a Mobile Data Network for emergency services calls in the greater Melbourne metropolitan area.

Another factor encouraging greater emphasis on outsourcing is the fact that, after the sale of major government trading enterprises, future privatisations are likely to involve a higher proportion of 'general government' agencies, particularly those involved in the human services area.

Yet the form of privatisation which is likely to be more important in the next decade is franchising—an arrangement whereby governments don't exactly sell a government agency, but allow others to operate it (or operate in similar fields). For example, in 1999, the Victorian government sought bidders to acquire franchise contracts for the operation of the state's trains and trams. The arrangements will involve transferring the management of rail and tram operations to the private sector, with the government buying back services on behalf of the public. The term of the franchise contracts will vary—with some lasting seven years, and others lasting fifteen years where major new investment is planned. Operators will be required to continue to operate a full range of services according to fares and timetables determined by the government (*1999–2000 Victorian Budget Paper No. 2*).

So what are the next candidates for outsourcing or franchising?

Jails and correctional services? To many, this might seem one of the last areas appropriate for privatisation. Yet, within Australia, it was one of the first. In the major states, some correctional facilities are now being managed by commercial operators (with varying degrees of success).

Community services? At the end of 1999, the NSW Department of Community Services was seeking to contract out the management of group homes for the intellectually disabled—a proposal which aroused much debate and opposition because of a concern that the quality of service would fall.

Health services? Already a wide range of health services have effectively been privatised. The obvious cases are the use of BOOT schemes to fund new hospitals (as was the case with NSW's Port Macquarie hospital, now almost universally seen as a bad deal for government). There has been discussion about extending the scale of localised privately-owned 'health centres' to full-scale 24-hour emergency centres. Meantime, other forms of privatisation are occurring gradually through the mechanisms of pricing and health insurance.

Police services? Promoters of sporting events have been pressured to replace police with private security guards. Some degree of outside involvement in certain activities undertaken by police may make sense: one doesn't need fully trained policemen to perform essentially clerical operations, or to fix car radios, or even to service speed cameras or record fingerprints. But privatisation of the investigation of criminal offences would be a sinister prospect.

Public safety? Already there has been speculation that air traffic control services might be privatised (*The Australian*, 20/8/98). Some air-sea rescue is already contracted out. One can expect that commercial interests might wish to run fire prevention services (though commercial interests are already subsidised by the minimal charges imposed for responses to faulty alarm systems). Already rural fire services (and State Emergency Services) are 'privatised', in so far as they are staffed by private sector volunteers. Commercialisation of fire services could be expected to establish disincentives for voluntarism.

Human services? The Federal government restructured its job-search services for the unemployed into corporations, under the oversight of a board of directors. It also forced the newly corporatised business to enter into contracts to provide services to the unemployed—with other contracts going to private operators or non-government organisations. The next step was to not renew the contracts to government-owned businesses, with most going to agencies run by church organisations, on the basis of their allegedly superior performance. The details of the relative performance of these agencies were not published or debated.

Education? The Australian community has long debated the case for retaining systems of public secular education. Some advocates of privatisation (notably Michael Porter of the Tasman Institute) have claimed that public schools should be sold off in the interests of efficiency (*The Australian*, 27/4/98). Others see the privatisation of tertiary education as inevitable, in the wake of funding cuts to universities and the consequential reliance by universities on revenues from full-fee paying students, who are subject to different admission criteria from government-funded enrolments.

Museums, art galleries and libraries? The management of monuments, and all items of scientific, historic or cultural significance? Business licensing? Tax collection? If one takes the view that government is 'too big', or that the private sector always does things better, nothing is sacrosanct.

For their part, zealous promoters of privatisation have yet to propose any limits to downsizing the public sector through contracting—or to suggest that any areas of government activity which should be off-limits.

Privatisation in stages?

If recent experience is any guide, the next decade may see further efforts to reduce the involvement of the public sector in many traditional areas of government activity, using a combination of devices to achieve this outcome—often in the name of 'competition' or 'contestability'.

The example of the Federal government's job-search contracts illustrates how privatisation can be secured through a series of linked steps. In this case these were: corporatisation of the government organisation, followed by defining the nature of services to be provided through contracts; opening up opportunities for service provision to other providers; the choice of specific criteria for evaluating the performance of contractors; and then a loss of business to public sector agencies, compelling downsizing of the government-run organisation.

Variants of this model can involve corporatised entities being empowered to bid for new business from the private sector, until they become so commercial in character that the case for their retention as public sector entities is diminished.

Another model for privatisation involves a combination of reduced funding for public sector activities, the use of 'user pays' pricing for those who wish to avail themselves of those services, and elements of 'franchising'—all in the name of 'competition'.

An example of this process is currently in progress in the area of tertiary education. The Howard government's policy of dramatically reducing funding has forced universities to rely more and more on student fees. Financial pressures have forced universities to redesign courses so that many are little more than industry-specific vocational training. Cash-strapped universities are compelled to 'cost' their activities (the offerings of individual schools or departments, or even enrolments in research degrees) to assess which are 'paying their way'. Moreover, universities have been required by financial pressures to establish lower admission standards for foreign, fee-paying students. In summary, universities are becoming less dependent on government funding than on their own-source revenues, and are being turned into commercial operations, whose prime function is to sell educational services. Increasingly, course offerings are biased towards the popular and the profitable.

Meantime, governments are 'promoting competition' by enabling organisations other than universities to offer courses which may be described as 'degrees' (a label previously protected). There are demands from some universities that they be allowed to set their own fees, setting the scene for a return to the days when only the children of affluent families could afford a university education. The end result: the government will have 'privatised' the tertiary education sector. (There may be collateral damage. Even now, universities are less able to attract or retain talent, since academic salaries have declined in relative terms from the days when professors' salaries were roughly equivalent to the remuneration of Supreme Court judges. The pressure for university courses to meet the needs of industry and commerce will marginalise the activities of those whose research interests relate to matters of concern to the community. The quality of all university programs will decline—already there is unspoken recognition that 'demanding' courses may be unpopular, leading to reduced enrolments and placing academic jobs at risk.)

In other words, without greater pressure from politicians and the media and the community, the trend towards the privatisation of public sector activities may proceed, but in different ways. Some may see these changes as more subtle. Others may describe it as privatisation by stealth.

There may be situations where these processes make good financial sense, and can actually lead to an improvement of services to the public sector or the community. In other situations, these exercises only satisfy an ideological agenda.

What is important is that no government should be allowed to initiate privatisation without being held accountable for its actions.

3

Touting Privatisation

A SUCCESSION OF self-styled reformers have set out to make their mark by promoting changes to the way the public sector operates, in the name of promoting efficiency, securing value for money, or just shrinking the size of the public sector. The main advocates of privatisation have been from the ranks of consultants, media commentators, public servants and politicians.

A succession of consultants have sought visibility by publicly advocating one or other 'reform', or the application of some 'new' technique, in the hope of getting new jobs (and thereby enhancing their incomes). Some consultants are merely rebadging old ideas, but few openly acknowledge the fact, preferring to think of themselves as being at the leading edge of reform.

A cohort of media commentators has been at the forefront of disseminating arguments about the rationale for the latest (often recycled) ideas about reforming the public sector. Many commentators do little more than repeat the contents of media releases, or rewrite cliches about such matters as the evils of public sector debt or the need to transform sleepy, inefficient and unprofitable government enterprises into dynamic businesses which will miraculously provide better services for customers at cheaper prices. The basic tool of many commentators is the telephone interview. Hence they disseminate ideas picked up from interviewing consultants and politicians with an idea to sell. Few commentators have demonstrated a capacity to check facts or examine basic source documents.

As for public servants: leading bureaucrats are not entirely cynical in their promotion of new nostrums for 'reform'. But some, having accepted an idea, have become advocates or zealots. Others function like weathervanes, dutifully noting which way the political wind is blowing, and behaving accordingly. Still others just react to circumstances as it suits their interests. If a bureaucrat is appointed to head a new organisation, contracting out or privatisation is the way to go. If it works, they can claim victory; if it doesn't work, they can blame the contractor; and if a government rejects contracting out or privatising service delivery, that can be used to explain poor performance.

Politicians who have actively promoted privatisation have often done so on the basis of ideology rather than from careful consideration of evidence and analysis. Most politicians don't have the skills to analyse financial advice provided to them by public servants. However, politicians are probably no different from ordinary mortals when it comes to responding to information they would like to hear; they just have more highly developed responses. Some politicians have been less interested in the pros and cons of privatisation than with promoting themselves as tough economic managers—with half an eye to a potential career *after* politics.

A review of the marketing material distributed by consultants and the public statements of politicians or other insiders, suggests some recurring themes. The promotion of privatisation is usually preceded by commentaries about a *crisis in public finances*, or about *public sector inefficiency*, and the need to expose the provision of services within the public sector to the forces of *competition*.

Embedded within these discussions are a series of basic arguments—or, more commonly, claims or assertions. There are minor variations in the way they are presented—but the main arguments for privatisation in its various forms can be classified as claims that:

- there is a need to repair government finances (claims which are often associated with rhetoric about the burdens of 'debt' and 'deficits');
- government agencies are irredeemably inefficient, and that privatisation will produce better services at lower cost;
- the proceeds of privatisation through asset sales (or the harnessing of private sector capital through infrastructure development schemes) are urgently needed to fund new initiatives.

To this list can also be added some recent, rather curious claims that some existing government activities should be sold:

- to enable the management of those enterprises to pursue their ambitions to operate in potentially risky and profitable markets interstate or overseas;
- because retention exposes the government to financial risk (and, presumably, potential rewards—though these are rarely mentioned);

- because other governments are not engaged in those activities, or have already sold them.

Each of these arguments needs to be considered on its merits. This chapter examines the main classes of claims favouring privatisation.

Crisis in government finances

There are occasions when privatisation through the sale of government trading enterprises (GTEs) may make good sense. Private sector businesses have benefited from selling-off non-performing or non-core assets to meet financial obligations or to fund promising new ventures. But those occasions depend on a careful balancing of the financial and non-financial costs and benefits of a range of options. In contrast, the arguments disseminated about how privatisation could repair or avert a crisis in government finances have been crude, and often quite misleading.

Indeed, the very idea that there is a crisis in government finances has often been deliberately manufactured to suit the interests of individual governments. A key element has been the establishment of short-term enquiries into government finances to report on a government's financial position (and to dump on predecessors). Gary Sturgess, who was a pre-election political strategist to incoming NSW Premier Greiner (and later appointed head of the NSW Cabinet Office) has explained the formation of the 1988 'Curran' Commission of Audit as follows:

> ... it was a marketing exercise ... In March 1988 there was no great feeling that New South Wales's finances were in drastic shape, so why would you need a government shake up? ... at that point in time people just did not see the need for it, people couldn't see the point of user pays. The whole idea of downsizing and putting these things on a commercial basis, there was just no basis for that. Nobody had done it. So we had to create a popular demand for that kind of reform (Interview, December 1994, as reported in *Laffin & Painter*).

The Curran Commission duly reported that

> New South Wales has been living beyond its means!

and the device of having a short-term 'Commission of Audit' talk about a crisis in government finances became a model for incoming governments—leading to similar reports being produced in Tasmania (1992), South Australia (1994), Western Australia (1993), Victoria (1993), Queensland (1996) and the Commonwealth (1996).

Box 3.1
VICTORIA'S FINANCIAL CRISIS—
AS CREATED AND SOLVED BY ACCOUNTING CHOICES 1993–95

A statement of financial position for Victoria was presented by the outgoing Treasurer in 1992, but substantially revised by a 'Commission of Audit' appointed by the incoming Kennett government. Reported liabilities were increased from $53.8 billion to $69.8 billion, asset values were reduced, and the Commission claimed that Victoria had negative net worth. When the incoming government prepared a public sector balance sheet three years later, the representation changed yet again.

Victoria—State Public Sector
Consolidated statement of assets and liabilities

Financial position as at:	Treasurer's Report 30 June 1990	Commission of Audit 30 June 1992	Government Report 30 June 1995
	$m	$m	$m
ASSETS*	93,743	64,450	74,268
LIABILITIES			
Borrowings	27,353	39,227	37,556
Unfunded superannuation & employees' entitlements	17,247	18,573	17,221
Accounts payable, accrued expenses, other liabilities	9,201	5,654	13,354
Outstanding claims liability	–	6,368	**
Total liabilities	53,801	69,822	68,131
NET WORTH*	39,941	(5,372)	6,137

* The Victorian Commission of Audit noted that 'substantial assets' had not been recognised in its balance sheet—including public land, heritage assets and the value of hardwood forests, though it did include assets and liabilities of universities. The 1995 State of Victoria report excluded the assets and liabilities of universities but included other 'assets to be valued over the next two years (estimate)—$10,000 million'.
** Accounting policies re this item were not disclosed.

In explaining its approach the Commission of Audit claimed that the definition of liabilities in earlier publications was 'too narrow', that it had chosen to ensure that transactions were accounted for 'in accordance with their economic substance not their legal form', and that 'the accounting treatment should reflect the distribution of economic risks and benefits'.

The main differences in accounting treatments between successive reports were:
- the 1990 financial statement treated the state's net investment in financial institutions as a single line-item while the Commission of Audit included the

> separate assets and liabilities of those institutions. Hence moneys deposited with government-owned financial institutions were recorded as borrowings. (Arguably the single line-item approach was to be preferred, since it ensured that the balance sheet focussed on borrowings entered into by the government in the course of managing the state's finances);
> - obligations from operating leases were recorded as liabilities in the Commission of Audit's version (contrary to Australian accounting standards which prescribe that only *finance* leases should be recorded in that fashion—a practice re-adopted in 1995);
> - the Commission of Audit included a $1.7 billion estimate of future losses associated with long-term supply arrangements of electricity between the State Electricity Authority of Victoria and the owners of aluminum smelters, and a $6.4 billion liability for 'outstanding claims' attributable to the Accident Compensation Commission and the Transport Accident Commission.

The Victorian experience deserves special attention. The outgoing Kirner Government must have sensed that it was at risk of losing office and that an incoming Kennett government might use the 'Commission of Audit' device to damage its reputation. The main author of the Curran report, the retired NSW Treasury official Don Nicholls, was hired to repeat the exercise for Victoria. Nicholls' 1992 report on Victoria's finances showed relatively moderate levels of state debt and liabilities. But the Kennett government duly appointed a new 'Commission of Audit'. This Audit Commission produced an alarmist report which depicted a financial crisis, mainly through its choice of consolidation practices and a contentious treatment of the 'substance' of certain transactions, at times contrary to the requirements of Australian accounting standards. Whereas the Nicholls' report referred to 'debt net of financial assets', the Audit Commission's figures highlighted *gross* liabilities. The end result was to add some $36 billion to the headline figures of state debt reported only months earlier.

It is of more than passing interest to note that when the Kennett government later produced financial statements to depict its financial position in 1995, it did not follow the Audit Commission's approach to identifying liabilities, but reverted to the practices used in reports from the previous government (see Box). No effort was made to estimate the 'liabilities' arising ('in substance') from the Kennett government's involvement in infrastructure financing schemes. In 1993, the Audit Commission claimed to be examining 'substance over form'; in 1995, the Kennett government's reports emphasised 'form' rather than 'substance'.

Claim: 'The proceeds of privatisation could reduce the budget deficit'

This is advocacy of privatisation at its crudest. It relies on the artificial way that governments have traditionally reported their financial activities: by focusing only on cash transactions, and by aggregating the effect of 'capital' and 'recurrent' spending. Having said that, it is one of the arguments most commonly-advanced in the political arena to justify the sale of GTEs.

To evaluate this argument, it is important to understand what a budget 'deficit' (or a 'deficit budget result') actually represents.

Budgets are forecasts, based on a series of assumptions about future revenues and future expenditures. 'Budget results' represent the actual financial consequences of a government's operations in a financial year. One can turn a budget forecast from good to bad, or from bad to worse, simply by varying the assumptions about what will happen in the future. Recent Australian experience suggests that after elections, incoming governments often prepare the ground for privatisation by suddenly announcing that they have inherited a 'black hole' in their budget, involving billions of dollars.

Some readers might interpret references to 'holes in the budget' as indicating that the government has actually incurred cash shortfalls—even running up overdrafts with its bankers. But all that has happened is that Treasury officials have changed their estimates about the level of future *revenues* from taxation and charges (and dividends from government-owned businesses), without correspondingly varying assumptions about future levels of *expenditure*. The whole point of monitoring budget results is to alert a government about the need to defer expenditure or increase charges if things are not turning out as expected. The claims about 'budget black holes' are thus emotive and misleading. Worse, references to 'black holes' are often said to refer to a period 'over three years' (or even some longer period). In other words, at best, the estimates do not relate to a current year deficit but about a highly hypothetical cumulative shortfall after three or five years in the event that the outgoing government had chosen not to respond to new information. At worst, the revised assumptions are unduly pessimistic, and misleading. Politicians continue to refer to an inherited multi-billion 'black hole' as if it was a real deficit for the current year.

Further—and this is more technical—a deficit budget only reflects the forecast results of a sub-set of public sector activities—those undertaken within the 'general government' or 'budget sector'. The concept of 'general government' is defined in rules issued by the Australian Bureau of Statistics for the preparation of so-called 'Government Finance Statistics' (GFS)—and those rules, in turn, are based on the United Nations 'System of National Accounts (SNA)' (*United Nations*, 1968, 1993). In broad terms, general government agencies are those which are primarily dependent for their funding on sums allocated by parliament from the consolidated fund. 'Public trading enterprises' (more commonly described as 'government trading enterprises'), on the other hand, are primarily dependent on fees and charges levied on the community for services rendered.

In most cases, government owned businesses are treated as part of the public trading enterprise (PTE) sector—though there are exceptions. For example, a public transport system which receives more in subsidies than in fares would be classified as 'general government'. So too would a government 'business' (such as an internal audit bureau) which receives the bulk of its revenues from charges levied on government departments.

To complicate the matter, there is a further category of government businesses recognised in Australia—'financial enterprises'.

Finally, it is possible to report on the activities of governments overall—the 'whole of government'. However, such reports may exclude Trusts and off-budget financing schemes.

On the periphery is a range of 'trust accounts' holding funds on behalf of individuals rather than for the benefit of the government.

To further complicate the matter, some governments refer to the 'budget sector' and the 'non-budget' (or government trading enterprise sector), and establish the boundaries of these sectors in a manner which departs from GFS standards. The following diagram sets out these relationships.

BUDGET RESULTS DEPEND ON BUDGET COVERAGE

Privatisation

The point to be made is that, generally, calculations of budgets (or budget results) only concern the 'general government' or 'budget' sector. (These sectors are shown as different but overlapping in the diagram because state governments in Australia persist in manipulating their reported budget results by avoiding use of the international definitions for budget coverage.)

Moreover, creative accounting and financing arrangements (involving transfers of funds between sectors) can be used by governments to avoid reporting a budget deficit or even to 'smooth' reported budget results, so that those results provide better news in the lead-up to elections.

So far as arguments about privatisation are concerned, the suggestion that the proceeds of sale will reduce a budget deficit should be restated as a claim that privatisation will

> reduce the *reported* budget deficit.

After all, a 'budget deficit' is simply an artefact, created by the choice of methods used to calculate budget results. Currently, budget results are usually calculated on a *cash* basis—as opposed to the *accrual* basis of accounting commonly used by private sector firms. When a cash basis of calculation is used, the receipt of the proceeds of privatisation will be recorded as a 'revenue', reducing the reported or forecast budget result—which is simply the difference between cash receipts and payments during a period. This is a bit like someone who has sold their house during the year (and not yet bought a new one), describing the proceeds of the sale as part of their 'income'.

For better or worse, cash-based results combine the impact of transactions of a 'recurrent' and 'capital' nature.

In contrast, on an accrual basis, operating results are confined to results from operation and largely exclude the financial consequences of dealings in major assets. An accrual-based financial result for the general government sector might be affected by privatisation, but only to a minor extent. The sale of a government trading enterprise would be viewed as exchanging one asset (the GTE—or shares in the GTE if it had already been 'corporatised') for another asset (cash). If the proceeds differed from the book value of that asset, then only that difference would be recorded as a gain or loss.

In any case, one could well challenge the claim that privatisation will reduce the [reported] deficit by saying,

> So what? Deficits are not necessarily bad.

> **Box 3.2**
> **USE OF INTER-SECTOR TRANSFERS BY GOVERNMENTS TO MANIPULATE BUDGET RESULTS**
>
> One smoothing device involves 'parking' sums in Special Deposits Accounts (a form of 'Trust' account) at the end of one financial year, and then bringing the money back into the general government (or budget sector) in the first days of the next financial year (*Nicholls*, 1992).
>
> The most common device to enhance budget results involves the payment of 'dividends' from government trading enterprises to the budget sector.
>
> For example, in 1991, when the then (Coalition) NSW government was facing an embarrassing budget deficit, it demanded a $400 million 'special dividend' from a government trading enterprise, Elcom (later renamed Pacific Power). Elcom, in turn, was compelled to borrow from Treasury Corporation (a non-budget sector agency) to pay the dividend (*SMH*, 1/4/91). As a GTE, the borrowings of Elcom were not counted as part of the budget sector, and the illusion was presented that the government had avoided deficit financing.
>
> During 1993–94 the device was used again: Sydney Water was required to pay a $100 million 'special dividend'. Then a second $100 million payment was made. There had been strong media criticism of the earlier 'special dividend' (which roughly matched cash raised but unspent from an 'environmental levy'). This second $100 million transaction was then described as for the purchase by the government from Sydney Water of a golf course ('wetlands') and a storm water canal (*Walker, SMH*, 23/2/93). The NSW Auditor-General later expressed reservations about the basis on which these assets were valued.
>
> After the use of such devices led to criticism of state budget presentations, at the 1991 Premiers' Conference all governments agreed to present their supplementary information in their budget papers about what their budget results would have been had they been prepared on a standard GFS basis. That meant presenting budgets to cover the 'general government' sector, as defined by the Australian Bureau of Statistics. That was progress, and some state governments began presenting their budget information on a GFS basis. But even now, Australian governments do not always comply with GFS rules in presenting their budgets. Readers must refer to the fine print about what budget results *might have been* had they been compiled on a GFS basis. Or, better still, readers could examine later Australian Bureau of Statistics publications which show those results after the ABS has checked them (in ABS Catalogue 5501.0, *Government Financial Estimates—Australia*).

A government may have recorded a substantial cash deficit because it has just invested heavily in new infrastructure, which will produce positive cash flows (or other benefits) in subsequent years. (Some Australian governments separate the effect of capital and recurrent transactions when reporting budget results, but journalists and economic commentators tend to look at the combined effect of these transactions—giving rise to the term 'headline result'.)

A public company's cash outflows in a period may exceed its cash inflows, yet the company may still record a profit in terms of 'accrual accounting'. At the same time, the cash deficit will not be hidden, but openly reported in an audited 'statement of cash flows'. Corporations may make massive investments in particular projects, leading to short-run cash shortfalls, with the aim of generating positive cash flows in later years.

Some corporations experience clear-cut cycles of negative and positive cash flows as they enter new projects and then later enjoy the fruits of those investments. Security analysts are accustomed to interpreting the financial performance of private sector corporations by examining a series of financial indicators (such as rate of return on assets, rate of return on equity, earnings per share, the ratio of debt to equity, trends in market share, the relationship between operating profit and operating cash flows). Other indicators are examined when firms are operating in particular industries (be it manufacturing, retail, or financial services).

In contrast, published analyses of the financial performance of governments are often relatively unsophisticated, and tend to focus on a limited number of financial indicators (such as, 'the deficit', or 'the size of government debt'). Media commentators rarely look beneath these figures to understand what is going on.

There is a tendency to regard deficits as 'bad', and a series of deficits as 'very bad'—often without assessing budget outcomes in the context of broader economic conditions. Moreover, there is a tendency to condemn governments which record budget deficits regardless of how the deficit has arisen. There is a big difference between deficits which arise because of heavy expenditures on capital works (which will have some ongoing benefit to the community), and deficits because of gaps between revenues and recurrent expenditure (such as wages and salaries of public servants).

Classic examples of ill-informed commentaries about the performance of an Australian government were provided by politicians and a number of supposedly 'expert' media commentators on the relative performance of the Victorian and NSW governments during the late 1980s (see Box)[1]. It seems that Victoria was not alone in making poor financial decisions—though it did not conceal its financial difficulties as well as some other states.

The point is that reported budget deficits can be misleading

---

1 This example should not be interpreted as a defence of Victoria's financial policies in that period. Victoria got into financial difficulties from a combination of poor decisions, including ill-judged investments in GTEs, some speculative banking ventures (which did not attract attention from the then state Auditor-General until they had almost failed) and from a reluctance to raise fees and charges, even to the point that charges for electricity and other services lagged movements in the CPI.

> **Box 3.3**
>
> **NSW AND VICTORIA IN THE EARLY 1990s:
> DEFICIT OR SURPLUS?**
>
> In 1991, the then NSW Premier Nick Greiner claimed that he was running a 'balanced budget', while Victoria had a billion-dollar deficit. Yet in one sense, both these claims were demonstrably wrong.
>
> Victoria's budget presentations covered a set of entities which were close to what the ABS defines as 'general government'. On the other hand, NSW budget presentations only related to the smaller set of transactions of the 'consolidated fund'—in effect, the pot of money into which revenues from taxes, fines and charges were paid, and from which funds were allocated to departments.
>
> The ABS has long published statistics representing the financial results of the 'general government sector' of the Commonwealth, state and territory governments. Sometimes the figures reported in these publications differ substantially from what governments have reported as their budget results. Yet in the early 1990s, some well-known economic commentators seemed unaware that the ABS made these adjustments. Those commentators usually wrote laudatory or critical reports of the performance of NSW and were critical of Victoria.
>
> Yet, as was pointed out in 1991, if NSW reported its budget on the same basis as Victoria, it would have recorded a budget deficit as big (if not bigger) than Victoria's (*Walker*, 2/5/1991). It was perhaps unfortunate that shortly after this article was published NSW Premier Greiner chose to announce an early election. But not before he personally briefed journalists with claims that even so, Victoria was worse off than NSW. The press only took this as confirmation that the original comments about NSW's hidden $1 billion deficit were correct.
>
> It had also been claimed at the time that Victoria was 'borrowing money to pay public servants'. That may have appeared to be the case from reports covering Victoria's budget sector, but this only covered part of the state's financial dealings. A fuller view was provided by 'whole of government' consolidated statements.
>
> One of the earliest sets of these financial reports was prepared by Coopers & Lybrand and published in the 1993 *Report of the Victorian Commission of Audit*, a body established by the incoming Kennett government. The statements showed that in 1991-92, Victoria had borrowed $2.456 billion—but had invested $2.497 billion on infrastructure. In those circumstances, a cash deficit was not necessarily bad news.

indicators of financial performance: as a consequence of ambiguous coverage of the budget, of the way figures are reported in the press (the so-called 'headline results') and also because budget results are generally reported on a cash basis, not accrual. To be fully informed about government finances, we need both cash and accrual reports, together with both reports separately covering the 'general government' sector, the 'public trading enterprise sector', and 'whole of government'. And then there is a need to look at all that data in detail.

If deficits are not necessarily 'bad', then correspondingly, the sale of government businesses is not necessarily 'good'.

Privatisation transactions will not necessarily strengthen a government's financial circumstances. Having sold a GTE, the government will lose a future stream of revenues (from dividends, interest and internal charges). Even if a GTE was sold for a good price—and evidence suggests many are sold too cheaply—then the question of whether a privatisation was a good or a bad financial deal will depend on the size of the lost revenue stream. More on this in Chapter 4.

Claim: 'The proceeds of privatisation could reduce government debt'

A second, crude argument about how privatisation could repair government finances is based on the alleged need to reduce government debt. This argument is often coupled with claims about the burden of interest costs and the need to protect (or restore) a government's credit rating. Arguments in this form have been frequently advanced by various 'commissions of audit', appointed by incoming governments. Reports on these reviews generally have advocated the privatisation of at least some government enterprises—though without exploring the possibility that retention might produce better financial returns than sale.[2]

The idea of debt reduction is commonly presented as an end in itself—not as a means to an end. Those who argue for debt reduction never really explain why having 'debt' is so bad, and why 'debt reduction' is so good.

They also ignore the fact that selling government businesses in order to pay off debt may actually lead to a deterioration in the financial circumstances of the government, due to:

- the fact that the loss of dividend revenue from a government business may exceed any savings from reduced interest costs;
- the costs of implementing the transaction—which involve not only the fees and marketing costs, but also so-called 'social bonuses' and other incentives which often have to be provided to

---

2 See NSW Commission of Audit, *Focus on Reform*; Independent Commission to Review Tasmania's Public Sector Finances, *Tasmania in the Nineties*; SA Commission of Audit, *Charting the Way Forward*; Independent Commission to Review State Finances [WA], *Agenda for Reform* Vol 2; National Commission of Audit, *Report to the Commonwealth Government*. One notable exception was the Victorian Commission of Audit, which advocated sale of 'non-core activities', but also noted that privatisation of the state's major businesses could have 'a negative impact on the budget position', since 'the loss of dividends, tax-equivalent payments and other contributions would outweigh the savings in lower interest payments made possible by applying the sale proceeds to debt retirement' (Vol. 1).

Touting Privatisation

interest groups or regions, in order to get sales through parliament (such as the more than $1 billion required to secure the support of the Senate for sale of 16.6 per cent of Telstra).

In the private sector, no one regards borrowing as a problem if the financial returns from a venture financed by those borrowings are stable, low risk, and exceed borrowing costs. In fact, the sale of government assets often leads to an increase in private debt when individuals borrow to buy shares in a government float.

So perhaps the alleged virtues of 'debt reduction' should not really be taken too seriously: perhaps one should just accept that politicians are making a superficial pitch to an ignorant electorate. One might hope so—for otherwise the politicians who are advocating zero debt are taking an extreme stance about the way governments should contribute to the management of modern economies.

In effect, the advocates of continued 'zero debt' could be saying that fiscal policies are useless. They are saying that national governments, having attained zero debt, should thereafter never run into budget deficit—because to do so would mean going back into debt. In effect, they are also saying that governments should not borrow to kick-start an ailing economy, or to meet expenditure required after natural disasters, or to try to reduce the burden of unemployment.

Fortunately, when the advocates of 'debt elimination' are compelled to place their proposals in writing, it seems that they don't really believe in zero debt after all. They are careful to include major loopholes. They confine their advocacy of debt elimination to 'budget' or 'general government' sectors, thus ensuring that government businesses and government-owned financial institutions can still borrow (and, if necessary, continue to pay 'special dividends' to the consolidated fund). They also say that debt should be eliminated—save for 'exceptional circumstances'. (See the following box for examples of what these circumstances might be.)

In its 1999–2000 Budget brought down on 6 May 1999, the West Australian government announced that it would pump $800 million of borrowed funds into a record capital program. The West Australian Premier and Treasurer Richard Court denied that he had abandoned his quest to wipe out state debt by 2008 and described the borrowing as a 'one-off' to stimulate the economy in the face of falling business investment and low commodity prices. However, this 'one-off' action will have the effect of increasing net debt from $5 billion in 1998–99 to $5.8 billion in 1999–00 and peaking at $6.2 billion in 2000–01.

In other words, claims about the evils of debt do not appear to

Privatisation

> **Box 3.4**
> **CHANGING INTERPRETATIONS OF**
> **'DEBT REDUCTION' IN NSW 1994-99**
>
> 'Debt reduction' and 'balanced budget' laws are always a bit of a con: no government has the power to bind the actions of future governments. The only way governments could be bound in this way is through constitutional changes effected through a referendum. However, this has not stopped a succession of governments from using legislation as a symbolic statement of their commitment to fiscal responsibility. At the same time, just in case they were in office when things went bad, they have been careful to incorporate loopholes.
>
> The NSW government's State Debt Control (Balanced Budgets) Bill 1994 stated that the proposed legislation would control budget sector net debt 'by requiring the maintenance of balanced Budgets'. The Bill provided the following let-out:
>
>> However, a State budget may contain a fiscal forecast of a budget sector deficit if the deficit is due to exceptional circumstances (for example, a natural disaster or a major economic recession) (section 59).
>
> In announcing this Bill former NSW Premier Fahey and former Treasurer Collins claimed that balanced budget legislation would ensure that from 1997, NSW governments would 'no longer be able to run huge debts to be paid by their children' (*Media release*, 13/9/94).
>
> By the time the Carr Labor government came to office in NSW, alternative legislation was renamed the General Government Debt Elimination Act 1995—and redefined the concept of a 'balanced budget' as applying not one year at a time but over an entire economic cycle. It also extended the list of circumstances in which balanced budgets could be avoided: governments were to have 'regard' to:
>
>> (a) the structure of expenditure and revenue of the budget,
>> (b) the outlook for the State's credit rating, keeping as an objective the achievement of the highest rating possible as judged by internationally recognised rating authorities,
>> (c) exposure to budget risks,
>> (d) demographic and social trends that will impact on the budget.
>
> A difficulty in implementing this approach is: the future is uncertain, and it is hard to predict how long the ups and downs of an economic cycle will last. Another major difficulty (for politicians) is that economic cycles are not synchronised with elections. Faced with an election, politicians might just be tempted to put re-election ahead of debt reduction.
>
> During the 1999 NSW election, the Coalition promised that if elected it would legislate to guarantee that NSW remained debt-free. The Opposition Leader stated that 'No government will be able to blow the budget again except, of course, in some exceptional circumstances.' These Coalition exemptions repeated its 1994 list of 'major natural disasters and severe economic downturns', but this time added 'war' (*SMH*, 16/3/99).

be taken too seriously by politicians themselves: debt is bad, but it is all right to borrow under certain circumstances.

'Gross debt' versus 'net debt'

More importantly, when politicians make extravagant statements about 'wiping out debt forever more', it should raise questions as to whether (a) they really understand what they are talking about, or (b) they are deliberately making meaningless, populist claims.

Take the statements made in May 1999 by federal Treasurer Peter Costello in relation to the Commonwealth budget. The sale of a further tranche of Telstra shares for around $16 billion together with a planned series of budget surpluses in the near future were said to ensure that the Commonwealth could 'totally eliminate debt' by 2003. Weeks after the sale of the 16.6 per cent of Telstra, Costello was claiming that the sale of the remaining 50.1 per cent will return Australia in the first few years of the 21st century to the debt-free state in which it began this century. However, such an outcome would be impossible on the basis of the figures reported in the budget papers:

- the Commonwealth reported debt amounting to $96.67 billion (*1999–2000 Budget Paper No.1*);
- $96.67 billion of debt simply could not be eliminated with the projected $16 billion proceeds from the sale of a further tranche of Telstra shares and the forecast aggregate budget surpluses of around $5.2 billion–$7.2 billion in the following years.

However, the Commonwealth also reported 'financial assets' of $52.96 billion. Apparently the Treasurer had in mind the target of eliminating *net debt*—gross debt less financial assets—by 2003. When Treasurer Costello told Parliament:

> the Commonwealth Government could be debt free (*1999–2000 Budget Speech*)

it seems that he either

- had not read the figures, or
- had read them but did not understand them; or
- thought that financial assets could be used to pay off debt—leaving the government without any working capital; or
- really meant to say:

> The Commonwealth government could have debt levels no greater than its holdings of financial assets.

In other words, the Commonwealth Treasurer, while describing the evils of debt, intended to retain Commonwealth borrowings at around $53 billion. He only wanted to *reduce* debt—not *eliminate* it. (In effect, he was proposing that the Commonwealth sell shares in Telstra in order to invest in interest-bearing financial securities. Paradoxically, during the same week that the government put its bill for the sale of a second tranche of Telstra shares through parliament, a leading funds manager began airing television commercials aimed at encouraging retirees to do the reverse: to invest their savings in equities rather than interest bearing securities. According to the commercial, the 'biggest mistake' many investors made was 'retiring' their money.)

In any event, the Commonwealth's reported figures for 'debt' were understated, since formal 'debt' had already been shown net of financial assets 'acquired for debt management purposes'. In other words, instead of the balance sheet reporting actual levels of debt, they had been reduced by the amounts of cash and other securities supposedly held for the repayment of debt or for trading purposes. That is not the way that balance sheets are supposed to be prepared. Indeed, Costello's balance sheet seems to have breached Statement of Australian Accounting Standards AAS 23, which states that liabilities and assets may only be netted off in balance sheets if there is a formal 'right of set-off' recognised at law or in equity. That would not normally apply to assets held for 'debt management purposes'.

The presentation in the Commonwealth budget papers was arguably the most audacious use of 'set-offs' in a balance sheet for more than a decade, since the time that the failed Hooker Corporation used similar devices in association with a debt defeasance transaction (see 'Hooker's $141m book exercise', *Australian Business*, 20/1/88). Hookers' reporting practices earned the fury of the National Companies and Securities Commission and prompted the accounting profession to produce a draft accounting standard on the subject of 'set-offs' in balance sheets within six weeks (smashing all previous records for speed).

In 1999, accounting standards on the subject of set-offs had been issued for a decade, and were legal requirements for corporations. By 1999, the Commonwealth Treasury had itself assumed responsibility for accounting regulation. Hence the Commonwealth's use of the device of showing debt net of financial assets was, arguably, more reprehensible than Hooker's use of set-offs more than a decade earlier.

Similar observations about the deliberate misrepresentation of 'debt' as 'net debt' can be made about NSW Opposition claims in 1999 that the sale of electricity assets would make the state 'debt-free'. The facts are:

- NSW gross state debt had been reported as $29.98 billion (*1998–99 NSW Budget Papers*);
- the sale proceeds of the sale of electricity assets had been variously estimated as $18.6 billion–$25 billion.

Hence, the sale could not possibly eliminate *all* debt.

However, according to the NSW Public Sector Consolidated Statements, the state held financial assets (cash, receivables and investments) of around $9.5 billion at 30 June 1998. Again, it seems that the proposed asset sales could not possibly wipe out *total debt*—only *net debt*.

Sadly, the media generally base their reports on politicians' press releases and a few telephone calls—and fail to check the figures. Take the editorialising of one Sydney newspaper, the day before the 1999 NSW election. The leader article expressed support for the Opposition, stating:

> The sell-off of the power industry would allow the retirement of state government debt (saving hundreds of millions of dollars annually in interest charges) and leave a small but significant surplus to fund infrastructure projects . . .
>
> Mrs Chikarovski deserves to win because she has the policy substance as distinct from Mr Carr's purely tactical flair. But this is more an endorsement of a policy than of a party (*SMH*, 26/3/99).

The 'policy substance' so enthusiastically endorsed by the editorial was illusory. While not everyone can read a balance sheet, editorial writers in the quality press might be expected to check their facts.

'Debt' versus 'liabilities'

A basic flaw of the 'debt reduction' argument is that it refers to the need to reduce 'debt', not 'liabilities'. The term 'debt' refers to formal borrowings from bankers or through the issue of government bonds. Debt is only a sub-set of 'liabilities'—which also covers amounts payable to suppliers and employees. For Australian governments, non-debt 'liabilities' include some big-ticket items, notably employee entitlements for long-service leave and unfunded superannuation commitments for public servants (and, of course, politicians).

When Costello was talking about the merits of the Telstra sale and the possible reduction over time of around $43 billion in 'debt', he neglected to mention that the Commonwealth general government sector actually faced total liabilities of some $187 billion— of which $75 billion was associated with 'employee entitlements' (including the generous benefits payable to politicians from defined benefit superannuation schemes). All the rhetoric about wiping out debt forever only related to less than 23 per cent of the Commonwealth's aggregate liabilities.

From the perspective of taxpayers, ratings agencies, employee groups and other stakeholders, data concerning 'debt' is of minimal relevance, compared with data concerning 'liabilities'.

Yet governments have chosen to avoid giving prominence to

liability data, preferring to highlight trends in aggregate 'debt'—even highlighting such obscure financial indicators as 'changes in real budget sector net debt'.

'Budget sector debt' versus 'General government debt' versus 'Total government debt'

Until 1993, Australian governments, with one exception, only systematically reported on the 'debt' incurred by their 'budget sector' (or 'general government'). The one exception was NSW, which in 1989 pioneered the publication of a series of Public Sector Financial statements, which encompassed the 'whole of government' and were prepared on an accrual accounting basis.

Starting in 1989, the ABS started publishing data relating to 'gross debt' and 'net debt' of the 'non-financial public sector' (i.e. excluding state banks, though not central borrowing authorities) for the Commonwealth, and for state and local governments (combined). The data reported in this publication (and its successors) was acknowledged to be incomplete (it excluded such items as unfunded superannuation commitments and commitments to pay long service leave). The ABS chose to include monies held on trust as liabilities (and also as assets, for the purpose of calculating net debt). The rationale for reporting 'net' debt remains obscure—particularly when the offsetting items (financial assets) could include non-monetary items such as shares in other enterprises.

'Government debt' versus 'national debt'

It is worth noting that 'government debt' (or liabilities) is a different concept from 'national debt'. Some pro-privatisation politicians (notably Peter Costello) seem to either confuse the two concepts, or else (fallaciously) cite *national debt* data as evidence of an impending crisis in the national economy, before presenting arguments about the need to reduce *public sector* debt.

In principle, the concepts of 'government debt' (or 'government liabilities') refer to the obligations of the public sector. 'National debt', on the other hand, concerns sums owing by all entities within the economy.

Unfortunately, references to government debt (by politicians, by ratings agencies, and in international compilations of financial data) often use the term in an inconsistent way. It is not always clear whether 'government' debt encompasses the debt of GTEs, or local government, or government-owned financial institutions. And, as one might expect by now, sometimes it is described as relating to gross debt (or liabilities), and sometimes as relating to a net figure (after off-setting holdings of cash and other financial assets). High levels of government debt could be a problem for the community if it means that a high proportion of taxpayer resources are being applied to pay interest rather than to provide services. On the other hand, there is a case for spreading the burden of paying for long-lived infrastructure over a number of years (even 'generations').

High levels of 'national debt' can reflect a variety of phenomena, though there are occasions when politicians choose to interpret national debt data as bad news. For example, following the release of the ABS estimate of foreign debt of $180.5 billion on 30 August 1995, the then Shadow Treasurer, Peter Costello said that:

> foreign debt was now eight times greater than when Labor came into power

and that:

> debt was the equivalent of $10,000 borrowed by every person in Australia

However, as noted by the then Treasurer, Ralph Willis:

> the claim was 'ludicrous' because the people who have to repay the debt are those who borrow it, which is predominantly private companies.
>
> some of the debt was used to finance the purchase of foreign equity (*SMH*, 31/8/95).

We did not hear much from Costello when by December 1998, net foreign debt had risen 31 per cent above 1995 levels to $236.8 billion, or around 41 per cent of Gross Domestic Product, and net foreign liabilities reached $343.8 billion (*The Australian*, 3/3/99). Nor did we hear from Costello later when these indicators deteriorated further.

However, one cannot ignore the possibility of the negative impact that too much foreign debt can have on the economy through currency value movements. For example, one consequence of external debt is the imposition of real costs on Australians when borrowing overseas. These costs, it is claimed, arise because high levels of foreign debt are commonly associated with depreciation of the currency. If this occurs then, when the borrowings become due, considerably more will be owed than would have been the case in the absence of depreciation. This means that external debt has real costs (*Stewart*, 1994).

The point made here is simply that changes in 'national debt' can arise from such factors as the way that Australian businesses are financing their activities offshore, or the way they are financing their investments in new plant and equipment for use within Australia.

Moreover, while the proceeds from the sale of government businesses may be used to reduce government debt, this is likely to be at the expense of raising private debt in the case of a float. For example, the purchase of shares in the next tranche of Telstra may be financed through borrowings. This means that while government debt may fall, national debt would increase.

When are government debt (or liability) levels dangerous?

Judging from some political rhetoric, all debt is dangerous. When analysed, the rhetoric can be restated as a claim that some debt is okay, but net debt is dangerous. It cannot be emphasised too strongly that such claims would be regarded as nonsense in the private sector, where debt-financing is seen as a fact of life, and choices about a firm's capital structure can improve returns to shareholders.

International comparisons of debt levels are regularly undertaken as an indicator of the financial standing of governments. The focus of these reports is generally on 'debt' rather than 'liabilities', for the simple reason that data about public sector 'liabilities' has been unavailable for most countries. In has to be acknowledged that, in some jurisdictions, the difference between the two figures may not be significant.

For the purpose of international comparisons, levels of debt are commonly related to the benchmark of Gross Domestic Product—to provide a crude index of 'affordability'. At state level, levels of debt are related to Gross State Product.

It is clear from published international comparisons that Australian public sector debt levels are very low by international standards. According to the 1999–2000 Commonwealth Budget papers, net government debt in Australia is expected to fall to 8.2 per cent of national product in 1999–2000. This compares with average debt levels of around 43 per cent of GDP for OECD (Organisation for Economic Co-operation and Development) countries since the mid-1990s (*1999–2000 Budget Paper No. 1*).

The OECD survey, based on figures provided by the various member countries, shows a net debt figure for Australia as a percentage of GDP at 7.2 per cent for 2000. This compares with 40.6 per cent for the United States, an average of 44.9 for the OECD, and an average of around 55.6 per cent in the European Union. Details are shown in the table below.

To further place Australian debt levels in context, it may be useful to consider the attitude of European countries to government borrowings. The Maastricht Treaty governing the activities

Table 3.1
GENERAL GOVERNMENT NET FINANCIAL LIABILITIES AS A PERCENTAGE OF NOMINAL GDP
Estimates and projections

	1997	1998	1999	2000
United States	44.0	41.9	41.6	40.6
Japan	18.5	30.3	38.2	46.4
Germany	46.5	47.3	47.9	47.9
France	41.8	43.6	45.0	45.6
Italy	108.8	107.0	105.1	102.8
United Kingdom	42.7	41.1	40.3	39.7
Canada	64.7	60.8	56.2	51.1
Total of above countries	**45.1**	**46.0**	**47.1**	**47.8**
Australia	20.4	16.1	11.0	7.3
Austria	43.9	44.2	45.1	45.4
Belgium	117.9	114.7	111.9	109.0
Denmark	38.2	35.7	31.9	27.7
Finland	-3.5	-4.1	-5.8	-7.4
Ireland	36.6	33.2	31.1	28.9
Korea	-23.8	-23.0	-20.7	-18.0
Netherlands	52.8	51.0	49.9	49.0
Norway	-41.6	-45.7	-49.1	-52.8
Spain	53.2	50.6	49.6	48.3
Sweden	21.6	18.7	16.7	14.1
Total of above smaller countries	**31.1**	**29.2**	**27.9**	**26.7**
Total of above OECD countries	**43.1**	**43.7**	**44.4**	**44.9**
Total of above European Union countries	**57.3**	**56.7**	**56.3**	**55.6**
Euro area	**59.9**	**59.6**	**59.3**	**58.6**

Source: Organisation for Economic Co-operation and Development, *OECD Economic Outlook 64*, December 1998.

Note: According to the 1999-2000 Commonwealth *Budget Paper No 1*, all data are for the total general government sector (i.e. the aggregate of all levels of government, including the social security sector but excluding the PTE sector). The OECD average data relate to only the 18 countries included in the *OECD Economic Outlook 64*. The European Union average data relate to only the 11 member countries of the EU included in the *OECD Economic Outlook 64*.

Data up to 1997 are outcomes, except for Japan where 1997 data is an estimate. The OECD data for 1998 to 2000, and the data for Australia and New Zealand for 1999 and 2000, are estimates. For Australia and New Zealand, data refer to the year ending 30 June.

of the European Community included requirements that member states take steps to ensure that their debt and deficits were to be within a nominated percent of gross domestic product (Article 104c(2)). A Protocol on the 'excessive deficit procedure' calls for alarm bells to be rung when a planned or actual government deficit exceeds 3 per cent of gross domestic product, or when government debt exceeds 60 per cent of gross domestic product, at market prices. In this context, 'government' encompasses central government, regional or local government and social security funds, but excludes commercial operations. Implementation of this Protocol has been deferred.

Against those benchmarks, comparable Australian government borrowings are at a comfortable level and certainly do not represent a debt crisis.

According to the 1999–2000 Commonwealth Budget Papers:

> The fiscal surpluses in prospect in each of the forward estimates years, along with expected proceeds from Commonwealth asset sales, provide for further substantial reductions in net debt ... the Government's target of halving the ratio of Commonwealth general government net debt to GDP over the five years to 2000–01 is expected to be exceeded by a substantial margin. Indeed, with the further sale of Telstra, by the end of the forward estimates period in 2002–03 Commonwealth general government net debt could be completely eliminated (*Budget Paper No. 1*, May 1999).

The question might be raised: does it make sense to base Federal government policies on financial targets rather than on targets for the provision of services to the community? Why should the Federal government aim to halve the ratio of general government net debt to GDP, given that existing levels are comfortably manageable, and that the country faces needs for further investment in social and physical infrastructure?

Claim: *'The proceeds of privatisation could reduce the burden of interest costs as a result of a reduction in debt'*

This argument presumes that current interest costs are a 'burden'—a very slippery concept indeed. To examine this argument, one needs to consider the following questions:

- What is a reasonable level of interest costs? Should it be expressed as a percentage of total revenues, or total budgetary outlays?
- If there are benchmark levels of interest costs, does this imply that governments move to privatise assets when interest costs go above a pre-determined threshold? If so, what explains the enthusiasm for privatising GTEs at a time when interest rates are low?

Generally, advocates of privatisation steer away from these questions.

Claim: 'The proceeds of privatisation by reducing debt will maintain (or improve) our credit rating and keep interest costs down'

Credit ratings measure an organisation's or a government's creditworthiness. That is, credit ratings show the 'ability and willingness to repay debt in a timely manner' (*Nicholls*, 1991). Two credit rating agencies rate governments in Australia—Standard and Poors (formerly Australian Ratings), and Moody's Investors Service.

State debt has been rated since the mid-1980s. Until June 1990, all states had the highest rating possible on domestic debt, that is, 'Triple A' or 'AAA'. The rating of state foreign currency debt has a ceiling of the Commonwealth's rating.

In June 1990, Victoria's credit rating was downgraded (it has since been upgraded again) and, later, all states except Queensland and New South Wales have received lower ratings. Since that time, there has been a major preoccupation with credit ratings.

Some identities place a great deal of importance on a government's credit rating. For example, on 12 November 1993, the then NSW Treasurer, Peter Collins, was enthusiastic at the confirmation of the state's credit rating by Standard and Poors. He said:

> In confirming the State's AAA rating, Standard and Poors has acknowledged that NSW continues to maintain manageable debt levels and that ongoing improvement can be expected in key debt indicators.
>
> S&P has expressed the view that the State sector net debt can be managed within the context of the State's financial profile and that the outlook for the AAA rating remains stable.

And, just before leaving his position of Secretary of the NSW Treasury after 18 years of service, Percy Allan listed as one of his three major policy achievements:

> the retention of the State's Triple A credit rating ... (*Weekend Australian*, 7–8/5/94).

The 1999–2000 NSW Budget claims that the benefits of adhering to its medium-term fiscal targets include the following:

> Ensure New South Wales strengthens its AAA rating, which will help attract business investment to the State and minimise interest expense (*1999–2000 NSW Budget Paper No. 2*).

Since NSW already has the highest possible credit rating, it is difficult to see how that can be strengthened.

And following the election of a new Labor government in Victoria, one commentator said:

> Maintaining the AAA rating is one of the keys to survival for Bracks ... (*The Australian*, 21/12/99).

When these agencies 'rate' governments' borrowings, they are essentially making judgments on political decisions. Indeed, the rating agencies have begun to comment on issues which go beyond the issue of creditworthiness: Hayward & Salvaris noted that the agencies

> have offered a view on whether Sydney can afford to have the Olympic Games (The Australian Financial Review, 12 November, 1993); praised the Kennett government for its public sector austerity program (The Australian Financial Review, 15 November, 1993); supported the Fahey government's decision to sell the NSW State Bank (Sydney Morning Herald, 3 September, 1993); and even offered views on whether the Australian Senate should delay passing the Federal budget (The Age, 25 October, 1993) (*Hayward & Salvaris*, 1994).

They also argued that rating agencies 'have come to acquire considerable influence in Australian state politics, yet their actions are based on narrow and contestable financial criteria which are applied inconsistently and often inappropriately to the public sector'. The agencies, in their view, 'do not carry out impartial and objective assessments of the public sector'.

> we agree wholeheartedly with Michael Pusey (1991) when he says that the whole credit rating process when applied to governments is a 'potent ideological fiction' (*Hayward & Salvaris*, 1994).

Whatever one's views about the political dimension of the work of ratings agencies, a close observation of the timings of announcements that they are looking closely or reviewing the status of individual governments suggest that they often appear to be reacting to media reports, rather than the earlier publication of relevant source data about government finances.

State credit ratings were recently as follows.

Table 3.2
STATE CREDIT RATINGS

State	Moody's Investors Service		S&P Ratings Group	
	Short term	Long term	Short term	Long term
New South Wales	P-1	Aaa	A-1+	AAA
Victoria	P-1	Aa1	A-1+	AAA
Queensland	P-1	Aaa	A-1+	AAA
Western Australia	P-1	Aaa	A-1+	AAA
South Australia	P-1	Aa2	A-1+	AA
Tasmania	P-1	Aa2	A-1+	AA-

Source: *1999–2000 NSW Budget Paper No. 2.*

Compared to other countries, the credit ratings of Australian States are high. For example, ratings of states in the USA range from AAA to as low as BBB. Even after Moody's Investors Service downgraded Victoria by an unprecedented (for Australia) two notches in October 1992, to A1, Moody's spokesman said:

> Victoria is still six notches away from being scarey (sic) (*AFR*, 29/10/92).

Even one of the conservative business writers, Terry McCrann, having said

> It should be clearly understood how close Victoria is to the precipice

then went on to say:

> A1 remains an exceptionally high rating (*Daily Telegraph*, 24/10/92).

The high credit ratings of Australian state governments may be contrasted with the arguments of those who advocate the sale of government assets for the sake of reducing debt in the name of improving credit ratings. Note that the credit rating agencies apparently accept that not all debt is bad for an economy. Of course, if debt was 'bad', they would not have anything to rate—they would be out of business.

Yet the credit rating of state governments has assumed the status of a potent political symbol. For example, the 1999–2000 NSW Budget Paper No 2 stated:

> New South Wales, Queensland and Western Australia have the highest ratings on both indexes.

Before that, the 1998–99 NSW Budget Paper was proud to report that:

New South Wales and Queensland are the highest rated on both indexes and therefore reap the benefit of lower interest costs.

But what would a fall in credit rating really cost a state?

In 1991 TCorp (the New South Wales Treasury Corporation) estimated that a downgrading of NSW's credit rating by one notch (to AA+) would increase borrowing costs by 15 to 20 basis points, an extra cost of $30 to $40 million per annum (*Nicholls*, 1991). (Note that one basis point is equivalent to one hundredth of one per cent.)

According to the 1994–95 NSW Budget Papers, during 1993–94, the average yield differential between triple A and double A rated securities was between 0.25 and 0.35 per cent.

> This implies that a downgrade from triple A to double A would increase new debt costs by around 1/3 per cent per annum. This would add slightly under $20 million to the New South Wales public sector interest bill in the first year, building up to over $50 million after five years. However, these costs reflect a marked fall from the previous financial year, possibly reflecting a decline in investors' concerns about credit differentials.

So according to the 1994–95 Budget Papers, a downgrading of the NSW credit rating by two notches—from AAA to AA—would have added less than $20 million to the NSW government interest bill in the first year. Presumably, it would have been less than $10 million for a one notch downgrade. This was at a time when Gross State Debt was reported to be almost $31 billion.

The 1999–2000 NSW Budget Papers claim that retaining a Triple A credit rating saves NSW up to $30 million per annum compared with a credit rating one level lower. This is at a time when gross state debt is estimated at over $32 billion.

In the event of a downgrading, existing borrowings would be unaffected and the financial impact of any re-rating would only be incurred as existing debt was rolled over. A government's debt would never be rolled over in a single year (as assumed by calculations of claimed savings from retaining Triple A ratings). Yet these arguments about credit ratings and interest costs seem to have been influential—but the sums involved are fairly trivial in the context of overall state spending. For example, a $10 million potential cost of a downgrade to NSW would only represent about 0.04 per cent of current total budget expenses; and a $30 million potential cost would represent 0.1 per cent of total expenses.

Investing in other things

Claim: *'The proceeds of privatisation could be used by governments to do things sooner'*

Everyone knows that it is easy to spend money. The hard bit is paying for it. Governments like delivering presents to their constituencies. Some of those presents are expensive, and cost more than is available from that year's revenues.

Governments are in an unusual position: their credit rating is, by and large, pretty good. They can readily borrow because they are in the position to raise money from taxes and charges. Even so, their financial affairs are subject to review and scrutiny by financial markets and the media. This oversight (however rudimentary) imposes some restrictions on their capacity to go on spending sprees. For politicians, once the notion of privatisation had some respectability, the sale of assets offered a way to buy presents without having to borrow to do so.

Every student of accounting or economics is taught the basic techniques of project evaluation. If a business has $10,000 to spend, and has to choose between two projects of similar risk which promise differing patterns of profits and cash flows in future years, then the way to choose between those projects is to 'discount' those cash flows to their present values, using a given rate of interest. Students learn to apply these techniques to rank projects which may generate cash flows over time horizons of ten, twenty or thirty years.

The choice of time horizons becomes of real significance when architects or engineers are designing or repairing infrastructure assets. Should a school be built to the same standards as cheap domestic housing, or should it be built of more durable materials, with the hope that it will last (with modest refurbishment) for 60, 80 or 100 years? Should a stretch of damaged waste water pipe be repaired (with the prospect of other sections of the same pipeline needing later repairs), or should it be replaced in its entirety? Architects and engineers choose 'design lives', having regard to such matters as the immediate cost of the alternatives, and costs over the whole of the expected life of those assets (and, one suspects rarely, some non-financial factors, such as inconvenience to the public if the same stretch of pavement is excavated on a series of occasions).

While architects and engineers and economists and accountants may assess projects in terms of long-term time horizons, politicians as a class are notorious for their short-term perspective. Some cynical observers describe the time horizons of politicians by asking:

Privatisation

How many days are there before the next election?

But resources are in short supply. Indeed, it is remarkable how little of a government's budget is available for discretionary allocation in the short term. Many government departments spend around 70–80 per cent of their budget on wages and salaries, and a large proportion of the remaining funds are often already committed because of past contractual arrangements. The capacity of an incoming government to make radical changes is severely limited.

Yet politicians in government tend to believe that bold initiatives—particularly on capital projects—are vote-winners. Some governments simply *announce* new capital projects (roads and bridges, railway lines, and so forth) just before an election. If these governments get returned to office, they are under pressure to honour these commitments. Whatever the history, governments wishing to embark on new initiatives often find difficulty in funding those projects.

This creates incentives for governments to raise money through sale of existing activities or businesses. A government can claim that a private sector purchaser will continue to provide the same services to the community. Then it can use the money raised from privatisation to fund something new, and vote-catching.

In principle, there is nothing wrong with this approach. There is no real reason for governments to simply accumulate assets. The coercive power of government may be necessary to get important national projects underway—otherwise private sector operators may be unable to gain access to corridors for pipelines or telecommunication cables or other infrastructure projects. Sometimes governments need to provide seed money to certain projects in the face of 'market failure' (e.g. the private sector has failed to provide a service because of perceptions of relatively high risks relative to low returns). Having seen construction of national infrastructure projects, or having demonstrated that other risky ventures could be successful, then government could well contemplate moving on—selling a business and reinvesting the proceeds in new ventures which promise to benefit the community.

But this leads us back to explore the basis of the claim that the proceeds of privatisation will enable governments to *do things sooner*—such as accelerating much-needed investment in capital works.

Although this is the claim, governments do not always spend the proceeds on what they say they will. Take for example the

NSW Coalition government. Between 1988 and 1994 the Coalition government raised almost $6 billion from the sale of public sector assets. This included the sale of the GIO in 1992 and the sale of the State Bank of NSW in 1994, as well as an unprecedented level of sales of 'surplus' government properties. However, contrary to promises in government-funded advertising campaigns that the proceeds of asset sales would be directed towards the renewal of infrastructure and debt reduction, neither actually occurred during the Coalition's term of office. According to published data for 1988–94, Public Sector Expenditure increased by $7.14 billion, of which increases in capital expenditure amounted to only $0.97 billion. At the same time, state 'debt' (whatever concept one chooses) actually increased.

Table 3.3
DEBT AND LIABILITIES OF THE NSW PUBLIC SECTOR

	1988 $b	1994 $b
Budget sector debt	14.66	17.60
Net budget sector debt	12.46	15.58
Gross state debt	25.27	30.82
Net state debt	20.14	21.86
Liabilities	46.75	57.42*
Liabilities as % GSP	44.9%	39.3%
Liabilities per capita	$8,194	$9,489

* The 1994 figure represents reported figures, plus $1.9 billion for FANMAC Trusts, as per the Auditor-General's 1994 qualified audit report. NSW Treasury did not include these liabilities on the grounds that these Trusts were not controlled entities; however, since that time, a reconstruction can be taken as confirming the Auditor General's assessment that these Trusts were 'controlled'.

Governments can always borrow to finance projects if they are important enough. They don't always need to sell assets in order to make new investment. But it is only prudent to maintain levels of borrowings within the bounds of 'affordability'.

That's what large corporations may choose to do in order to finance expansion—subject to the constraints that increasing levels of borrowings mean higher leverage which may mean higher returns to investors if things go well, and lesser returns (even losses) if things go worse than projected. For that reason, lenders may well demand higher returns as corporations become more highly geared. On the other hand, modest changes in levels of borrowings may well be ignored. Indeed, there is no body of research suggesting otherwise. Certainly modern finance theory has yet to develop any models to predict the impact on interest rates of changes in levels of borrowings. The impact of changing levels of borrowings on the returns demanded by lenders (as reflected in the prices for government bonds when they are traded in the securities market) appears to be minimal.

So why should governments prefer to sell assets rather than increase borrowings? Politics is all about shaping perceptions. So too, in many situations, is the practice of accounting. Given that governments and politicians and media commentators are all accustomed to focus on 'budget results', the sale of productive assets may be preferred to borrowings as a means of funding new ventures precisely because of differences in the way that these transactions are reported.

Cash-based reports of budget results will show the proceeds of asset sales as 'improving' reported performance, regardless of whether the assets were sold for a good or a bad price. But under accrual accounting, the sale of an asset for cash will be primarily reported as a change in the composition of a government's portfolio of assets. If the sale was equivalent to 'book value', then the transaction will have no effect on the budget result whatsoever. If the sale was at a better price, then only the difference between the proceeds and book value will be shown as a revenue. Conversely, if the sale proceeds were less than book value, the transaction will give rise to a recorded 'loss'—thus showing a poorer budget result.

The method of accounting used by governments does not affect the substance of past transactions; it only affects how they are reported. But at the same time, ways of reporting financial transactions create incentives for politicians to engage in certain types of transactions which will make their performance look good.

When private sector managers use these accounting devices they are said to be 'managing earnings'—or, less kindly, to be engaging in 'creative accounting'. Yet when the same practices are undertaken in the public sector, politicians (or ill-informed) media commentators often describe these transactions as prudent and responsible.

As already noted, not everyone can read a balance sheet. Even so, it is curious that media commentaries on public sector financial issues have been so preoccupied with the dollar value of a government's past borrowings—without considering whether funds borrowed in the past were applied to capital works of enduring value, or were simply spent on day-to-day operating expenditure.

One might well ask: what's wrong with a government borrowing money? Particularly if borrowings are invested in infrastructure which will produce benefits over the next 10–100 years?

Claim: 'The proceeds of privatisation could be spent on alternative ventures'

This is currently the theme propounded by some politician-touters (from either side of the fence) in a bid to attract votes in targeted electorates. They argue that funds from privatisation will be used on (what they hope are) popular projects. Or they suggest that, without the sale of a nominated enterprise, government will not be able to afford those projects.

For example, Prime Minister Howard—not known for his sensitivity to environmental issues—pledged an extra $250 million for the Natural Heritage Trust if the Senate allowed the sale of another 16 per cent of Telstra. Funds would be spent on forests, land care, rivers and fisheries (*SMH*, 11/9/98).

Later, Senator Richard Alston, the Federal Minister for Communications, Information Technology and the Arts, amplified the list of projects and benefits that (he implied) could only be funded if further shares in Telstra were sold:

> The benefits of the sale are obvious.
> At the current share price of about $8.50, selling the remainder of Telstra would allow us to come close to wiping out all Commonwealth Government debt, thereby freeing up billions of dollars of interest payments for other worthwhile economic and social projects.
> The sale of another 16 per cent of Telstra provide, for example, $671 million for (among other things) improvements to the environment, to provide untimed local calls for even the most remote subscribers, to provide SBS-TV to more than one million regional households, and to provide Internet access at local call rates for all Australians (*The Australian*, 4/3/99).

By 21 June 1999, the day before the sale of the next tranche of Telstra was approved by the Senate, the so-called 'social bonus' had increased to $1 billion earmarked for heritage and telecommunications programs, especially for the bush.

On the basis of the experience of spending following the sale of the first tranche of Telstra, one may be excused for treating these promises with suspicion. Following a request by the Federal Opposition the Auditor-General announced on 27 August 1999 that he will inquire into allegations that the Federal government misused a $70 million Federation Cultural and Heritage Projects (FCHP) program to the advantage of Coalition seats. This program is part of the Federation Fund set up following the sale of the first tranche of Telstra.

It has been revealed that two days before the 1998 Federal election was called, the Prime Minister approved the 60 projects

Privatisation

recommended by Senator Alston and Senator Robert Hill, the Minister for Environment and Heritage, under the FCHP program. The Ministers' recommendations overrode an independent assessment process to include 16 projects which scored poorly. Apparently, at least 114 others were assessed more highly than the 16 which the two Ministers upgraded.

During the election campaign, the government announced 32 of the winners; of which 26 were in Coalition seats (11 of these in marginals). Of the announcements before the election relating to marginal seats, roughly three quarters were in Coalition held electorates.

By December 1999 (when this book was finalised) the Auditor-General's report on this issue had not been issued.[3]

In NSW, the Coalition's *Energy Reform Plan* released just before the March 1999 election, stated that part of the proceeds of the sale of the NSW electricity industry would be used for:

> infrastructure renewal throughout regional NSW;

It stated:

> The Coalition will use proceeds from the $2.6 billion Millennium Fund to revitalise regional NSW.
>
> Proceeds from the fund will be used for new infrastructure projects which will provide job opportunities to regional NSW.
>
> Financial assistance will be made available from the Millennium Fund to provide:
> - employment development programs;
> - funding for small business incubators;
> - industry training centres;
> - land for industrial estates;
> - seed-funding for new industries; and
> - tax concessions and exemptions.

---

[3] The report, *Examination of the Federation Cultural and Heritage Projects Program* was eventually published in February 2000. It disclosed that the Ministers had 'later documented, but did not make public, the reasons for their decisions'. Ministers had taken two months to document their decisions, and had relied on 'memory and notes taken at the time, and which were not retained'. The report observed that 'it is difficult to engender confidence in a system of open and transparent decision-making, as part of a sound framework of public accountability, if access to documentation, explaining the reasons for approving particular projects, is not reasonably forthcoming'. Further, 'if Ministers are to control the announcement process [for grants], it would seem important, from the perspective of sound public administration, that it is done in such a way that there is no perception that the timing of announcements is being used for party political purposes'.

What should alarm all who hear these messages is that the politicians in question are often proposing to sell off revenue-earning assets, and to invest the proceeds in assets which will not earn revenues (and may even require funds to maintain). Rarely are these proposals questioned in terms of their medium-to-long-term financial impact. Obviously the overall purpose of public sector is to provide services to the community—not to make profits. But short-term populist proposals like these could, in time, impose burdens on future generations or even current generations.

Some privatisation proposals deserve serious consideration. If only financial considerations were relevant, then the sale of a government enterprise could be justified if reinvestment in an alternative venture (or ventures) would provide a better return to the community than retention of that enterprise in public ownership. For example, public sector resources can be used as 'seed money' to initiate projects which might not otherwise attract private sector investment capital. Once established (the argument goes) these ventures could attract private sector investors, thus enabling resources to be reallocated for other purposes (see e.g. *Independent Commission to Review State Finances* [WA], 1993, Vol 2).

The establishment of regional electricity distribution systems or water treatment plants is a case in point. With a sparse population, the prospective returns (and associated risks) did not attract private sector investment. Rather, the public sector was left to make an investment in these utilities. Possibly, governments of the day saw that there were votes to be won. Collectively, the community accepted the legitimacy of governments investing in infrastructure so that people living in regional communities could have access to those services. Decades later, when those electricity utilities are self-sustaining, the financial arguments for continued retention of those agencies deserves respectful attention, particularly if there is a pressing need for new investment in new forms of infrastructure.

However, it does not follow that the optimal way for a government to finance new ventures is necessarily to sell existing profitable businesses. At some point, the sale price of an existing business might be so low as to make the switching strategy unattractive. In some cases, it may be more attractive to retain existing enterprises, and to use the cash flows generated by those businesses to service and repay any borrowings required to fund new ventures.

Moreover, the evaluation of the options of sale or retention of a government-owned activity can never be entirely based on financial considerations. The initial reasons for government investment in trading enterprises often involve non-financial factors. For example, governments did not invest in water treatment plants to make a profit, but to safeguard public health. Government did not invest in public transport systems to make a profit (they usually don't!) but to provide members of the community with opportunities to obtain access to shops, health or education services, or places of employment.

Just as non-financial factors were important considerations when governments chose to make investment decisions, so too should they be important considerations when disinvestment (through privatisation) is being given even the most fleeting of consideration.

Some touters of privatisation give multiple reasons. For example, John Talbot, a director of the Australian Council for Infrastructure Development (an industry association self-described as 'promoting the role of the private sector in public infrastructure') stated:

> privatisation should not be a dirty word. It frees up public funds for the benefit of the community. It also transfers business risk to those whose profit motive should ensure better management of those risks, improved operating efficiency and, therefore, in the case of electricity, cheaper power (*SMH*, 4/3/99).

More on these reasons later.

Reducing risk

Claim: *'The sale of government trading enterprises would avoid involvement in risky enterprises'*

As noted above, one of the more recent arguments advanced in favour of privatisation is the claim that sale of government trading enterprises (or other activities) refers to risk, and the management of risk. It has been argued that when considering private sector involvement in the construction of infrastructure, ownership should rest with whichever sector (public or private) could best manage risk:

> If the circumstances suggest that the private sector is better placed to manage the risks incident to ownership, the public would be better served by eschewing public ownership (*Harris*, 1998).

This is an interesting argument, given that to date the greatest area for private sector investment in infrastructure has been in tollway schemes—and because this is an area where government is better able to handle risks than the private sector. (The government already controls alternative roads, alternative forms of transport, and motor vehicle licensing—and is in a position to cap liability claims.)

Similarly, it suggests that there are strong grounds for the public sector to control infrastructure when it is the sole 'user':

> Sydney Water is the sole customer of the water filtration plants built in the last several years at Prospect and elsewhere. Sydney Water is also in the best position to manage water consumption, and indeed is obliged to act reasonably to reduce consumption of filtered water. Under these conditions it is better placed than the private sector constructors, operators and maintainers of those plants to bear the risks incident to ownership (Harris, 1998).

However, the argument about risk-sharing is most commonly advanced by promoters of privatisation—and usually, without any articulation of the 'risks' supposedly now faced by the government.

Fred Hilmer, in his capacity as an adviser to the Commonwealth government in the early 1990s, promoted the idea of 'national competition' by making GTEs subject to the same tax regimes as private sector corporations (if only notionally), and the idea of exposing government enterprises to competition from the private sector. Both Commonwealth and state governments embraced these ideas. Possibly the states were compelled to go along since the Commonwealth made plain they would receive a lesser share of Commonwealth tax revenues if they did otherwise.

The whole exercise meant that governments which ran businesses operating in regional monopolies were to be exposed to competition from the private sector—and this meant they would also be exposed to risk. There was the risk that GTE prices in profitable city markets would be undercut by new entrants—leaving GTEs to service unprofitable country and regional customers. The prospect of these activities occurring was described as discussed in the context of the recognition of 'community service obligations' (CSOs) or 'universal service obligations'. It could equally have been identified as a source of 'risk' for the shareholder/investor.

Hilmer had earlier proposed the break-up of Pacific Power to promote competition. Later, as chairman of the newly-competitive Pacific Power, he emphasised the 'risk' argument for privatisation. According to Hilmer, the NSW government could not afford to retain its investment in Pacific Power because it was now a risky business. On the Channel 9 *Sunday* program, he said:

> The government is flat out providing schools, the hospitals, the roads, the level of spending services that this state needs. They've just had another Budget blow with the excise decision and to go along to this owner and say 'please sir we would like another billion dollars', a lot of which will be spent on high risk projects. For example, we're currently

doing work in Vietnam, doing work in India, doing work in China and doing the commissioning of a power station in Malaysia and so to say 'please sir we would like state government money to undertake those risky kind of investments' is simply not on and I can't see our Board and our management putting that to the government (5/10/97).

Similarly, the current Federal Finance Minister, John Fahey, in advocating the sale of Telstra stated:

> The Coalition government believes it should not expose taxpayers' money to the risk associated with a commercial business venture.
>
> It was appropriate to use taxpayers' money to fund the expansion of telecommunications across an isolated country at a time when the private sector was unwilling or incapable of taking on the risk. The private sector is now capable and prepared to take on that risk. The 'no-risk returns' the government once enjoyed in a monopoly are increasingly open to erosion, especially since the former Labor government opened up telecommunications to competition (*The Australian*, 28/7/98).

There seems to be an element of 'bait and switch' in this succession of arguments. Competition was presented as being a good thing for governments to do because it would lead to better outcomes for the consumer. But, once competitive arrangements were in place, competition was bad for governments with investments in GTEs, because it meant that taxpayers were now facing unacceptable levels of risk.

Yet, on the face of it, governments are in a very good position to manage financial risk associated with GTEs because they can regulate not only the prices and conditions of sale, they can also regulate the activities of their competitors. Academic research studies have suggested that regulated industries are viewed by the stock market as less risky than unregulated businesses—presumably because the whole apparatus of price regulation legitimises price increases to compensate for increased costs, and prevents individual players from using their market power to drive out smaller firms.

So, on the face of it, Hilmer's (and others') arguments are curious, to say the least. Closer inspection reveals some of the sources of potential risk. Electricity generation is a fairly stable technology, and access to sources of coal for NSW's coal-fired generators is not an issue. Arguably, the possibility of regulatory responses to concerns about greenhouse emissions is a risk factor for any coal-burning generator. But to Hilmer, the risk was not associated with problems in upgrading generation equipment. Hilmer explained that Pacific Power wanted to get involved in overseas infrastructure projects, and it was those projects that were risky.

Many would think that a state government would be ill-advised to invest taxpayers' funds on risky investments in other countries. Indeed, Hilmer's statements appear to be one of the first occasions that anyone has dared to presume that GTEs have a right to invest scarce capital provided by taxpayers in offshore entrepreneurial activity, rather than in expanding services to their local communities. Worse, Hilmer went on to talk about possibly missed employment opportunities if Pacific Power did not sell its services in offshore markets.

Ironically, it later emerged that Pacific Power had indeed been engaging in risky businesses through its dealings in the newly-competitive energy market. No doubt staunch advocates of privatisation might see this as support for their contention that the electricity business is too risky to remain in government ownership. However, on the basis of publicly available information, it appears that the risks in this case were unrelated to ownership issues but arose from inadequate management controls established within the organisation (see Box).

As noted above: many Australian GTEs were established because of 'market failure'—because the private sector had not delivered adequate services (often because of the scale of capital investment required, or because the prospective returns from that investment were not commensurate with the risks. Initially governments built electricity distribution systems, water treatment plants, and airports. Over time, demand for these services has stabilised and increased and many have become both profitable and of low risk. It is precisely because some of these GTEs are now viewed as being of relatively *low risk* that they are attractive to private investors.

There are occasional illustrations of this phenomenon. In July 1998 an executive from a US corporation was in Australia investigating opportunities for the establishment of a spaceport. Asked why the private sector was interested in such a business, he explained that government bodies had borne the risk of developing the technologies. Now that they were *low risk*, it was time for the private sector to become involved.

So, some advocates of privatisation say government should not be in activities because they are high risk, while some businessmen see things the other way around.

Maybe the biggest risk for government is that of *advisory risk*: whose advice can be trusted?

Privatisation

> **Box 3.5**
> **PACIFIC POWER'S LOSSES FROM ELECTRICITY TRADING—A FAILURE OF MANAGEMENT? OR STRICTLY BOARDROOM?**
>
> A combination of the break-up of state-based electricity businesses into generators and distributors, the privatisation of some entities, and the establishment of a state-based (and, later, a national market for electricity in December 1998) significant changed the nature of the risks faced by those businesses—and highlighted the need for astute management.
>
> Distributors in the new market were competing to secure long-term contracts to supply major customers, while being compelled to purchase electricity from a pool, in which spot prices for half-hour periods were very volatile. Generators would receive a wholesale price determined by the interaction of supply and demand. Participants in this market sought to reduce their risks of fluctuating returns by entering into 'commodity derivative contracts' to buy or sell notional quantities of energy over specified periods—with periodic financial settlements between the parties being based on the prices which actually emerged in the market. The NSW government-owned Pacific Power entered into a series of trades with a privatised and foreign-owned Victorian distributor, Powercor Australia, which was seeking to enter the NSW market, in competition with other NSW distributors which were allowed to compete for customers on a progressive basis. A dispute arose as to whether eleven of these futures contracts had been validly consummated and were enforceable. In the Victorian Supreme Court it was held that the contracts were valid (*Powercor Australia Ltd v. Pacific Power* [1999] VSC 110). The extent of Pacific Power's potential losses has yet to be established, but were estimated possibly as costing $300m–$400m over the 10 year life of the contracts, depending on prevailing power prices (*The Australian*, 21/12/99).
>
> The facts of the case seem remarkably similar to the problems which befell the electronics manufacturer and trading company AWA Ltd in the late 1980s and which led to extensive litigation, and debate about the relative responsibilities of auditors and company directors. A trader had engaged in long-term speculative dealings rather than short-term hedging. Records of these dealings were poor. Directors were not acquainted with the extent of financial exposures from these dealings, and management had not established adequate controls. After AWA incurred losses of $49.8 million, it sued its auditor for negligence but it was held that the auditor was entitled to a reduction in damages because of the contributory negligence of the company (AWA Ltd v Daniels [1991] 10 ACLC 933). It was later held that AWA's chief executive officer was liable for contributory negligence (AWA Ltd v Daniels [No. 2][1992] 10 ACLC 1,643).
>
> In the light of the AWA decisions, Fred Hilmer (then at the Australian Graduate School of Management) was invited by the Sydney Institute to review the role and responsibilities of company directors. The major theme of the report, *Strictly Boardroom* (1993) was that the focus of corporate governance should be on corporate profitability and wealth creation, and that the key role of a board should be to ensure that corporate management is continuously and effectively striving for above-average performance. In the process, *Strictly Boardroom* aggressively contested the emphasis placed in previously-published reviews of corporate governance on the need to upgrade regulatory arrangements and controls.
>
> Pacific Power's experience suggests that some of the lessons of the 1980s were not learned, and that it is wise for directors to ensure they regularly review delegations, internal controls and reporting arrangements.

Increasing efficiency/Reducing costs

Claim: *'Privatisation is necessary because government trading enterprises are inefficient and more efficient private sector firms can provide the same services at lower cost'*

This is the basic argument put forward by proponents of privatisation and advocates of smaller government. It amounts to a series of cliches, since such claims are not the product of systematic research into the performance of GTEs and the sources of any alleged inefficiencies. In fact, such claims also ignore the many productivity gains achieved by government businesses in the last decade or so, particularly through the use of computer technology.

There is no denying that politicians and other players are attracted by the appeal of simple, populist messages. In his book released in May 1999, George Stephanopoulos, a former senior adviser to the US President Bill Clinton, describes how the President came to declare:

> the era of big government is over.

According to Stephanopoulos, it was another former adviser to the President, Dick Morris, who got Clinton to make this statement. Similarly, Morris is claimed to have persuaded President Clinton to bomb Bosnia so the President would 'look strong' (*Stephanopoulos*, 1999).

At another level, proponents of privatisation invoke economic analysis, arguing that competition amongst profit-maximising firms means that services will be provided at the lowest cost because private providers are more cost effective than government agencies. Often those who put forward these arguments are engaged to represent the interests of the same profit-maximising and supposedly efficient private sector firms (which are seeking more business).

For example, John Talbot of the Australian Council for Infrastructure Development has advocated the sale of the NSW electricity industry in the following terms:

> if the private sector values the business at more than the Government does, that creates an opportunity that should be exploited. Private sector capital is more likely to drive cost reduction leading to lower prices for the consumer and higher profits—regulators can ensure a fair balance between the two (*SMH*, 4/3/99).

The suggestion that lower priced services will automatically be provided by an efficient private sector ignores:

- the risk that, if government is the sole or major purchaser of services, it may become hostage to the inefficiencies of single sellers of services;
- the tendency of private providers to service only the easy and profitable customers, while the difficult and unprofitable are neglected—a process called 'creaming';
- the creation of opportunities for bribery or kickbacks when government buys from the private sector (a phenomenon well documented by the NSW Independent Commission Against Corruption, since 56 per cent of its reports have concerned dealings between individuals from the private sector and 'public and elected officials'—see *ICAC, 1999*);
- the potential for private contractors to seek to influence political decisions, exploit contract incentives, and engage in cost overruns (outcomes which have been evident in American experience in the defence industry, highway construction, and medical care);
- the advantages of competition, following privatisation, result from lower wage levels and the greater use of casual workers with lesser employee entitlements.

Moreover, when an activity is privatised, a government may lose control of activities it is financing. The end result may be to affect the benefits of the most needy in the community.

At the very essence of the often-emotive arguments about the better run and more profitable private sector versus the less efficient and less profitable public sector GTEs, lie the methods and procedures used to assess performance.

There is little evidence to suggest that when politicians decide to sell a GTE, they do so on the basis of a detailed financial assessment of the performance of that business. Nor do political decisions appear to take account of the different conditions under which those GTEs operate, compared with those of the private sector.

For example, two years after coming to office then NSW Premier and Treasurer, Nick Greiner, announced a price freeze in real terms on government rates and charges which impact on households. The freeze meant that 'increases in specific charges are to be kept to a minimum and, in any event, are not to be increased beyond the Consumer Price Index level'. The freeze applied to the State Rail Authority and the State Transit Authority (passenger fares), water authorities, electricity generators and distributors, the Department of Housing (rentals on public housing), local councils (rates were pegged), and the Roads and Traffic Authority (in relation to private vehicle registration and drivers' licences (*Premier's Announcement*, 9/2/1990). Two months later Greiner announced the establishment of a Pricing Tribunal. He said:

> the Tribunal would have the twin effects of getting prices right on services provided by Government enterprises whole at the same time putting pressure on them to keep their operating costs down through greater efficiency and productivity

and:

> Criteria for recommending maximum prices will include:—
> - Protection for consumers.
> - The rate of inflation applying at the time.
> - The need for greater efficiency.
> - Protection of the environment.
> - An appropriate return on public sector assets (*Media Release*, 9/4/90).

Private sector firms are never subject to such wide-ranging controls and constraints.

In addition, while the proponents of privatisation highlight the economic benefits, they often ignore issues of accountability, equity of access to services, and the quality of those services.

Selling like the rest

Claim: *'The sale of a government trading enterprise is necessary because part of it has already been sold'*

The logic is obviously questionable. Because of some significant partial privatisations of government owned enterprises, some use this position as the reason for the sale of the remainder of the enterprise. The Federal Minister for Communications, Richard Alston, in criticising the Federal Opposition's criticism to the sale of the remainder of Telstra, said that the Opposition was prepared to 'leave Telstra in no-man's land', and to leave the government

> with a fundamental conflict of interest as both shareholder and regulator (*The Australian*, 4/3/99).

Similar comments were made by Frank Blount, Telstra's former chief executive, during the course of promoting his book (written with former Westpac chief Bob Joss), *Managing In Australia*. While noting that Telstra was performing 'admirably well, given the conflict of having to lose market share gracefully up to a point',

Blount claimed that 'unless this company can be freed from government ownership it's going to continue to slide'. The government, he claimed, has a conflict of interest in remaining a shareholder:

> It's a huge conflict. Here's the Minister responsible for communications policy which basically means taking the market share away from Telstra to get the industry to be stronger, and at the same time he's the shareholder representative. That's crazy (*Sun-Herald*, 24/10/99).

There is a temptation to quote the story (perhaps apocryphal) of the former Queensland politician, who, when asked if his role as a minister procuring goods from a family company constituted a 'conflict of interest', demurred:

> I think it's more a *commonality* of interest.

In that case an individual was in a position to exploit the joint role for his own benefit at the expense of taxpayers. That was a conflict of interest.

Similarly few would disagree that Commonwealth ministers who hold shares in companies subject to regulation by their departments appear to be facing a conflict of interest—in appearance, if not in fact. But one might well ask, what's wrong with government exploiting relationships for the benefit of taxpayers? If governments (as shareholders) reap rewards as shareholders of GTEs, then those benefits accrue to the community, not to ministers.

Claim: *'The sale of a government trading enterprise is necessary because the industry is privatised in other countries'*

The fallacious reasoning is self-evident. Yet such an argument has been actively advanced during the debate about the privatisation of various agencies.

For example, both Treasurer Peter Costello and Communications Minister Richard Alston have claimed that Telstra should be fully sold because other comparable countries have taken the same path. In early July 1998, Alston told the Senate:

> Every man and his dog has gone down that path and the only crowd that's left is North Korea.

Costello put the same argument in mid-July 1998 on ABC Radio's AM program:

> There is no reason why governments should be investing their money in phone companies. It is not in the US; it's not in England; it's not in Europe; it's not in Asia.

Touting Privatisation

When challenged on his claims that these countries had sold all of the public sector equity in telecommunications carriers, Costello insisted, 'Oh yes they have, yes they have.'

Then in March 1999, Senator Alston again claimed that communication carriers are owned by the private sector in other countries.

> Very few countries around the world see a reason for government to own high-technology telecommunications carriers—including 25 out of 29 OECD countries, as well as Cuba, South Africa and Albania (*The Australian*, 4/3/99).

The facts do not support these claims. The latest (1998) survey of the Organisation for Economic Co-operation and Development (OECD) of the communications sector in its industrialised member nations, shows that 100 per cent private ownership of phone companies is far from common. In only six of the OECD's 29 member countries—US, UK, Canada, Denmark, Mexico and New Zealand—are the telecommunications network operators fully privately owned. Partial privatisation appears the norm in most of the industrialised world—including Japan, the countries of Eastern Europe, France and Germany.

The form of fallacious reasoning known as 'appealing to authority' is well known, and well-used in political debate. Usually those who deliberately employ this technique in argument try to cite examples where those 'authorities' have thoroughly researched an issue, or where policies have already been adopted without inappropriate or unexpected outcomes, or where those policies remain relevant.

None of these might seem relevant when citing the experience of Albania or Cuba as being relevant 'authorities' on which to base Australia's communications policy. The economic and political circumstances of those countries are very different from that of Australia. Moreover, the explosive growth of the internet, of e-commerce, and the coming applications of digital technologies all suggest that the context in which other governments may have chosen to sell telecommunications carriers is not relevant to the current circumstances of this country.

Privatisation

Selling before the price falls

Claim: ***'The sale of a government trading enterprise is necessary because if it isn't sold now, its price will fall'***

Arguments favouring privatisation often include efforts to stampede acceptance on the basis that

> If we don't act now, the value will decline.

This is an interesting approach. It avoids scrutiny of estimates of retention value on the ground that whatever it is, it is falling fast.

It is instructive to watch the way the 'sell now before it is too late' argument emerges. Consider the sequence of events concerning NSW electricity assets (see Box).

The 'let's sell before it's too late' argument continues to be used by advocates of privatisation. In the same week that the $40 billion estimate of the proceeds of NSW electricity privatisation appeared, the principal author of the Hogg Report was heard to claim that, with competition, the government's investment in electricity

> is losing value all the time.

John Talbot, lobbyist of the Australian Council for Infrastructure Development, also continued to advocate sale of electricity businesses:

> In the new national market for electricity generation, many of the NSW generators do not rate well against their potential Queensland (government) and current Victorian (private) competitors.
>
> These more efficient competitors threaten to displace NSW Government generators from the market so the value of the NSW Government generators is likely to be eroded over time (*SMH*, 4/3/99).

It seems that some years ago there was no shortage of advocates of the benefits of competition to make public sector agencies more efficient. Competition would be good for GTEs. Now that competition is occurring through a national market, it is being argued that government-owned businesses are in so much trouble because of competition they should be sold for what is currently a good price. (Apparently the price can only go one way—down.)

Of course, there are serious doubts about the validity of some estimates of the proceeds from sale of electricity GTEs. Yet while advocates of privatisation have been warning that electricity businesses should be sold before they lose value, their estimates of the likely proceeds of sale have doubled.

Box 3.6
SELL NOW BEFORE IT IS TOO LATE

- 1995 (September): NSW Treasurer and Energy Minister Michael Egan announced that the NSW government ruled out privatisation of Pacific Power when he released a report on that organisation's future by Fred Hilmer. The Hilmer Report recommended disaggregating Pacific Power into two or three competing groups in order to achieve effective competition.
- 1997 (February): two long time advocates of the privatisation of the public sector, Percy Allan and Michael Lambert (both former heads of the NSW Treasury department) were quoted as calling for the privatisation of the State's *$20 billion* electricity industry because:

    > If not sold, privatised Victorian rivals would steal business from NSW generators and distribution companies, slashing their value and deepening Budget problems (*SMH*, 17/2/97).

- 1997 (May): NSW Treasurer Michael Egan proposed privatisation of the NSW electricity industry, because it is now competitive and there is no need for the government to own it. The sale estimate was *$22 billion*. Egan said:

    > The sale of our electricity utilities would raise up to $22,000 million, according to accounting firm, Arthur Andersen.
    > This would allow us to completely eliminate our budget sector net debt. That would mean annual savings to the Budget (i.e. the difference between interest paid and dividends received) of around $500 million each year.
    > In other words, we could have around and extra $500 million each year for better schools, better hospitals, better public transport and roads, a cleaner environment, safer streets and neighbourhoods, and better community services.
    > In addition, we'd have around $3,000 million left over for almost immediate new capital investment in social and economic infrastructure and environmental enhancements.

- 1997 (August): Deutsche Morgan Grenfell estimated for the 'Hogg' Committee of Inquiry into the Sale of NSW Electricity Assets that the 'the most likely sale value' of the electricity assets was *$25 billion*. Accordingly the Committee's 1997 report stated:

    > DMG conservatively estimate that the sale of the six distribution, three generation and the transmission businesses owned by the NSW Government is around $22b. Their view was that the most likely sale value would be $25b.

- 1999 (February): then NSW Shadow Treasurer Ron Phillips also proposed privatisation of the NSW electricity industry and claimed that the sale proceeds [to be used to 'repay debt' and to build new schools and hospital, etc.] would be *$25 billion*. He argued that privatisation of electricity was now urgent:

    > while the market was strong.
    > while the market's this good we should get on with it (*The Australian*, 5/2/99).

- 1999 (February): Mr. Alan James, described as Deutsche Bank's global head of utilities and energy, said there was 'potential to realise up to *$30 billion*' (*SMH*, 16/2/99);
- 1999 (February): NSW Deputy Leader of the Opposition George Souris claimed that the proceeds of electricity privatisation would be *$40 billion* (*SMH*, 16/2/99).

Ironically, within four years of the break-up of major Australian electricity businesses into smaller entities, in the interests of promoting competition, it has become clear that in overseas countries the power industry is doing the opposite, and going through a spate of mergers and acquisitions. For example on 12 October 1999, the board of New York's largest power company, Consolidated Edison, decided to buy Northeast Utilities, New England's largest power company for US$6.8 billion ($10.4 billion). Con Ed also bought Orange & Rockland Utilities, a New York gas and electric utility, for US$1.5 billion in July 1999. What the experts are saying is that 'big is best in the power industry'. As one expert, Robert Rubin from Bear Stearns & Co, put it:

> Size matters in the electricity transmission and distribution business. Consolidation of wires is inevitable (*The Australian*, 14/10/99).

This explains why overseas corporations have bid high to get a foothold in the Australian market.

This also brings to mind the comments of one former Treasury economist (over lunch, on the occasion of his departure for a new career in merchant banking). Ruminating on the policies of privatisation and restructuring of government trading enterprises then being promoted in the name of 'reform', he commented that some of his former economist colleagues were often 'extraordinarily naive':

> They've been sold the idea that private sector involvement means competition. They forget that private sector businesses generally work as hard as they can to *eliminate* competition.

It would indeed be ironic if policies of privatisation saw the replacement of government-owned regional monopolies with a smaller number of larger, privately-owned firms seeking to secure the benefits of monopolistic pricing

Summary

There is merit in some of the arguments for improving productivity through privatisation. However, there are also other ways of improving the productivity of government agencies.

Private sector involvement in delivering services for government does not need to come through privatisation. It can also come from private sector alternatives such as contracting, partnerships or joint ventures. These alternatives could be useful when a government is expanding a service or adding a new function, especially in areas where in-house capacity has not been developed and private sector firms are already providing similar services.

Touting Privatisation

However, many of the claims made for privatisation have little substance, and are reflect the misleading nature of current methods of reporting the financial results of governments. Traditional methods of presenting 'budgets' and 'budget results' have emphasised cash transactions—so that the proceeds from sale of government businesses produces budget surpluses (or smaller deficits). Yet often these apparent improvements in the financial stewardship of governments are illusory.

4

Government Trading Enterprises Have Been Undervalued

WHILE 'PRIVATISATION' CAN involve a variety of transactions or arrangements, the most commonly-understood form of privatisation involves the sale of government trading enterprises. Many will recall how the Commonwealth government sold shares in the former Commonwealth Bank of Australia, the Commonwealth Serum Laboratories (CSL Limited), and Telstra, or how the NSW government sold 100 per cent of the shares in the GIO. In those cases, the sale took the form of an offer of shares in a company through a public float. But privatisation can also occur through the sale of a government enterprise to private sector firms already operating in that industry (a 'trade sale'). In NSW, this was the way that a Coalition government privatised the State Bank of New South Wales Limited—by selling to Colonial Mutual.

Those cases are familiar because the privatisations involved corporations whose shares are publicly traded on the Australian Stock Exchange and press reports about their performance provide daily reminders of the activities of what were formerly government businesses. As shown in Chapter 2, some of those floats have done very well for the new shareholders.

Privatisations can be popular events for those who manage to secure large parcels of undervalued shares in an initial public offering. Large investors, and participants in the financial services industry, are usually the best placed to obtain large parcels of undervalued shares (though this is not peculiar to privatisation proposals: the same held true for the 1998 initial public offering of shares in Cable and Wireless Optus).

Some politicians have argued that the sale of shares to the public at low prices is necessary to obtain public support for privatisation. This argument could be a cynical attempt to buy votes, and thus further the proponents' own ambitions. Or it might simply reflect confusion between means and ends: resulting in the belief that privatisation—in any form and in any circumstance—is an end in itself, rather than a means to the end of providing services to the community.

But (as shown in Chapter 2 and as will be explored in more detail in the next chapter) any sale which produces a massive profit to those with funds available for investment is effectively a transaction which is producing a loss to the broader community. Potential beneficiaries face incentives to promote these wealth transfers—and not to publicise them too much.

Indeed, some sales of government businesses happen relatively quietly. They do not give rise to daily reminders of gains to shareholders and losses to vendors. Several of these sales have been to local corporations whose shares were not listed or publicly traded. The owners of those businesses had expertise in the industries concerned—commercial cleaning, equipment maintenance, or grain handling—and recognised an opportunity. Other little-publicised sales have been to foreign companies, notably firms anxious to gain a foothold in Australia's water and electricity industries, and in the management of airports.

These 'trade sales' of public utilities have often produced higher proceeds than local analysts had expected—underlining the strategic significance of an initial investment in an industry which promised more opportunities from further privatisations. Those events highlight the risk that the sale of regional public sector monopolies may lead to the emergence of larger and more powerful private monopolies.

Meantime, at the time of writing, advocates of privatisation are proposing the sale of electricity businesses in NSW and Tasmania, and greater involvement of the private sector (if not outright sale) in water businesses throughout the country.

As mentioned in Chapter 3, the idea of 'privatising' government trading enterprises or other agencies has gained momentum and been popularised by a variety of interest groups and politicians from across a wide range of the political spectrum. Yet there has been little published analysis of the *financial* implications to vendor governments (and, ultimately, the real owners, the public) of privatisation.

Governments are bound to go through the formal process of seeking parliament's authorisation of Budgets which detail proposed expenditure on 'programs'—sometimes for modest amounts of $1,000 or so. Yet governments can enter into privatisation transactions involving hundreds or even thousands of millions of dollars, often without any requirement for prior parliamentary scrutiny or approval.

Assessing the case for privatisation

The merits (or otherwise) of privatisation must be assessed on a case by case basis. But this becomes quite a complicated exercise, for three main reasons.

First, the case for or against privatisation depends on the type of industry involved, the significance of that industry to the well-being of the community, and the number and market power of participants in that industry after privatisation. Proposals to privatise labour-intensive government businesses, which act as suppliers of stationery items to government departments, may well deserve respectful attention. These activities are essentially internal housekeeping activities of government, and have minimal effect on the community. Technological changes—notably in e-commerce and the development of integrated management information systems—have made central government stores and warehousing facilities expensive anachronisms. Retention of these 'businesses' is likely to add costs to government without adding value to the services provided by the public sector.

On the other hand, proposals to privatise government trading enterprises (GTEs) in the water industry must be looked at in light of the role that water and waste water distribution systems play in providing basic services and in the maintenance of hygiene in urban communities. Water utilities are natural monopolies since it is impractical to establish other systems of pipes and treatment plants to serve a given community. If they were privately owned, there would still be a need to establish systems to monitor water quality and to subsidise the provision of these services (in the interests of protecting the health of the whole community), to regulate pricing practices, and to ensure that infrastructure investment is consistent with changing demography and government policies for town planning and regional development.

A second reason for the need to examine privatisation proposals on a case by case basis has to do with the state of the existing stock of assets. Technological change or ordinary wear and tear may place GTEs in the position of having to make massive investments in re-equipment, or to allocate substantial sums to refurbishing infrastructure. Sometimes these looming funding problems are the outcome of individual management decisions which went wrong, or generally a poor standard of financial management. Often they reflect a failure of the public service to properly inform governments and the community about emerging needs for reinvestment in infrastructure.

Governments, for their part, might prefer to allocate the funds demanded by GTEs to other projects. External events or crises have a way of changing priorities. In those circumstances, when retention of some government business activities will place demands on a government's future cash flows, there may be a case for diverting scarce resources to other projects promising better returns.

The third reason to look at privatisation proposals on a case by case basis arises from the way in which GTEs do their accounting. This issue is explored in some depth, because information about the past financial performance of Australian GTEs has often been distorted in a way that suggested that Australian GTEs were unprofitable and inefficient.

In fact, many of those GTEs were highly profitable by private sector standards, but had only *reported* low levels of profitability. This occurred because Australian GTEs were required to adopt radical methods of accounting—methods not used anywhere else in the world.

How 'GTE accounting' differs from private sector accounting

Most government trading enterprises in Australia have long used 'accrual accounting'—the form of accounting used by listed public companies. (Queensland GTEs are an exception: until recently they used a system of 'jam jar' or cash accounting—which meant that spending on long-lived assets such as buses or trains or electricity generators was treated in the same way as payments for wages and salaries.)

Accrual accounting differs from cash-based accounting in several ways. The totals of cash transactions involving revenues and expenses for a period are adjusted to take account of moneys owing and owed at the beginning and end of that period. Second, 'capital transactions'—those involving borrowings or investment in new assets—are excluded from the calculation of surplus or deficiency (profit or loss) during a period. Third, adjustments to the values of assets and liabilities are made each year. Some of those changes are counted as revenues or expenses, and included in the calculation of surplus or deficiency for the period. Currently, international accounting practices differ in the treatment of these adjustments—particularly the treatment of increases in the value of assets through changes in prices. By and large, accounting practices prescribed for public sector agencies by the Australian accounting profession are similar to those prescribed for private sector firms.

However, there are some important differences in the way private sector and public sector entities value their assets. It is not widely recognised that since the late 1980s, Australian GTEs have used a system of accounting which is radically different from that used in the private sector accounting. This has produced radically different financial results.

Traditional accounting techniques require assets to be initially measured at 'cost'. Long-lived or 'non-current' assets are subsequently then usually valued at figures based on 'historical cost'—in the sense that the initial cost is then allocated as an expense over the estimated useful life of the asset, with balance sheet values showing the residual of unallocated cost. Hence, an asset which cost $10,000 and which has an estimated useful life of ten years would be valued at $9,000 one year later, and the amount written off the asset value ($1,000) would be recorded as 'depreciation' expense for the period. The next year the asset would be valued at $8,000, and another $1,000 depreciation would be expensed—until after ten years the asset would be totally written down to zero. (This example assumes use of so-called 'straight line' depreciation, whereby depreciation charges are even throughout the asset's life. There are other methods: for example, tax laws permit use of 'reducing balance depreciation', which produces higher depreciation charges—and hence more tax deductions—in the early years of an asset's life.)

Not every asset is 'depreciated' in this way. Some assets—such as land - may be viewed as having an indefinite life, and hence their values do not have to be adjusted each year through depreciation. These asset values may be adjusted in other ways.

Australian companies periodically revalue assets upwards. Directors may decide that balance sheet values for certain assets are understated, and hence direct that these assets be revalued to estimates of current market values (or, perhaps, 'directors' valuations'). In this respect, Australian accounting practices differ significantly from those used in the USA. From the 1930s, the USA's Securities and Exchange Commission (SEC) set out to eradicate the practice of upward asset revaluations—and managed to do so mainly through its administration of registration processes, without ever having to issue a formal rule banning asset write-ups (*Walker*, 1992).

In Australia, upward asset revaluations have been used to ensure that recorded balance sheet figures are not misleading through understatement. Generally, the assets which are revalued upwards by private sector firms are items like land, patents, brand names or television licences—items which do not have to be 'depreciated'.

Government Trading Enterprises Have Been Undervalued

At this point, it should be emphasised that changes in asset valuations can have a significant effect on reported profits and balance sheet figures. Contemporary accounting practice is a mishmash of different practices in identifying assets and liabilities, and differences in valuation practices mean that balance sheets can seemingly involve adding up apples and oranges. Putting all that to one side, and adopting the economist's heroic assumption of 'all things being equal', we can then consider the impact of an upward asset revaluation on key indicators of financial performance.

Two key indicators of financial performance are *rate of return on assets* and *rate of return on equity*.

Rate of return on assets can be represented as:

$$\frac{\text{Profit for period}}{\text{Aggregate value of assets}} \times \frac{100}{1}$$

Suppose that a company had reported a profit for the year ended 30 June 2000 of $1 million. If the company's assets were valued at $5 million at 1 July 1999 (and there had been no additional investment from shareholders during the year), that would represent a rate of return of 20 per cent per annum. However, if on 1 July 1999 the company increased the recorded values of some of its assets (say, land) to $7.5 million, then the rate of return would be only 13.3 per cent.

The second key indicator of financial performance is rate of return on equity. Equity—the ownership interest—represents the difference between the aggregate values of assets and liabilities. Rate of return on equity is therefore:

$$\frac{\text{Profit for period}}{\text{Value of assets less value of liabilities}} \times \frac{100}{1}$$

Suppose in the above example, liabilities of the entity totalled $1 million, so that before the asset revaluation the equity was ($5 million–$1 million), or $4 million. The rate of return on equity would thus be 25 per cent per annum. After the upward asset revaluation, the rate of return on equity would be reduced to 15.4 per cent.

During the 1970s and early 1980s, the Australian accounting profession flirted with the idea of using a system of 'current value accounting' which involved regularly revaluing assets to estimates of 'current written down replacement price'. After some colourful debate, the profession eventually abandoned the proposal. The Commonwealth government made plain it would not accept any such system for taxation purposes. A few corporations experimented with supplementary 'current cost accounting' reports for a few years, but business support eventually evaporated. The accounting profession bravely kept a set of guidelines on how to implement CCA on its books (*SAP 1*), and 'strongly recommended' that entities present CCA reports as supplements to conventional financial statements. Yet private sector firms ignored these guidelines, and no Australian listed companies currently publish CCA reports.

Yet when a Coalition government was elected in NSW in 1988, and required all agencies to adopt full 'accrual accounting', it chose to introduce a form of CCA for asset valuation, rather than adopt private sector methods. The first step required GTEs and some other agencies to record all of their 'assets' on the balance sheet—some had not assigned values to infrastructure assets acquired in earlier decades—and these newly-recorded assets were valued at current replacement values. Then the use of this basis of asset valuation was extended to government departments.

A NSW Labor government had earlier introduced performance agreements between ministers and agencies, and some of these required GTEs to earn at least a minimum rate of return. But upward asset revaluations to current replacement prices increased the denominator in rate of return calculations. Moreover, while private sector firms tended to undertake upward revaluations for assets which did not have to be depreciated in terms of accounting standards—such as land, television licences, patents, and other intangibles—the public sector's upward revaluations often involved depreciable assets, leading to higher depreciation charges. Hence the revaluations also affected the *numerator* in rate of return calculations. They made rate of return targets harder to achieve in the public sector.

Some of the asset revaluations had a dramatic impact on reported asset values:

Example 1:

> Elcom's 1989 annual report disclosed that the Commission had undertaken substantial revaluations of property, plant and equipment. Book values had increased from $4,503.6 million in 1988 to $5,600.2 million in 1989. The book values of hydro-electric equipment at Brown Mountain, Burrinjuck, Hume, Keepit, Shoalhaven and Warragamba dams—some of which dated back to 1938—had been revalued upwards from $41 million to $134 million i.e. by 287 per cent. The NSW Auditor-General later noted that the revaluations had contributed $101.99 million in extra depreciation charges in the 1988–89 financial year.

Example 2:

The 1989 write-ups by Elcom were followed by further revaluations: during 1989–90 Elcom revalued its 132 kilovoltage transmission lines, underground feeders, substations and transformers of 132 kv and above, from historical cost to depreciated replacement value. That increased book values by $904.4 million.

Example 3:

Even larger write-ups were recorded in 1990 by the Sydney Water Board, which wrote-up some of its infrastructure assets by more than $2.5 billion—arguably the largest balance sheet revision ever undertaken in a single year by an Australian business. The write-ups involved pipes and tunnels which were said to have been only 18.5 per cent of the Board's infrastructure assets (presumably the calculation was based on prior book values); in those terms, 81.5 per cent of the Board's infrastructure assets await revaluation. The write-ups were said to have increased depreciation charges during the year by $35 million over what would have been charged had valuations based on historical cost been retained for the full year.

NSW had not pioneered the use of rate of return targets linked to values obtained from current cost accounting—that honour belongs to Victoria (see *Victorian Government*, 1986). But the Victorian approach only involved the use of supplementary disclosures in annual reports of 'rate of return' performance. Likewise the Commonwealth had used rate of return targets, though it did not establish across-the-board target rates of return, and did not report the results publicly. The Commonwealth's calculation of rate of return data did not use published accounting figures, but was based on adjusted data (see *Department of Treasury*, 1990). Representatives of the Commonwealth Department of Finance have advised that target rates of return were generally 'negotiated' between ministers and GTEs in their portfolios.

This changed when in the early 1990s other Australian governments were persuaded to follow the NSW example, in the interests of promoting efficiency in the GTE sector.

How efficient are Australia's GTEs?

The Special Premiers' Conference agreed in July 1991 to a proposal to establish a system of performance monitoring 'to assist governments in their efforts to achieve and sustain improvements in the ... efficiency and client responsiveness of GTEs'.

The idea of monitoring the performance of GTEs was hardly new—the Commonwealth and states each have central agencies which have a responsibility for oversighting the performance of departments and GTEs. Each government should have established systems to monitor the performance of GTEs, including comparisons with the performance of similar agencies elsewhere in Australia (or elsewhere). In fact, industry associations had already been established to do just that in the water and electricity industries.

So the question might well be asked: what advantages might flow from a coordinated national approach to monitoring? The states each needed to maintain their own monitoring arrangements, but a centralised operation might improve the quality of that work and extend its coverage. In practice, the Industry Commission simply reproduced materials provided by the states, and did not seem to have independently analysed the data provided by individual agencies. It seems possible that the whole exercise was designed to place political pressure on GTEs to improve their efficiency. A commendable objective, perhaps, but no substitute for informed and careful analysis of their activities at the local level.

The Industry Commission proposed that a range of performance indicators would be used, 'including accounting, economic and non-financial indicators' with the focus initially to be on providing 'accounting and non-financial measures of performance'. Comparisons were to be made between GTEs and 'comparable' private sector firms.

Around this time one of the authors was invited to a seminar in Albury at the headquarters of TUTA (the Trade Union Training Authority—since unfunded by the Coalition government). An economist from the Industry Commission presented a progress report on the development of sets of performance indicators for GTEs. Being unfamiliar with financial indicators of performance, the Industry Commission staff had apparently looked in their library, and found a work of excellence on which to base their analysis. It was, sadly, not the product of academic research. It was not even an undergraduate text on financial statement analysis. Rather, it was a publication designed for persons unsophisticated in financial matters who found themselves needing rudimentary information on the subject: an Australian Institute of Company Directors publication, the *Company Directors' Handbook* (*Morkel*, 1990).

Accordingly, the draft proposals were for the Steering Committee on National Performance Monitoring of GTEs to assemble data from GTEs about the 'current ratio' and the 'quick

Government Trading Enterprises Have Been Undervalued

assets ratio'.[1] Those indicators are highly relevant to small retail or manufacturing businesses trying to manage their working capital, but were not at all relevant to assess the financial performance of billion dollar enterprises managing most of the nation's infrastructure. There seemed to be little comprehension of the difficulties associated with comparing the financial performance of agencies which used different accounting methods to record developers' contributions, to expense or capitalise expenditure, to handle the recording of unfunded superannuation commitments, or to establish the bases for asset measurement and depreciation.

In any event, conventional methods of financial analysis often shed little light on 'efficiency'. Often one needs to look at the circumstances of individual industries and the business and physical environment in which they operate—to 'know the business'— before making judgments about efficiency.

A case in point concerns the profitability of one NSW electricity distributor. The pro-privatisation Greiner government established a committee to review this agency, and it essentially advocated 'corporatisation' of this distributor on the basis of findings about past inefficiencies and poor financial performance. Yet at that time, the government (as owner of the generator) also controlled the wholesale price of electricity. The government also established the mark-ups which distributors were allowed to impose on different classes of consumer. These mark-ups had changed over time, falling from an average mark-up of 33.9 per cent in 1982 to 26.6 per cent in 1989.

The following table presents data relating to changes in the operating income of the electricity distributor over a ten year period. These figures have been taken from published annual reports, but were subject to some adjustments—for example, eliminated was the effect of changes in accounting methods affecting depreciation expense. The most fundamental change was to translate 'electricity purchases' expense to the hypothetical amounts that would have been paid *if gross mark ups on bulk electricity were held stable at 27 per cent* during the ten year period.

---

[1] The current ratio, or (current assets/current liabilities), is a crude indicator of the capacity of an entity to pay its debts as and when they fall due. The quick ratio, or (current assets—inventories/current liabilities) is intended to indicate capacity to pay debts in the short term.

Privatisation

Table 4.1
PROSPECT COUNTY COUNCIL
PROFIT & LOSS STATEMENTS 1982–92
(hypothetical—as if wholesale margins had been standardised)

	1982 Dec	1983 Dec	1984 Dec	1985 Dec	1987 Jun	1988 Jun	1989 Jun	1990 Jun	1991 Jun	1992 Jun
	$m	$m	$m	$m	$m	$m	$m	$m	$m	$m
REVENUE										
Rates & charges	333	400	407	440	477	545	606	691	793	826
Less: Electricity purchases	243	292	297	321	348	398	442	504	579	603
GROSS MARGIN (assumed: 27%)	90	108	110	119	129	147	164	187	214	223
Other income, grants	18	21	18	21	23	26	39	37	38	49
Total oper. revenue	108	129	128	140	152	173	203	224	252	272
EXPENDITURE										
Subtransmission distribution	34	37	42	54	48	48	78	79	85	76
Customer service administration	43	49	53	57	62	59	38	38	42	43
Depreciation	8	11	11	11	15	17	19	24	31	32
Total oper. expend.	85	97	106	122	125	124	135	141	158	151
OPERATING INCOME	23	32	22	18	27	49	68	83	94	121
Operating income %* (change year on year)		43%	-32%	-19%	52%	83%	37%	22%	14%	29%

Amounts reported here have been rounded; percentages reported are based on raw data.
Source: R. G. Walker, *The Curran Report*—a Response, January 1993.

Gross mark-ups were outside the control of the electricity distributor. Yet, if margins had been held constant, operating income would have steadily increased over the period—by roughly 25 per cent per annum.

Back in 1992, the Greiner government's Curran Committee argued that Prospect was inefficient, and that only modest improvements in efficiency had been secured. Subsequently the Greiner government had established performance agreements to place Prospect (and other electricity distributors) under pressure (see *Curran Committee*, 1992). But analysis of the data presented above suggests that operating performance actually soared in 1987 and 1988 (probably as a consequence of changes in work practices and staff cuts made before the Greiner government came to office).

Overall, the above table suggests that the Curran Committee's claims about a track record of only modest gains in efficiency were fundamentally wrong. Major productivity gains had just been secured from the introduction of new technologies. Discussions with supply engineers and other staff confirmed this hypothesis: major investments in new technology in the early

1980s meant that the distributor could rapidly locate faults centrally (rather than by sending out gangs to look for fallen wires). Computer aided design replaced the work previously performed by hundreds of draftsmen. Investment in technology had enabled the automation of billing and accounts payable functions, which in turn had contributed to significant reductions in spending on customer administration.

Correspondingly, the Curran Committee's recipe for improving the productivity of this electricity distributor—through forced redundancies rather than through attrition—were also flawed.

But all that is history. The broader point is that an analysis of the productivity or efficiency of GTEs needs to be undertaken with care and with some appreciation of how underlying data have been compiled and what they reflect in terms of the physical or financial operations of those businesses. Sadly, that has not always been apparent in many government-sponsored analyses of the GTE sector. And if policy decisions are based on flawed data, the policies which are subsequently adopted by governments stand a good chance of also being flawed.

Initial analyses of Steering Committee on National Performance Monitoring of Government Trading Enterprises

The first set of reports produced by the Steering Committee on National Performance Monitoring of Government Trading Enterprises were assemblages of materials provided by state and territory Treasuries. They focused on financial indicators of performance, though mention was made of a series of Working Groups preparing non-financial indicators for each of six industry groups and some unclassified GTEs.

As the Steering Committee acknowledged, there were major differences in the way that performance information had been compiled, particularly with indicators based on asset valuation information. Hence there was a need to exercise caution in making comparisons across both GTEs and between the public and private sectors, on the basis of these initial results (*Steering Committee*, 1993).

Given that the Steering Committee's host organisation, the Industry Commission, had itself only recently made a series of comparisons between the performance of public and private sector organisations (all adverse to the public sector) this cautionary note was a concession of sorts. Unfortunately, the message came too late, and was not heeded.

Efforts to standardise GTE accounting

It appears that comments offered on the approach of relying on the *Company Directors' Handbook* were effective in sensitising Industry Commission staff that they did not have quite the right set of indicators, just yet. In true bureaucratic style, the Steering Committee established a 'working party'. The Working Party on Asset Valuation then enlisted the support of the accounting profession's Australian Accounting Research Foundation (AARF).

The staff of AARF could hardly have believed their luck. Several had experienced the failed attempt to introduce Current Cost Accounting in the 1970s—and were probably still feeling bruised by the experience. But now: they were being invited to advise all Australian governments about how they should value their assets. Some economists (encouraged by NSW Treasury's asset valuation guidelines) were arguing for assets to be valued at current values. A recipe was at hand—the previously ignored guidelines on CCA. In due course, the Working Party produced a paper outlining 'Draft Guidelines on Accounting Policy for Current Valuation of Assets for Government Trading Enterprises'. This paper endorsed the use of asset valuations based on replacement values.

Perhaps mindful of the strong feelings which emerged during the accounting profession's failure to introduce CCA in the 1970s, this time there was virtually no discussion or debate within professional journals or the technical literature about these proposals which would radically change public sector accounting in Australia. Further, public servants seemed nervous about the possible adverse reaction if they openly adopted the once-discredited CCA. The Working Party on Asset Valuation convened regular meetings at venues which provided members with suitable inspiration about ways of reforming public sector administration. When meeting in Launceston, it agreed that the label CCA was 'too aromatic'. So the Working Party hit on the term 'deprival value' to describe those techniques.

The draft guidelines were polished and refined and then issued by the Steering Committee on National Performance Monitoring of Government Trading Enterprises as a red-covered booklet, *Guidelines on accounting policy for the valuation of assets of Government Trading Enterprises* (1994). It was authoritative advocacy of the use of 'deprival values', though actually it reflected a misunderstanding of that concept as originally outlined in the technical literature on asset valuation: deprival value was an insurance concept. It refers to the basis on which an insured party can be compensated if deprived of an asset through theft or natural disasters or other misadventure.

Indeed, the papers issued by the Steering Committee and by its host organisation, the Industry Commission, echoed debates in the 1970s and reflected a lack of awareness of recent advocacy of the use of current replacement prices in asset valuation. One Industry Commission paper (*Temple-Heald*, 1991) included 26 references, a respectable indicator of scholarship for the 29 pages of text. But most of these were to other papers written by public servants, not by technical specialists. Only two papers were from the technical literature on accounting (one published in the early 1950s).

The major omission was a failure to recognise that recent advocacy of the use of current replacement prices was that for consistency, the amounts by which asset values were increased should be brought to account in the operating statement as revenues (or unrealised gains). Adoption of this model of 'clean surplus' accounting would have meant that poor rates of return would have been converted into good rates of return.

As it happened, the end result of the Working Party's ill-informed activities was that Australian GTEs were told to adopt a system of accounting which produces figures for 'profit' and 'rate of return' which differ substantially from the figures which would be produced by private sector firms using private sector accounting methods. If there had been openness about the debate, and more engagement with the academic and business communities, the outcome might have been different.

The Steering Committee had set out to ensure that the accounting methods used by GTEs would enable comparisons to be made between the government-owned businesses and 'comparable' private sector firms. They ended up promoting a system that ensured exactly the opposite.

Impact of accounting methods on reported profits of GTEs

Throughout the privatisation debate, there has been little public debate or media recognition of the way that audited financial reports have conveyed distorted representations of the profitability of GTEs.

Indeed, it is virtually impossible to unpick the effect of a range of accounting treatments upon the profitability of GTEs. It must also be recognised that public sector auditors have generally failed to comment on the issue. So far as the auditing profession is concerned, a financial statement audit assignment involves only providing reassurance about the quality of financial information presented. By and large, auditors see their job as being performed if financial statements comply with Australian Accounting Standards and relevant legislation. Since there are no accounting standards prescribing particular methods of asset valuation (or proscribing CCA) then auditors are generally content so long as financial reports are accompanied by suitable notes which adequately describe the accounting policies adopted in their preparation.

Some have had misgivings. In his 1990 report to parliament, NSW Auditor-General Ken Robson devoted some attention to the revaluations by the Sydney Water Board, and other agencies, and the effect of those revaluations on reported 'costs':

> It is the flow-on effect of additional depreciation charges following asset revaluation which is my major concern. This effect is displayed by increased costs and depressed operating results in the Income and Expenditure Statements.
>
> My concerns in this area are that costs will be overstated, that increased prices will be more easily justified and that depreciation charges will in time exceed original cost.

Since Ken Robson had only two years earlier claimed that accrual accounting would show 'the true annual cost of services', this was a courageous statement. It was described in friendly terms at the time as a 'Paulian conversion'—'except that on his road to Damascus, he has lost his faith' (*Walker*, 13/12/90), a description the NSW Auditor-General did not enjoy. He explained later that he had always understood accrual accounting to involve the use of historical cost valuation.

There has been little academic or media interest in the radical and controversial accounting methods used by some of Australia's largest enterprises. Hence there are little data available about the impact of these accounting policies. But there may be enough to demonstrate the impact of the new accounting on published balance sheets and operating statements.

The scale of the upward revaluations undertaken by three NSW GTEs in the period 1987–1995 is reported in Table 4.2. Sydney Water wrote up assets by $9 billion in this period; Pacific Power by more than $7 billion; and Prospect by around $1.5 billion (though some of these write ups—notably by Prospect—were reduced by same-year write-downs).

Table 4.2 also tracks the effect of these asset write-ups on reported rates of return on 'assets' and 'equity'. These rate of return indicators declined over time for both Sydney Water and Prospect—but as a result of book entries rather than changes in the way those businesses were run. Pacific Power's reported profitability has been consistently strong, though in part this reflected

Government Trading Enterprises Have Been Undervalued

the impact of a series of accounting changes which had the effect of 'managing' what was reported as earnings—though always within the rules established by accounting standards.

Table 4.2
KEY FINANCIAL DATA FOR SELECTED GTEs*

	1987/88 $000	1988/89 $000	1989/90 $000	1990/91 $000	1991/92 $000	1992/93 $000	1993/94 $000	1994/95 $000
Sydney Water								
Total assets	5,102,104	4,726,141	7,813,598	13,414,813	14,273,217	14,626,537	14,930,919	13,569,566
Revaluations	0	0	2,565,240	5,505,212	696,570	207,280	107,710	-1,676,917
Total liabilities	3,034,915	2,466,757	2,596,669	2,423,392	2,421,476	2,403,424	2,402,822	2,430,772
Total equity	2,067,189	2,259,384	5,216,929	10,991,421	11,851,741	12,223,113	12,528,097	11,138,794
EBIT	412,304	360,495	485,444	557,258	429,433	321,223	372,841	299,312
Revenue from operations	809,315	944,668	1,066,416	1,210,022	1,275,855	1,284,343	1,288,205	1,333,916
Operating surplus	129,381	142,287	251,124	197,965	140,356	122,222	189,176	145,069
Depreciation	76,489	80,844	113,728	244,782	305,096	291,249	292,897	248,395
Return on assets	8.4%	7.3%	7.7%	5.3%	3.1%	2.2%	2.5%	2.1%
Return on equity	7.7%	6.6%	6.7%	3.9%	1.8%	0.6%	1.1%	0.6%
Prospect Electricity								
Total assets	550,209	653,663	833,617	893,007	1,527,143	1,957,002	1,538,231	1,594,246
Revaluations	0	0	0	0	701,108	446,744	-470,087	47,399
Total liabilities	298,126	301,716	382,963	360,930	342,909	350,307	485,733	487,081
Total equity	252,083	351,947	450,654	532,077	1,184,234	1,606,695	1,052,498	1,107,165
EBIT	41,166	53,975	93,593	99,533	-30,050	56,646	78,413	99,012
Revenue from operations	547,599	622,297	705,814	815,202	857,913	891,812	893,557	873,379
Operating surplus	24,465	36,370	70,776	83,784	81,749	63,853	77,169	79,567
Total expenses (incl dep'n)	543,664	599,102	654,839	748,709	910,274	851,642	822,907	798,785
Depreciation	26,936	18,835	23,549	30,719	54,713	64,957	58,327	64,425
Return on assets	7.8%	9.0%	13.4%	11.5%	-2.5%	3.3%	4.5%	6.3%
Return on equity	10.8%	12.0%	20.3%	17.1%	-5.7%	0.6%	4.3%	5.8%
Pacific Power								
Total assets	6,473,646	7,129,286	7,564,791	7,668,164	10,463,194	10,526,724	11,753,363	8,196,690
Revaluations		61,688	1,145,964	904,571	0	2,095,523	127,034	1,609,229	-1,474,300

Privatisation

	1987/88 $000	1988/89 $000	1989/90 $000	1990/91 $000	1991/92 $000	1992/93 $000	1993/94 $000	1994/95 $000
Total liabilities	6,440,705	5,962,015	5,797,190	5,887,267	6,469,994	6,192,405	5,625,726	4,127,193
Total equity	32,941	1,167,271	1,767,001	1,780,897	3,993,200	4,394,316	6,127,637	4,069,497
EBIT	441,562	622,741	724,396	910,952	1,284,488	1,344,028	1,314,409	1,052,461
Revenue from operations	2,324,350	2,578,456	2,832,536	2,983,455	3,181,845	3,372,255	3,226,700	3,042,065
Operating surplus	21,436	71,574	201,351	345,532	564,756	704,126	790,116	629,851
Total expenses (incl dep'n)	2,374,506	2,565,627	2,724,698	2,735,397	2,713,894	2,618,795	2,437,412	2,444,705
Depreciation	248,060	401,308	436,335	390,987	473,387	562,459	441,120	410,801
Return on assets	6.8%	9.2%	9.8%	12.0%	14.2%	12.8%	11.8%	10.6%
Return on equity	-21.0%	5.3%	10.8%	18.0%	20.8%	10.7%	9.90%	8.3%

*Definitions: EBIT—earnings before interest and tax; Return on assets—Earnings before interest and tax/average total assets; Return on equity—Operating profit after tax/average total equity.
Source: Compiled from data reported in *Walker, Clarke & Dean*, 1997.

Indeed, Table 4.2 provides some evidence of how public sector managers learned to minimise the burdens of a combination of tough rate of return targets and upward asset revaluations (though some of those adjustments were netted off against upward revaluations reported here). Managers found ways of writing assets down again—partly through taking advantage of the flexibility of the CCA system, and partly through some creative interpretations of the CCA rules, and newly-introduced accounting standards which formally stated that assets should not be recorded at amounts in excess of 'recoverable amount'—defined as 'the net amount that is expected to be recovered through the cash inflows and outflows arising from its continued use and subsequent disposal' (AAS 10).

The CCA rules were nothing if not flexible. Managers looking at 'current written down replacement values' could virtually pick a number—any number. Technological changes meant that existing infrastructure could be constructed or rebuilt in different ways. Estimates of the cost of reconstruction were always going to be crude estimates. Deductions for wear and tear also involved crude estimates. Allowances for the value of the enhanced functionality of modern technology introduced even further arbitrary adjustments.

CCA requires valuation at the modern engineering equivalent of an asset, making allowance for changes in technology. Suppose that a business owned an electric typewriter, which was believed to be 50 per cent worn out. The current replacement value would be considered in relation to the current cost of word processing equipment.

Government Trading Enterprises Have Been Undervalued

Suppose a personal computer with printer and software costs $5,000. One way of working out the current replacement price of the electric typewriter in this subjective and arbitrary system of accounting would be to make assumptions about the difference in productivity between a word processor and typewriter. But that depends on whether you are using the equipment to produce hundreds of standard letters, or to write a book. Suppose an electric typewriter has 1/50 of the service potential of a word processor. The CCA values of the typewriter could then be calculated as 1/50 of $3,000 (or $60) divided by 2 (since the typewriter is half worn out—giving a figure of $30. But if one assumed that a typewriter was not 1/50 but 1/3 as 'productive' as a word processor, the value of that used typewriter would be $500—more than 1500 per cent higher. A key element in the valuation process—the identification of relative productive capacity or service potential—is arbitrary and subjective.

Another adaptation introduced in the 1990s application of CCA (or 'deprival value') was to introduce the idea that the correct valuation was the 'optimised deprival value'. Suppose that an electricity distributor has 1000 sub-stations each containing three transformers which cost an average of $2,000 each, but now have a book value of $1000 (after depreciation), or $3 million. Two of the transformers are in use at any time, the other is 'back up'. Application of this form of 'current value' accounting meant that the transformers had to be written up to $5,000 each, or $15 million. But this approach establishes tough rate of return targets. Enter the creative accountant, who decides that the optimum number of transformers needed by the electricity distributor was only two transformers at each sub-station, plus another 'spare' on a truck which could be moved from place to place when there were breakdowns. That means that the assets could be written down to 2/3 of their current written down replacement prices, that is, $10 million, plus the value of the mobile unit.

A further device used by GTEs to reduce recorded asset values was conveniently supplied by the accounting profession in 1991, when it amended accounting standards dealing with asset valuations.

The problem the profession was trying to address concerned the overstatement of the valuations of properties in the balance sheets of listed companies. So it introduced the 'recoverable amount test': non-current assets should not be shown in the balance sheet at figures in excess of their 'recoverable amount'. Unfortunately 'recoverable amount' was defined ambiguously, so that the RAT test (as it became known) could be interpreted at will. 'Recoverable amount' was said to be the value of the proceeds to be derived from using an asset and its eventual sale. If a firm had a property which cost $100 million but could be sold now for $40 million, what was its recoverable amount? Commonsense suggests $40 million, the current proceeds of short-term sale. But property owners could decide that recoverable amount was the likely sale price when the property cycle had recovered (say $100 million in five years) plus net rentals to be received over those five years.

One major difference between the public and private sector applications of the 'RAT test' was that in the private sector, 'recoverable amount' could be ascertained by reference to the proceeds of abandonment of an unprofitable project, whereas in the public sector, agencies had limited scope to abandon areas of service delivery. That restricted assessments of recoverable amount to the value of projected cash flows.

Creative interpretations of the RAT test enabled electricity distributors to make material reductions to asset values. Industry accountants collectively decided that the recoverable amount of an electricity distributor involved examination of the cash flows from operating their 'system', including the negative cash flows associated with expanding services in new subdivision areas. Many accountants would regard the installation of additional poles and wires as adding to assets, not as a reduction in value of an existing asset, the 'system'. Still, that kind of interpretation appears to have underpinned Prospect's write down of system assets by $1.18 billion in 1990–91 (reducing the effect of other upward asset revaluations in the same year).

Even NSW generator Pacific Power, under the chairmanship of competition and privatisation advocate Fred Hilmer, seized on the RAT test to reduce reported asset values and so make rate of return targets less burdensome.

Pacific Power had undertaken one of the largest write-ups of 'depreciable' assets in Australia's corporate history. Consequently its reported rates of return had slumped (see Table 4.2). Yet in an interview with ABC's Stateline presenter, Quentin Dempster in September 1997, it was apparent that Pacific Power's then chairman Fred Hilmer was unable or unwilling to discuss the effect of those write-ups on reported profits (see Box 4.1).

Even so, in 1994–95, Pacific Power then reversed the accounting treatments by writing assets *down* by $1.5 billion (or 13 per cent). It was claimed that the write-downs brought asset values to their 'recoverable amount', following 'the organisation's future entry into a competitive national market (*1995 Annual Report*). Again in 1995–96 there were further write-downs of $848 million. Hilmer, as chairman, had signed these accounts which, in effect, reported that competition had meant a loss of value to the shareholder.

Few Australian companies have written down their assets by $1.5 billion or $848 million in a single year. Normally write-downs

Government Trading Enterprises Have Been Undervalued

> **Box 4.1**
> **PACIFIC POWER FINANCIAL POSITION—**
> **PROFITS OVERSTATED OR UNDERSTATED?**
>
> **Dempster:** Pacific Power was reporting increasing profits until 1995. Would you agree that even those high reported profits were reduced by excessive depreciation charges after assets were written up by $5.5 billion to current replacement prices? Companies like BHP don't value their assets at current replacement values, do they?
>
> **Hilmer:** I can't really comment Quentin because I don't have those numbers in front of me. So I just don't know the answer to that question. I mean that's a fairly technical question. If you gave me the annual report I'm happy to talk to you about it. But I can't comment on that question. All I can say is that the profits up to 1995 that is prior to deregulation reflect profits when pricing was something that the government just set.
>
> **Dempster:** But what about the revaluing of the assets?
>
> **Hilmer:** Well I'm just not familiar . . . I don't have the specifics. I mean companies revalue assets. I'm on the board of a number of companies. It's good practice to keep your assets in line with real values and lots of companies do that.
>
> **Dempster:** The point of the question is you can minimise your reporting of profits because of the accountancy involved.
>
> **Hilmer:** You can, but you can also overstate it and I would have to go back in history if you wanted to have that discussion and look at the extent to which the accounting was fair. All I can tell is the accounting goes through a fairly rigorous auditing process from the Auditor-General. As far as I'm aware the accounts have never had anything but a clear bill of health.
>
> **Dempster:** I'm not suggesting they did, that they've had anything but a clean bill of health.
>
> **Hilmer:** No but you're suggesting that the profits have been overstated.
>
> **Dempster:** Or understated I think.
>
> **Hilmer:** Or understated. I wasn't sure which. All I can say is that as a member of the Board for the last few years, each time the accounts were prepared we've done so in accordance with accounting principles that an independent auditor tells us are an appropriate way to report what is he says a fair and true profit and I think that's been the tradition of the organisation. But you know if there were technical questions about the accounting I'd be happy to talk with you about them if I was given notice and had a chance to look at them.

on this scale reflect catastrophic losses to shareholders, and attract tabloid headlines. But Pacific Power's owners were 'only' NSW taxpayers, and these events passed unnoticed.

While some GTEs have tried to make rate of return targets less burdensome (by finding new reasons to reduce asset values), the overall effect of the use of replacement price accounting has been to materially reduce the reported profits of GTEs, relative to what would have been reported if those agencies consistently calculated their profits on a private-sector accounting basis. (For a fuller review of this evidence, see *Walker, Clarke & Dean*, 1997.)

Profitability of GTEs—using private sector accounting

Some years ago one of the authors was invited to contribute to a collection of essays on the Australian water industry—and to assess the financial performance of Australian water authorities (*Walker*, 1993). The approach adopted was to try to assemble data concerning operating results, and then to adjust that data so that the figures could be compared with the financial performance of listed public companies in the industrial sector. This involved identifying the year and amount of asset write-ups, and estimating the depreciation charges, which would otherwise have been recorded as expenses if the GTEs concerned, had not written up depreciable assets.

Adjustments were also made for the accounting treatment of unfunded superannuation commitments, since it was found that several GTEs had been recording as an 'expense' sums which recognised not only the cost of superannuation for the current financial year, but additional sums to compensate for under-recorded expense in prior years.[2]

However, in the course of the exercise the need for a further set of adjustments became apparent—to standardise the accounting treatment of 'donated assets'.

A significant proportion of the assets of water authorities has been acquired through compulsory 'donations' from property developers. An industry association, the Australian Water Resources Council (AWRC) had noted that developers' 'donations' were potentially 'an important source of capital for the industry' (*AWRC*, 1990) and reported that preliminary data collected in 1989 suggested that approximately 12 per cent of the water industry's assets had been provided by developers. The Industry Commission (1990) suggested that 12.5 per cent of the water industry's assets were acquired from this source, but added 'the actual figure is likely to be lower than this'. Yet it turned out that the 12.5 per cent represented a crude estimate of 1/8 of newly-acquired assets: the AWRC, in personal correspondence (21 September 1992) acknowledged that there was no intention to imply 'an accuracy of 0.5%'.

---

2 This treatment was consistent with the recommendations of actuaries that agencies should progressively 'fund' superannuation commitments over time. However, from an accounting perspective, the correct accounting treatment would have been to immediately recognise accrued liabilities for superannuation, while recognising part of that sum as an adjustment to the ownership equity in GTEs.

From an accounting perspective, the receipt of these 'donations' meant that water authorities had to record an increase in their assets—but most authorities recorded the receipt of these assets as an increase in 'reserves' rather than a source of revenues—the treatment indicated by the accounting profession's statements of accounting concepts. Having recorded increases in assets, water authorities then wrote-off those assets through depreciation charges (which were treated as expenses, and hence reduced reported profits). The combination of these treatments meant that the more donated assets received by those GTEs, the lower their reported profits.

The Industry Commission had criticised the 'low real rates of return' achieved by water authorities (1990) and reported that their earnings for the 1987–88 year was only 1.5 per cent per annum.

Similarly EPAC had claimed that the average rate of return on total assets earned by GTEs (in all industries) during the 1980s was actually negative (*EPAC*, 1990). Later EPAC estimated that the (positive) earnings of all GTEs was around 6.5 per cent in 1990–91, which was described as well below the long-term average of 10 per cent per annum for companies listed on the Australian Stock Exchange (*EPAC*, 1992). As for water authorities, EPAC claimed that they 'achieve quite low rates of return'—citing an average rate of return during 1990–91 of only 4.74 per cent, and 'profitability' (defined as rate of return on total assets) of only 2.36 per cent.

The same theme about the inadequacy of the rates of return being recorded by GTEs was pursued by the NSW Treasury in a 'research paper', *Public Authority Pricing in New South Wales* (1992). Subtitled 'Case studies of existing policies and their likely economic, social and political consequences', this document included reviews of the financial performance of a number of GTEs. In relation to the Sydney Water Board, for example, the document states:

> The Board expects to make a real rate of 3.1 per cent on its assets in 1991–92; this is low by commercial standards.

Given that this NSW Treasury document was published more than a year after the NSW Auditor-General had pointed out the impact of revaluations on depreciation and reported profits, the claim that the Sydney Water Board's rates of return had been 'low by commercial standards' reflected, at best, an astounding lack of understanding of the way that NSW agencies had been calculating their profits. Or perhaps NSW Treasury's research simply relied on the prior studies by the Industry Commission and EPAC.

Replication of those prior studies, to correct their misuse of accounting data, produced quite different results and put such claims into perspective.

Both the Industry Commission and EPAC had taken reported asset valuations and profit figures at face value, even though GTEs were using different accounting treatments for donated assets, Commonwealth grants, and catch-up provisioning for employee pension entitlements. EPAC in particular had compared the profitability of water authorities with private sector firms—even though private sector firms do not write-up depreciable assets.

Adjustments were made in some major areas. The aim was to ensure that data concerning the profitability of GTEs were comparable with that published by private sector corporations. It was possible to convert the GTE results to be consistent with methods used by private sector firms, but not vice versa (since no information was available about the current replacement prices of the assets of all listed companies). One set of adjustments removed the effect of upward revaluations of depreciable assets. Other significant adjustments corrected the accounting treatment of donated assets. Some minor adjustments standardised the treatment of reported operating profits (e.g. by deducting investment income from reported results from operations, in order to focus on the operational performance of GTEs).

The exercise of restating the reported results of ten GTEs was not easy—it consumed more than a hundred hours of detailed data recording and analysis. It is not an exercise that could be undertaken without expertise in accounting and a detailed knowledge of public sector accounting practices.

The adjusted data for 1991 presented a quite different profit picture of water industry profits.

	Water authorities %	ASX-listed corporations %
Return on equity	15	4.5
EBIT/total assets	12	7.4

Notes: Return on equity is before interest and taxes. EBIT = 'earnings before interest and taxes'. ASX data relates to industrial corporations and is from Australian Stock Exchange, *The Stock Exchange Financial and Profitability Study*, 1992. Reported data have been adjusted to present pre-tax returns, using average tax rates payable by listed companies.

In other words, on a 'standardised' accounting basis, water authorities were far more profitable than listed industrial companies. (That is not to be interpreted as advocacy of historical cost accounting—far from it. See *Walker, Clarke & Dean*, 2000.)

Lest readers think the validity of these calculations is debatable or questionable, it is worth recording that the accounting treatments used for donated assets were prescribed for NSW GTEs from 1992 (*NSW Treasury Circular* G1992/3), and in 1996 were formally endorsed by the Australian accounting profession's Urgent Issues Group. For a sense of the effect of prior accounting practices on reported profits from use of this one technique, one need look no further than the *1992 Annual Report* of Sydney Water. This disclosed that the previous treatment of donated assets had understated SWB's reported profits in prior years by no less than $1,052.02 million.

Yet Commonwealth-funded 'think tanks' had uncritically interpreted published data about the financial performance of water authorities as demonstrating the inefficiency of GTEs, relative to private sector enterprises (*EPAC*, 1990; *Industry Commission*, 1990, 1992).

Similar comments had been made about the supposed inefficiency of electricity authorities—by bodies like the Industry Commission and EPAC, and at state level in NSW, by committees of inquiry established to review the performance of individual electricity distributors.

Yet, those GTEs had also been revaluing depreciable assets upwards and failing to record the 'donation' of assets as revenues. For example, after upward asset revaluations required by NSW Treasury, Prospect Electricity had been reporting rates of return on operational assets of less than 5 per cent per annum. After making two adjustments to reported data (counting donations of assets as revenues and eliminating the effect of upward asset revaluations of depreciable assets) it was found that Prospect's financial performance, as measured by 'earnings before interest and taxes', represented an average rate of return of 10.67 per cent per annum over a ten year period. After further adjustments, mainly to retrospectively adjust for changes in accounting policies, that average rate of return on a 'private sector' accounting basis increased to around 14 per cent per annum (*Walker*, January 1993).

The study was extended to compile some key performance indicators for the 1991 financial year for other electricity distributors, with the following results.

Privatisation

Table 4.3
KEY FINANCIAL INDICATORS
FOR NSW ELECTRICITY DISTRIBUTORS 1991

	Sydney Electricity	Prospect Electricity	Melbourne Electricity	Shortland	Illawarra	Oxley	S. Mitchell
EBIT to total assets	15%	14%	12%	8%	16%	9%	9%
Rate of return on equity	33%	22%	14%	10%	23%	11%	9%
EBIT per employee	$18,034	$38,961	$15,848	$22,240	$27,959	$18,779	$39,683

Notes: EBIT—'earnings before interest and taxes'. All data obtained from 1991 annual accounts, except for S. Mitchell County Council, for which the latest available accounts (1989) were used.
Source: R.G. Walker, *The Curran Report—a Response*, January 1993.

The above data should again be related to the performance of ASX listed companies, which reported comparable rates of pre-tax returns on assets of only 7.4 per cent in 1991, or rates of return on equity of only 4.5 per cent.

Proponents of privatisation often make much of the alleged inefficiency of the workforce of GTEs, so the above data regarding earnings before interest and taxes per employee are of interest. Comparable 1991 data for companies listed on the Australian Stock Exchange were as follows: average net profit per employee after tax, $3,191 (equivalent to around $6,624 per employee before tax, after adjusting the NPBT figures for the year's average effective tax rate.) In these terms, electricity distributors appeared relatively efficient, compared to average industrial companies, but part of the explanation for those differences probably lies in the fact that electricity distributors are highly capital intensive organisations. But if one accepts that explanation, where does that leave claims by EPAC, the Industry Commission, and a range of advocates, that privatisation will have a material effect on overall efficiency?

One might have hoped that publication of these papers might have led to some rethinking by economists of their analyses and also of their strong conclusions about the inefficiency of GTEs. Both Commonwealth think tanks had claimed, on the basis of their rudimentary analysis of rates of return, that privatisation could lead to more efficient infrastructure provision (*EPAC*, 1992; *Industry Commission, Draft Report*, 1992). If their facts were wrong, surely their analysis would now change?

That was not to be. The conclusions remained. Only the argument in support was changed. At a commercial seminar one economist employed by EPAC put it this way:

Of course water authorities make high profits.

They are monopolies.

High profits by monopolies are not necessarily an indicator of efficiency.

It seems that staff of Australia's economic think tanks knew what were acceptable conclusions—e.g. that GTEs were inefficient—even though they had a bit of trouble sorting out what facts could be used as a demonstration of the findings of their research.

Understatement of GTE profits

Reviewing the last decade, it seems that an unusual conjunction of events promoted the view that Australian GTEs were inefficient, and that the community would be well-served if they were privatised. This created opportunities for ideologues to strut their stuff, for some ill-informed commentators to mindlessly endorse the rhetoric about privatisation—and for some well-informed individuals who could benefit from privatisation to engage in what might be kindly described as 'opportunistic behaviour'.

Consider the following.

- The Commonwealth Labor government was anxious to promote its credentials as a good economic manager, and used bodies like the Industry Commission and EPAC to promote reform—while endorsing proposals to drive efficiency in government enterprises through 'national competition' and efforts to compare the performance of individual GTEs throughout the country.
- Economists in the public service who were working on microeconomic reform were generally untrained in accounting (or tax, or finance) and were ill-equipped to analyse published financial statements, and hence to assess the performance of GTEs.
- Since many public servants lacked commercial knowledge about accounting, finance and tax, they lacked the skills to manage privatisations and to point out the potential financial risks to the public sector of allowing purchasers to negotiate guarantees and indemnities or to structure contracts of sale in a tax effective way.
- The accounting profession, after initially not wanting to get involved in public sector issues, decided that there were opportunities for revenue growth in that sector, after representatives had noted in the late 1970s that 'governments are big business'.
- NSW elected a Coalition government in 1988 with aspirations to 'reform' public sector financial management, and supported the accounting profession's proposals for the wider application of

accrual accounting in the public sector—which included trying to show the current value of assets held by GTEs. GTEs in the electricity and water industries were already using conservative accounting policies to record revenues from developer contributions; the valuation of assets at current replacement prices made the reported profitability of those agencies look even worse.
- The Commonwealth promoted the establishment of a system of national performance monitoring of GTEs—and the economists managing that process soon realised they were unable to resolve accounting issues—but sought the involvement of staff of the Australian Accounting Research Foundation, who just happened to be a cohort of 'true believers' on one side of a 1970s debate about current value accounting.
- Merchant bankers, major accounting firms, business-sponsored think tanks and other 'reformers' were not averse to using distorted financial information to promote their arguments about the inefficiency of the public sector and the need for privatisation.

One of the authors had first hand experience with the responses of a merchant bank to his suggestions that the profitability of the water industry had been distorted through the choice of unusual accounting policies. After an essay on this subject had been published, he received a call from an employee of a Melbourne-based merchant bank, ANZ McCaughan, who wanted to organise a meeting with his boss to discuss these issues, when he was next in Sydney. A meeting was duly arranged. The merchant banker explained that the timing of the paper was embarrassing: ANZ McCaughan had just prepared a publication advocating privatisation of the water industry. Would I be interested in a consultancy, to edit or update the text so that it covered those points (while still pushing privatisation)?

The offer was politely declined.

It was some months before the ANZ McCaughan publication appeared, under the title *The Australian Water Industry—Future Ownership Options* (1993). The report referred to its estimates of the current replacement values of assets in the industry ($80 billion for the whole industry, $40 billion in major urban water agencies)—though since not all GTEs were then using CCA, it is not clear how those estimates were derived. It also referred to the 'non commercial culture of operators', based on reported operating results.

> Consistently poor financial returns have been achieved with the [Australian water industry] for many years. This reflects an historically non-government culture of ownership of water agencies under government ownership ... The rate of return for the metropolitan water agencies as a whole is 2.8%.

Government Trading Enterprises Have Been Undervalued

It seemed that ANZ McCaughan had lost interest in updating the text to include adjusted profit figures—despite the fact that some water authorities had just openly acknowledged that prior profit figures had been understated through their treatment of developers' contributions. (Recall that Sydney Water had reported in 1992 that it had previously understated its reported profit by $1,052.02 million.) The only reference to the contestable nature of the quoted 2.8 per cent rate of return was an obscure footnote—located not at the foot of the page, not at the end of the chapter, but 117 pages further on. This footnote (in very small print) explained that the 2.8 per cent rate of return represented 'reported profit before interest, divided by the written down replacement cost of assets'. The source of those estimates was not explained.

All this suggests that advocates of privatisation do not bother to let facts get in the way of a good story. One can only wonder how many politicians or public servants were influenced by the thought that, in government ownership, massive businesses were earning less than one could obtain by putting money in the bank.

Certainly the debate about privatisation has been comprehensively won in some states—notably Victoria. So it is of more than passing interest to record that, by the time the Coalition government had lost office in 1999, Victoria (once the pioneer in reporting rate of return data on a current value basis) now led Australian governments in no longer requiring the reporting of replacement price data for its remaining GTEs—most of which are in the water industry. Rather (as the following Table suggests) Victoria (and to a lesser extent Western Australia and Tasmania) are retaining conventional, private sector accounting methods—valuing assets at historical cost less depreciation.

Table 4.4
USE OF 'CURRENT VALUES' BY AUSTRALIAN GTEs 1995–96

Industry	GTEs using current values		GTEs using historical cost	
Electricity	19	90%	2	10%
Gas	2	67%	1	15%
Water	14	70%	6	30%
Urban transport	7	70%	3	30%
Rail	2	33%	34	67%
Port authorities	8	57%	6	43%
Other	2	40%	3	60%
Totals	54	68%	25	32%

Privatisation

	GTEs using current values		GTEs using historical cost	
Jurisdiction				
New South Wales	19	100%	0	–
Victoria	5	43%	7	58%
Queensland	10	91%	1	9%
Western Australia	2	33%	4	67%
South Australia	4	100%	0	–
Tasmania	5	56%	4	44%
Aust. Capital Territory	1	50%	1	50%
Northern Territory	1	50%	1	50%
Commonwealth	8	100%	0	–
Totals	55	75%	18	25%

Source: adapted from data reported in *Steering Committee on National Performance Monitoring of GTEs* (1997). Totals differ apparently because of the classification of GTEs engaged in joint activities (e.g. water distribution and electricity generation).

Why? It's probably not because former Premier Jeff Kennett had strong views about accounting theory. If you are selling a business, then you want the highest price. That means you want potential buyers to think they can acquire a good earner. That is not the time to use CCA accounting, since CCA accounting depresses reported profits.

So, the likely explanation is that, having won the debate about the need to privatise GTEs, the Victorian government has reverted to conventional accounting methods and conventional asset valuation practices for its remaining businesses as part of the process of preparing them for sale.

In fact, with some exceptions (notably perennially loss-making railways) if GTEs are still using historical cost methods of asset valuation, that could be interpreted as signalling that the owner-government has targeted that GTE for privatisation.

How can the performance of GTEs be assessed?

The difficulties of analysing the financial performance of GTEs are considerable but not insurmountable. A key step involves standardising the basis of asset valuation and other accounting methods.

For government agencies which have not previously brought all of their assets to account, it may be necessary to find some basis for initial valuation (since available records may not even reveal what was spent in constructing those assets). But it is also worth bearing in mind that many of those assets are immovable, highly specialised, and of little value other than in their present use.

Government Trading Enterprises Have Been Undervalued

Regular asset revaluations of infrastructure assets is likely to ensure that the stream of reported operating profits of GTEs would be affected by changes in the replacement prices of assets—assets which may not need replacement.

Box 4.2 illustrates this point—and also the difficulties confronting anyone trying to assess the performance of GTEs on the basis of accounting reports. Box 4.2 illustrates a hypothetical case where management made an investment decision which promised to earn an internal rate of return of around 11 per cent. Those expectations were met perfectly. But accounting representations of profitability do not show a rate of return of 11 per cent per annum for each year. Using conventional methods of accounting (whereby assets are valued at historical cost less 'depreciation'), reported rates of return on assets escalate in the later years of the project as reported asset values decline.

However, applying CCA/deprival value accounting produces a different series of profit figures, and suggests that management performance was poor as a consequence of changes in the current replacement price of the assets used in the project. Using CCA in conjunction with the 'recoverable amount test' gives different results again. Under accounting standards, assets must be written down if the cash proceeds from use and sale exceed book value—but the standards are silent as to whether the 'recoverable amount: represents the gross sums expected to be received, or their present value'. On the assumptions provided in this illustration, use of the RAT test in Panel D produced a zero rate of return in later years, whereas in Panel E the RAT test produced a rate of return exactly equal to the discount rate selected to calculate the recoverable amount in 'present value' terms.

In short, Panels B, C, D and E show how different impressions of profitability can be obtained using different accounting methods. For public sector managers, they show how the use of CCA accounting means that reported profits can be affected by matters entirely outside their control. The manager who made a good investment decision which worked out perfectly can be shown to have produced a poor profit result under CCA.

If the system of accounting established for GTEs is intended to assist interested parties to track changes in the financial performance of GTEs over time, it is important to focus on results from operations—and to exclude the impact of changes in replacement prices on calculations of depreciation expense. Changes in replacement prices are outside the control of public sector managers.

Accordingly, while it may be desirable to record the current values of infrastructure assets (if only to ensure that reported rates of return have some contemporary significance) it may be inappropriate

Box 4.2
HOW ACCOUNTING METHODS AFFECT REPORTED RATES OF RETURN

PANEL A—Investment and subsequent cash flows

	t_0	t_1	t_2	t_3	t_4	t_5
Initial Investment (residual value: nil)	1000					
Operating cash flows		+270	+270	+270	+270	+270
Internal rate of return = 10.9% pa						

PANEL B—Conventional accounting

	t_0	t_1	t_2	t_3	t_4	t_5
Revenue		+270	+270	+270	+270	+270
Less depreciation		-200	-200	-200	-200	-200
Accounting profit		70	70	70	70	70
Asset values	1000	800	600	400	200	–
Rate of return on assets		**7%**	**9%**	**12%**	**17%**	**35%**

PANEL C—Current Cost Accounting*

	t_0	t_1	t_2	t_3	t_4	t_5
Revenue		+270	+270	+270	+270	+270
Less depreciation		-200	-200	-400	-400	-400
Accounting profit		70	70	-130	-130	-130
Asset values (revaluation at t^2)**	1000	800	1200	800	400	–
Rate of return on assets		**7%**	**8.7%**	**-11%**	**-16%**	**-32%**

* ignores recoverable amount test.
** assuming that the cost of replacing the assets has doubled at t_2 to $2000. Current written down replacement value at t_2 is (3/5 × $2000) = $1200; straight line depreciation applied for remaining useful life.

PANEL D—Current Cost Accounting with RAT test (without discounting)***

	t_0	t_1	t_2	t_3	t_4	t_5
Revenue		+270	+270	+270	+270	+270
Less depreciation		-200	-200	-270	-270	-270
Accounting profit		70	70	–	–	–
Asset values	1000	800	810	540	270	–
Rate of return on assets		**7%**	**8.7%**	**0%**	**0%**	**0%**

*** current written down replacement value at t^2 of $1200 is further reduced to gross amount of projected future cash flows ie. (270 × 3) = $810.

Government Trading Enterprises Have Been Undervalued

PANEL E—Current Cost Accounting with RAT test (using discounting)****

Revenue		+270	+270	+270	+270	+270
Less depreciation		-200	-163	-187	-211	239
Accounting profit		70	107	83	59	31
Asset values	1000	800	637	450	239	–
Rate of return on assets		7%	13%	13%	13%	13%

**** current written down replacement value at t2 reduced to net present value of projected future cash flows; discount rate assumed to be 13% per annum.

to regularly revise those valuations at short intervals. Contemporary regulatory requirements encourage listed companies to revalue properties every three years. For GTEs, a longer period (say 5–7 years) between revaluations would ensure that reported profits and rate of return present meaningful trends about operational performance. The reporting of profits and rates of return on an 'old' and new' valuation base in transitional years would ensure performance could be tracked without breaks in the series.

At the same time, it must be recognised that financial results only provide a partial picture of GTE performance. Most GTEs have little ability to adapt the nature of their operations and the clientele they serve. For example, a water authority cannot decide to stop servicing suburbs which have an unfavourable topology. Any decisions of that nature—including decisions about whether to invest in the extension of services to new areas—usually involve some kind of political directive.

For that reason, efforts to compare the financial performance of water authorities in (say) Sydney and Adelaide are unlikely to be very meaningful because of differences in the sites of those cities. Some may point to differences in financial results as evidence of managers to achieve 'world-class' performance. But Sydney's hilly sandstone terrain covers more than twenty catchments, and hence Sydney's water and waste water systems are likely to be more expensive to construct and operate than those in Adelaide, which is sited on a gentle slope running towards the sea. To put it another way: there are no such things as 'world-class' geography or demography.

The best one might hope for when assessing the performance of GTEs is to be able to track trends in performance of individual agencies—and to compare the efficiency of *aspects* of a GTE's activities with those of similarly-sized entities operating in similar environments and serving a population with a similar geographic distribution.

However, even then, adjustments would need to be made for the way in which the capital structure of a GTE had been established, and the way in which those enterprises were required to pay taxes, interest, or other charges to the consolidated fund.

Effect of capital structure on reported profits of GTEs

To illustrate just one of these points: suppose that the Commonwealth had two hypothetical GTEs, both with an equity investment of $10 million, and both producing earnings (before interest or taxes) of $900,000 per annum. GTE 'A' provides a much-demanded service but its clients are not concerned about the prices they are charged. GTE 'B' is in a politically sensitive area. There is concern that consumer groups may start media campaigns about excessively high prices. Hence it is proposed to change the capital structure of GTE 'B' so that the government's equity investment of $10 million is changed to be described as $5 million 'debt' (on which interest of 10 per cent per annum is charged) and $5 million 'equity'. These paper transactions transform the reported profitability of GTE 'B':

	GTE 'A'	GTE 'B'
Earnings before interest	$900,000	$900,000
Less interest		600,000
Reported profit	$900,000	$300,000
Equity	$10,000,000	$5,000,000
Borrowings from government	–	$5,000,000
Rate of return on equity	9% pa	6% pa

The example is hypothetical, but the use of these techniques is real enough. For example, when the Australian Telecommunications Corporation (Telecom) was a wholly government-owned entity, politicians faced incentives to avoid reporting that this public utility was earning high profits. Accordingly, the government's interest in Telecom was described as partly debt and partly 'equity'. This reduced reported rates of return at a time when the government was sensitive about the level of prices charged for phone calls.

Yet in substance, when looking at the returns paid to the government, there was no difference between 'profits' and 'interest' paid to the Commonwealth—both should be included in assessments of the returns being received by a public sector owner. If a GTE was

Government Trading Enterprises Have Been Undervalued

paying notional company tax to its owner-government, that too was just as much a return as an interest payment.

Profits versus dividends

Mention might also be made of a rather sneaky way that proponents of privatisation have talked-down the benefits being enjoyed by governments from current public sector ownership of GTEs. Whenever private sector analysts refer to the financial returns being obtained from investments in securities, they include both the cash streams generated from those investments, and the gains being enjoyed (or losses incurred) from increases in the market value of those securities.

For example: if you bought a government bond for $95 which was redeemable one year later for $100, and, in the meantime, paid interest of $4.50, then the return earned from that investment would be around 10 per cent per annum—a return of $9.50 ($4.50 interest plus $5 gain in the value of the bond) on an investment of $95. (It might be slightly more than 10 per cent per annum, depending on when the interest was paid.) Similarly, the rates of return earned on investments in shares is calculated by taking into account a combination of dividends, and increases in the value of those shares.

Yet some proponents of privatisation often provide a distorted set of numbers—and refer only to the dividends paid out by GTEs thus ignoring the effect that an accumulation of undistributed profits would have on the value of that enterprise.

This kind of fallacious analysis is often used in combination with other forms of distortion and misrepresentation. For example, some promoters of privatisation have pointed to the difference between *dividends received* from GTEs, and the savings in *interest payments* which might be made if a GTE was sold and the proceeds used to reduce government debt. Such a comparison is flawed because it:

- focuses only on dividends and ignores undistributed profits;
- ignores the gains being made by a government as owner of a GTE which is increasing in value;
- also ignores other returns received from a government owner in the form of interest, tax equivalents, guarantee charges and taxes or tax equivalents;
- assumes that the proceeds from sale will be very high—on the basis that private secret bidders are likely to value a privatised GTE on the basis of its overall earnings, not just its 'dividends':
- also assumes that private sector buyers will understand that the

earnings of the GTE may be far higher than those reported from the use of 'GTE accounting'.

Postscript

The foregoing description of how the reported profits of GTEs had been systematically understated was somewhat contentious when first published (*Walker*, 1993). But since that time, individual GTEs have changed their accounting to record the receipt of 'donated' assets as revenues, and the accounting profession has now required these practices. There has been some modest debate within the academic community about the unusual nature of GTE accounting practices, and the themes outlined above have not been challenged. Even economists at the Industry Commission appear to recognise that it was not possible to make direct comparisons between the reported financial results of GTEs and private sector firms.

The Industry Commission's series of annual publications of performance indicators for GTEs have now been concluded (as has the Industry Commission). Changes in the text of these are revealing.

Having first claimed that the performance indicators for GTEs could be compared with those calculated for private sector firms in Australia and elsewhere (*SCONPMGTE*, 1993), the last volume (issued by the newly-established Productivity Commission) acknowledged that 'in certain circumstances, comparisons between the [return on equity] between the private and public sectors may be invalid' (*Productivity Commission*, 1998).

Since the Commission's predecessor (the Industry Commission) had earlier made those same kind of invalid comparisons, and thereby prepared the political ground for privatisation on the basis of false analysis, this was all a bit late and a bit low-key as an admission of past error.

Indeed, to explain the reason why inter-sector comparisons of profitability were invalid, the Commission resorted to mendacious explanations. Instead of referring to the prior incorrect treatment of donated assets from land developers, or to the effect of upward asset revaluations on depreciation charges, the Commission claimed that since some government grants were treated by GTEs as revenues 'this addition to revenue raises the apparent ROE of GTEs *vis a vis* private sector entities' (*Productivity Commission*, 1998). However, this accounting treatment was not uniformly adopted by GTEs until prescribed by the accounting profession's Urgent Issues Group in 1996. Yet the Commission's report was discussing GTE performance from 1991–1997.

In a remarkable display of recalcitrance, the Productivity

Government Trading Enterprises Have Been Undervalued

Commission then repeated the same old observations about GTEs earning unacceptably low rates of return. It claimed that 'for many GTEs, returns to equity capital have been below rates obtainable from other investments'.

The Commission's members and staff should have been aware of the contested nature of rate of return data. They should also have been aware of the fact that comparisons of yields from alternative 'investments' customarily take into account the effect of holding gains on properties or securities—something which the economic think tanks had conspicuously failed to do when they sought evidence to suit preconceived ideas.

Worse, they then offered an explanation:

> This either suggests that financial performance was inadequate, or that the value of assets has not been written down sufficiently to reflect their true economic value.

No thought was given to alternative explanations. No mention was made of the treatments of donated assets, or of the impact of upward asset revaluations on depreciation. No mention was made of other factors: how the profitability of some GTEs had been affected by short-term charges for superannuation commitments incurred decades earlier, or by provisions for redundancies (for staff yet to be declared redundant), or of how some GTEs had been burdened with excessive levels of debt (in order to pay 'special dividends' to reduce reported budget deficits).

One can forgive ignorance of the subtleties of accounting and finance. But one must still despair at how an agency which is supposed to be a source of economic advice to the country's leaders can reduce complex phenomena to a series of simple certitudes—and then get it so wrong. Further, press comment has continued to uncritically echo claims that GTEs have been earning poor rates of return—without recognising that most Australian GTEs are using a system of accounting which is not used anywhere else in the world.

For example, on 1 November 1997, the *Sydney Morning Herald* reported that the NSW electricity industry was only earning 4 per cent on capital employed. The source of this claim was unstated—the 4 per cent rate of return was presented as fact. All this underlines the point that accounting can be quite creative. It can create illusions of profitability, and vice versa. Accounting can be used to shape perceptions.

The term 'creative accounting' is commonly associated with the way that private sector entrepreneurs have been able to create illusions of profitability through a combination of paper transactions and financial engineering. The same term might well be applied to the way Australian GTEs have been required to adopt unusual accounting methods which reduces their reported profitability.

The intentions might have been honourable—to place managements under pressure by imposing tough performance targets, and to drive efficiency so as to achieve a better deal for the community. But in the end, those responsible may have deceived themselves, as well as shaping perceptions about the unprofitability of businesses built with the use of taxpayers' money.

Unfortunately, with privatisation, governments have only one chance to get it wrong.

5

To Sell Or Not To Sell: Financial Implications

PRIVATISATIONS MAY INVOLVE a substantial financial loss to the community.

Some examples were provided in Chapter 2 of how many privatised government enterprises were sold at bargain prices. Possibly politicians are careful to provide investors with bargains. They may fear that disgruntled investors may become disgruntled voters. Hence they may set the price of initial public offerings of privatised businesses at a level lower than what their advisers consider the market would be prepared to pay. That means that initial investors get bargains—and the proceeds of privatisation are less than what might have been achieved if the shares were more keenly priced.

However that is only part of the story—possibly only a small part.

Even if sale prices were set at the *maximum* that the market might be prepared to pay, privatisations may still involve a further, substantial financial loss to the community. That is because the net proceeds of privatisation, plus the present value of cash flows from post-privatisation taxes and charges, will generally be less than the value of those businesses if retained in the hands of the public sector.

Financial factors are only some of the matters which are relevant to decisions about selling or retaining public sector enterprises— just as initial government involvement in particular activities and enterprises would have been based on factors other than the evaluation of costs and benefits in purely financial terms. The approach outlined here is, in effect, an 'economic rationalist' analysis of financial issues relevant to the privatisation decision.

In order to focus on the fundamental differences in the circumstances of public sector and private sector enterprises, a series of simple scenarios are presented in which a hypothetical government trading enterprise (GTE) will generate a known stream of future cash flows. This enables the 'value' of a GTE to a private sector purchaser to be examined under a range of assumptions—and for that value to be compared with 'retention value'.

Mainly because of differences in the circumstances of government-owners and private-sector purchasers, the present value of a future stream of cash flows to the government (i.e. retention value) will generally be greater than the present value of the same stream of cash flows to a prospective purchaser. The difference in values is more serious for state-government vendors than for the Commonwealth because the latter can earn taxes on future profits of privatised entities.

The following simple scenarios illustrate this relationship between sale and retention values, and then explore the extent to which the outcomes can vary depending on such matters as whether a private sector buyer believes he can earn more by improving operational efficiencies, or whether a vendor-government enables the purchaser to take advantage of generous tax minimisation opportunities.

Reference to a hypothetical GTE also avoids the necessity to make judgments about such matters as the current financial position of a specific agency, the validity of past reports on its profitability, the extent of any past cross-subsidisation, the prospects of the particular industry in which that GTE operates, and its need for additional investment.

Analysis of cash flows

As explained earlier, the reported profits of GTEs do not necessarily provide a good indicator of whether they are efficient or inefficient, and accordingly, whether it makes sense for those enterprises to be privatised. Reported profits of government activities may be seriously affected by choices of accounting techniques and financing arrangements. Moreover, public sector organisations are just as likely as some listed public companies to engage in 'creative accounting' or financial deals to enhance reported rates of return. Or (unlike their private sector counterparts) they may seek to disguise their underlying profitability.

A more relevant basis for evaluating the financial implications of privatisation of GTEs is provided by analysis of the cash flows likely to be received by a vendor-government if a particular GTE was retained, or sold.

The accompanying diagram illustrates the sources of cash flows arising from either retention or sale.

To Sell Or Not To Sell: Financial Implications

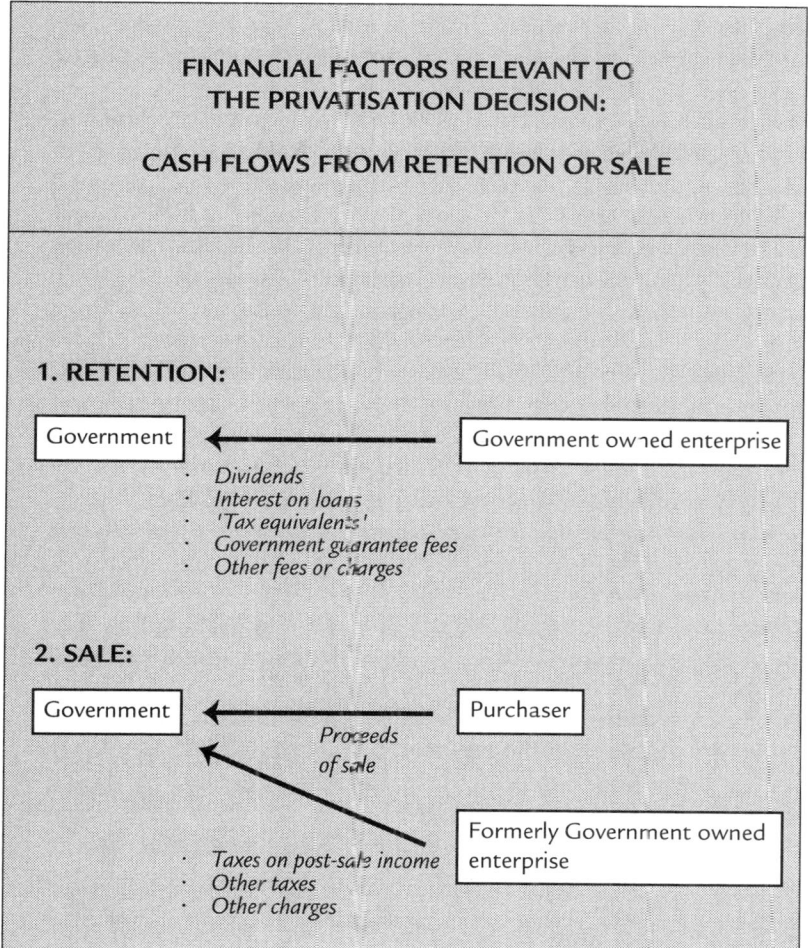

(1) Cash flows from retention

As 'owner', a government may enjoy the benefit of cash flows from a government enterprise in several forms: dividends, interest revenues, tax equivalents, guarantee fees and other charges. In some situations a GTE may have built-up excessive holdings of cash or other assets (particularly in light of the existence of any government guarantees for borrowings, which reduce the need to retain a 'cushion' of cash reserves in case of downturn or misadventure).

Conversely, a government-owner may be obliged to make contributions to an enterprise to enable the latter to undertake major capital works, or to initiate new ventures—just as listed corporations in the private sector resolve to make rights issues in order to raise additional equity capital.

Dividend distributions by a GTE will generally be related to enterprise profitability—though this is not necessarily the case. In NSW, for example, the government has demanded and received 'special dividends' from GTEs (notably the former Sydney County Council, Prospect Electricity, and the Sydney Water Board) which substantially exceeded the current profits of those agencies.

A government may also receive interest on loans to GTEs. Some of these loans may reflect decisions to describe a government's pre-existing investment in a GTE as part 'equity', part 'debt'. This practice reduces the reported profits of those agencies by the amount of interest charged on 'debt'. This practice may be attractive for governments which wish to avoid suggesting that some GTEs are excessively profitable and are exploiting monopoly power.

In these situations, the choice of capital structure (i.e. the relative percentage of debt and equity) would not affect the aggregate returns to the government, as owner/lender. The same would not be true in the private sector, where interest is tax deductible. For private sector firms, the choice of equity structure would have real effects on tax payments and, hence, on cash flows to the owner/lender. Obviously the higher the level of interest-bearing loans from the government, the less the reported profits of a GTE.

For the purpose of analysing the cash flows generated by a GTE to the government, it is appropriate to treat cash flows in the form of dividends and cash flows in the form of interest payments on the same basis.

Similarly, it is appropriate to include cash flows described as 'tax equivalents', guarantee fees, or capital charges. Even though government enterprises may be exempt from Commonwealth income taxes, some states have established a regime whereby government enterprises are required to pay the equivalent of taxes to the consolidated fund. The claimed rationale for levying these notional taxes was to place GTEs on the same footing as private sector enterprises, and enable more direct comparisons to be made of the financial performance of enterprises from either sector. Later, these practices were extended to all state governments, in the name of 'national competition policy'.

Likewise, arguments about the supposed need for a level playing field have provided the rationale for governments to levy a 'guarantee charge' on enterprises which have borrowed with the benefit of government guarantees. The guarantee charge may be pitched at a rate which brings the financing costs of a government-owned enterprise into line with the rates of interest payable by comparable private sector firms. Whatever the rationale, these charges provide additional cash flows to the owner-government while reducing the reported profits of a government-owned enterprise.

Overall, the government may be enjoying a stream of cash flows from its ownership of a GTE. These cash flows would cease if an enterprise was sold (though, as discussed below, for the Commonwealth government a new source of cash flows should subsequently arise in the form of taxes on the profits of the new owner).

(2) Cash flows from sale

The amount a prospective purchaser would be prepared to pay to acquire a GTE will depend, to a large extent, on the purchaser's expectations about the cash flows which can be generated from that enterprise in the future.

Managers of a private sector corporation contemplating the purchase of a GTE may believe that they can earn financial returns superior to those earned under public ownership. They may plan to apply improved technologies, or to secure synergies from linking their existing activities with those conducted by the GTE. They may believe they can introduce 'efficiencies' through reduced staffing, less expensive employment arrangements, and the avoidance of unprofitable activities which governments deem 'community service obligations'.

Undoubtedly there will always be scope for any organisation to introduce marginal efficiencies. Further, it may be possible for private sector managers to increase prices more than might be feasible under public ownership (where governments are subject to targeted pressure from constituents). Indeed, some governments may view privatisation as a way of avoiding the political problems which routinely arise whenever attempts are made to increase the prices of certain services.

The extent to which a change of management after privatisation might lead to 'efficiencies' would depend both on how effectively the GTE has been managed in the past, and the nature of its operations (e.g. there may be greater opportunity to introduce 'efficencies' in labour intensive activities than in capital intensive activities which utilise a small workforce).

There are some other, fundamental factors affecting the price which might be offered by a private sector entity to acquire a GTE. In principle, a private sector buyer will not bid more than the 'value' it ascribes to an enterprise, where 'value' represents the present value of the cash flows expected to be derived from that investment.

In some situations, private sector buyers may be anxious to enter a new market—and may look upon a bid price as a strategic investment which may lead to more profitable opportunities in later years. In that case, buyers may well compare the expected returns and the expected outlays associated with a chain of investments. The buyer's analysis of the purchase decision is, in principle, similar to the analysis outlined in the simple case described here, save that the buyer may view the acquisition as a privatised enterprise as involving purchase of the cash flows expected to be derived from that investment, plus an 'option' to make further investments in the same industry.

A more fundamental factor affecting the pricing of government businesses on privatisation is that the circumstances of governments and private sector purchasers are different.

Private sector purchasers of government businesses face *a higher cost of capital* since they must provide an equity return to their shareholders while also paying higher rates of interest on borrowings than are faced by sovereign governments. (A fuller discussion of arguments relating to the 'cost of capital' is in an Appendix.)

Because of these differences, the present value of the cash flows to be derived from a GTE is likely to be significantly less to a private sector purchaser than it is to the government-vendor. That means that the maximum price a private sector purchaser can afford to pay to buy a GTE will be *less* than the value of that enterprise to the vendor-government (and hence to the community which that government represents).

Moreover, private sector purchasers *are liable to pay company tax (and other taxes and charges)* whereas Commonwealth and state statutory authorities are exempt from company tax, and may be exempt from other state or Commonwealth charges, and local government rates. Some bidders may have carry-forward tax losses which will affect the cash flows they can derive from the investment. Others may adopt tax minimisation strategies.

There is some disagreement in the technical literature about what the impact of taxes and charges should be on the cost of capital and on valuations. Often those commentaries are normative arguments, based on assumptions made about what kind of outcomes are desirable in the interests of economic efficiency (assuming the existence of perfect knowledge or other conditions associated with perfect markets). The approach adopted here involves looking at the circumstances of owners or potential owners under a series of more realistic conditions.

For example, there may be differences between the circumstances of different bidders. Some bidders will have better credit ratings (and hence face different interest costs) than others. Bidders will also differ in their assessments of what is the relevant 'cost' of equity capital. The extent of the gap between value to a purchaser and value to a government vendor may be affected by the vendor providing tax concessions, or by the buyer adopting tax minimisation strategies, as well as prospective efficiencies or synergies which the buyer believes he can secure.

Buyers may also assess the extent to which they may be able to increase the prices currently being charged by a GTE, once they have purchased it. They may also make allowance for the likely cost of dealing with government agencies established to regulate prices, trade practices, or environmental issues.

The price paid by a purchaser will exceed the proceeds received by the government, because of transaction costs. The benefit from these transaction costs (such as the preparation of prospectus, and the marketing of a float) will go to intermediaries: lawyers, accountants, advertising and marketing consultants, underwriters and brokers.

There are likely to be some economies of scale in relation to transactions costs: the larger the transaction, the less the level of transactions costs as a percentage of gross proceeds (*Woo & Lange*, 1992). UK experience indicates that the expenses of privatisation have ranged from 2.8 per cent to 11.2 per cent of gross proceeds (*Vickers & Yarrow*, 1988; *National Audit Office* [UK], 1992; *Walker & Howard*, 1992). Experience with some major Australian privatisations has been mixed. The expenses of the 1991 sale of around 30 per cent of the Commonwealth Bank appears to have constituted 2.9 per cent of the gross proceeds; however, given that much of the work was undertaken in-house, this estimate may be a little conservative. On the other hand, the privatisation of the NSW Government Insurance Office (GIO) cost over $71 million, or 5.94 per cent of the proceeds (*Walker & Howard*, 1992).

(3) Cash flows after sale

A national government which privatises a GTE can normally expect to receive cash flows after the sale from taxes levied on the profits of the newly-privatised enterprise. GTEs may also be exempt from sales tax, but may be liable to pay sales taxes after a change of ownership.

State governments which sell off their business activities will not receive taxes on the profits of those newly-privatised entities; any cash flows from company taxes will go to the Commonwealth. Hence the Commonwealth has provided Victoria and NSW with compensation following the sale of the State Bank of Victoria, and the Government Insurance Office, respectively. In 1991 the Commonwealth indicated that compensation was to be based on the expected increase in Commonwealth tax revenues following privatisation. However, in 1993 the Commonwealth announced that these compensation payments must be viewed as 'one-off' since, henceforth, the Commonwealth would only provide compensation for one privatisation of a bank or insurance company per state, while promising to examine other proposed privatisations on a case-by-case basis.

On the other hand, state governments could receive cash flows from state payroll taxes or land taxes following privatisation. Correspondingly, the newly-privatised entity will face increases in expenses from these items, and, in addition, will lose its prior exemption from local government rates.

Private sector firms can be expected to undertake tax-minimisation strategies. Indeed, the more a purchaser can minimise the amount of tax payable on future revenue streams, the higher the price it will be prepared to pay for an acquisition. Conversely, if the vendor-government allows purchasers to choose the vehicle to be used in the acquisition (rather than bid for shares in a previously-established corporation), or to exercise discretion over the way in which the assets acquired are valued for tax purposes, then the vendor may be effectively trading off a higher 'headline' sales price against lower future cash flows from company taxes.

'Modelling' the privatisation decision

In order to examine the financial implications of privatisation, the following extended illustration adopts a series of simplifying assumptions about a hypothetical GTE. They are:

- the operations conducted by the GTE are capital intensive;
- the GTE has recently invested in infrastructure which is not capable of alternative uses;
- the technology is extremely durable, so that the GTE's assets do not physically 'depreciate';
- the GTE has no borrowings;
- the GTE's revenues are received entirely in cash;
- the GTE generates a profit/operating cash flow of $100 million per annum;
- the GTE is expected to continue to generate that profit, without further investment or the need for additional staffing, into the foreseeable future;
- all profits are distributed as dividends.

Let us also adopt a number of assumptions about interest and earnings rates, taxes, and transaction costs:

- the long term government bond rate for the owner-government is 8 per cent per annum;
- interest rates required by investors in debt securities issued by private sector corporations will be higher—it is assumed that corporate borrowings can be undertaken at 9.5 per cent per annum;
- since equity investors face higher risks than lenders, they expect a higher return than that payable on debt securities. It is assumed that contributors of equity capital seek a rate of return of 14 per cent per annum (before tax);
- company tax rates are 33 cents in the dollar;
- transaction costs will be approximately 4 per cent of the gross sale price on privatisation.

Retention value

The retention value of the GTE to the government is the amount which would otherwise have to be invested in order to generate a return of $100 million per annum. Using the marginal government borrowing rate of 8 per cent per annum as the appropriate discount rate for a project of equivalent risk (the choice is discussed in detail in the Appendix to this chapter), retention value would be $1,250 million.

Proceeds of sale

The value of the same business to a prospective private sector purchaser would be much less than retention value to the government, since (a) the cost of capital of a private firm would be far higher than the rates appropriately applied by a government, and (b) the net cash flows to a private sector purchaser would be less because of a range of taxes and charges (for which the public-sector vendor would be exempt).

In practice, prospective purchasers may under-bid, seeking a bargain purchase. Moreover, whatever the bid price, sale proceeds to the government will be reduced by transaction costs.

Scenario 1: Purchase financed by equity

Suppose that a potential purchaser could finance an acquisition without borrowing. Since the GTE generates $100 million per annum, and the purchaser seeks a pre-tax return to equity investors of 14 per cent per annum, then the maximum price that the purchaser would pay would represent the present value of projected pre-tax cash flows discounted at 14 per cent per annum—i.e. $714 million. With transaction costs of 4 per cent, the net proceeds of sale would be $686 million. This would represent only 55 per cent of the GTE's retention value.

Scenario 2: Purchaser financed by debt and equity

In practice, a purchaser may take advantage of debt finance. Given that interest paid on borrowings is less than the returns demanded by contributors of equity capital, and that interest payments are tax-deductible, a prospective purchaser can expect to secure a higher rate of return for shareholders by borrowing.

The higher the level of borrowings, the higher the risks faced by equity investors (and hence, in turn, the higher return demanded by those investors). However, the hypothetical GTE has regular and positive cash flows, and as such is 'low risk'. It seems reasonable to assume that in these circumstances a prospective purchaser would be prepared to finance the purchase with 50–60 per cent debt finance, perhaps higher. To illustrate the impact of using debt finance, it is (initially) assumed that a purchaser proposes to raise $500 million from borrowings, and the balance through equity.

The purchaser would assess the prospective cash flows to be derived from the enterprise, as follows:

Earnings before interest and taxes	$100m pa
Less	
9.5% interest on $500 million borrowings	48m pa
Net profit before tax	52m pa
Company tax on $52m at 33c in $	17m pa
Net profit after tax	35m pa

The maximum proceeds from sale of the GTE would be:

Maximum purchase price	
Financed by borrowings	$500m
Financed by equity	371m
	871m
Less transaction costs	35m
Net proceeds to Government	$836m

A comparison of Scenarios 1 and 2 shows that the net proceeds are a higher percentage of retention value (67 per cent) where a purchaser utilises debt finance than where the purchaser relies wholly on equity finance (55 per cent).

Both Scenarios 1 and 2 assume that the rate of return 'demanded' by equity investors is 14 per cent per annum. Table 5.1 shows the sensitivity of the financial returns from privatisation to both different levels of 'borrowings', and differences in the returns sought by equity holders.

Table 5.1
MAXIMUM PROCEEDS AS PERCENTAGE OF RETENTION VALUE

Borrowings	$300m	$400m	$500m	$600m	$700m	$800m	$900m
Debt as % total investment	35–40%	44–51%	55–60%	64–69%	73–77%	81–84%	89–91%

Return sought on equity							
16.00%	57%	60%	64%	67%	70%	73%	76%
15.00%	60%	62%	65%	68%	71%	74%	77%
14.00%	62%	65%	67%	70%	72%	75%	77%
13.00%	65%	67%	69%	71%	74%	76%	78%
12.00%	69%	70%	72%	74%	75%	77%	78%

The data in Table 5.1 suggest that the maximum proceeds from sale of a GTE may only be 57–78 per cent of retention value, depending on the capital structure of the acquiring firm. In practice, the returns demanded by equity holders will not be independent of the gearing of the privatised enterprise. The higher the gearing (the proportion of debt relative to equity), the higher the risk and hence the higher the returns demanded by equity investors—and vice versa. The technical literature has yet to develop a basis for predicting the cost of debt capital with changes in gearing, but it is reasonable to assume that there is an association. It is speculated that the relevant values are likely to be within the band of unshaded cells. That suggests, in this simple model (and on the assumptions adopted for the purpose of this exercise), that *the maximum proceeds from sale of a GTE may only be in the range of 65–77 per cent of retention value.*

Conversely, *the initial loss to the government from privatisation is likely to be 23–35 per cent of retention value.* Again, in practice, a purchaser may bid well below the 'maximum' bid price, so that the loss may be greater.

Privatisation

As already noted, part of this 'loss' may be recovered by post-privatisation tax revenues if the vendor is the Commonwealth government.

Scenario 3: Impact of post-privatisation taxes

Since company profits are subject to tax, the cash flows to the Commonwealth government arising from privatisation of a GTE will comprise sale proceeds, and the stream of company taxes to be paid after privatisation.

Using the data in Scenario 2, and assuming there is no 'leakage' of tax revenues through use of tax-minimisation strategies, the maximum value of the tax stream to be derived under the foregoing assumptions would be:

Present value of revenue stream of $17.3m pa discounted at 8% pa	$216m

Hence the overall minimum residual loss from privatisation of a Commonwealth GTE would be:

Value to government from retention		$1,250m
Less		
Maximum sale proceeds	$836m	
Maximum present value of tax stream	216m	1,052m
Minimum residual loss from privatisation		**$ 198m**

Whereas the use of debt finance increases the maximum proceeds on sale, the overall net proceeds to government (from sale proceeds and tax streams combined) actually decline as borrowings increase. Table 5.2 illustrates this phenomenon.

The data in Table 5.2 suggest that the sale proceeds would be only 81–92 per cent of retention value. Conversely, *the minimum net loss to the Commonwealth (after counting post-privatisation tax receipts) would be between 8–19 per cent of retention value.*

To Sell Or Not To Sell: Financial Implications

Table 5.2
AGGREGATE PROCEEDS & TAX AS PERCENTAGE OF RETENTION VALUE

Borrowings (at 9.5%)	$300m	$400m	$500m	$600m	$700m	$800m	$900m
Debt—as % of total investment	35–40%	44–51%	55–60%	64–69%	73–77%	81–84%	89–91%
Return sought on equity							
16.00%	81%	81%	81%	81%	81%	81%	81%
15.00%	83%	83%	83%	82%	82%	82%	81%
14.00%	86%	85%	85%	84%	83%	83%	82%
13.00%	89%	88%	87%	86%	85%	84%	83%
12.00%	92%	91%	89%	88%	86%	85%	83%

However, a rational purchaser will seek to minimise or defer payment of company taxes. For example, a purchaser may:

- revalue assets to 'current values', giving rise to higher tax-deductible depreciation charges, thus reducing payments of company tax;
- structure the acquisition to take advantage of any carry-forward tax losses;
- elect to use accelerated depreciation methods for tax purposes, which will defer the timing of cash payments and hence reduce their value to the government;
- finance the acquisition through borrowings from an off-shore associate. This would enable the purchasing entity to treat some of the cash flows earned from the newly-acquired business as tax-deductible interest payments to an off-shore associated company. As those payments would only be subject to 10 per cent withholding tax, this arrangement would reduce the cash flow to the Commonwealth.

These examples do not exhaust the range of income-tax minimising strategies which might be adopted by a prospective purchaser, or strategies which might divert profits earned in Australia to off-shore corporations. Only one will be examined in any detail: the use of off-shore financing arrangements.

This device substantially reduces the financial returns from

Privatisation

privatisation to the Commonwealth. Table 5.3 illustrates the impact on returns to the Commonwealth of off-shore borrowings subject to withholding tax.

A state government may be able to produce higher sale proceeds by assisting a purchaser to adopt tax minimisation strategies (e.g. through increased depreciation charges). In effect, a state government can increase its sale proceeds at the expense of the Commonwealth.

Table 5.3
AGGREGATE (AFTER TAX) LOSS AS PERCENTAGE OF RETENTION VALUE
(assuming use of off-shore financing)

Borrowings	$300m	$400m	$500m	$600m	$700m	$800m	$900m
Debt as % total investment	35–40%	44–51%	55–60%	64–69%	73–77%	81–84%	89–91%
Return sought on equity							
16.00%		20%	20%	20%	20%	20%	21%	21%
15.00%		17%	18%	18%	19%	19%	20%	20%
14.00%		15%	16%	16%	17%	18%	19%	20%
13.00%		12%	13%	14%	15%	17%	18%	19%
12.00%		8%	10%	12%	13%	15%	17%	18%

Scenario 4: Effect of post-privatisation 'efficiencies' on government revenue streams

It is commonly suggested that privatisation could lead to greater efficiencies. This leads to the suggestion that governments could benefit from increases in profitability through increased taxes on the revenues of the privatised GTE.

There are usually pockets of inefficiency in every business; likewise it must be conceded that a change of management can often revitalise an organisation. The performance of both public sector organisations and private sector organisations can change (for better or for worse) with a change of management. However, there are grounds to be sceptical about suggestions that privatisation will produce such a quantum leap in efficiency that it will compensate government-vendors for the loss of value on sale through post-privatisation tax streams.

To Sell Or Not To Sell: Financial Implications

To illustrate, let us compare two GTEs. Both generate profits of $100 million per annum. However, one has a small workforce and a large investment in infrastructure assets; the other has only minor investment in equipment, and a large workforce:

	Scenario E	Scenario F
	Capital intensive GTE	**Labour intensive GTE**
Earnings	$100m pa	$100m pa
After charging		
Wages & salaries	$3m (100 employees)	$90m (3000 employees)
(average $30,000 pa)		
Net Assets	$1,000m	$100m

Let us suppose that the prospective purchasers of these GTEs believe that they can find ways of producing the same level and quality of goods or services as are presently being provided by those two organisations, with a reduction of the workforce of 20 per cent. In other words, assuming no change in demand for the goods or services provided by those entities, the purchasers estimate that the future sustainable earnings of the two organisations will be as follows:

	Capital intensive GTE	Labour intensive GTE
Earnings when govt. owned	$100m pa	$100m pa
Add		
Projected reduction in expenses	$0.6m pa	$18.0m pa
Projected earnings after privatisation (before interest and taxes)	**$100.6m pa**	**$118.0m pa**

Even adopting such extreme assumptions about the possibility of cuts in operating expenses, the expected 'efficiency gains' still do not eliminate the loss of value on privatisation for the capital intensive GTE. To illustrate, the following example adopts the same underlying assumptions about interest rates, equity returns and tax rates as in earlier Scenarios (save that here the purchasers finance their acquisitions with 50 per cent debt and 50 per cent equity).

	Capital intensive GTE	Labour intensive GTE
Value to government:	$1,250m	$1,250m
Value to purchaser	$856m	$957m
(financed 50% debt, 50% equity)		
Maximum proceeds From sale	$822m	$919m
(after transaction costs)		
Max. present value of tax stream	$247m	$290m
Total proceeds & tax	$1069m	$1254m
Loss (gain) to govt	**$188m**	**($4m)**

Here, the initial losses from privatisation are greater for the capital intensive than for the labour intensive enterprise. Again, for the capital intensive GTE, only part of these losses can be recouped from post-privatisation tax revenues, despite massive efficiency gains.

On the other hand, the final outcome from privatisation of the hypothetical labour intensive GTE is in fact a surplus for the Commonwealth government, relative to retention value. Indeed, on the numbers presented here the break-even point for the government from sale of the hypothetical labour intensive GTE would only occur when there was a profit improvement of around 16 per cent. While many authors have claimed that privatisation can lead to efficiencies, there are few cases where gains of that scale have been achieved. One of the most comprehensive international studies of privatisation found that only 55 per cent of privatised firms showed an improvement in operating performance, and that overall the mean change was only a 0.16 per cent improvement in the reported rate of return on equity (*Megginson, Nash & Van Randenborgh*, 1994).

Moreover, attribution of those gains to privatisation is in itself contentious, since it assumes that any efficiency gains obtained by private sector managers could not have been secured if GTEs remained in public ownership. The evidence from some studies suggests otherwise (*Domberger & Piggott*, 1986).

Implications of analysis

The foregoing discussion and illustrations suggest that in most circumstances, it would not make good sense to privatise GTEs which are capital intensive, and producing positive cash flows.

The major findings are:

(i) *The privatisation of government trading enterprises, and the application of the proceeds to debt reduction, does not necessarily confer financial benefits on the community.*

The attractiveness or otherwise of such transactions depends on the relative returns earned by the government from a GTE's dividend distributions, taxes and related charges, relative to the cash flows avoided by reducing interest commitments.

(ii) Because a private sector purchaser faces a higher cost of capital than a government, the proceeds from privatisation are likely to be substantially less than retention value.

Using a range of representative assumptions about the 'gap' between interest rates payable by government and private sector borrowers, and the rates of return sought by private sector investors, the findings were that the maximum likely to be bid by a private sector purchaser would be in the range of 57–78 per cent of the retention value of a GTE.

The scale of the immediate losses incurred on privatisation will be related to, *inter alia*:

- interest rate differentials between a government and a private sector borrower;
- the capital structure adopted by the purchaser;
- the return sought or ('demanded') by equity investors 'over and above that payable on debt finance'—which will affect the ceiling bid prices;
- the level of transaction costs.

Moreover, bidders may seek to make bargain purchases, and they may make allowances for the anticipated costs of dealing with regulatory agencies.

A final qualification: it is not suggested that governments should never dispose of any business activity—nor is it suggested that governments should nationalise every business.

Assumptions about the relative costs of public sector borrowings, private sector borrowings and the returns demanded by private sector investors in equities are fundamental to the foregoing analysis. The relative costs of finance might change if (for example) a government embarked on a major borrowing programme and was investing in high-risk ventures. However, it is reiterated that the rates used in these illustrations presented above were similar to those selected by a number of consultants in reports advocating the privatisation of publicly-owned enterprises in the early 1990s.

(iii) Post-privatisation tax collections may recover only part of the 'loss of value' arising from sale

Commonwealth company tax collections may constitute a material component of the set of cash flows derived by government after privatisation—but the present value of these cash flows will not outweigh the 'loss' incurred on sale. State governments may mitigate their losses through post-privatisation payroll taxes, land taxes and other charges, but only to a relatively minor extent.

Little weight should be given to suggestions that privatised entities will generate a higher revenue stream to the government from taxes because, as private sector entities, they will be more 'efficient': and hence earn higher taxable profits.

Many government-owned enterprises are capital intensive, so that supposed private sector 'efficiencies' would only have a minor effect on post-privatisation profitability. Opportunities for improvements in profitability may be greater in labour-intensive organisations, but such improvements would have to be very substantial to compensate the vendor government for the loss of value on sale.

Moreover, it is only to be expected that private sector purchasers will adopt tax minimisation strategies—which in turn will reduce the post-privatisation revenue streams of the vendor.

Of course, governments may adopt strategies to minimise 'leakage' of tax revenues. In the early 1990s there was little evidence that Commonwealth public servants engaged in privatisation fully comprehended the tax implications of different arrangements for the sale of a GTE. Later some initiatives were undertaken: for example, 'thin capitalisation' rules were applied to foreign-owned entities generating revenues in Australia. These limited the use of high levels of borrowings from off-shore related entities so as to reduce corporate tax payable in Australia. However, other tax minimisation practices can still be used—and 'thin capitalisation' was only one of a repertoire of devices available to shift profits off-shore.

Indeed, one suspects that governments have tended to turn a blind eye to some tax minimisation strategies, possible believing that the involvement of major multi-national corporations in local manufacturing generates sufficient benefits in the form of commercial activity and employment as to warrant disregarding the low level of corporate tax they pay within the country. Notable examples are the financial results of Australian subsidiaries of Japanese motor manufacturers, which have consistently recorded high sales in Australia and increased their local investment, while reporting minimal profits and therefore paying minuscule corporate income taxes.

(iv) Governments may increase the sale price on privatisation by initiatives which reduce post-privatisation cash flows.

The sale of a GTE may stimulate media attention and prompt criticism from parties who consider that the consideration in such transactions is inadequate.

Conversely, governments which otherwise would report a deficit on their budget results face incentives to maximise the sale proceeds on privatisation transactions. The greater the sale price, the greater the reduction in the reported deficit—and, correspondingly, the less the increase in government 'debt'. While it might be argued that these indicators are less significant than others (e.g. the surplus or deficit for the 'whole of government', or trends in the quantum of aggregate 'liabilities', or trends in investment in infrastructure assets) media commentators tend to focus on the traditional, cash-based budget results.

The desire to report improved budget results may encourage governments to introduce sale conditions which may lead to higher prices on sale, but lower cash flows later. Examples of such initiatives are easy to find. For example:

- The NSW government's proposals to privatise the State Bank of NSW included the condition that existing borrowings by the SBNSW would continue to be subject to a government guarantee until maturity. Moreover, the NSW government agreed to indemnify the purchaser against bad debts above a specified threshold.
- The Commonwealth's *One Nation* statement in 1992 announced the introduction of 'infrastructure bonds', interest on which would be non-assessable in the hands of the bondholder—an initiative which has been described as promising 'cost effective' funding for certain strictly-defined projects 'land transport, ports and electricity generation' (*P. Robinson*, 1994).
- The Commonwealth's 1994 *Working Nation* statement moved to encourage more private sector investment in infrastructure by offering a tax rebate of 33 per cent as an alternative to non-assessable income to encourage taxpayers with marginal tax rates below 33 per cent to invest in infrastructure bonds. It also extended the eligibility for infrastructure bonds to aviation, electricity transmission and distribution, gas transmission facilities, water and sewerage treatment projects and other water infrastructure.

Similar initiatives were revived by the new Coalition Commonwealth government.

Other initiatives take the form of leaving tax loopholes which establish tax minimisation strategies for prospective purchasers, and so increase the likely headline prices on privatisation. For example:

- Proposals for the sale of the Commonwealth-owned Pipeline Authority did not constrain the purchaser from revaluing assets upwards, thus enabling a purchaser to record increased depreciation charges and, hence, lower taxable profits after privatisation.
- Proposals for the sale of the Housing Loans Insurance Corporation permitted the purchaser to amend the HLIC's deferral of revenue recognition on single-premium mortgage insurance policies—thus also deferring tax collections on that deferred income.

All such initiatives reduce the cash flows to be derived by governments, post-privatisation.

Estimating retention values—in practice

Since these arguments were first outlined (*Walker*, 1994, 1995; *Quiggin*, 1995) a variety of interests have accepted at least part of this analysis. Commentaries on privatisation now routinely refer to 'sale' or 'retention value', and frequently raise questions as to whether the savings on interest through debt reduction from the proceeds of privatisation will really exceed revenues from retention. Press reports occasionally note inconsistencies between earlier claims that elimination of debt from privatisation 'would mean annual savings to the Budget', and Budget figures showing that projected dividends from privatisation targets would exceed projected interest payments (e.g. *SMH*, 24/6/99).

Governments have occasionally produced reports on the merits of privatisation, incorporating 'expert' assessments of likely sale and retention values. This is progress, of a kind. It does, after all, provide the community with opportunities to scrutinise major proposals for asset sales—opportunities long available in the private sector to shareholders contemplating the merits of takeover bids, or proposals to sell company assets to related parties.

A case in point was the ACT government's proposals to privatise ACTEW, the Territory's water and electricity utility. The government commissioned merchant bankers ABN AMRO and DGJ Projects to examine issues associated with 'the structure and ownership' of ACTEW. The resultant report found, rather delicately, that 'maintaining ACTEW's current structure and relationship with the ACT government ... is not in the best interests of the ACT community'. In other words, ACTEW should be broken up and sold. Publication of this report (which included assessments of 'sale' versus 'retention' values) enabled concerned citizens to question the analysis—even though critical slabs of the report dealing with efficiencies supposedly obtainable under private ownership were withheld as 'confidential'. The Canberra-based Australia Institute produced a report which systematically analysed the advice received by the ACT government, described defects, and vigorously contested the recommendations (*Quiggin, Saddler, Neutze, Hamilton & Turton*, 1998). ACTEW has not been sold.

Many sophisticated shareholders are conscious of the fact that while some experts jealously guard their reputations as a source of independent and thorough advice, others may be better described as 'guns for hire', who deliver reports favourable to those who pay them. There have been many occasions when litigation to block the distribution of shareholders' notices on contentious corporate matters has been successful—with applicants successfully arguing that the information proposed to be disseminated to shareholders was misleading or that it omitted material facts. Indeed, on occasions courts have been moved to observe that the authors of such reports were 'neither independent nor expert'.

It should not surprise, therefore that some 'experts' reports' commissioned to support privatisation proposals are subject to the same array of flaws that one might expect to find in reports distributed to the shareholders of listed companies. Indeed, less discipline is imposed on reports produced to support government privatisation proposals. In the private sector, major shareholders are often prepared to challenge the distribution of misleading reports through the courts. In the public sector, opponents of privatisation proposals may use parliaments and political processes to some effect, but they are generally unable to harness the resources required to ensure that dubious reports are thoroughly scrutinised.

Some recent expert's reports on sale or retention values have not even applied standard valuation methodologies in a consistent manner.

Others have done their best with a difficult task. When trying to analyse actual privatisation proposals, an obvious difficulty is that GTEs do not generate their earnings entirely in cash (as assumed above), so that it is necessary to estimate future cash flows from operations. Such estimates of future cash flows need to allow for *growth* in revenues—and this demands analysis of trends in industry activities.

In practice, analysts usually only calculate net present values for revenue streams for a period of 10–20 years—and then add in the present value of the assumed 'sale value' of the business at the end of the selected period. That calculation in turn is often based on a crude multiple of earnings at the level reached 10–20 years ahead.

A further point to note is that GTEs do not distribute all of their earnings as dividends—they re-invest some of their cash flows in new equipment or other assets. Some flawed 'expert' analysis of privatisations—and some political tracts advocating privatisation—have wrongly linked retention values with dividend streams rather than underlying earnings. This is tantamount to ignoring increases in the value of the business during the period under examination. This does not alter the basic approach outlined above, though the cash flows to be taken into account need to be adjusted to allow for negative cash flows associated with reinvestment.

It is difficult for anyone outside an industry (and without access to in-house records and expertise) to develop reasonable projections of future cash flows, especially on the expenditure side. Only in-house engineers have a good appreciation of the likely economic life of infrastructure assets, and what it would cost to maintain those assets in future, or to upgrade them to higher standards of functionality. When privatisation proposals are in the offing, experts are given access to internal business plans, and are able to use these in estimating projected future cash flows.

There is a risk that GTEs which have been stripped of cash to pay 'special dividends' may have a backlog of maintenance and upgrading expenditure. If these are incorporated in business plans as short-term negative cash flows, this could seriously reduce calculated retention values. Regrettably, existing rules governing financial reporting by GTEs do not require summary reports on the state of infrastructure, and what it will cost to fix or upgrade it, and the likely timing of major expenditures to perform remedial work.

Another difficulty in assessing specific privatisation proposals is that bidders (particularly overseas bidders) may be prepared to pay higher prices to acquire an individual GTE in order to get a foothold in an Australian industry. If governments proceed to sell-down Australian water or electricity businesses, buyers have the opportunity to buy up former GTEs and thus develop larger businesses with considerable market power—more than was ever enjoyed by local county councils or state-owned GTEs. Market power translates into the capacity to increase prices in the future—thus generating extra revenues to the owners of those businesses. Bidders may be prepared to pay a premium to get a foothold in those industries.

The prices received from the sale of Victorian electricity assets are consistent with that hypothesis—privatisations provided higher returns that even optimists predicted. Further support for the 'foothold' hypothesis has been provided by some recent amalgamations of privatised GTEs.

Critical assumptions about 'the cost of capital'

Arguably the most significant factor in the determination of estimates of 'sale' and 'retention' values is the choice of the discount rate.

The foregoing modelling of the privatisation decision assumed that the relevant discount rate to calculate retention values to government was less than the discount rate ('cost of capital') to be used by private sector purchasers in the estimation of what they could afford to bid to acquire a GTE.

In practice, experts' reports have routinely adopted the same discount rates in the calculation of sale and retention values. The effect of this choice is to strongly reduce estimates of retention values, thus favouring privatisation.

The most commonly stated rationale for this practice is that the relevant discount rate *should* reflect the risk associated with a project, and such risks are (or *should* be) independent of whether the owner is in the public or private sector.

Another way this is expressed is a claim that the 'cost of capital *should* be the same for the public sector as for the private sector'.

Mark use of the words, '*should*'.

These claims are normative, ideological statements. They reflect someone's opinions about how the world should be run. They also reflect a fundamental misunderstanding of the underlying rationale for the estimation of a 'cost of capital' to guide the ranking of capital projects or to estimate the value of businesses. They are at odds with an established body of literature from the disciplines of economics and finance. For those with the patience to explore these issues further, see the appendix at the end of the book.

6

Contracting Out/ Outsourcing

Governments can't do everything, and nor should they try

Governments have always bought goods and services from the private sector, simply because it made good business sense to do so.

Contracting out or outsourcing often made sense in relation to the provision of support services. For example, while governments have always owned buildings, it was cheaper and easier for governments to have the lifts in those buildings maintained by external suppliers—simply because the suppliers of lift cars and associated machinery had a comparative advantage in obtaining spares, training staff and maintaining the equipment.

On the other hand, when governments were bulk users of particular types of equipment (such as buses, railway rolling stock, or police vehicles) decisions were made in the past to have government-owned workshops handle that maintenance.

Sometimes highly specialised equipment (such as that used in large-scale electricity generation or water treatment) was only used by public sector agencies. In many cases, that equipment had been designed by government engineers. Hence, in the absence of any private firms with equivalent experience, decisions were made to have that equipment maintained by government employees. Overall, public sector agencies tended to outsource activities where private sector firms had a comparative advantage, and to provide services themselves where the work involved specialist activities, or where the scale of demand could support in-house service provision.

However, if a government had established an agency to provide services to the community in a particular area, those 'core' services were not outsourced. This was largely because governments had only become involved in some fields of service delivery—be they social services, or advice to farmers—because of 'market failure'. If the private sector had failed to provide adequate or comprehensive or reasonably priced services, then governments had intervened to fill the void. And of course, governments became involved in some areas of activity—assisting the aged and frail, or persons with intellectual or physical disabilities—simply because it was seen as the right thing to do. It wasn't a question of whether the private sector was or was not providing services of that nature. Often a range of voluntary organisations were doing their best. But more resources were needed.

Times (and markets) change—but sometimes, the public sector doesn't

Decisions made decades ago may have been well-founded at the time. But that does not mean that those decisions should not be revisited later on.

It may have made good financial sense to have government garages maintaining vehicles—until car manufacturers extended warranties to something close to the economic life of a government vehicle. (Governments buy cars free of sales tax and often sell them after two years or 40,000 km at a profit.)

It may have made good financial sense for governments to employ clerks to make up payrolls and keep personnel records. Electronic banking has reduced the need to employ so many in this back-office activity. Now, private firms provide payroll, transaction-processing and record-keeping services, thus presenting a new alternative to in-house service provision.

It may also have made good financial sense for government to buy stationery by the truckload, and store it in warehouses before distributing it around the country to schools and hospitals and offices. That is, until competition developed in the office supplies market. Major stationery suppliers not only compete on price, but on service. Now many big customers—such as leading accounting and legal firms—don't employ armies of clerks to order stationery and to distribute it around their offices. Nor do individual branch offices buy the stuff themselves. The stationery suppliers now provide an integrated service: they automatically replenish stationery cupboards, and provide their clients with a single account detailing the purchases of individual offices or units, together with details of variances and abnormal usage, so that office managers can watch for waste or pilferage. These arrangements reduce the paperwork to be handled by both suppliers and customers. That means that the supplier can operate on lower margins. Deals like this can be a win-win for both sides of the transaction.

Many governments are still operating sector-wide contracts in procurement. The agencies managing these contracts claim to be saving a lot of money—and compared to standard retail prices, possibly they are. But large-scale purchasers rarely pay standard retail prices. Some observers claim that traditional government procurement practices can be laborious and expensive. Public servants with recent private sector experience have been heard to reject claims that government contracts are saving money—explaining that their previous private employers cut even better deals despite the government's greater purchasing power.

Where many governments still handle routine clerical tasks in traditional ways (often passing bundles of paper from hand to hand to hand) private firms have long-since streamlined processes, or outsourced non-core activities to firms which have the skills and technology to provide those services faster and reliably and at lower cost.

There is some evidence that large and bureaucratic agencies may not be quick to change—and may not even regularly review their activities. In the late 1980s and early 1990s, NSW Premier Greiner could tell rollicking yarns about inefficiencies his review teams had unearthed. For example:

State Rail Authority—Tall Tales But True!

- Until recently Narrandera had 26 people on the SRA payroll. 11 were train crew, but there were no trains. 3 were there to drive the train crews to and from trains, of which there were none. 6 were employed on the station and platform selling a total of $87,985 worth of passenger tickets a year at a rate of 5 tickets per day. The remaining 6 were 'relief staff'.
- State Rail operated passenger trains 6 days/week between Tamworth and Armidale. Three days a week when the train was loco-hauled, only 15 people got off at Armidale. On the three days it was an XPT, less than 30 people got off at Armidale. That didn't fill half of one carriage of a seven carriage XPT train.
- On the Queanbeyan–Cooma line (114km of track), State Rail hauls 8,000 tonnes of freight a year! In the Hunter Valley they haul up to 40 trains a day, many with 6,000 tonnes of coal on each. The Hunter Valley does before breakfast what it takes a whole year to do on the Queanbeyan–Cooma line.

- Tenterfield until recently had four enginemen on the payroll—for one freight train a month.
- The track between Glen Innes and Tenterfield used to carry about 5,000 tonnes of freight a year. But more than 90 per cent of the traffic was the SRA's own timber sleepers. The SRA was putting sleepers under the track in order to haul sleepers over the track.
- And one NSW town had one employee costing over $30,000 in wages and overheads, who sold 37 tickets in a year, valued at $700.

State Transit Authority

- The STA was operating a tramways workshop, even though trams haven't run in Sydney since 1961!
- As it had done since the tram days, the STA was completely rebuilding its buses, at a cost of $20 million a year. The only problem is—modern buses don't need to be rebuilt.

Maritime Services Board

- For two years the MSB employed a field clerk at Goat Island when the only person he was responsible for was himself.
- Until recently, it took seven different tradesmen to remove an outboard motor from an MSB patrol boat—a task a normal boat owner could do single-handed.

(*NSW Government*, 1990)

Some of these stories are plainly exaggerated or distorted. Take the last: a boat owner might easily handle a 6 HP outboard motor on his own, but not the massive outboards on patrol boats, unless working with cranes or special equipment. But if any of these stories from the 1980s were true, they are cause for concern. They don't say much about the merits of insourcing or outsourcing. Rather, they point to poor management.

Public sector managers would (or should) have been aware of such inefficiencies, but apparently chose not to make a fuss about it. If that was the case, then the stories may also suggest that there had been poorly-designed arrangements for monitoring performance within those organisations. Possibly some managers kept quiet out of concern that they might be doing workers out of a job. If so, that may reflect a deeper problem: that the public sector has failed to establish effective arrangements for the mobility of its workforce, particularly between agencies, as employment needs change.

But plainly advances in information technology, and changes in market conditions, suggest the need for the public sector to re-think the way it does some things (as well as rethinking whether it really needs to do some things at all). Services that were once provided internally might well be provided more cheaply and more efficiently by external providers.

And vice versa. Some activities which have been out-sourced could also be returned to the public sector because they can be provided more cheaply and more effectively that way.

The trick is identifying which things should be changed, and when, and by how much.

The rhetoric of outsourcing

But the advocates of outsourcing don't see it that way.

As with all forms of privatisation, advocates of 'contracting out' rely to a large extent on rhetoric about the alleged need for smaller government, and for competition in service delivery. Occasionally, advocates of contracting out recount anecdotes about the high cost of internal service provision versus the cost of obtaining similar services from external suppliers.

The examples cited in these internal debates may seem persuasive, but can often be criticised as unrepresentative, or as focusing unduly on financial considerations rather than speed and quality of service.

> Consultants examined the costs of a workshop run by a Victorian electricity generator, and concluded that it should be closed down and maintenance services obtained from external contractors. An example cited by the consultants was the cost of re-wiring a small electric motor: the time taken by in-house staff plus on-costs exceeded quotes from external contractors, plus freight.
>
> Union representatives argued that the example was both unfair and unrepresentative. The re-wiring job had been undertaken by an apprentice under supervision from a tradesman as a training exercise at a time when there was a low workload. The charges recorded included the time of both tradesman and apprentice, plus 'on-costs' which were allocations of overheads incurred elsewhere within the organisation, and which were outside the workshop's responsibility and control.
>
> The workshop had been established to maintain infrastructure and to have the capacity to undertake major and urgent tasks. Closing down the workshop would lead to extensive delays in repairing facilities when repairs were most needed.

It is interesting to contrast the perspective of a private sector consulting firm about the efficiency of a public sector operation, with the observations of a private sector consulting firm about its own costs and fee structure. A high-flying lawyer working in

Contracting Out/Outsourcing

mergers and acquisitions once commented about his firm's fees:

> Some people say we charge a lot. But they overlook the fact that we have to keep a lot of highly qualified staff on the payroll so that when a big job comes up we can throw a team onto it, and work night and day to see it through.

To one firm of consultants, the government-owned workshop was inefficient because of high labour costs from overmanning. To the other firm of consultants, maintaining the capacity to undertake big and urgent jobs was good business.

Plainly, one needs to look at a range of financial and non-financial factors to assess whether or not government agencies can be more efficient and effective—and whether outsourcing would be even more efficient and effective.

The modelling of the decision to sell or retain government-owned businesses in Chapter 5 suggests that usually there may be a stronger case for contracting out *labour intensive* activities than *capital intensive* activities. An additional factor, which needs to be considered carefully, is whether public sector agencies are as good at managing their affairs or motivating a workforce as private sector employers.

If public sector agencies are poor managers of finances and poor managers of human resources, then these two factors suggest that *all* labour intensive operations may be candidates for privatisation. But this is an oversimplification.

Before one can validly conclude that outsourcing is the 'solution', one needs to know more about the 'problem'.

If evidence suggests that the public sector is a relatively poor (or expensive) service provider, then possible reasons should be explored. Are there differences in workplace arrangements between the public sector and private firms? Does the public sector tend to establish layer upon layer of supervisory staff and management? What incentives are established by public sector organisations to encourage efficiency, and reward high quality service? What feedback is provided when things go well, or badly?

Stories are told about the massive savings which were realised when activities previously provided by government agencies were contracted out. Yet the same evidence can often also be interpreted as pointing to poor management, or to a failure to negotiate sensibly with the workforce in order to lower costs and improve service quality.

Of course, advocates of 'contracting out' are not the sole source of emotive rhetoric. Union representatives who are opposed to reductions in public sector employment often make much of the mistakes made by private sector firms after activities have been contracted out. They neglect to mention any of the mistakes made when services were provided by public sector agencies.

Steering not rowing

An influential set of proposals for a shake up of the (US) public sector was set out in Osborne & Gaebler's *Reinventing Government*. The authors presented a suite of management ideas about how to revitalise jaded and hierarchical bureaucracies. The ideas were not entirely new, but they were well-packaged. They include familiar admonitions. Empower employees. Question old ways of doing things. Look for alternative solutions to old problems.

Much of the appeal of *Reinventing Government* lay in its anecdotes about public sector inefficiency—which probably reminded readers of similar problems and issues which have arisen within their own workplaces (and, for other readers, confirmed their prejudices). Osborne & Gaebler coupled these stories with motivational passages about how energetic employees found ways to cut red tape or redesign processes. Undoubtedly Osborne & Gaebler found a receptive audience in the Clinton administration, which embraced the idea of trying to 'reinvent government' with a vengeance (and a website, and the direct involvement of Vice President Al Gore).

One of the Osborne & Gaebler themes was the idea that even though governments may be committed to provide services to the community, they do not need to actually be the *provider* of those services, just the *funder*. What really mattered was that a service was provided, not who provided it. They added a metaphor: governments needed to steer, but they did not have to *row*.

As Osborne & Gaebler acknowledged, the idea of 'steering not rowing' actually came from an earlier book on privatisation by E.S. Savas:

> The word government is from a Greek word, which means 'to steer'. The job of government is to steer, not to row the boat. Delivering services is rowing and government is not very good at rowing.

Well, this was a pretty crude and selective translation. There is a Greek word $\kappa\upsilon\beta\varepsilon\rho\nu\omega$ (pronounced 'keeverno') meaning to govern. However, where 'steer' is shown in dictionaries as a synonym, it is only in relation to steering a ship. A key element of both 'steer' and 'govern'—$\delta\iota\varepsilon\upsilon\theta\upsilon\nu\omega$—can mean 'manage', 'oversee', 'direct' or 'lead'. In government, those who 'lead' don't have to stand up the back watching others do the work: they can also lead from the front.

Savas, and then Osborne & Gaebler, started from the assumption that government was not very good at 'rowing'. They could equally have started from the assumption that government was not very good at *managing*—which might have led them to explore ways of improving public sector management rather than proposing the 'solution' of outsourcing.

Yet governments can actually be very good at service delivery. One should keep in mind the fact that many of the things that are done by government are things that the private sector had earlier found to be unprofitable, or just too difficult. Sometimes members of the public aren't even aware of what public servants in a range of occupations actually do for the community—until they themselves encounter the caring of nurses, or the compassion of police to accident or crime victims, or learn about the challenges and stresses faced by community workers.

Of course, sometimes governments provide services which are so good that services of that quality may not be affordable.

The idea that governments should 'steer not row' was very attractive to advocates of 'smaller government', and also to Treasuries and other central agencies wanting to exert greater influence over resource allocation.

If governments only *funded* the provision of services, and did not necessary have to *provide* those services, then the public sector could be downsized, and government could simply pay private sector firms to provide services. Where governments already provided grants or subsidies to non-government organisations (NGOs), the *funder/provider model* established a rationale for establishing contractual relationships between the government and NGOs regarding the nature and quality of services the latter were to provide. (It is something of a surprise to learn that such basic arrangements had not been established earlier.)

Within the public sector itself, the funder/provider model established a rationale for separating the roles of those who managed resource allocation and those who provided services.

In some instances, the funder/provider model was used to justify the establishment of whole new government departments which would be funders, while other departments and private sector organisations would be providers.

The underlying idea may have some merit, but it was often introduced into a context in which neither the departments which were currently 'providers', nor central agencies, had a good grasp of what volume of services were currently being provided, let alone what they were costing and what was their quality. Moreover, they did not have a good idea about how to write contracts which embodied incentives to improve performance. Hence, in at least some cases, the introduction of the funder/provider model had the effect of increasing rather than reducing the total costs incurred in providing services. It led to the establishment of new agencies, the enlargement of others, and generally slowed down administrative processes because of the need to work through additional layers of bureaucracy. Where the Commonwealth government jointly funded programs, the burden of bureaucracy increased even further.

Teams of public servants wrote letters to each other, convened inter-departmental or Commonwealth/state meetings, prepared agendas and discussion papers and then wrote up lengthy minutes and distributed the drafts for comment, before starting the whole cycle all over again.

Despite this investment of time and energy, in many cases the public servants involved in these highly stylised encounters were working in the dark. They did not have information about such basic matters as the number of clients being served or the number and type of services provided, let alone high-quality financial information about the cost of providing those services and running their agencies. After a few years' experience, numbers of these funder/provider arrangements have been found wanting.

There have been few published analyses of the effectiveness of the funder/provider arrangements, and the high incidence of departmental restructuring undertaken by all governments makes it difficult for outsiders to assemble cost information from published annual reports or budget papers. However, major increases in the costs of administering programs seem to have occurred in some instances—in the range of 10 per cent to 30 per cent—without compelling evidence of corresponding increases in service quality.

At the same time, government dealings with the NGO sector seem to have been indiscriminate. No one can quarrel with requests for NGOs to be accountable for their use of government funding. But just as private sector firms are subject to systems of differential disclosure—listed public companies have to disclose far more financial information than small private companies—the same approach should be applied to NGOs receiving government assistance. In practice, some small voluntary organisations have been required to provide as much paperwork to their 'funders' as larger charities receiving subsidies of millions of dollars. This red tape just imposes costs on voluntary workers.

The over-zealous application of the funder/provider model can have painful consequences. If charitable organisations are treated as 'contractors' to government, which have to be accountable for money and time, then the first casualty may be the spirit of voluntarism. A case in point: a young university graduate (first class honours, university medal) was contributing his spare time as honorary treasurer of a Sydney charity. The charity had received funds for a pilot program to help street kids. Then came the paperwork: the conditions of government grants required copious data to be compiled and reported about the background of each individual client so that funding could be justified in terms of the conditions of the grant. As the (now, former) honorary treasurer described it:

> They seemed to expect that when social workers made contact with street kids at 3 or 4 in the morning they were supposed to take them to an interview room and run them through a questionnaire. It was ridiculous—at that time in the morning the kids were pretty strung out, and should have just been calmed down and given a bed. From my point of view, it meant putting systems in place to compile all this data and report back to the funder. That was just one example. My role started to involve a lot more work, and with all this paperwork I was looking at spending as much as three days a week ... I had to resign.

Efforts to formalise accountability mechanisms between governments and NGOs need not be so heavy-handed. But episodes such as these are by-products of other events: use of the idea of 'steering not rowing' to justify the establishment of contractual arrangements within and between organisations. Often these arrangements oversimplify complex phenomena. But they also prepare the ground for more and more outsourcing.

As noted above, governments cannot do everything, and there are many situations where outsourcing is sensible and likely to produce better outcomes for the community.

Private sector firms have explored the same options, and outsourcing has been accepted as a cost-effective way to obtain services.

Sadly, to some politicians and public sector bureaucrats, the outsourcing of services has become an end in itself, not a means to an end.

The hit-or-miss way some governments have gone about outsourcing

The late 1980s and 1990s saw a number of Australian governments painting themselves as administrative reformers. Reform meant reducing the size of the public sector, through outsourcing. It was simply *assumed* that the private sector was more efficient than the public sector, so that outsourcing would mean cost-savings. In many cases, public sector agencies had not been monitoring the quality of services being provided in-house. Hence they were not in a good position to prepare contracts which would bind external suppliers to specified standards of service.

Little or no attention was given to more strategic questions as to likely changes in supply arrangements three, five or ten years down the track. The short-term imperative was to downsize, and to outsource.

Possibly the activities of Auditors-General placed some pressure on governments to curb perceived inefficiencies in service delivery. During the 1980s, the role of Auditors-General steadily expanded beyond the traditional functions of providing reports on financial statements and the adequacy of financial controls. Encouraged by parliamentary Public Accounts Committees, public sector auditors began reviewing the economy, efficiency and effectiveness with which government services were being delivered. By the end of the 1990s, performance audits had become a significant element of the work of Auditors-General in Australia.

At a time when the techniques of 'performance auditing' were poorly developed, several Auditors-General chose relatively safe targets for projects to review, and topics like school cleaning or the management of car fleets were seen as manageable. In several jurisdictions, reports to parliament concluded that in-house services, such as cleaning, were more expensive per square metre when provided by the public service than when provided under competitive conditions in the private sector.

Reports of this type provoked examples of what would later be described as debates about 'economic rationalism'. For example, one Auditor-General concluded that the government of the day appeared to be paying too much for school cleaning. At a conference of members of parliamentary Public Accounts Committees, the Auditor-General (who had provided a paper on the subject of value for money auditing) found himself being criticised by government politicians for evaluating school cleaning practices solely in terms of cost:

> It's our policy to employ janitors. Of course school cleaning costs more than in the private sector, because school cleaning is only part of the janitor's job. He's also there to keep an eye on the children before and after school.

The Auditor-General, it was argued, was wrong to evaluate school cleaning only on economic grounds. He was, in effect, only criticising the government's policy which was to employ full-time janitors.

The same tensions between economic analysis and a broader concern with service quality have been reflected in a host of subsequent debates about outsourcing proposals.

Contracting Out/Outsourcing

The initial targets were often 'hotel-type' services: notably cleaning, catering and building maintenance.

Two prominent proponents of outsourcing were the leaders of NSW Coalition governments between 1988–95, Nick Greiner and John Fahey. Greiner's enthusiasm for public sector reform was reflected in a 1991 proposal to pursue competitive tendering and, 'where appropriate' contracting out of services currently provided in-house by government departments and authorities. In a later *Premier's Memorandum to Ministers (Memorandum 91–24)* Greiner explained that existing in-house providers would be given the opportunity to bid for the provision of services. Greiner also proposed that savings from contracting out would be shared 50:50 between budget sector agencies and consolidated revenue. (This wasn't much of an incentive. Before then, agencies could have kept 100 per cent of any savings.)

Greiner indicated that agencies had to develop broad strategies for contracting-out, establish annual savings targets, and supply information on progress to a steering committee. In 1993, a survey was undertaken of savings achieved to date. Another survey was administered in 1994, and Treasurer Peter Collins asked agencies to submit 'action plans' which were to be reviewed by a steering committee.

In other words, the government of the day was saying to its senior managers: the onus is on you to outsource as much as possible. Then it set about checking on whether its directives were being followed by sending out questionnaires about how many activities had been contracted out.

Correction, it engaged a *consultant* to send out the questionnaires. Prof. Simon Domberger was engaged by NSW Treasury in 1992 to design, perform and evaluate surveys into contracting out in the NSW public sector. Domberger carried out this work between 1992 and 1998.

(Later, NSW Auditor-General Tony Harris reported that, in engaging Domberger, Treasury had breached NSW government *Guidelines for the engagement and use of consultants* [March 1996] in two fundamental areas: it had failed to call for tenders, and there was no evidence of any formal evaluation of the work undertaken on contracting out by this consultant. Harris reported that 'Treasury has indicated that for future engagements of consultants in this area, competitive tendering will be followed' [*1998 Report to Parliament, Vol 2*].)

In 1986, Domberger, in conjunction with Prof. John Piggott of UNSW's School of Economics had undertaken a careful and considered analysis of claims and counter-claims about contracting-out.

However, in the same year, Domberger (in conjunction with two UK colleagues) claimed that contracting out of refuse collection services by local councils had produced savings of 'broadly 20 per cent' (*Domberger, Meadowcroft & Thompson*, 1986). These claims were an extreme and unsupportable interpretation of the evidence provided by the authors, and the validity of that analysis has been seriously contested by a succession of authors (e.g. *Ganley & Grahl*, 1987; *Paddon*, 1991; *Hodge*, 1996). The evidence presented on refuse collection did not indicate any significant differences in the efficiency gains achieved from contracting out as opposed the gains achieved by in-house teams which feared having their jobs outsourced. This distinction was neatly fudged by the authors when they referred to savings *through* (rather than *from*) contracting (*Domberger, Meadowcroft & Thompson*, 1988). But, as will be illustrated below, the claim of '20 per cent savings from contracting out' became part of the repertoire of catchphrases favoured by privatisation advocates.

Perhaps encouraged by this, Simon Domberger's later, solo work could be readily described as advocacy. Indeed, Domberger became a leading promoter of the benefits of outsourcing, establishing his own consultancy firm, and actively marketing the virtues of outsourcing through that firm's Internet site—even to the extent of using commendations from brave (or foolish) Treasury officials in his firm's marketing material.

Meantime, some NSW Ministers were absolute zealots in their quest to reduce public sector employment by contracting out. But those Ministers were mainly in control of public trading enterprises, not budget sector agencies. While NSW government trading enterprises (GTEs) drastically reduced staff numbers, employee numbers in government departments remained virtually unchanged.

It later became apparent that some of the newly-employed 'contractors' to GTEs were former employees who had been declared redundant, paid out, and then re-engaged on better pay to perform their old jobs. Arguably, the exercise had increased rather than reduced costs in some areas of the public sector (though sacking these employees may have reduced pension costs—a matter discussed below).

But overall, the strategy of asking agencies to develop plans and respond to surveys was not likely to produce a strong response. This was especially the case where agencies were unaware of what it was costing them to produce services or perform functions, because their internal management information systems were still essentially limited to recording cash expenditure and comparing that with 'budget'. As the NSW Council on the Cost of Government found in 1996, the management information systems in most agencies were incapable of tracking trends in spending on 'line items' (like salaries and wages), let alone trends in spending on 'activities' (such as accounting, management of information technology or human resources).

Misinformation about the benefits of outsourcing

Nevertheless, Domberger's commissioned studies soon claimed massive savings from contracting out. Those claims were repeated by the Federal Coalition in its 1991 *Fightback* document (with Domberger's work cited in support):

> Contracting out will improve efficiency in production and distribution, provide clear definitions of services costs and a mechanism to monitor them, accelerate the delivery and reduce internal restrictions and cost impediments.
>
> Empirical evidence (Domberger 1989, Rimmer 1991) suggests that contracting out can conservatively save 20 per cent in the costs of service provision. Domberger suggested these savings could be made in transport, maintenance, construction, cleaning and printing not already out-sourced (*Fightback!* 1991).

As noted above, the principal basis of those claims was a study by *Domberger, Meadowcroft & Thompson* (1986) of the costs of refuse collection of a sample of UK local councils. This study was undertaken at a time when private firms were actively lobbying the Thatcher government to make competitive tendering compulsory and were offering their services to some councils (*Paddon*, 1991). The claim of savings of 20 per cent was inferred from data from 'a self selecting group of Councils which were already convinced of the benefits of contracting out and favourably disposed towards its procedures' (*Paddon*, 1991). *Ganley & Grahl* (1987) pointed out that some of these contracts appeared to have been won by loss-leading behaviour, or had involved serious deterioration in the quality of services provided—citing evidence of firms seeking to increase their charges within the first year of winning tenders, of complaints from residents, or of penalties imposed by councils in response to failures to meet standards of performance. *Hodge* (1996) noted that the main analysis presented in Domberger's 1986 paper did not produce any statistically significant association between contracting out and the overall cost of service provision—the main explanatory variables were the 'number of units' to which services were provided (suggesting economies of scale) and whether collections were more than once per week. Further,

Finding that the costs differences between contracting 'out' and contracted 'in' service was not statistically significant, Domberger *et al.* concluded that both resulted in cost reductions 'of around 20%'. This is the origin of the now much quoted '20% cost reduction rule' used as a basis for contracting out and competitive tendering in public sector policy (*Hodge*, 1996).

The obvious point to be made is that if roughly 20 per cent savings could be achieved by *improving in-house performance*, then the case for contracting out was not compelling. Possibly the savings resulted from exposing these activities to competition, or the threat of contracting out; if so, possibly the same level of savings could have been achieved though better management of in-house operations.

Yet the claim of '20 per cent savings from contracting out' was reiterated as fact—notwithstanding the existence of a series of published studies presenting conflicting evidence. For example, NSW Treasury were happy to translate the questionable Domberger claims as a finding from 'experience':

> Extensive analysis has been undertaken both in Australia and overseas of the potential for contracting out and the savings and other benefits that can be achieved. Typically, experience shows that savings of the order of 20 per cent can be achieved after account is taken of all transitional (sic) costs (*1991–92 NSW Budget Paper No. 2*).

The picture which emerges from an accumulating series of studies on contracting out is as follows:

- claims about savings from contracting out usually fail to take account of compensation payments to redundant employees, other transaction costs, and subsequent costs of contract supervision;
- public sector agencies have achieved savings from outsourcing in some situations, but not in others;
- savings from contracting out are not only achievable when the *public sector* contracts out to the *private sector*: savings have also been achieved when private sector firms outsource functions to other private sector firms; similarly savings have been achieved when public sector agencies have outsourced functions to other public sector agencies;
- the threat of competition or outsourcing has been sufficient to encourage cost cutting in some situations;
- public sector cost savings through contracting may not be passed on to the community but may be absorbed 'through greater numbers of management positions and other rewards to the organisation' (*Hodge*, 1996).

Nevertheless, Domberger (still funded in part by NSW Treasury) produced a series of reports presenting further 'evidence' and extolling the virtues of outsourcing. He reported that a 1993 survey of NSW agencies 'reported savings of approximately 20 per cent compared to previous expenditures' (*Domberger*, 1994). NSW Treasury later reported that *average savings on the cost of services prior to contracting was 18 per cent* (NSW Treasury, May 1996). Then, on the basis of Domberger's survey work, it was claimed in 1996 that contracting-out across the NSW public sector had produced annual savings of approximately $266 million 'without sacrificing quality of services' (*NSW Treasury*, September 1996).

The basis of these claims about savings are in stark contrast with the 1996 findings of the NSW Council on the Cost of Government that the NSW government's management information systems could not provide basic data about trends in expenditure on 'line items' or 'activities'. Accordingly, sceptical readers might wonder how the respondents to Domberger's surveys could arrive at estimates of major savings from outsourcing (particularly when overall spending on departmental programs had been steadily increasing).

It seems that respondents to Domberger's NSW surveys were simply asked to provide their own estimates of savings—at a time when much publicity had been given to claims that savings of around 20 per cent were achievable from contracting out.

In terms of methodology, Domberger's approach was a textbook example of 'reactive research' (*Webb, Campbell, Schwartz & Sechrest*, 1966). Evidence was collected from surveys of senior public sector managers, most of whom would have been on short-term contracts. Managers were asked, in effect, whether they had implemented government policies. Those managers would be unlikely to report that they had defied the government directives, or that their own efforts as managers had been less than successful.

As for the scale of savings secured by their efforts: NSW Treasury was saying that 20 per cent was achievable, and the designer of the survey had already publicly claimed that 20 per cent was an average saving. No one would be surprised if respondents to Domberger's surveys claimed savings of around 20 per cent. But many researchers would suggest that survey responses collected in these circumstances could have been influenced by external events.

One can speculate about the incentives that were faced by public sector managers, particularly if they were to surrender 50 per cent of any savings. For many, the easiest response would have been to outsource some small-scale activities, and then to report savings of around 20 per cent of prior spending. That way they appeared to be diligently complying with government policy, without damaging their agency's budget. The evidence appears consistent with this speculation. The average size of the more than 82,000 contracts described in Domberger's 1994 survey (*NSW Treasury*, 1994) was less than $13,000 per annum; if 68,000 legal aid contracts were excluded, the average was little more than $72,000 per annum.

In the event, Domberger's estimates of savings were based on figures provided by a small minority of respondents and covering only 1.3 per cent of his sample, after excluding legal aid contracts (*NSW Treasury*, 1994). The estimates were not based on data extracted from accounting records, but from respondent's recollections of questionable data. It appears that Domberger's respondents were only asked to compare annual costs of providing a specific service *before* and *after* contracting—without counting the costs of establishing and administering the contracts, or the costs associated with paying out redundant employees.[1]

This was flimsy evidence. It was pathetically flimsy when viewed as the basis for policies which would affect the livelihoods of thousands of public sector employees and their families.

If Domberger's analysis was based on poor quality information, he was at least brave enough to recommend that existing guidelines on outsourcing should be revised to emphasise the importance of contract management and the need to establish systems for monitoring performance (*NSW Treasury*, 1996). Yet this seemed a case of 'do as I say, not what I do' (or, perhaps, 'what I have been asked to do').

Certainly Domberger's recent book *The Contracting Organization* (1998) avoided any systematic discussion of how to 'cost' services. Strangely for a work of academic pretensions, it also ignored published works which had attacked the quality of his analysis. Academics are normally quick to respond to such criticisms, if they have the evidence. Domberger even went so far as to dismiss the relevance of rigorous financial analysis of proposed outsourcing arrangements, by making the extraordinary claim that:

> a purely economic accounting (sic) approach to contracting is more suited to understanding *ex post* outcomes than as an aid to decision making (*Domberger*, 1998).

This stance might be restated as 'don't let the facts get in the way of a good decision'.

---

[1] Some respondents to a later Domberger survey could estimate the costs of managing their contracts. Contract management costs for this small sample (only 1.5 per cent of the total number of contracts) were estimated to be 2.7 per cent of contract value (*NSW Treasury*, February 1997). Again, this Domberger study did not report how these costs had been estimated.

When providing this message through speaking engagements, Domberger was also able to report his findings about client attitudes regarding the quality of services being provided by private sector providers. At one function, Domberger displayed bar charts showing how many respondents considered that contracts were 'successful' or 'very successful'. Apparently no one thought the contracts were 'unsuccessful'. A suspicious questioner asked that the chart be shown again, and enquired why the responses only added up to around 90 per cent of contracts? The speaker explained that the other contracts 'did not satisfy contractual requirements', but then declined to discuss whether a 10 per cent failure to meet contractual requirements was acceptable.

Ideologically-based (rather than factually-based) approaches to contracting out were bound to generate suspicion and resistance from trade unions—which in turn would impede discussions about ways of introducing workplace efficiencies.

A NSW Joint Parliamentary Committee report on its inquiry into *Competitive Tendering and Contracting in the NSW Public Sector* (1998) was highly sceptical about whether the analysis underpinning proposals for more extensive outsourcing was independent:

> The Committee remains concerned that the government relies heavily on CTC research obtained through a limited number of consultants. This trend also raises concern about bias and whether researchers have a vested interest in the outsourcing industry themselves.

The observations of this parliamentary committee only highlighted the fact that large-scale contracting out had been undertaken without effective oversight and scrutiny—and that many decisions to outsource had been made in the basis of incomplete, partial, or poor quality information.

Shortcomings in public sector management information systems don't help

A legacy of the public sector's use of cash-based budgeting and cash-based accounting systems is that public sector management information systems (MIS) are sub-standard.

The tradition of simply counting expenditure to date and comparing it against budget meant that public sector managers neither had to be skilled in financial management, nor had any need to hire staff who were trained in financial management.

While public sector disclosure requirements commonly require agencies in the general government sector to report on aggregate spending against budget, and to disclose levels of spending in broad categories (salary related expenditure, depreciation, other) many agencies would find difficulty in compiling a report which presents information on *trends* in spending on individual items of expenses (such as overtime, travel, telephone or supplies).

Managers of those agencies (and some senior officers in central agencies) would probably argue that financial information is not very relevant when a Minister is demanding answers to questions about day-to-day operational issues. They would probably suggest that they have major issues of public policy to deal with than minor issues about trends in spending on 'line items'. They would probably claim that analyses of variances in expenditure were not worth doing provided that overall spending was 'within budget'. All of which amounts to an abrogation of responsibility for the efficient and effective use of taxpayers' funds.

The same managers may often play the game of 'good idea' budgeting—seeking enhanced budgetary allocations because of a 'good idea' about how to provide some new type of service. Practitioners of 'good idea' budgeting rarely ever explore whether new initiatives could be funded by scaling back other activities which are not working effectively, or for which demand has fallen.

Public sector budgetary arrangements in the public sector involve a formal process whereby parliaments allocate funds to be spent on 'programs'. In practice, many agencies simply pool the monies so allocated and don't use budget allocations to programs as a means of managing scarce resources within their organisations. Indeed, some appear to regard the budget process as a bit of a game, and proceed to reallocate those resources within their agencies to regions or other internal units. Then at the end of the year, staff are asked to provide estimates of the time they have spent on programs. Figures are then compiled which miraculously demonstrate that the pattern of spending by the agency conformed almost exactly to the figures nominated within the budget. If the allocation of staff time doesn't do the trick, then a series of internal transfers can be made, charging programs for overheads in a fashion which may not really reflect underlying cost drivers. Some public sector financial managers gain their power and authority from the ability to orchestrate these internal transfers—and seem to actually *prefer* internal management information systems which do not reveal the underlying patterns of expenditure to others within their organisation—let alone to Ministers or external stakeholders.

But the real shortcomings of public sector management information systems concern the manner in which they fail to track patterns of spending (and other aspects of financial performance) within individual agencies and across government.

Undergraduate text books on management accounting introduce

students to the concepts of 'fixed' and 'variable' costs, 'direct' and 'indirect' costs, of ways of calculating the unit cost of products or services, and the techniques needed to manage organisations on the basis of information about the relationships between categories of costs as levels of activity change. These notions are extended to develop ways of monitoring the contributions of divisions or product lines or geographically distributed production facilities. More advanced undergraduate texts explore ways in which cost and operational information can be used strategically—to identify ways of adding value to the firm. In practice—at least in many large private sector organisations—information systems empower managers at all levels of responsibility to examine financial and operational data about the performance of the units under their control. Further, modern software enables managers to drill down into their firm's data base to seek information which may enable them to explore ways of continuously improving firm performance.

The public sector counterpart of these concepts and ideas would suggest that, as a minimum, government agencies should know the cost structure of their organisations: what has been spent (through wages and salaries and other direct costs such as rent and communications), and how many staff are engaged in direct service delivery and in ancillary functions. Managers of programs or regional offices should also have information to enable them to benchmark their performance against others and to explore ways of maximising the effectiveness of the way in which resources are expended in the interests of the community.

In practice, MIS currently operating in government agencies fall far short of these basic requirements. Even at head office, agencies don't monitor spending on administrative overheads as distinct from service delivery, and don't track spending on activities (such as accounting, human resources management, property management, and information technology).

As an example: when in 1996 the NSW Council on the Cost of Government (COCOG) set out to explore the sources of major increases in spending during the term of office of the previous government, it found that agencies could not supply basic information about trends in spending on line items. A survey found that, in a sample of 95 agencies, 82 operated different financial systems, using 48 different software packages (of which five were developed in-house), and that there was almost total diversity in coding expenditure items like wages and salaries. When COCOG set out to find how much was being spent on corporate services within the general government sector, it found that agencies could not provide this information from their accounting systems. Data had to be collected by distributing questionnaires.

There are grounds to believe that such problems are not confined to NSW (though the other large states of Victoria and Queensland have both been very active in recent years in upgrading their internal management information systems).

With management information systems like these, one can understand that governments are not in a good position to assess what is being spent on specific activities within agencies, let alone understand the cost structure of those activities, let alone assess whether those activities are being undertaken efficiently. Yet such basic costing information is necessary if governments are to be able to make informed assessments of whether it makes good sense to continue to provide services from within the public sector, or whether they should close-down internal operations and buy-in services from external contractors or suppliers.

The NSW Council on the Cost of Government returned to this question in 1999—and found little cause for optimism about improvements in management information systems (and intra-agency financial analysis) in the last four years.

The Council surveyed NSW agencies and invited them to nominate an activity from among those they were presently undertaking, and to indicate the extent to which they could provide advice on the costs of those activities in a timely fashion (i.e. within two weeks). The gentle design of the survey afforded agencies an opportunity to make themselves look good, since they could select an activity for which cost analysis was 'easy'. In fact, in 1997 the NSW government had issued directives that agencies should strive to know their costs and to drive efficiencies (COCOG, 1997). If agencies had heeded those directives, the material sought in the survey should have already been on file.

This exercise produced the disturbing news that 54 per cent of the agencies that responded lacked the capacity to calculate the costs of major activities. One would expect that most of the agencies which failed to respond would have reported low capability (COCOG, 1999).

Further, of the respondent agencies 'only 33 per cent provided a financial analysis of some kind, and many of these were rudimentary'. The Council reported:

> The implication is that complex financial analysis is neither common nor commonly well done within the general government sector (COCOG, 1999).

Anecdotal and other evidence suggests that this deficiency is fairly common through the Australian public sector. One favourite story concerns the hospital which thought its running costs were within budget until it was realised that the hospital's 'accountant' had assumed that there were only three quarters in a year (since three fours make twelve).

Financial analysis and accounting distortions

Undergraduate courses in accounting commonly include exercises designed to highlight the need to examine reported cost and profit data with care, and to look beneath reported figures. These exercises appear in many forms and many guises. The following is but one example.

The theme is that bad decisions can be made if they are based on an uncritical reliance on internal cost data. While the 'cases' described in Box 6.1 refer to proposals to downsize a commercial business, the underlying theme is equally applicable to proposals to outsource activities in public sector agencies, on the basis that internal costings show that those activities are more expensive than the use of external contractors. The internal costings can be grossly misleading.

While this is just a hypothetical example, there is plenty of anecdotal evidence of private sector managers taking accounting numbers at face value. Because they did not understand how cost-allocations can distort reports of the profitability of business units, they sold off their most efficient or inherently profitable businesses.

The way to avoid such misinterpretations is to focus on the contributions made by business units towards the 'recovery' of overheads and hence to profits. This is possible so long as accounting systems are well-designed and are used to generate reports which reveal underlying cost structures and cost-volume-profit relationships.

Application to the public sector

None of the government-issued guidelines on analysing the costs of in-house versus out-house service delivery canvass the need to analyse cost structures in this way. Indeed, the guidelines issued by the Commonwealth's Department of Finance and Administration (1998) reflect an astonishing lack of knowledge of these issues. They list as further reading on 'costing activities' the accounting profession's Statements of Accounting Standards. This is a farcical statement, since those documents, while sounding authoritative, have virtually nothing to say about the assignment of costs to units or activities.

The lessons about the potentially misleading nature of internal costings may be readily translatable to the public sector. This is especially so for GTEs, where the performance of public sector

Box 6.1
HOW INTERNAL COSTINGS CAN MISLEAD

Case 1
A business has three divisions—A, B and C—with operating results as shown below. Management is concerned about falling profits. Should the company sell or close down Division C?

Year ended June 19x1	Total $'000	Division A $'000	Division B $'000	Division C $'000
Sales revenues	10,000	4,000	3,000	3,000
Less				
Cost of sales, selling and administrative expenses	5,000	1,000	2,000	2,000
Trading profit	5,000	3,000	1,000	1,000
Less				
Division office expenses	1,000	400	200	400
	4,000	2,600	800	600
Less				
Central office expenses	2,100	700	700	700
Net profit (before tax)	1,900	1,800	200	-100

On the face of it, Division C is recording a loss of $100,000, and so the sale of Division C could seem a good idea. But Division C's profit is *after* the allocation of central office expenses, totalling $2.1 million. If Division C is closed down, and central office costs continue to be incurred at the same level, then the overall profit performance of the firm will get worse, not improve.

Case 2 shows the profit performance of the firm for the following year, after the sale of Division C—assuming that divisional sales and costs and central administrative expenses have remained unchanged:

Case 2

Year ended June 19x2	Total $'000	Division A $'000	Division B $'000
Sales revenues	7,000	4,000	3,000
Less			
Cost of sales, selling and administrative expenses	3,000	1,000	2,000
Trading profit	4,000	3,000	1,000
Less			
Division office expenses	600	400	200
	3,400	2,600	800
Less			
Central office expenses	2,100	1,050	1,050
Net profit (before tax)	1,300	1,550	-250

If managers now decide to sell off Division B because it was showing a loss, then they will make matters worse, as shown in Case 3. Net profit declines even further.

Case 3	
Year ended June 19x3	**Total**
	(Division A)
	$'000
Sales revenues	4,000
Less	
Cost of sales, selling and administrative expenses	1,000
Trading profit	3,000
Less	
Division office expenses	400
	2,600
Less	
Central office expenses	2,100
Net profit (before tax)	500

managers is evaluated in terms of the profitability of business units, and where those units themselves generate revenues from directly selling services to the community. Or perhaps in many cases it is too late. A range of government-provided services have been closed down—without any public disclosure of the financial analysis which underpinned those decisions.

Occasionally some internal documents fall off the backs of trucks (or photocopiers). Some have been sighted which advocated the sale of depots or business units on the basis of projected 'savings', which included supposed 'savings' on internal charges for overheads. As explained in the cases presented above, these savings may be illusory. Those responsible for analysing such actions must have been poorly trained, or unintelligent—they were certainly unaware of basic principles of cost-volume-profit analysis, such as are routinely taught to second-year students in most business studies courses.

A particular concern is the way that claims are made about the alleged inefficiency of notional business units, which have been established within public sector organisations on the basis that they will charge other business units a fee for their services.

Such practices—often undertaken in the name of 'commercialisation'—can establish meaningful monitoring arrangements and be useful complements to the establishment of incentives for improved performance. Conversely they can prepare the ground for downsizing or outsourcing arrangements when in-house accounting systems deem those units to be unprofitable.

As outlined in Cases 1–3 above, such judgments can be illusory where accounting methods involve the arbitrary assignment of costs which are not controllable by the business units whose performance is being evaluated. If those units are directed to set internal charges at a level which ensures 'full cost recovery' (including recovery of someone else's overheads), then they may be virtually doomed to be setting their charges above market rates.

The stage is then set for someone to come along and demand that the activity be contracted out, because it is too expensive and/or unprofitable.

The purpose of these comments is not to suggest that appalling errors have been made by public sector managers in closing down business units. Without a comprehensive review of all such decisions it is not possible to say how extensive such practices may have been. However, the quality of the training of many financial managers throughout the Australian public service is not high.

The NSW Council on the Cost of Government recently surveyed agencies about their efforts to track spending on activities and to compare those costs with the alternative costs of outsourcing.

The approach was very softly-softly. Agencies were invited to provide their best examples of internal financial analysis—in the form of information they have provided (or could provide) to Ministers in relation to some query.

Even so, the Council reported:

The ... survey revealed

- knowledge of costs and outputs varies markedly
- financial analysis skills need strengthening—many of the responses showed little understanding of how to identify and analyse relevant 'costs' ...

Some of the financial analyses received showed that agencies benefit from analysing their costs, but many were rudimentary. The relatively few analyses provided suggests that either, analyses are not undertaken, or that agencies did not wish the quality of their analyses to be reviewed. This, together with the general quality of the analyses, suggests that the answers given about the quality of information which could be provided to Ministers are based more on optimism than on actualities (COCOG, December 1998).

Given that many senior public sector managers have been heard to propose outsourcing, findings like this raise questions about how effectively those public servants may have managed their agencies—let alone how they came to identify outsourcing as an optimal strategy.

It seems highly likely that many proposals to outsource activities have not been made on the basis of careful analysis, but simply follow from earlier patterns of managerial behaviour involving both denial and blame.

If senior staff of an agency have avoided the hard work of monitoring an agency's financial and operational performance, but also deny any personal responsibility for rising costs and unsatisfactory service, then the only way they can avoid personal responsibility is to blame their workforce. If they are unable to deal openly with the workforce by providing credible facts and figures about where performance needs to be improved, and how they propose to drive improvements, then they have little option but to maintain a culture of blame. Having blamed the workforce for poor performance, bad managers have painted themselves into a corner. Their only remaining option may be to propose outsourcing, while promising cuts in costs (generally after a lengthy transitional period, by which time new initiatives can be found to justify claims for additional funding).

Moreover, some of the guidelines published by Australian governments on the evaluation of proposals to outsource government activities give no grounds for confidence in past analyses. The content of some of those guidelines is technically flawed.

The outsourcing decision—financial considerations

The decision as to whether or not to 'outsource' should, in principle, be preceded by analysis of

- the efficiency of in-house service provision; and
- the quality of those services (including assessments of such issues as the extent of availability or access to those services to different groups within the community).

Indeed, one would expect good managers to routinely assess the relative costs of providing some types of services 'in house', or using contractors.

Developments in information technology, in particular, have allowed many private sector firms to cut their costs by outsourcing routine transaction processing (for payrolls, accounts receivable and accounts payable). Some major Australian banks and insurance companies have entered into joint ventures in order to get the benefit of economies of scale in routine transaction processing.

A major difficulty for public sector managers is that traditional cash-based budgeting and accounting systems were not designed to track spending on 'outputs' or 'activities'. Even though governments have decreed that agencies should use accrual accounting, these techniques have been introduced in a half-hearted manner, with the main use of those accounting systems being to compile little-read annual reports.

As has been documented by the NSW Council on the Cost of Government, most public sector accounting systems are unable to collect and routinely report information about the costs of key activities, or the unit costs of service delivery. Hence it may be difficult for managers to monitor trends in the costs of in-house service delivery, let alone compare those costs with the cost of outsourcing to external suppliers.

A second consideration is the need for managers to understand how their internal costings have been undertaken.

When accounting systems report on the costs of a given service or activity, a range of assumptions have been made about how costs are to be traced, or how costs which are common to two or more services are to be allocated between those services. Then assumptions are made about the way that the cost of past purchases of long-lived assets (such as cars or computers) are to be apportioned between periods, through charges for depreciation.

The product of these calculations may be useful in analysing the internal costs, but these numbers may not be relevant when considering whether to retain or outsource a particular activity. As suggested by Cases 1, 2 and 3 outlined above, managers might actually make bad financial choices if they focus on reported numbers without understanding what they represent. Indeed, if it appears that internal processes are costing far more than might be obtainable from outsourcing (or other arrangements) then it becomes necessary to look very carefully at the costings before concluding that outsourcing is the answer.

In fact—and this may be hard for some to accept—it would be absolutely wrong to simply compare

(a) the costs of in-house service provision (as reported by internal accounting systems) with
(b) estimates of the cost of obtaining equivalent services from an external supplier.

It would be wrong for a range of financial reasons, including:

- in-house costings may include depreciation on previously acquired assets—which may have a minimal value if scrapped or sold;
- some costs which have been allocated to the service under scrutiny may still have to be paid regardless of whether delivery of those services is maintained or abandoned;
- termination of in-house service delivery may immediately crystalise the need to make redundancy payments to employees.

(It may also be wrong because of a range of non-financial factors—discussed further below.)

In principle, the appropriate cost comparisons would focus on projected cash flows, not accounting entries, and would compare:

(a) the cash flows which would be *avoided* by outsourcing; and
(b) estimates of the cash flows to be incurred by obtaining equivalent services from an external supplier

using discounted cash flow analysis to calculate the present values of alternatives.

Some of the implications of this approach are that any analysis should:

- ignore depreciation charges (which are internal bookkeeping entries);
- disregard internal allocations of overheads or service charges or 'on costs';
- ignore accounting calculations of 'full costs';
- treat the acquisition of assets (such as through the replacement of equipment) as the same as any other cash outlays;
- include as costs any new expenses which may be incurred (e.g. through contract management) as a result of outsourcing.

(For a fuller explanation of the avoidable cost methodology and some worked examples, see *COCOG, 1997*.)

One of the paradoxes which emerges from identifying and analysing avoidable costs is that an agency may be better off continuing with in-house service provision even though the agency's accounting system suggests that the costs of those services are greater than the costs of outsourcing.

On the other hand, much depends on the choice of the time period used for the analysis. The longer the time horizon selected, the more the items of cost which will become 'avoidable'. For example, outsourcing payrolls may leave an agency with surplus office space for the term of a lease, so that rents previously allocated to the payroll function are not avoidable. However, in the medium to long term, those rental costs are avoidable. Conversely the longer the time frame the greater the difficulty in assessing the costs of obtaining payroll services from contractors—since suppliers of payroll services would not want to enter into long-term fixed price contracts.

Arguably the appropriate time horizon should at least match the life cycle of major assets or contractual arrangements. Outsourcing may be financially more attractive *just before* major items of equipment need to be replaced or upgraded than *just after* asset replacement. But that statement must be accompanied by the economists' disclaimer, 'all other things being equal' (and other things are rarely equal).

Mention might be made of proposals for certain agencies to be subject to compulsory competitive tendering (or CCT). The foregoing observations about cost structures and the behaviour of costs over time often mean that CCT is a crude instrument, which is potentially costly to taxpayers.

If an agency is compelled to put its activities out to tender at a time when it has just reinvested in equipment, under conditions that a private sector tenderer can acquire that equipment at fire sale prices, then the exercise may involve significant wealth transfers from the public purse to a select and fortunate private sector business.

If an agency is compelled to put its activities out to tender, and in-house teams are required to tender on the basis of full cost recovery (including overheads) then in-house teams are severely (and probably, fatally) handicapped. A private sector bidder could readily win new business if it sets its bid on the basis of recovering its marginal costs. That pricing structure may not be sustainable in the long term—but in the long term, the private sector bidder may have grown in size, driven out competition, and be able to earn monopolistic profits. For the agency embarking on compulsory competitive tendering, short-term gain may generate long-term pain.

Flaws in some government-issued guidelines on outsourcing

There is an old accounting maxim, *different costs for different purposes*.

There are many ways that accountants can trace, accumulate, allocate and attribute costs—to functions, to line items, to divisions, to products or activities, or to processes. In most of those cases no single calculation is necessarily 'right'. Indeed, it is not even possible to assess which calculation is heading in the right direction without examining the context in which calculations are made and the purpose of the exercise.

Australian governments have prepared guidelines for use by agencies in assessing the case for (or against) contracting out. Guidelines (or drafts) have been issued by the Commonwealth (*Department of Finance & Administration*, 1998), and in NSW (*NSW Premier's Department*, 1991, 1992; COCOG, 1997), South Australia (1995), Western Australia (*WA Treasury*, 1995; *WA*

Public Sector Management Office, 1996), and Victoria (*Victorian Department of Treasury & Finance*, 1995). Queensland has issued guidelines on the assignment of costs to 'outputs' (*Queensland Treasury*, 1998), which do not directly deal with outsourcing, beyond suggesting that managers should 'benchmark and compare output costs between suppliers and other providers'.

Several of these documents appear to have been prepared as guides on *how to justify outsourcing*—not how to evaluate whether outsourcing made sense. For example, guidelines issued by Victoria simply directed staff to prepare a 'business case' for outsourcing, by identifying potential external service providers. The WA Guidelines went further, providing advice on *how to implement* outsourcing, including a pro forma 'deed of severance' for employees accepting redundancy payments, and a pro forma 'letter of resignation for employees moving to private sector employment'.

Several of these guidelines tried to do too much. They set out to be do-it-yourself kits on cost accounting (for readers without any understanding of relevant accounting concepts). The contents pages told the story: they listed guidelines for costing services for use in 'output budgeting', or for preparing performance indicators, as well as for preparing a business case for outsourcing. As such, these publications were often confused, and confusing to a readership which may not have understood the maxim, 'different costs for different purposes'.

In so far as published government guidelines on 'costing' referred to the outsourcing decision, several contained technical flaws—flaws which usually biased any analysis in favour of 'outsourcing'. As such, these guidelines reflected a misunderstanding of three basic principles associated with the evaluation of alternative courses of financial action.

First, the costs and benefits of those alternatives should be evaluated by using estimates of *future cash flows* (not historical accounting information, or even projections of that data) and discounted cash flow analysis.

Second, the cash flows which should be examined are those (and only those) *which will be affected by the selection of one or other alternative*. When considering alternatives to in-house service provision, the relevant concept of 'cost' to be considered relates to those expenditures which can be *avoided* by outsourcing, together with any additional costs that may be incurred as a consequence of outsourcing.

Third, an emphasis on financial factors should not mean a lack of concern for the *quality of services available from alternatives*. None of the sets of guidelines had much to say about how to measure the quality of service currently being provided, or how to assess or define the standards of service potentially available from external contractors. (The failure of government agencies to establish and monitor quality performance measures—a key element of the success of contract management—has subsequently been the subject of critical attention—see *Commonwealth Auditor-General*, October 1999).

The flaws in the guidelines relating to the selection of techniques of financial analysis are technical. In brief, some of these flaws are:

- guidelines have emphasised the need to look at the 'full' cost of providing a service. But, whatever methods were used to calculate 'full costs', the fact remains that in many instances, overheads will continue regardless of the outsourcing of one or other activity. Even though the 'full costs' of in-house service delivery may be higher than the costs quoted by external suppliers, outsourcing may not be the optimal financial outcome. (It would amount to a practical illustration of the hoary tales of mismanagement illustrated in Box 6.1 above.) Quite different solutions might be identified if the analysis focused on 'avoidable' costs—and analysed data representing cash flows rather than accounting accruals;
- virtually all guidelines proposed analysis of the *on-going* costs of service delivery from in-house or out-house suppliers—and ignore the short-term costs of staff redundancies. Recent Commonwealth draft Guidelines (1997) avoid discussion of redundancy costs by outlining approaches to the analysis of the costs of service delivery on a *long term basis*. In other words, given political imperatives, these guidelines could be saying that it would be wrong to assess the impact of outsourcing within (say) a five or ten year timeframe, because the numbers might not favour outsourcing;
- conversely, some guidelines illustrate the analysis of costs from in-house versus out-house service delivery by suggesting use of an overly *short* time horizon for analysing costs—so that the analysis might then exclude the cash flows associated with the periodic replacement of equipment. Indeed, a common failing of the guidelines was to indicate what principles should guide the selection of the contract period. One exception was the Commonwealth's 1998 contribution, which suggested that the duration of a contract should be determined with regard to the likelihood of 'policy changes';
- similarly several government guidelines count as part of the costs of service delivery the salaries and overhead costs associated with the management of in-house service delivery, but then fail to

include the costs of preparing detailed contracts, and then of supervising the work of external contractors;
- some guidelines propose that the 'full cost' of services should include allowance for the use of capital through a 'capital charge'. They then suggest that projected costs should be subjected to discounted cash flow analysis. This is simply double-counting, since the time value of money is already taken into account in discounted cash flow analysis.

Some might view these flaws as quite sinister: that the authors of these guidelines have deliberately set out to slant any analysis in favour of outsourcing. But the overall impression to be gained from a critical reading of these documents—some running to hundreds of pages—is that they reflect muddled thinking. Possibly that arises from the fact that several of these guidelines were attempting to provide government-wide advice on costing practices.

One might ask a second question: why was there a need to prepare these guidelines when finance professionals should have already been aware of basic accounting concepts and basic forms of financial analysis? The fact is that the Australian public sector has failed to recruit well-qualified staff to senior positions in financial management. Some argue that this is a legacy of the long tradition of cash-based budgeting and accounting. One did not need a university degree in accounting to work out whether total monthly cash spending was more or less than an annual budget divided by 12. Hence many chief financial officers in major government agencies have minimal qualifications, and have 'learned on the job'. Many are not members of professional accounting associations (and, if they are, may have been admitted through the back door, on the basis of the seniority of their position, without ever passing an exam).

In many situations the publication of 'guidelines' served more than the provision of useful memory joggers and checklists. The guidelines were often providing basic education to unqualified staff—albeit without any obligation for neophyte financial analysts to actually study these materials in detail, or work through practical exercises, or obtain any feedback on their efforts.

This was brought home when the NSW Council on the Cost of Government prepared revised guidelines on 'service competition policy' in 1997. They were issued to outline the Carr government's policies regarding contracting out. Rather than requiring CEOs to outsource as much as possible, the guidelines required CEOs to know their costs and to operate efficiently. If market testing (through informal enquiries or formal benchmarking exercises) indicated that a particular activity was inefficient, relative to the costs of obtaining services from alternative suppliers, then CEOs were obliged to find out why, and do something about it. If these efforts failed, outsourcing was to be considered as a live option. An appendix to the guidelines outlined issues concerning the calculation of net avoidable costs, and provided spreadsheet templates which could be used to analyse those costs.

The document referred to concepts that are usually mastered by second-year undergraduate accounting students. It was therefore somewhat disturbing to receive a letter from the chief financial officer of one agency (annual budget in excess of $1 billion) asking that the guidelines be reissued in a 'less technical' form.

Non-financial considerations

Since the public sector is intended to provide services to the community, it is of more than passing interest to consider the quality of services provided by *in-house* or *out-house* providers. There is little point in government cutting costs by outsourcing if the end result is substandard services.

One hears a host of stories about some early disasters in outsourcing.

- Hospitals which terminated their staff cleaners and engaged contractors found that vomit in hallways might not be cleaned until the contractors arrived at their scheduled times. Moreover it became apparent that the now-dismissed staff cleaners, apart from cleaning, had also provided a valued social contact for often-lonely long-term patients, by chatting as they went about their work.
- School cleaning also suffered similar difficulties as contractors performed their tasks after school hours—leading to complaints from parents about unhygienic conditions in toilet blocks.

No doubt it would be argued that such cases reflected initial inexperience on the part of public servants in specifying contract conditions. Lessons were learned from those experiences, and outsourcing contracts were later improved.

Perhaps they were, though some tender documents (with page after page of specifications on the cleaning of washrooms) could have gone too far in the opposite direction. The two pages devoted to scheduling requirements for the cleaning of mirrors were probably too detailed and complex to be useful to those who would actually do the work.

Arguably there has been a tendency within the public sector to present the financial arguments for outsourcing, and then to only pay lip service to the idea that issues relating to service quality and delivery should also be considered. Most published research in contracting out has reinforced that approach, by emphasising the extent of cost savings which might be achieved from contracting out—very few studies have looked at service quality (see *Hodge*, 1996, for a review).

There are three main reasons why a preoccupation with immediate cost savings can fail—even if agencies have been thoughtful and careful in pre-specifying the terms and conditions of contracts. First, such an approach may have too narrow a focus on a specific area of service delivery, without regard to 'second order effects' which flow from an initial decision to outsource.

- Several governments have outsourced management of corrective services institutions because of perceived savings in costs. One government established a new privately-run low-cost gaol in a rural area. Its operating costs were lower. But corrective institutions are intended to foster rehabilitation of offenders. A key element in rehabilitation is the maintenance of contacts with families and friends. The service experimented with charter buses to assist low-income families in metropolitan areas to maintain contact with prisoners—but it became too expensive, and eroded most if not all of any operational savings from outsourcing. Then, to save money, the prison came to be used to house prisoners who did not have many visitors (such as sexual offenders).

The same kind of second-order effects need to be considered with a host of routine management decisions:

- Savings from securing low-cost rental accommodation for government agencies may be eroded by higher travel costs and wasted staff time as public servants commute between meetings with Ministers or other agencies.

But government policies which put pressure on managers to outsource as much as possible increase the probability of counter-productive effects.

Second, a focus on the circumstances of an individual agency may produce good solutions for that agency which are actually sub-optimal from a whole-of-government perspective.

> Individual agencies may outsource payrolls and other routine transaction processing functions and so secure savings relative to prior patterns of expenditure—but less savings than could have been achieved if all agencies had collectively standardised their procedures and developed shared service centres within government.

> A transport authority might select a form of electronic ticketing using available smart-card technologies which was a good solution for that authority, but would represent a wasted opportunity so far as the entire public sector was concerned, since alternative technologies could also been used for handling fee collection in hospitals, payment of traffic fines, and the sale of other products or services.

Third, it is a fact of life that no matter how carefully one tries to pre-specify the terms and conditions of contracts, there will always be a need to adapt those terms and conditions in the light of changing circumstances.

NSW Auditor-General Tony Harris once illustrated the problems which can arise when one can't specify all possible contract requirements and conditions in advance:

> It's a bit like having a building company renovate your kitchen. You can draw up detailed plans and specifications, call for quotes, and pick the best price. That's competition. But once the job is started, and you want to change any of the materials or details, your kitchen company is now a monopolist. It will charge you monopoly prices.

(One suspects that this example reflected personal experience.)

In the private sector, it is said that the auditing profession is prone to 'low balling'. Auditors may put in cheap bids when a corporation puts its work out to tender, in the hope of later picking up the more profitable work associated with management advice, staff recruitment and taxation services. The audit might cost less, but (from the audit firm's perspective) the opportunity to charge high prices for additional services should more than compensate.

Contracting out may not necessarily lead to lower costs to government. It doesn't just depend on whether a private sector service provider can operate more efficiently than public sector service providers, but on whether the supplier is in a position to charge for 'add-ons' or variations to the original contract.

The reality is that private sector firms which operate in competitive markets often seek to drive out competition—so that their own profitability can improve through increased market share and possibly through freedom to increase prices (having regard to the responsiveness of demand in the face of price changes).

Some private sector firms deliberately pay more than necessary in the short term, in order to maintain some semblance of competition. A former mine manager gave the following example:

> We had two local suppliers of explosives in the local market, and one was more expensive. We gave the expensive one around 30 per cent of our orders, simply to keep them in business. The alternative would have cost us more in the long run.

Another market reality is that competition between suppliers may not solely concern 'price'. Proposals to outsource simply because an external supplier promises to provide services for a cheaper unit price does not necessarily mean that the public sector (and hence the taxpayer) will get better value for money. A range of factors need to be considered:

- Will the quality of those services be the same (or better) than those provided in-house?
- Will service delivery be as timely—or, if not, will delays dislocate other activities?

Even if one focuses on financial factors, a range of issues require consideration:

- Is it possible to pre-specify all of the features of the services to be provided by an external contractor? If not, how will modifications be priced?
- What will it cost to administer outsourced contracts, to ensure that services meet pre-specified quality standards?
- What will be the state of competition in future years if the government abandons the field to a cartel of private sector firms?

In some fields (such as school cleaning) governments which have outsourced have simply created a series of regional monopolies in country areas.

In part, these outcomes were probably predictable given that the analysis undertaken by public sector agencies was crude, commercially naive and pre-determined to recommend outsourcing. It is astonishing to find that governments have issued guidelines which reflect a lack of awareness of long term possibilities beyond a first outsourcing contract (or, for that matter, in the early years of any form of privatisation).

Another non-financial matter deserving consideration is the *manner* in which potential contractors will deliver their services. Governments are often fairly good employers, particularly in relation to occupational health and safety issues. Probably this reflects the negotiating power of public sector unions.

A focus on financial factors may suggest that governments would benefit from contracting out. But this then raises questions, in some situations, as to whether a private sector firm is able to provide services more cheaply because of lesser attention to such issues as occupational health and safety:

Union representatives have claimed that low-cost maintenance contracts have been associated with unacceptable short cuts in safety arrangements with workers operating near high-speed road traffic, and a series of fatalities in rail track maintenance.

Looking at the 'big picture', there are grounds to believe that many of the gains claimed for outsourcing can be attributed to staff reductions and a winding-back of the conditions of employment of public sector employees.

There has been minimal analysis of these questions—which is not in itself surprising since governments of all political persuasions face incentives to wind-back some employment conditions with a minimum of fuss.

Arguably the most significant changes are those which reduce a government's financial commitment to pay for employee pensions.

Public service pensions and outsourcing

In some respects outsourcing activity can be viewed as a way of transferring wealth from employees to the government (to be spent for favoured purposes). That arises from the way that outsourcing leads to job losses, which push public servants out of defined benefit superannuation schemes—leading to a loss of their accrued entitlements.

Around 1974 the Whitlam government decided to 'index' pensions payable to public servants by Commonwealth defined benefit superannuation schemes, and other states soon followed. Defined benefit superannuation schemes are those which provide benefits determined by some formula (such as percentage of pre-retirement salary). In contrast, the benefits payable by accumulation-type schemes are linked to the value of contributions and the investment performance of the funds into which employers' and employees' contributions have been paid.

Problems arose when improvements in benefits payable by defined benefit schemes were introduced without corresponding increases in levels of contributions. It soon became apparent that the value of the assets accumulated by those schemes was less than the estimated value of the accrued entitlements of employees and their beneficiaries—the schemes were not fully 'funded'.

The scale of the emerging liability for unfunded superannuation was examined in 1983–84 by the NSW Public Accounts Committee (PAC), which reported on the unexpected scale of commitments facing NSW statutory authorities (*NSW PAC*, 1984). Subsequently NSW, and most Australian governments, chose to close down defined benefit schemes to new entrants. Notable exceptions to this trend have been the defined benefit schemes for judges and politicians, which have been retained.

Even so, by 1996, the NSW government's aggregate liability for unfunded superannuation had grown to $15.4 billion. Arguably the major reason for this rapid growth was the low level of employer contributions to the schemes—including a period in which NSW Premier Nick Greiner had claimed to have been 'reducing debt', while unfunded superannuation liabilities were escalating dramatically.

Similar experiences were recorded in other states and the Commonwealth. In 1996 the Commonwealth's liability for unfunded superannuation and other employee entitlements (such as long service leave) reached $120 billion. Arguably, during the 1990s the aggregate liabilities incurred by Commonwealth and state governments for employee entitlements rivalled the scale of the *national* foreign debt. By late 1999, the Commonwealth government had yet to close down its defined benefit schemes to new entrants (though a bill had been prepared to enforce that step).

Meantime the Commonwealth's experience provides a telling example of how contracting out and consequential downsizing can reduce the government's financial obligations associated with defined benefits superannuation schemes. Since it came to office, the Howard government has slashed public service employment, largely through the sale of government businesses and outsourcing. Commonwealth employees totalled 352,000 in February 1996 (just before the Coalition came to office), but were cut to 248,000 by February 1999 (*ABS*, 1999). In the process, the Commonwealth's liability for employee entitlements fell from $120 billion in 1996 to $79 billion in 1999 (see *'Trial' Public Sector Consolidated Statements*, 1995–96; *Consolidated Financial Statements* 1998–99).

This $41 billion reduction in the Commonwealth's liabilities may involve a number of factors, including changes in actuarial assumptions about future rates of salary increases, inflation, and investment earnings of superannuation funds. It also reflects the fact that employees' entitlements were paid out, when those employees were retrenched. But it is also likely that a proportion of the $41 billion 'gain'; to the Commonwealth arises from the fact that payouts on retrenchment were less than what was already owing to those employees (in an accounting sense) from their past service.

In other words, governments have made big savings from outsourcing by retrenching employees before their retirement age.

It must also be recognised that some element of 'loss' by the employees is probably inevitable whenever individuals are dismissed for poor performance. For younger employees, the switch from a defined benefit to an accumulation type superannuation scheme may not involve great hardship. Moreover, the sweeteners paid by some governments to encourage members to move to an accumulation scheme may be attractive to those employees who do not plan to remain in the public sector for the rest of their careers. For some older employees with children, the switch might also be attractive as a means of providing greater certainty about the sums payable to surviving family members in the event of misadventure. Yet there must be concerns about the equity of governments sacking career public servants with 30 years or more of service, only a few years before they would have become entitled to pensions or a steep rise in the value of their lump-sum payouts.

What lies ahead?

Many government activities have already been outsourced—see Box 6.2 for an illustration. Some of the activities listed in Box 6.2 are only support services. Few would seriously argue that government should employ their own sign writers or vehicle maintenance staff if these services could be provided at a similar standard by private firms, for less money. The outsourcing of other activities—such as the management of jails—raise questions about whether it is the role of government to run cheap prisons or (possibly more expensive) 'correctional facilities'? Should the provision of services for the unemployed be treated as just another business—and if so, what are the likely outcomes of this policy for the community as a whole? One senses that some politicians see outsourcing as a means of changing long-standing policies without prior policy debate—in the name of saving money or improving efficiency.

In that form, contracting out can be a crude (and cruel) management tool. In many situations it underscores the failure of managers to reform inefficient processes through improved performance. Contracting out can reflect belated recognition of inefficiency and poor-quality services—or it can be prompted by external pressures to cut budgets.

Seen in this light, bad management practices in the public sector have exposed employees to the risks of unemployment from outsourcing. Arguably a major shortcoming has been the failure to monitor the costs of in-house service provision and to benchmark those against the costs of other agencies or private sector providers.

Even in the area of human services, government agencies have often closed their eyes to the way in which non-government organisations have been providing services very similar to those provided by public sector agencies, but at lower costs, not through reliance

Box 6.2
ACTIVITIES WHICH HAVE BEEN CONTRACTED OUT BY SOME AUSTRALIAN GOVERNMENTS

Accounting	Event management	Photography
Actuarial services	Facilities management	Printing
Administrative services	Financial analysis	Prison management
Advertising	Fleet management	Probation & parole services
Aircraft maintenance	Grounds maintenance	Project management
Architectural services	Medical supplies	Publication production
Audio-visual	Help desks	Research
Audit	Home detention	Records management
Bailiff services	Human resource mgt.	Removal services
Building construction	Industrial relations services	Revenue collection
Building maintenance	Information systems design	Road maintenance
Call centres	Internal audit	Security services
Cash collections	Inventory management	Signage services
Catering	Janitorial services	Software development
Cleaning	Laundry	Staff training
Computer maintenance	Legal services	Storage
Cost-benefit analysis	Library services	Toll collections
Counselling	Management services	Transport
Courier services	Marketing services	Valuations
Debt management	Medical services	Vehicle maintenance
Employment counselling	Parking services	Veterinary services
Engineering	Payroll	Waste management
Equipment maintenance	Personnel administration	Web site development

Sources: include WA Government Competitive Tendering and Contracting—Framework and Guidelines (1995), various media reports.

on unpaid volunteers, but through more sensible management practices.

There's an old saying, popular with auditors, engineers and lawyers, that among the professions, medical practitioners are the most fortunate: they can bury their mistakes. Public sector managers who advocate contracting out may also be trying to bury their mistakes.

It is difficult to avoid the conclusion that the push for contracting-out is largely driven by ideology. Managers can readily advocate contracting out and readily find support from politicians who are ideologically disposed to contracting out and other forms of privatisation because they have been persuaded by rhetoric rather than the facts of particular cases.

The last decade has seen the ascendancy of this ideological position, and the consequence of outsourcing and downsizing decisions has been demoralising for the workforce. As social commentator Hugh Mackay has observed, downsizing and outsourcing in many organisations all over the country is 'breeding defensive and insecure employees':

Employees now accept that employers intend to employ as few of them as possible. If you have a job, the new folklore says, it's because they haven't yet thought of a way of doing without you. More than 20 per cent of Commonwealth Government employees have lost their jobs in the past two years (to say nothing of the massive staff cuts in banking, airlines and manufacturing), so the folklore is grounded in reality (*SMH*, 22/8/98).

The consequences have been even more devastating for those displaced from employment, particularly for middle-aged workers who, having made career choices to work in the public sector, found themselves casualties of political debate about the relative efficiency and effectiveness of different approaches to service provision by governments.

Having said all that, outsourcing can make good sense in many situations—because money saved on outsourcing can be better used to provide services to the community. Correspondingly, financial costings should not be the be-all and end-all of decisions on whether services should be sourced from in-house or out-house. Governments need good financial information to assess efficiency. But just as important is information about the *quality of services* currently being provided by in-house service providers.

Caution needs to be exercised whenever private firms promise to provide the same services at lower costs, in the absence of contractual commitments which protect the interests of those to whom services are to be provided, or the community. Experience has shown that private firms can bid low to capture new business, but then may not always be capable of delivering services to the same standard as had previously been provided.

For example, a US firm successfully won a tender to dispose of hazardous medical wastes from hospitals. The usual method of disposal involved high temperature incineration. The contractor cut costs by dumping these wastes in the ocean—a practice which only became evident when waste materials washed ashore on beaches.

Complaints were made about the poor standard of bed linen and towels made available to a government-run institution. The agency had accepted the lowest price for providing these services, unaware that some commercial laundries adopted the practice of grading their linen and towels, with the newest product going to high quality hotels, the relatively worn product going to motels, with the used and thinnest product going to nursing homes and similar facilities. If the government agency wanted fluffy towels, it should have specified higher standards; alternatively it could have purchased its own bed linen and towels, so that materials in differing stages of wear were made available to clients, emulating the experience of most households.

But, if it is possible to design contracts which ensure that equivalent standards of service can be provided by in-house providers or external contractors, and if available information is available about the costs of those service from internal or external sources, then some more difficult decisions have to be made.

At the extremes—where one sector outperforms the other in terms of both criteria—then the sensible (non-ideological) decision is clear. If the private sector can provide better services at lower cost, then (all other things being equal) the rational decision is to consider outsourcing. And vice versa: if the public sector can do better than the private sector, it is sensible to retain the status quo.

But if the results are mixed (as set out in scenarios 2 and 3 below) the appropriate response may be more problematic.

Service delivery in-house produces:	Possible response:
Scenario	
1 Lower costs and better services	Retain
2 Lower costs but poorer services	?
3 Higher costs but better services	?
4 Higher costs and poorer services	Consider outsourcing

Scenarios 2 and 3 suggest that difficult judgments have to be made about what are *acceptable* standards of service, and whether contracts can be devised which establish incentives and penalties for deviations from those standards.

Note that the rational response to scenario 4 is not 'outsource' but only 'consider outsourcing'. The reasons for higher costs should be considered before reaching conclusions that outsourcing is the solution. It may be, for example, that some costs were not controllable by the public sector providers, but were incurred because of the actions from others.

Moreover, consideration might also be given to whether redesigning processes might be a better course to adopt than obtaining the same kind of services from external suppliers. A case in point: a central agency advocated the privatisation of security services—notably the services provided by police in escorting prisoners from jails to courts. Those involved in courts administration preferred the use of video conferencing for remand and other procedural matters, so that prisoners could remain in the relative comfort of their own cells rather than be transported to a court and be held in court cells until their matter was heard. Video conferencing would reduce the need for escort services.

In practice, it seems that few public sector agencies have actually monitored and analysed in-house service delivery and hence are ill-prepared to either write contracts for outsourcing purposes or to monitor the performance of contractors.

By the late 1990s, it seems that the ideological commitment of some politicians and public servants to outsourcing was leading to extreme initiatives. The idea of 'steering not rowing' was being re-thought: after all, 'steering' (in the sense of making decisions, or managing) can be hard work too.

Within the public service, in a new era of short-term contracts and performance assessments, many senior managers have tried to protect themselves by hiring consultants to provide formal advice on all key decisions. Whatever savings might be made from outsourcing, some part of those savings is being wasted elsewhere by managers who are, in effect, contracting out their own jobs.

Some agencies which were simply *managing* outsourcing are being closed down. Removals Australia, the Commonwealth agency which operates a $95 million relocations brokerage business for government agencies, is to be sold in favour of total reliance on private contractors (*Minister for Finance and Administration Media Release*, 27/4/99).

Even the training of public servants has been largely outsourced. This may make sense in some specialist areas, but may not be effective in relation to a range of in-house matters. Former NSW Auditor-General Tony Harris observed (in an unreported retirement speech) that senior public servants were largely unaware of their own legal obligations in terms of the law governing their jurisdiction.

Worse, there have been efforts to outsource basic elements of the accountability of governments to parliament—notably the work of an Auditor-General.

The efforts of the Kennett government in Victoria to downgrade the responsibilities of the Victorian Auditor-General through requiring the use of private sector audit firms to conduct private-sector style audits became an election issue and has been the subject of extensive, and often well-meaning but ill-informed, comment. The Kennett government was hardly breaking new ground, since audit offices in other Australian jurisdictions (notably the Northern Territory) have always been established with a minimal staff and have been required to outsource audit work to private firms. In the Commonwealth, the Hawke government introduced legislation to permit government trading enterprises to appoint private firms as auditors rather than be subject to review by the Commonwealth Auditor-General. A more subtle way of diminishing the role of an Auditor-General is to encourage the use of private sector auditors to act as highly-paid internal auditors, or to undertake some aspects of an audit, while the Audit Office remains responsible for the overall audit at a much reduced fee. This means that the external auditor is taken out of play as a reviewer of internal systems and procedures, with a role being largely reduced to expressing an opinion on financial statements.

Overall, the significance of outsourcing audit services turns on issues of independence and issues of service quality. Private sector audit standards are relatively lax compared with the practices which have been adopted by Australian public sector auditors. For example, if an audit reveals that internal controls are poor, or that staff have been engaged in illegal activity, a private sector auditor who follows the accounting profession's Auditing Standards is only obliged to report on these matters in confidential letters to management (or, if one exists, to an audit committee). Public sector auditors, on the other hand, generally place such findings on the public record. This subjects public sector agencies to external scrutiny and greater pressure to respond to the issues raised in an audit report.

The major hazard associated with outsourcing the public sector audit function is that the scope of audit work will be reduced, and audit reports on financial statement audits will be reduced to stereotyped, standard-form statements, providing little comfort to parliament and the community that taxpayers' resources have been properly used.

Further, private audit firms have minimal experience (and no real comparative advantage) in the conduct of 'performance audits', whereby assessments are provided to parliament about the economy, efficiency and effectiveness with which financial, human and physical resources have been utilised. To date, the accounting profession's standards on the conduct of performance audits are flimsy, and provide little assurance that the product of any outsourced audit work in this area will be effective in alerting parliament and the community to waste or mismanagement, let alone the failures of government programs to produce outcomes consistent with stated objectives.

Put bluntly: few politicians (or public servants, for that matter) are keen to subject themselves to rigorous accountability arrangements, and the push to make the providers of audit services subject to commercial pressures may be intended to achieve more favourable outcomes for the incumbent government.

The result of the 1999 Victorian election has been interpreted by some as a repudiation of the Kennett government's policies regarding eroding parliamentary accountability. Hence efforts to outsource public sector auditing may be more subtle and circumspect in future. But it seems unlikely that the incentives facing politicians in government will change. Expect more of the same.

It is difficult to predict where the trend to outsource government activities will end. Some have argued that the biggest benefit from policies requiring public sector agencies to consider outsourcing has been that agencies have been compelled to think about what they are there to do—what are their 'core functions'.

That may be one of the benefits of outsourcing policies—provided agencies are not pressured to outsource, for the sake of it, and provided it is not left to agencies themselves to decide what are their 'core functions'. That is a responsibility of government and ultimately, the parliament.

7

Private Sector Infrastructure Development

Private sector use of 'financial engineering'

During the 1980s, some high-flying entrepreneurs disguised the extent of their borrowings by using what were known as 'off balance sheet' financing arrangements. Those in the business of arranging such deals delicately referred to their work as 'financial engineering'.

Here is an overly-simplified example. A company may have paid too much for a piece of real estate—let's say it cost $100 million. Directors are reluctant to write it down to market value of (say) $80 million (and show a loss of $20 million). Instead, the property is 'sold' to a friendly associate for $156 million, of which $80 million is in cash and the balance is payable in three years. That allows our vendor to record a book profit of $56 million (rather than a loss of $20 million). The catch is, the property was not really 'sold'. The purchaser also acquired a put option which entitled it to sell the property back to the vendor in three years for $156 million in cash.[1] In substance, the deal was a loan of $80 million which was repayable after three years together with $76 million representing accumulated compound interest at 25 per cent per annum. But the $80 million initial borrowing (which escalated in value over the three years) would not appear as a liability—it was structured to be *off balance sheet*.

---

1 US accounting standards would not permit the recording of revenue from a contingent sale'. See the Financial Accounting Standards Board's Statement of Financial Accounting Standards FAS 48, 'Revenue recognition when right of return exists', June 1981. No equivalent rule or guideline prohibiting the recording of revenues from contingent sales has been issued by the Australian Accounting Standards Board, the Australian Securities and Investments Commission, or any professional association or regulatory body.

One of the most prominent examples of the use of the technique of 'sale with an option to repurchase' was undertaken by Bond Corporation Holdings just after the stock market crash of 1987. As later revealed by the ABC's *4 Corners* program, Bond Corporation recorded paper profits by selling companies whose underlying assets were real estate in Rome, and Sydney's Hilton Hotel. The fact that the 'profit' on these transactions could be reversed through the exercise of options was not disclosed in Bond's accounts; nor was there any disclosure of the extent to which the sale with an option to repurchase had contributed to Bond Corporation's reported profits (*Walker*, 1989).

During the 1990s, the financial engineers turned their attention to the public sector.

While Australian governments have started preparing balance sheets using the techniques of accrual accounting, media commentators and politicians have paid little attention to these forms of report (often quite justifiably, given the arbitrary, variable and often contentious way those reports have been compiled). In the eyes of the community, the key financial documents produced by governments are annual budgets, and subsequent reports of 'budget results'.

That's why Australian governments have got away with financing arrangements which are both *off balance sheet* and *off budget*.

The role of the Loan Council

To fully understand the origins of such schemes one needs to have a working knowledge of the way the Loan Council once operated to co-ordinate and ration borrowings by Australian governments. The financial arrangements for private sector involvement in infrastructure development were initially undertaken to enable governments (or individual agencies) to embark on major capital projects while avoid borrowing restrictions imposed by the Loan Council.

Proposals to co-ordinate government borrowings were voiced prior to Federation (but assumed greater significance by 1919, when 'both levels of government were borrowing heavily: the Commonwealth to redeem or convert war debt, and the States for development', and this involved intense competition for borrowings in domestic markets (*Saunders*, 1989). These pressures led to the establishment of a voluntary Loan Council in 1923, aiming to agree on the timing of issues, interest rates, and other loan conditions. In 1927, the Commonwealth and states entered into Financial Agreement covering revenue redistributions, debt, future borrowings and transferred properties. In 1928, the Constitution was amended by referendum to empower the Commonwealth to 'make agreements with the States with respect to the public debts of the States'.

The so-called 'gentlemen's agreement' of 1927 set ground rules for establishing the maximum sums that Commonwealth and state governments could borrow. This aggregate global limit for borrowings was set with regard to macroeconomic policy, and the Loan Council allocated that sum between jurisdictions via a formula based on population. In broad terms, states were only allowed to borrow within these 'global limits'. That arrangement continued for 65 years.

The definition of 'borrowings' included any means by which an entity within the global limits obtains the capacity to finance expenditure which involves the creation of liabilities to entities outside the global limits. The provision of guarantees and other contingent liabilities did not count as borrowings as such, but were taken into account in determining whether a government could be regarded as bearing the greater part of the financial risks and hence controlled the entity or project.

The rules were delightfully ambiguous: the approach was a set of guidelines concerning what entities were subject to the global limits, and then a set of guidelines concerning what constituted a borrowing.

The determination of what entities were subject to the global limits was based on a test of 'control': the borrowings of all agencies under the 'control' of a government were to be included, with some exceptions. Public financial enterprises (such as the State Bank of NSW) were excluded from the global limits on the ground that their borrowings were used for 'financial intermediation' rather than to fund activities controlled by the government.

Borrowings were defined as including an obligation or a potential obligation to make a future payment arising from debt, equity or quasi-equity arrangements. The Loan Council claimed that the status of each financial transaction would be determined on the basis of its economic effect rather than the legal form.

Finding ways around the global limits

The global limits restricted the capacity of state governments to undertake what they saw as important (or electorally appealing) capital projects. Finding ways around the global limits became a serious sport.

The first serious foray was in NSW with the Wran government's financing of the Eraring power station through a lease. The Loan Council responded by paying special attention to lease transactions.

The international accounting profession has long distinguished 'operating' and 'finance' leases—the former are treated as simple rental arrangements while the latter are treated as being, in substance, purchases on credit. In other words, a finance lease is regarded as a borrowing. Particular attention was paid to the tests in Australian lease accounting standards, which classified leases in terms of whether, in substance, a contractual arrangement involved the transfer of substantially all the risks and benefits of ownership to a government agency, as lessee.

But financial engineers are continuously developing new products and proposing new deals. The Loan Council was obliged to assess a range of new financing arrangements.

In making those assessments, the Loan Council seems to have been relatively liberal to the states, allowing a number of financing deals to be regarded as outside the global limits. Some of these determinations may not have passed muster in terms of overseas accounting guidelines for interpreting what was the 'substance' rather than the 'form' of financial transactions in the private sector (e.g. *UK Accounting Standards Committee*, 1988, 1994). Possibly staff of the Loan Council, and their advisers, were unaware of these materials.

In such an environment, the financial engineers were active in proposing new deals. One 1988 proposal was for the Queensland government to sell its hoop pine forests, while simultaneously purchasing an option to repurchase the same assets five years later for a larger sum. A side deal involved the finance company receiving revenues from the sale of thinnings and paying for insurance and forest management services, with any surpluses to be paid to the Forestry Department. A feature of the arrangement was that investors could hope to enjoy their financial returns as a tax-free capital gain rather than as taxable interest revenues—all at the expense of the Commonwealth.

The overall arrangement was similar to what in the private sector had been described as an 'inventory buy back'. Private businesses could sell their inventories to a bank, only to buy them back at a higher price later on—thus both avoiding recording additional debt on their balance sheet, and enabling the business to book a profit on the deal, if they wanted to report higher profits to the market. Some indication of the popularity of such deals can be gauged by the fact that the Australian Accounting Standards Review Board had earlier listed inventory buy-backs as one of the creative accounting devices it would like to regulate (*1987 ASRB Annual Report*), though no such rule ever appeared.

In the Queensland government case, while the transaction

nominally involved the sale of assets, in substance it would have been a borrowing—at an effective interest rate of 11.74 per cent (*Walker*, 1988). That particular proposal fell through.

The most common forms of public sector off-budget financing have taken a different form. Rather than the sale of assets, they often involved proposals for the construction of *new* assets, to be funded by a government-underwritten stream of cash flows to the private sector financier. The Loan Council had to consider how such arrangements should be treated—and many deals apparently designed to avoid the global limits were ruled to be 'borrowings' (see Box).

In the event, the Loan Council determined that the sale of an income stream was to be treated as an asset sale rather than a borrowing where (i) the underlying source of the income stream was already an asset on the balance sheet of the government entity, and the asset is removed from the balance sheet as a result of the sale, and (ii) the government entity is not liable to repay the proceeds of the asset sale, directly or indirectly.

As soon as the Loan Council ruled against one type of financing arrangement, new arrangements were devised.

One was the 'take or pay contract', whereby a private firm constructed a pipeline or electricity transmission line, and was then entitled to receive a minimum financial payment from a government agency each year regardless of whether the pre-specified volumes of gas or electricity were actually carried during that period. The agency in turn could accumulate 'credits' to be drawn down when volumes increased in association with the economic growth anticipated to follow that investment in infrastructure. On the basis of such deals, the private firm could secure finance for the investment. The government was effectively guaranteeing the cash flow which would repay those borrowings. Arguably, in substance, the government was borrowing and undertaking to repay those funds, but the legal form of the transaction put the private firm up front as the borrower.

However, the most popular arrangements were BOOT schemes —an acronym for 'Build, Own Operate, Transfer'.

In a BOOT scheme, an asset would be constructed by a private sector firm, which would own and operate it, while receiving most or all of the fruits of the venture. The returns to private investors would be subject to some kind of government 'enhancement' or guarantee. After a predetermined period, ownership of the asset would pass to the government. The Loan Council struggled along for a while, trying to assess whether individual deals should be classified as 'borrowings' on the basis of which party bore most of the risks and rewards of the ventures.

Box 7.1
FINDING WAYS AROUND BORROWING LIMITS

Victorian Equity Trust

The establishment of this Trust in November 1988, costing millions in prospectus and legal fees, seems in retrospect to have been designed to raise funds without the Victorian government or its business enterprises having to borrow directly. The Trust was to acquire a share in the equity of some government business enterprises, and would receive dividends from those entities. The financial returns of investors were protected by an option to redeem their units at a price set by reference to the share price index. The overall effect of these arrangements was to avoid new borrowings adding to Victoria's budget deficit. Whatever accounting methods were used when calculating published budget figures, the Loan Council treated the deal as the fundraising of quasi equity, and hence the sums raised were counted as borrowings in terms of the global limits.

Tuggeranong Pre-Commitment Lease

Then there was a 1989 transaction whereby the Commonwealth Department of Administrative Services accepted a tender for the construction and financing of an office building in Tuggeranong to house the Department of Social Security. It was proposed that a private company would construct and own the building, with the construction financed by bonds issued to the private sector. The Commonwealth was to rent the building until the bonds were paid out, after which the Commonwealth could occupy the building rent-free or buy it at a nominal price. The Loan Council decided that the arrangement was in substance a finance lease so that the financing arrangement counted against the Commonwealth's global limit.

Perth Southern Suburbs Railway

A proposal before the WA government was also deemed a borrowing. The proposal concerned the financing and construction of a Perth Northern Suburbs Railway line. A private company would construct the line, and thereafter Westrail would operate it, with ownership passing to Westrail upon completion of financing arrangements. The returns to private financiers would be subsidised by the WA government.

The Loan Council argued that financing of the rail project was to be counted as a borrowing because, even though it was initially owned by a private sector firm, the project was controlled by the public sector and would eventually be owned by it and because the state government would subsidise it. It was noted that retention of ownership and management of the line within the private sector (even though Westrail trains might operate on it) would have put the project in the private sector.

New South Wales Toll Road Proposal

To illustrate the latter rationale, the Loan Council deemed a NSW toll road proposal to be a private sector borrowing arrangement. The toll road known as the F4 'Freeway' involved a private consortium building, owning and operating a toll road on land leased from the state government. The Loan Council explained that all project risk and management responsibility lies with the private sector participants 'since there is no government involvement in raising funds or

> guaranteeing returns on the project'. Ownership of the road passes to the NSW government at the expiry of the lease, but 'this is not in consideration for any public sector involvement'. In this case, the Loan Council decided that the project would not be controlled by the NSW government and therefore did not fall within the global limits.
>
> **NSW Housing Trust**
>
> The establishment in 1989 of the NSW Housing Trust remains one of the more curious arrangements. The Loan Council explained that the Trust was a private partnership to finance the acquisition of housing stock. Initially, the NSW Department of Housing, acting as manager and agent, was to lease houses to tenants from the public housing waiting list. Where necessary, the NSW government was to provide a subsidy in order to maintain the rental returns to the Trust. As houses were vacated by public tenants, the Trust would have the option of either renting those houses to private tenants or to sell them on the open market.
>
> In November 1989 the Commonwealth Treasurer wrote to NSW Premier Greiner agreeing that 44 per cent of the financing for purchasing the houses should count against NSW's global allocation. Why 44 per cent? Because that represented the estimated share of housing to be occupied by public tenants over the life of the project.
>
> Source: Loan Council of Australia, *Guide to the Global Limits*, May 1991.

How the Loan Council gave the game away

Then, in December 1992, the Loan Council gave the game away.

It announced a new system for monitoring and regulating the level of borrowings by Australian state governments. Australian states had been successfully evading efforts to ration their borrowings through the establishment of 'global limits', by their involvement in new forms of financing arrangements with private sector participants. Indeed, the Loan Council publicly conceded in 1993 that its 'global limits' approach was 'at the point of breakdown'.

Under a new approach, the Loan Council redefined what was to be counted as 'borrowings', and announced that it would require more 'uniform and more comprehensive reporting' of public sector finances. It explained that the new arrangements were designed to promote 'financial market scrutiny':

> The new arrangements are designed to enhance the role of financial market scrutiny as a discipline on borrowings by the public sector, and in so doing, build on the changes instituted in the late 1980s to enable the individual states and territories to be given the responsibility for managing their own borrowings and to be accountable to financial markets for their actions (Loan Council, 1993).

The Loan Council acknowledged that the increasing use of

sophisticated financing techniques raised concerns about the relevance of a government's budget deficit or surplus, and outlined plans to base a new set of borrowing controls on a combination of measures of cash-based budget results, and measures of what it called 'memo items'. These would include obligations arising from complex financial transactions. Under a new regime, financing arrangements would be 'risk weighted'. The effect was to abandon attempts to assess whether financing arrangements undertaken with private sector firms represented 'liabilities' of government.

The aggregate of the deficit/surplus and memo items would be known as the Loan Council Allocation (LCA). Hence, instead of the old idea of 'global limits', in future the Commonwealth and state governments would agree on Loan Council Allocations (LCAs). The plan was for each jurisdiction to nominate a proposed Loan Council Allocation (showing the deficit/surplus and details of individual memo items) for endorsement by the Loan Council. Later, each jurisdiction was to provide a quarterly report of its deficit or surplus, and of the aggregate changes in memo items, *vis a vis* the approved Loan Council Allocation.

In the context of public political debt, this was extraordinary. Some politicians had won office after campaigning about the need to reduce government 'debt'. Governments had enacted 'debt elimination' legislation, supposedly to bind future governments to avoid increasing borrowings (in full knowledge that such measures were purely symbolic, as a future government could simply repeal any legislation it found inconvenient). Yet, at the same time, representatives of all Australian governments were agreeing on measures to avoid debate about whether financing arrangements were in reality, backdoor borrowings.

The fine print in the Loan Council publications explained how this was to be handled. A Loan Council Allocation would henceforth comprise the budget deficit/surplus, plus the value of memo items, *after weighting for risk*. The Loan Council impact of an infrastructure project would not be the government's liability in that project, but a multiple of the project risk weighting (r) and the government liability (Lg). The project risk weighting would in turn be a function of three variables: the contract period over which the government faces penalty provisions, the extent to which the project was funded by borrowings, and the 'volatility' of the project.

The underlying idea was that the government's exposure associated with complex financial transactions (such as the popular Build Own Operate Transfer schemes) could be viewed not as the government's 'liability' in an accounting sense, but as the amount a government would need to pay a third party to assume the government's risk in respect of a project. Thus if a government guaranteed the returns to private sector participants in a $100 million tollroad project, and the risk weighting for a project of that time period, financed by a specified level of debt and equity, was deemed to be 10 per cent, then the arrangements could carry a Loan Council Allocation value of only $10 million.

The following Box reproduces one of the Loan Council's rather extraordinary illustrations of how a project financed by direct government borrowings of $50 million and a government guarantee of an additional $50 million of loan finance could be treated (for the purpose of rationing government borrowings) as being equivalent to new borrowings of only $29 million.

The Loan Council explained that 'the aim of the risk weighting approach is to estimate a jurisdiction's expected liability in relation to a project'—and to report this to the market. It did not publish a full description of the theoretical basis of the risk weightings; instead, it distributed a table indicating the weightings for projects of varying term, project volatility and project gearing. It is widely acknowledged that the new Loan Council approach relied heavily on proposals outlined in a commissioned paper prepared by consultants. Reputedly, the paper derives risk-weights from an adaptation of the Black & Scholes option pricing model, but how the writers picked estimates of (say) the volatility of investment returns for different types of public infrastructure (such as sewerage tunnels or hospital car parks) remains obscure. Shares in sewerage tunnels are not publicly traded in international securities markets. Yet (in the first round of disclosures in NSW Budget Papers) investments in hospital car parks and hydro schemes were assumed to have a volatility rating of 20 per cent, motorways 25 per cent, while sewerage tunnels were rated at only 10 per cent.

In effect, the new Loan Council arrangements reduced the restrictions on private sector involvement in infrastructure construction projects, while creating positive incentives for governments to get involved in such deals. But the incentives were perverse. They had more to do with concealing the extent to which governments were (in substance) borrowing than on revealing the scale and cost of the financing.

The first public disclosures were in 1994–95 budget papers, but only NSW reported details of six deals (asset values, project liabilities, volatility and risk weightings), while other governments (including the Commonwealth) simply reported aggregate 'allocations', without any description of the projects being financed in this fashion. Moreover, the disclosures only related to projects being undertaken in the current year—there was no disclosure of the total

Privatisation

Box 7.2
LOAN COUNCIL CASE STUDY—PRIVATE HOSPITAL

Project Description

The project involves a fully debt funded $100 million redevelopment of a private hospital by the private sector. The financing arrangements are:

- a fully government guaranteed $50 million bond issue; and
- bank finance of $50 million.

As part of the project makeup the government Health Department enters into a 25 year agreement with the private sector operator. Under this agreement payment by the Health Department takes two forms:

- $4.5 million per annum indexed, non cancellable for 25 years, and capped at $50 million; and
- a CPI linked payment of $35 million per annum under a hospital service agreement which is conditional upon the provision of public hospital services by the hospital.

In addition to the government guaranteed bonds, under the termination provisions in the project contract (operator default) the government is liable for the bank debt carried by the private sector.

Project Risk Weighting

Project Parameter	Comment	Assumed Value
Asset Value	Equal to construction cost based on the assumption that the benefit/cost ratio is greater than one and the project is the best alternative	$100m
Project Liability	The project is fully debt funded	$100m
Volatility	. . . the hospital sector has a low volatility rating	15%
Term	Given the payment arrangements and nature of the service agreement the term of the project is 25 years	25 yrs
Project risk weighting	A function of project gearing (1), volatility (*15%) and project term (25 yrs)	29%

LCA Impact

Government Liability (Lg)	Based on bond guarantees and termination clauses the government liability is the value of total debt carried on the redevelopment	$100m
LCA Impact = r * Lg	Project risk weighting is applied to the government liability	0.29 * 100 = $29m

financial exposure associated with prior off-budget, off-balance sheet transactions. Nor was there any disclosure of the re-financing of prior deals.

Certainly the new arrangements failed to provide key financial information to capital markets, or anyone concerned with monitoring the financial performance of governments.

Meantime, the Commonwealth added other incentives for private sector investment in infrastructure, in the form of tax-effective 'infrastructure bonds'. A task force was asked, among other things, to report on ways of removing any further impediments to private sector involvement in public infrastructure projects (*EPAC*, May 1995 and September 1995).

The report of the task force may have been disappointing. It concluded that infrastructure as a whole 'is not significantly tax disadvantaged compared to most other investments' and that there was no strong tax efficiency case for retaining infrastructure bonds. However, it observed:

> Private ownership of infrastructure can sometimes lead to ... efficiencies and thereby help the community to get more from its investments.
>
> Private financing of projects will also allow greater spending on infrastructure without the need to increase government borrowing. In principle, this should not be a compelling reason for private financing, as the macroeconomic effects are broadly similar whether the public or the private sector borrows the money. However, governments do not always feel free to increase borrowings, even if the money is earmarked for good investments (*EPAC*, September 1995).

Subsequent actions of the Loan Council enabled governments to undertake more back-door borrowings.

Further erosion of accountability

The initial reports by Australian governments about off-budget financial transactions were abbreviated and obscure. Even specialists in public finance could not interpret them. To understand the disclosures, readers needed access to a sheaf of technical papers explaining the underlying methodology, the transitional reporting rules, and details of the risks assumed to be associated with investment in different types of infrastructure projects.

It appears that even Treasury officials involved in the Loan Council process have difficulty understanding the reports: one described it as 'a black box—we just read off figures from a table provided by some consultants'.

While NSW Budget Papers provided brief descriptions of

projects which were the subject of 'memo items', the Commonwealth and Victoria only listed the aggregate amount of Loan Council Allocations attributable to these so-called 'memo items'.

Treasurer Ralph Willis reported in 1994 that the Allocations approved by the Loan Council for NSW and Victoria included '$196 million and $69 million respectively for government exposure to infrastructure projects with private sector involvement' (*1994–95 Commonwealth Budget Paper No. 3*). Those 'exposures' could translate to government liabilities five or even ten times greater than the sums reported. But that was the last time Commonwealth Budget Papers provided any quantification of the scope of these deals.

Fulsome statements continued to be made about the role of the Loan Council in promoting public scrutiny of government finances:

> The Loan Council arrangements introduced from 1993–94 are designed to enhance the role of financial market scrutiny as a discipline on borrowings by the public sector ...
>
> The Loan Council process is supported by uniform and more comprehensive reporting of public sector finances. Each jurisdiction provides to Loan Council, quarterly reports of performance against its budget time LCA and an annual statement of financial assets and liabilities, supplemented by footnotes on contingent liabilities. The resulting increase in transparency of government finances should assist Parliaments, financial markets, the media and the public generally to make their own judgments about each government's financial performance (*1995–96 Commonwealth Budget Paper No. 3*).

But the very next year the Commonwealth Budget Papers failed to report jurisdictions' exposures to infrastructure financing deals. This was despite the fact that the Budget Papers admitted that so-called 'memo items'

> have many of the characteristics of public sector borrowings but do not constitute formal borrowings (*1995–96 Commonwealth Budget Paper No. 3*).

The role of the Loan Council was redefined to include territory governments as full members and to 'remove anachronistic provisions of the previous Agreement'. Moreover, the two-year old 'risk weighting' approach was abandoned:

> Following a detailed review of the infrastructure guidelines, the Loan Council has agreed to change the basis on which jurisdictions report their exposure to infrastructure projects with private sector involvement from the previous risk weighted estimate to the full contingent exposure

measured by the government's termination liabilities.

In addition, subject to detailed consideration, the Loan Council has agreed in principle that these exposures would in future be disclosed as a footnote to, rather than a component of, LCAs. This reflects a concern that the inclusion of contingent exposures as part of the LCA is misleading as they would only be realised in the unlikely event of project failure and thus are materially different from actual borrowings ... (*1995–96 Commonwealth Budget Paper No. 3*).

The last sentence in this quote was particularly misleading. The Loan Council Allocations related to complex financial arrangements which were often, in substance, borrowings. The calculation of dollar value for a Loan Council Allocation disregarded this fact. The claim that 'underlying exposures would only be realised in the event of project failure' was misleading and irrelevant.

It was a bit like saying that the full amount owing on a housing loan with a bank only became due and payable if the home owners couldn't keep up with their monthly mortgage repayments.

The Commonwealth seems to have led a revolt against the Loan Council reporting arrangements. Despite having agreed 'in principle' to disclose information about private sector financing deals 'in footnotes' to the Budget Papers, the new reporting format was not followed in the Budget presented by Treasurer Peter Costello in 1995–96.

The following year the Loan Council 'confirmed this in-principle decision' (*1997–98 Commonwealth Budget Paper No. 3*) and indicated that a new reporting framework would not be implemented until 1998–99. Meantime, in a major change of policy, the Loan Council announced that public trading enterprises which were operating in a commercial manner and have a demonstrated track record of 'commercial performance' were to be entirely exempted from Loan Council coverage in future.

> The rationale behind the exemption criteria is that some PTEs operate with a sufficiently competitive environment that they respond to market signals ... in much the same way as private sector entities so as to substantially reduce or eliminate the need for their borrowings to be included in government aggregates subject to Loan Council oversight.

The technical language should not obscure the enormity of this change. While politicians had been publicly decrying evils of public sector debt, Australian governments were meantime agreeing to avoid disclosing information about any back-door borrowings undertaken by any government-owned businesses which could be described as operating 'commercially'.

This was an extraordinary erosion of public sector accountability. As one Treasury official put it, with a smile,

> we're giving the public all the information it needs to know.

Within the rarefied culture of Treasury departments, the public needs to know very little indeed.

Privatisation through off-budget financing of infrastructure projects

After five or six years of experience with different versions of the new arrangements, whereby the Loan Council does not bother to assess whether financing deals are, in substance, borrowings, two obvious conclusions can be drawn. The new arrangements:

- are very popular with both governments and the private sector;
- have concealed the full scope and scale of financial dealings of governments from both taxpayers and financial markets.

Governments have always involved the private sector in the construction of infrastructure, to a greater or lesser extent. No one seems to have any quarrel with the concept of governments inviting private firms to tender for the construction of buildings, roads, bridges or pipelines. The 1990s variant of these arrangements involved private firms being placed up-front and identified as the nominal financiers of the projects, when in substance, repayment of their loans was being 'ensured' (if not 'guaranteed') by the public purse.

The motivation for governments to enter into off-budget financing schemes may well have been to enable capital projects to be completed sooner, to enhance the re-election prospects of governments. But, in such a process, there is a basic risk that governments may be surrendering extremely valuable rights to the private sector. Any surrendering of rights (to future cash flows or profits) in situations where the government could have financed and managed projects themselves amounts to a loss to the community.

As outlined above, it is possible to view both 'take or pay' schemes and Build, Own, Operate and Transfer schemes as financial arrangements which conceal the underlying substance whereby a government is essentially borrowing money to acquire assets. Another way to look at these arrangements is that governments are essentially 'privatising' government activities, and in the process, transferring to private firms a series of benefits which would otherwise accrue to taxpayers.

This does not involve the sale of existing businesses, but the 'sale' of the right to enjoy revenues derived from the exercise of a government's coercive powers, particularly the power to resume or rezone land and thereby establish natural monopolies. Indeed, without government involvement, the private sector would be hard put to obtain the land corridors through which to build gas or water pipelines, tollways, tunnels, railways or other infrastructure.

BOOT schemes can be highly expensive

While, in principle, there is merit in the idea of involving the private sector in infrastructure construction, there is no need to use 'take or pay' contracts or BOOT schemes to harness private-sector expertise in design or project management or construction. All of these elements in the construction of infrastructure could be directly purchased by governments, through traditional tendering processes.

The essential attraction of BOOT schemes and similar arrangements to governments is that they avoid borrowings through the public budget process. But this can come at a price. Indeed, BOOT schemes can be an unduly expensive form of finance.

Australian governments are routinely able to borrow funds at lower rates of interest than private firms—a phenomenon that reflects market recognition that lending to governments involves low risk. In contrast, private sector investors would have to pay a higher rate of interest on borrowings used to fund their participation in BOOT schemes, and would seek an even higher pre-tax return on their own investment of equity capital.

As noted above, the international accounting profession accepts that finance leases are, 'in substance' purchases of assets on credit terms, and insists that they be reported as such. The international accounting profession has yet to accept that BOOT schemes should be treated in the same light (though there are movements in that direction). If BOOT schemes were treated that way, then the returns earned by private sector investors could be regarded as being, in substance, the interest paid by governments to those investors for use of their firms as financing vehicles.

'Mario D'Elia, a vice-president of BT Investment bank, says most BOOT projects make a net return of 11–13%,' reported Adele Ferguson in *Business Review Weekly*, 20 April 1998. That statement represents one of the few occasions that businessmen have canvassed the level of returns obtainable for involvement in those projects.

Arguably, the 11–13 per cent estimate was conservative. Perhaps it referred to 'real' returns (before inflation), since a feature of many BOOT contracts seems to be that they define the basis for any revenue-sharing between public and private sector participants as a threshold rate of return *after adjustment for inflation*. Even then, some deals appear to have promised higher (and almost obscene) financial returns.

Insights into the potential returns available from a BOOT scheme was obtained when one of the authors was asked by a Sydney journalist to review draft contract proposals for a BOOT scheme involving construction of a rail link between metropolitan Sydney and Mascot airport—set out in a document titled *Airport Link Feasibility Study—Summary Report on Detailed Feasibility Studies* (1993). The proposed contractual arrangements were complex, and analysis was necessarily based on the Study's assumptions concerning construction costs, projected passenger volumes and revenues, and the timing of both.

A summary of the projected cash flows and proposed revenue sharing arrangements as described in the Feasibility Study is set out in the accompanying box. Analysis of cash flows on the basis of this material suggested that there was a considerable disparity in the way that returns were to be shared between the private and public sectors.

On the face of it, the relative capital contributions of the private and public sectors were to be about 21 per cent and 79 per cent, respectively. The profit-sharing arrangements accelerated returns to the private sector consortium, which would have its original investment repaid in full between three and four years. On the other hand, the NSW government would not break even for 23 years.

The cash flows associated with the government's participation would produce an internal rate of return (in 'real' terms) of only 2 per cent per annum. The consortium stood to earn a 'real' internal rate of return of 21 per cent per annum.

These estimates are based on a key assumption that the proposed contribution of the private sector consortium—which in part was not in cash but in kind (in the form of design work)—was indeed worth the value ascribed to it. Engineering sources suggest that these fees might be around 12–14 per cent for this work, or between $57–$66 million for services relating to the public sector's expenditure on tunnelling and construction work. Allowing for a 'profit' component of around 30 per cent on these design fees, the consortium's cash outlays could be estimated to be not $125 million but around $103 million.

If it was assumed that the consortium's contribution was to be only $103 million (or around 15 per cent of the projected costs of the project) the internal rate of return earned by the consortium would be an astounding 25 per cent per annum over the 30 year project life.

The Study also reported that 'the patronage forecasts are ... highly conservative estimates'. If that proved to be the case, the returns earned by the consortium would be higher.

It must be emphasised that these calculations are based on the projections in the Feasibility Study. After the earlier publication of this analysis (*Walker*, 1994) the then NSW Treasurer Peter Collins protested that the deal had not been finalised and that

> a full contract summary will be available early next year and Professor Walker will be in a position to provide a more informed commentary based on fact at that stage (*SMH*, 26/9/94).

Some months later it was reported that the deal had been renegotiated and 'was several percentage points below first estimates' (*SMH*, 11/2/95). But even 'several points' below a projected real rate of return of 21 per cent per annum amounts to a high cost of finance for the government involved in such deals.

In due course—in October 1995—the NSW Auditor-General provided a brief report on a 'contract summary' prepared by the State Rail Authority on these arrangements. Neither the contract summary nor the audit report examined prospective rates of return. The information provided in this contract summary was insufficiently detailed to enable any reworking of the calculations set out in Box 7.3.

The contract summary did however include results of an economic benefit-cost study undertaken by two consultants. Presumably this exercise involved assigning dollar values to such benefits as time saved by passengers in travelling to and from the airport (though details of the analysis were not included). Both consultants concluded that the project produced a benefit-cost ratio of around 1.7 to 1— suggesting that the project was worthwhile. Indeed, no one seems to disagree that the extension of public transport links in this fashion was a good project for Sydney. What was intriguing was that both consultants assumed that the relevant discount rate to evaluate a project of this risk was 7 per cent (real)—significantly less than the implicit cost of finance effectively incurred by the government through use of a BOOT scheme, which was the 21 per cent (real) internal rate of return likely to be earned by private firms.

Another sequel was that several parties (ranging from urban lobby groups to senior officials) observed that the analysis had missed the point: the big profits being earned by the private sector were associated with the recent acquisition of land near the sites of new rail stations.

Box 7.3
SYDNEY AIRLINK BOOT SCHEME

In 1989, the NSW Coalition government promoted the idea of constructing a railway line joining Sydney's domestic and international airports with the existing metropolitan rail system. In March 1994 the Minister for Transport, Bruce Baird, told the NSW parliament that companies had been asked to formally tender for an extension of the existing metropolitan passenger network past the airport. Press reports revealed that at this stage, 'the companies objected rather strenuously to having to go to tender. They sought to sue the Government' (*SMH*, 5/8/94). Subsequently, after private mediation, engineering consultants were engaged to review the project's financing 'and concluded that construction prices were reasonable and the risks and benefits had been shared between government and the private sector in a "reasonable manner"' (*SMH*, 4/8/94).

On 3 August 1994 the NSW Premier announced that 'work will begin on the $600 million New Southern line project' (*News Release*, 3/8/1994). A consortium was to construct the railway line and associated infrastructure in terms of an arrangement whereby the government would contribute 'more than $470 million' while the joint venturers 'will spend (sic) $125 million for the construction and operating costs of the four new stations'.

As the media was quick to note, this announcement contrasted sharply with claims made by the NSW Minister for Transport in 1991 that the project 'will not require one cent of Government money' (Editorial, *SMH*, 5/8/94). The major participants in the consortium included two original competitors, Transfield and CRI, who were reported to have 'teamed up at the suggestion of the Government' (*AFR*, 4/8/94). The consortium also included a French contractor, Bouygues, and provided that Transfield and Bouygues would build the 10km line under a $470 million contract funded by the state government, 'but with the contractors carrying the construction risk' (*AFR*, 4/8/93). Those companies, with development manager CRI, would also build, own and operate four stations 'worth $125 million'. It was also claimed that, 'on a capitalised interest basis', the consortium was contributing between $150 million and $160 million (*AFR*, 4/8/94). The government's contribution was initially described as $470 million (*SMH*, 4/8/94), then the following day as $375.7 million expenditure, though this figure was said not to include interest costs (*SMH*, 5/8/94).

Baird was reported as saying that 'when the contracts were signed all details would be disclosed to the Public Accounts Committee for scrutiny' (*Daily Telegraph Mirror*, 9/8/94).

Proposed profit sharing arrangements

The Feasibility Study confirmed that the Airport Link project was to be a 'BOOT' scheme, with assets transferred back to the government after 30 years. The Study:

- indicated that the consortium's contribution in terms of a $124 million lump sum contract was to cover design, project management, insurance and commissioning of the railway extension, as well as the construction of railway stations;
- confirmed that the NSW government planned to contribute $474 million, giving a total budget for the Airport Link project of $598 million (in 1993 prices). Escalation clauses would shift the risk of increases in levels of inflation and construction-related costs for tunnels and the railway line extension to the government;

- revealed that the $474 million estimate of the public sector's costs did not include land resumptions expected to cost between $10 million–$15 million, and does not include $14 million for demolition and redevelopment of a multi-storey car park on the preferred site for the East Terminal Station at the airport. Nor did it include unspecified costs of roadworks, or the costs of diverting water, sewerage, drainage and electricity lines; and
- revealed (contrary to government suggestions that profits would be 'capped') that the distribution of cash flows will be determined by a complex formula, whereby the consortium's share of marginal cash varied in four distinct steps. Fare supplements of $6–$7 (in 1993 prices) were to be imposed for airport trips, on top of normal City Rail fares:
    1. 100 per cent of the cash flows from fare supplements would flow to the consortium, until these firms have recovered all of their initial investment;
    2. the consortium would then get 80 per cent of the fare supplements until it had earned a cumulative real rate of return of 15 per cent (presumably, before tax) on its initial, already repaid investment;
    3. thereafter the consortium would get 20 per cent of any additional surplus cash until it had earned a cumulative 22 per cent real rate of return on its initial (by then, repaid) investment;
    4. thereafter the consortium would enjoy the benefit of 10 percent of any additional surplus cash flows.

Analysis of projected cash flows

Since the Feasibility Study contains projections of capital outlays, and forecasts of both the revenues from fare supplements, and the estimated costs of running the railway stations, the likely cash flows to be earned respectively by government and the private sector consortium from the project could be analysed in detail.

The following assumptions or adjustments were adopted:
- that the Consortium's contribution would indeed be $124 million in cash, as initially suggested—even though on the facts stated, the Consortium's cash outlays may be less and the contribution would in itself include an element of profit;
- that the government's contribution was taken as including a conservative $26 million for land acquisition and costs associated with the preferred site for the Mascot terminal, bringing the government's projected outlays on the project to $500 million. This adjustment was in the mid-range of estimates cited in the Study, and still excluded costs associated with roadworks and the diversion of water and electricity services; and
- that passenger volumes would increase in a linear fashion between the dates for which the Feasibility Study reported cash flows from fare supplements (i.e. $36.6 million per annum in 1998, rising to $66.3 million per annum 31 years later, in 2028).

Findings

On the basis of the Feasibility Study's projections, it would take between three and four years for the consortium's investment to be repaid in full. The NSW government would not break even on its investment for 23 years.

The cash flows associated with the government's participation would produce an internal rate of return (in 'real' terms) of only 2 per cent per annum. In contrast, the consortium stood to earn an internal rate of return of 21 per cent per annum.

Privatisation

There have been other snippets of evidence concerning the profitability of BOOT schemes to private sector participants—and hence some indication of the financing costs to government of 'privatising' operational responsibility for infrastructure development to private sector operators.

A sample:

- Investors in Sydney's M2 motorway project stand to earn a pre-tax return of 24.4 per cent per annum if traffic forecasts are valid (*Auditor-General of NSW*, October 1994). (That return is after transaction costs, which are very high: a total of $28 million has been disclosed in the reports of the Roads and Traffic Authority and in the prospectus issued by Hills Motorway—all for a total private sector equity investment of only $156 million.)
- The private firm Statewide Roads, operator of Sydney's M4 tollway, enjoyed an immense increase in shareholder value. A former Commissioner of Main Roads was reported to be a director and shareholder in Statewide roads. A former NSW Premier was a director of a company that 'is an important shareholder of Statewide Roads'. The company had an initial equity of $500,000 but the reputed sale of 10 per cent of Statewide's shares to AIDC for $7.7 million suggests an overall estimated value of the company of $77 million (*Auditor-General of NSW*, October 1994).
- The prospectus for the Melbourne City Link project indicated that initial investors would expect to receive a real return over the expected life of the project of 17.5 per cent per annum *after tax* (see Box 7.4).

The period of BOOT schemes is getting longer and longer

Some BOOT schemes—such as that for Sydney's Olympic village—cover short periods of time (and in this case, the assets are to be transferred to private developers). But the period of schemes has tended to be longer and longer.

The arrangements in NSW for the construction of a hospital and the provision of hospital services by the operator, Hawkesbury District Health Service (May 1996) were nominally for a term of 20 years, while allowing the operator to extend the arrangement by a further five years (provided it was not in default of the agreement).

Transport schemes have tended to be longer. The NSW Southern Railway link was to be for a 30 year period, while the Sydney light

Box 7.4
MELBOURNE'S TRANSURBAN CITY LINK TOLLROAD
—PAYMENT IN CASH IS NOT ACCEPTABLE
(and don't ask what the consortium will earn, or what the project is costing the government)

The City Link project was designed to improve transport links to-and-from and within the Melbourne area. It was to involve 'expenditure of $1.5 billion in 1993 dollars over the years 1995 to 2000' (*Allen Consulting Group et al.*, May 1995). By the time a prospectus was prepared in 1996, project costs (including construction contract, equity infrastructure bond distributions, and contingencies) were expected to total $1.776 billion—not counting works funded by the state of Victoria.

The City Link project can also be seen as a case study of the ugly side of private sector involvement in public infrastructure. The project combined five ugly features. The Kennett government:

- provided a consortium of private firms with the economic benefits of a virtual monopoly, in the form of a dedicated transport corridor without effective alternatives—essentially providing the consortium with the powers to 'tax' road users through tolls;
- assisted the consortium to levy tolls in an oppressive form: requiring either the rental of electronic tollway passes, or by requiring one-time toll users to 'book' their trip through telephoned requests to charge their credit cards;
- legislated to impose fines on innocent or ignorant users who had not pre-paid—a form of government-imposed incentive not readily available to small businesses;
- withheld details of contractual arrangements with the consortium from the public, and expressly exempted matters relating to the tollway project from FOI legislation—virtually elevating a commercial transaction to a standard of privacy reserved for matters of national security;
- agreed to financial arrangements which appear likely to provide very high financial returns to the private sector consortium.

Arguably some of these observations could also be applied to tollway contracts previously entered into in NSW. But the revenue collection features and the FOI exemptions of the Transurban deal were unprecedented.

Transurban City Link's prospectus was lodged with the Australian Securities Commission in February 1996. The prospectus claimed that the Melbourne City Link project was the first major infrastructure development in Victoria in which the public will have an opportunity to participate. Formal contacts between the Victorian government and the Transfield and Obashi Joint Venture (TOJV) had been signed in October 1995. The project involved the design, financing, construction, operation and maintenance of two sections of toll road referred to as the Southern Link and the Western Link. This involved construction of 13.4 kilometres of new and upgraded roadway, the upgrade of the existing Tullamarine Freeway to eight lanes, a six lane elevated roadway to extend the Tullamarine Freeway, and other works. The Western link was scheduled to be open in April 1999, and the entire link by December 1999.

The prospectus was offering 'stapled securities': one share in Transurban City Link Ltd, and one unit in a Trust, together with 499 Equity Infrastructure Bonds. It explained that the nominal pre-tax internal rate of return for investors based on the projected cash distributions over the entire life of the project was

Privatisation

approximately 19 per cent (*Prospectus—Transurban City Link Limited and Transurban City Link Unit Trust*, 1996).

The public offer was for $63.5 million, while the offer to institutional investors was for $206.5 million. Transfield and institutional investors had directly subscribed $185 million. On the face of it, the public offer would provide Transfield and other direct subscribers with liquidity: a public offer would provide a spread of shareholdings, enabling the stapled securities to be listed on the Australian Stock Exchange, and hence allowing the initial investors to liquidate their holdings, hopefully at a profit. (Similar incentives apparently faced the promoters of the M2 freeway in Sydney: a prospectus costing more than $17 million was issued to raise funds of only $2.3 million.)

Tolls and their collection

The agreement with the government provided for tolls to escalate at the greater of 1.1065 per cent per quarter (equivalent to 4.5 per cent per annum) or the CPI for the first 15 years of the project. The prospectus disclosed that tolls on the Melbourne City Link 'will be collected by means of an Electronic Toll Collection System that can detect vehicles travelling at highway speeds'.

This system involves the installation of Transponders in vehicles that are regular users of the Link. The transponder identification is transferred through roadside equipment, via computer links, to the Link Control Site and the user's (previously established) account will be debited with the toll.

Other users have to purchase a Day Pass in advance for use of the link over a 24-hour period. There are restrictions on the number of Day Passes that can be purchased in any 12-month period. And heaven help those who forget or don't know.

According to the prospectus:

> A video camera system will record an image of the number plate of vehicles not carrying a Transponder. If the user has not purchased a Day Pass, the registration details of the vehicle will be supplied to VicRoads which may process the non-payment of tolls as an infringement.

Expert's report (Halcrow Fox): 'we are not aware of any toll road which relies entirely on AVI technology without alternative direct payment toll booths'.

Returns to investors: the cost of private sector finance

The Agreement between the Victorian government and the consortium was appended to (and ratified by) the Melbourne City Link Act, 1995. This Agreement defined the 'equity return' as the expected *real after tax internal rate of return* which a Notional Initial Equity Investor would receive on his investment over the entire concession period, in terms of a 'base case equity model'. The concession period was to be 33½ years after the date on which the project was expected to be completed. The term could be extended if there had been events which reduced revenues or increased outgoings, and hence adversely affected returns to investors.

The 'base case equity model' was not disclosed. However, other clauses in the agreement give some idea of the scale of the 'base case equity return'. One clause stated that the project could be terminated at the option of the state as early as 25½ years if all project debt had been repaid and the cumulative, *real after tax equity return to equity investors 'is or exceeds 17.5% per annum'*.

Not a bad return—especially after tax.

This 17.5 per cent real after tax rate contrasts with the 8 per cent rate assumed as the relevant 'cost of capital' by economic consultants Allen and Associates for their analysis of the City Link project. The consultants wrote:

> We believe use of this discount rate is conservative for this type of project. The overall benefits from infrastructure projects such as City Link are not very sensitive to the economic cycle (i.e. they have low risk or 'beta'), implying a lower rate (around 6 per cent real) could be justified

rail project is scheduled to be operated by the private sector for 30 years 6 months after completion. The standard BOOT scheme involves reference to a 'base case equity model', which sets out projected traffic volumes and 'real' rates of return to be enjoyed by the operator over the life of the project. Additional standard clauses provide that the life of the arrangement may be further extended if the operator has not enjoyed a *cumulative* minimum rate of return. So the actual term of a BOOT arrangement could be longer than the nominal term. Likewise, individual contracts might specify that the term starts when the project is actually completed, or from the date that the project is expected to be completed—subject again to exception clauses, depending on which party or the nature of the circumstances responsible for occasioning the delay.

For example, the Melbourne Transurban toll road was nominally for 33½ years after the expected completion date, with the possibilities of extension of this period, if specified events adversely affected returns to investors.

Sydney's recently opened Eastern Distributor was constructed in terms of a longer-term BOOT scheme. When private sector firms were originally invited to submit preliminary proposals in 1994, the process identified a preferred proponent (a company backed by a consortium of Leighton Holdings and Macquarie Bank). After some delays (occasioned by changes in Federal government policies on tax concessions for infrastructure borrowings) the NSW government announced a preferred proponent in August 1996. At that stage the proposal involved a 38 year concession term. However, the project was extended to encompass funding of three other projects—the widening of Southern Cross Drive, General Holmes Drive (south of the airport tunnel) and an estimated $65 million contribution for the construction of new roadworks, the M5 East. This change in the specification of the project led to a negotiated increase in the proposed toll (from $2.50 to $3.00 for cars), and an extension of the concession period from 38 to 48 years (*Eastern Distributor—Summary of Contracts*, September 1998).

Off-balance sheet financing arrangements affect urban planning

It is difficult to resist the conclusion that BOOT schemes and other financial arrangements for private sector involvement in infrastructure financing have changed the way priorities are being set for new capital works. The NSW Auditor-General has expressed concern at the lack of 'auditable controls or guidelines' for these financing schemes. In other words, the process is largely deal-driven.

There is a risk that this will lead to rapid (and possibly over-) investment in projects like toll roads, simply because they can produce a discrete stream of cash flows—and hence can be readily packaged as an off budget financing arrangement. Other worthwhile projects (such as upgrading the treatment of waste water, or repairing storm water systems) cannot be packaged in this form, and so could slip down the list of priority capital projects for this reason alone.

The extent of off budget financing arrangements

It is difficult to estimate the scale of off-budget financing arrangements for the simple reason that it is hard to measure what governments do not wish to disclose. The original disclosure arrangements proposed by the Loan Council promised to make this information public—but the lack of compliance with the spirit if not the letter of the original agreements saw that disclosure regime fail.

Nevertheless it is possible to glean some sense of the scale of these deals from a range of sources.

- The Reserve Bank of Australia reviewed the impact of the Commonwealth government's tax concessions to encourage private sector involvement in infrastructure. One such scheme was the Develop Australia Bond (DAB) scheme introduced in 1992, but frozen in late 1996 and ended in 1997 due to its cost to the Commonwealth Budget.

  According to the Reserve Bank, by the time the scheme was ended, 13 projects worth around $4.5 billion were approved. This involved the issue of around $2.8 billion in infrastructure bonds. The projects included three major motorways in Sydney and Melbourne (Reserve Bank, 1997).

- In 1994 one of the authors estimated that 47 NSW projects worth an estimated $8.4 billion were either underway, or had been announced or proposed (*Walker, SMH*, 18/10/1994). The biggest were in the Transport portfolio. Apart from the State Rail Authority's involvement with the airport rail link and a tilt train project, the Roads and Transport Authority accounted for seven projects worth $3.2 billion: the Sydney Harbour Tunnel, the M2, M4 & M5 tollways and extensions, and 'Motorway Pacific' (a project which has yet to appear). Other agencies involved were the Department of Housing (construction of housing projects) and what is now known as Sydney Water (water treatment plants and sewerage tunnels). Then there were a series of projects associated with infrastructure for the 2000 Olympic Games, plus arrangements for private sector firms to construct and manage correctional facilities.
- The NSW Auditor-General confirmed in 1994 that the NSW government had been using expensive private sector finance to fund infrastructure projects while trying to ensure that these arrangements were not counted as government liabilities, and were not scrutinised by parliament. He observed that in NSW

    ... almost 50 certain or mooted major transactions of this kind have been identified. *The aggregate present value of these transactions may be equivalent to almost 20% of the State's gross liabilities* and 10% of gross assets (as per the 1993 State Consolidated accounts) (*Auditor-General of NSW*, 1994, emphasis added).

The state's gross liabilities at June 1993 were $54.43 billion, so 20 per cent amounts to almost $11 billion.

Back-door financing avoids accountability to parliament and the public

Those who have lobbied for greater private sector involvement in public infrastructure projects have been strangely defensive about suggestions that details of BOOT contracts and other arrangements should be made public.

It has been argued that the contractual arrangements contain significant intellectual property. Yet the structure of these deals is little different from the arrangements for equity-enhancement contained in private sector financing arrangements involving (say) the securitisation of receivables. Possibly the consulting industry wants to keep the deals under wraps so it can extend the shelf life of its current financial engineering products.

Another argument opposing public disclosure is that private sector involvement in infrastructure schemes is not significantly different from other forms of contractual arrangements involving the public sector's procurement of goods or services. For example, one submission to a NSW Public Accounts Committee enquiry into infrastructure financing argued that

> if such contracts are to be open to public scrutiny then should not all other major contracts of public interest also be open in a similar manner, i.e. the acquisition or sale of buildings by the public sector, the entering into various contractual arrangements for the provision of services, the employment of senior officers of various agencies etc? How can it be argued that these contracts are any less significant to the public interest than (say) the building of a road? Can it logically be argued, for example, that the provision of railway services under a Build, Own and Operate structure should be transparent but the purchase of railway rolling stock under current tender practices not? (*Submission to NSW PAC*, Michael Perry, Infrastructure Development Corporation, March 1993).

Whatever the merits of wider disclosure of contractual arrangements affecting major items of public expenditure, particularly where there may only be a limited number of firms with the capacity to participate, the involvement of private sector firms in public infrastructure projects does have some distinguishing features.

Such arrangements often involve the use of material public assets or other resources. The arrangements may convey to private interests the advantage of a government-controlled natural monopoly. They may also convey the benefit of the government's powers of land resumption, and possibly the benefit of what amounts to a 'taxing' power (e.g. tolls or airport 'fare supplements' where there are no comparable alternatives).

The traditional approach to public sector accountability developed through the so-called 'Westminster System' involves prior parliamentary consideration of proposals from executive government for the expenditure of moneys raised from taxes, fees, fines and other charges. Governments have to present 'Budget bills' to parliament for debate and review. Parliamentary Estimates Committees may further interrogate public servants about past and proposed public sector expenditure. There are long-established requirements (often avoided by means of internal accounting devices) for variations from proposed expenditure to be recommitted to parliament for endorsement. And there are arrangements for reports on such expenditure (in the form of 'public accounts') to be audited and submitted to parliament, completing what was described in Gladstone's times as a 'circle of control' by parliament over public sector expenditure.

Now the extent of parliamentary control over public sector expenditure has been eroded by the way that government departments and public trading enterprises alike source their funds from the sale of services directly to the community. An enduring feature of the Westminster system, as it is applied in a modified form in Australia, is that parliament oversights annual budget allocations for cash expenditures.

BOOT schemes (and other financing arrangements) can largely bypass these systems of parliamentary accountability, because they do not involve expenditures from the Budget but the alienation of revenue streams from the public purse to the private sector.

At the same time, the public sector is essentially underwriting the financial returns of private sector investors. If investors have not enjoyed the cumulative rates of return specified in a BOOT contract, the public sector must defer receiving its share of the revenues—or take a smaller slice—until the private sector investors have been accommodated. If the contract has not delivered the promised cumulative real rates of return as originally promised in the contract, then the term of the contract may be extended until it does.

It seems absurd that relatively small amounts of proposed expenditure require parliamentary scrutiny and approval, while major contracts involving financial commitments stretching over 30 years can be handled in secret by executive government.

It is encouraging that in September 1999, when re-announcing an infrastructure development proposed for Sydney—an east-west cross-city traffic tunnel—the NSW government suggested that the tunnel would be fully self-funded by tolls—implying that the government would not enter into a BOOT scheme. Some years earlier, the NSW Treasury had argued that private sector funding would remove the financing of public infrastructure projects from 'the vagaries of the budgetary and political process'. It did not explore the implications of the alternative: the impact on taxpayers of the vagaries of *political processes* involving an unaccountable executive government. When choices have to be made between open or secretive political processes, the preferences of bureaucrats or ministers may well differ from those of ordinary citizens.

Arguably, one reason why politicians and private sector participants in these schemes want to keep contract particulars under wraps is that they are reluctant to let the public know how profitable the schemes can be. Possibly this underpinned the decision of the Kennett government in Victoria to amend Freedom of Information legislation to expressly exclude any materials relating to the Transurban tollroad project from the ambit of FOI enquiries.

Yet, without proper controls and scrutiny, the finances of a government could be burdened by guarantees and the loss of revenues which might otherwise be going to government coffers. Unfortunately it may take a decade or more before the impact of lost revenues is discernible in the finances of state governments in Australia—and even then such analysis will be partial (because all governments have indulged in privatisations to some extent in their quest for short term financial flexibility).

Several states have issued 'guidelines' for handling private sector involvement in infrastructure.

For example, in 1988, 1990 and 1995 successive NSW governments issued policy papers affirming support for private sector involvement and suggesting conditions under which it would be attractive (*NSW Department of State Development*, 1988; *NSW Treasury*, 1990, 1995). The 1990 guidelines emphasised that the government would adopt a 'flexible' approach to the sharing of risks and returns between public sector and private sector participants in infrastructure projects. Expressions of interest would be sought for particular projects, leading to the short-listing of three or four applications, to be followed by the development of more detailed proposals, followed by final evaluation by a committee and selection on the basis of committee recommendations by a minister or Cabinet, 'depending on the scope and sensitivity of the project'.

To date, there has been little transparency. One of the few occasions when the full details of a BOOT contract have been made available was when the private sector participants in one tollway contract sought to register a prospectus (see Box 7.5). Under Corporations Law requirements, material contracts must be produced for inspection by private investors. Even though the contract was available to potential investors, the then NSW Minister for Transport, Bruce Baird, refused to table it in parliament.

> **Box 7.5**
> **THE M2 MOTORWAY**
>
> The NSW government's deal on the proposed M2 Motorway for Sydney's northwest illustrates how parliamentarians can be left in the dark about private sector involvement in public infrastructure.
>
> On November 1994, the NSW parliament called on the Fahey government to produce to Auditor-General Tony Harris 'all legal documents' relating to the Motorway project, and asked for a report to be presented later that week. Transport Minister Bruce Baird had previously declined to table the documents.
>
> While parliament was debating an Opposition motion of no confidence in Baird, one of the authors exercised his right as a prospective investor to inspect the documents. The Hills Motorway Company and the Hills Motorway Trust had jointly registered a prospectus with the Australian Securities Commission. Registration of the prospectus meant that the Hills Motorway Company and the Hills Motorway Trust had to make copies of 'material contracts' available at their registered offices.
>
> The registered office of Hills Motorway was given as a floor of a building on Bond Street, Sydney. On arrival, it was found that all but two doorways on the floor were unlabelled, except for one marked 'private' and the other marked 'fire escape'. No one answered either door. Recourse to the directory in the entrance foyer indicated that the floor was held by Macquarie Bank. Macquarie Bank's receptionist was helpful, and a meeting was soon arranged with Hills Motorway's company secretary, who enjoined the author/prospective investor to wait in Macquarie's boardroom with impressive views of Sydney Harbour. Soon he returned with several boxes of documents.
>
> In effect, any member of the public could inspect documents which were being denied that very day to members of the NSW parliament. Not that the Hills Motorway Trust was entirely gracious about the request for access: permission to photocopy or purchase photocopies was refused. This was despite the fact that later, when Hills Motorway's 'stapled securities' (a combination of units in the Trust and shares in the Company) were listed on the Australian Stock Exchange, copies of material contracts had to be made available to the public through the Australian Stock Exchange.
>
> The contract documents contained detailed projections of likely revenues and operating costs of the tollway. The main 'project deed' referred to arrangements between the Roads and Traffic Authority and Hills Motorway, but largely by reference to another document. Several clauses deal with compensation for early termination of the contract, and with the circumstances in which the term of the contract may be extended. A particularly sensitive clause concerned an agreement that the substantial upgrading of 'an alternative road' would be a 'material adverse effect' for which compensation would be payable to Hills Motorway. All of these clauses refer to a 'Base case equity return'. This in turn is defined by reference to material which was not incorporated in the project deed. Rather, it was set out in a document 'which the parties have initialled for identification'.
>
> This document was only made available after Hills Motorway had obtained legal advice that it was obliged to release that information. (The company secretary explained that directors, not unreasonably, were concerned about their liability for publishing forecasts which might not be realised.)
>
> The document revealed that Hills Motorway expected $408.6 million in financial support from the NSW government. The support was to take the form of 'RTA promissory notes' to be issued between 1998 and 2025. Apparently these

> promissory notes relate to deferred payments for rent on the motorway land. Repayments (apparently with interest) are budgeted to be made between 2028 and 2042.
>
> The 'Summary of material contracts' in the prospectus made no reference to these promissory notes.
>
> However, the existence of this arrangement contrasts with claims made by the then Roads and Transport Minister Bruce Baird. Before surviving a no confidence motion, Baird told parliament that 'all the risk' of the Motorway deal would be borne by the private sector.
>
> Plainly the contractual arrangements meant that taxpayers faced (and continue to face) considerable risks. There is a risk of delays in receiving repayment of the $546 million principal and interest on the promissory notes before 2042. There is a risk that compensation will have to be paid by the RTA under a wide range of scenarios. And there is the risk that the RTA may not obtain much of a financial return on $179 million outlays for land acquisition and up-front capital payments.

Disclosure of contract summaries?

In the face of political and business opposition to the full disclosure of contracts involving the private sector financing of public infrastructure, the NSW Public Accounts Committee recommended that the essential elements of all projects with private financing 'be made transparent, preferably through contract summaries' (*NSW PAC, 1994*).

Similarly a task force to review infrastructure financing, established by Prime Minister Keating, observed:

> To build public acceptance of private provision of infrastructure, governments should provide contract summaries of major projects to Parliament. They should also give their Auditors General sufficient resources to properly and expeditiously review contentious contracts (*EPAC, September 1995*).

These proposed disclosures were only to be made *after* contracts had been finalised. Mere disclosure of contract summaries *after* deals have been completed is inadequate to ensure appropriate scrutiny and accountability in parliament.

In particular, contract summaries would only tell part of the story about the way in which the risks and rewards of such projects are shared. For a start, they may not reveal all of the government's past and projected expenditure in providing ancillary services to a major project. These can involve new roadworks to feed traffic onto tollways, bridges to enable local traffic to by-pass the tollway route, and the costs of moving wires, pipes and drains in the path of the tollway corridor.

Even then, the spirit of those proposals has not been fully

observed. Since 1995, NSW has adopted the practice of preparing contract summaries and associated cost-benefit analyses—apparently the only state to do so.

In NSW, contract summaries have been prepared by relevant agencies (e.g. State Rail Authority, Department of Transport) and then reviewed by the NSW Auditor-General, who has produced a 'special purpose' report on the contents of the summaries. The nature of the audit examination has been severely limited—to the point that the Auditor-General has asserted that it could not be properly described as an 'audit review', only a 'procedure' (see following Box for a review of the six contract summaries examined by the Auditor-General between September 1995 and January 1999).

These audit reports have been prepared for, and at the request of, the agency engaging in off-balance-sheet financing. There does not appear to be any mechanism to assure the release of contract summaries in a timely fashion. The documents have not been tabled in the NSW parliament, or lodged in the parliamentary library. They are not secret, but are only available if one knows where to look or ask.

The analysis of the contracts has also been limited. Most contain some form of economic cost-benefit analysis in a form which brings to mind the observation that such exercises can be described as 'nonsense on stilts' (*Self*, 1970). Economists' cost-benefit analyses may assign dollar values to community benefits (such as reduced waiting time in traffic, reduced car accidents) in an essentially arbitrary way. Moreover, such analyses often fail to clearly identify who will be responsible for the costs and who will be the recipients of the benefits. Statements such as 'the project will have a benefit: cost ratio of 2' are presented as self-evident justifications when the underlying analysis heroically assigns dollar values to only *some* costs or benefits (incurred or enjoyed by only *some* parties) while ignoring others.

Notably contract summaries of transport infrastructure projects have not included assessments of the rates of return likely to be earned by private sector operators. These rates of return indicate what governments are effectively paying to fund capital projects through BOOT schemes. The omission of this information is a fundamental shortcoming of the NSW practice of preparing contract summaries, and highlights the limited value of an audit review which has been undertaken in terms of procedures selected by agencies, rather than the parliament.

Box 7.6
NSW EXPERIENCE WITH THE PREPARATION OF CONTRACT SUMMARIES FOR PRIVATE SECTOR FINANCING OF INFRASTRUCTURE

NSW, alone among Australian states, has adopted the practice of preparing 'contract summaries' of private sector infrastructure financing arrangements, and has had them subject to a limited examination by the Auditor-General. Contract summaries have dealt with:

- The New Southern Railway (September 1995);
- Ultimo-Pyrmont light rail project (April 1996);
- Hawkesbury District Health Service Ltd (May 1996);
- Olympic Park Stadium (July 1997);
- Eastern Distributor (September 1998);
- Olympic Village (January 1999).

Form and content: The contract summaries ranged from 8 pages (the Eastern Distributor) to 48 pages (the Olympic Village), and generally contained a history of the project, the main features of the agreements, and a brief summary of an economic cost-benefit analysis of the project (usually prepared by a consultant). They also contained some tabulation of risk factors, and how they were addressed in the agreements or otherwise.

The cost-benefit analyses were highly summarised and abbreviated, and did not indicate the basis of assigning values to social benefits from (for example) reduced waiting times in traffic.

Notable omissions were any attempts to assess the effective cost of finance incurred by the government as a consequence of relying on private sector funding, or an outline of the assumptions and forecasts incorporated in 'base case models' which would be used to determine compensation payments payable to the private sector participants if the government sought to terminate the agreement.

Arguably the most informative report was that relating to the proposed private sector construction and management of a hospital by an element of the Catholic Church using the vehicle, Hawkesbury District Health Service Ltd. This included a systematically compiled financial analysis of contractual arrangements and risks, and outlined projected savings relative to the projected cost to a government agency of delivering equivalent services.

Audit examination: The review by the Auditor-General's office was limited to the procedures specified in the conditions of the engagement by the government agencies concerned. The audit reports took the following form:

1. A listing of documents covered by the contract summaries which had been obtained by the Auditor-General—ranging from 28 for the New Southern Railway, to 176 for the Olympic Village (the latter included such items as the 36th edition of Gregory's Street Directory);
2. A statement that the Auditor-General had obtained a copy of the NSW *Guidelines for Private Sector Participation in the Provision of Public Infrastructure* (dated September 1995);
3. A statement that the information contained in the contract summary had been compared with the documents listed, and with the recommended disclosure requirements of the Guidelines;
4. A report that 'nothing has come to my attention that causes me to believe that the [contract summary relating to the project]

> (a) does not fairly represent the substance of the contractual arrangements pertaining to the [project] between the private and public sector participants; and
> (b) does not comply with the disclosure requirements of the *Guidelines*';
> 5. A disclaimer of any responsibility for the 'adequacy or otherwise of procedures requested by [the agency requesting the audit review]'.
>
> The statement of 'disclaimer' from the Auditor-General warrants attention. The standard wording was
>
>> I disclaim any assumption of responsibility for the adequacy or otherwise of the procedures requested by you.
>
> The last of the series of contract summaries (that dealing with the Olympic Village) contained a more strongly-worded disclaimer:
>
>> The procedures were performed solely to assess whether the Olympic Village Summary of Contracts complies with the disclosure requirements of the *Guidelines for Private Sector Participation in the Provision of Public Infrastructure*.
>> Because the above procedures do not constitute either an audit or a review, no assurance is expressed. Had additional procedures or an audit or review been performed in accordance with Australian Auditing Standards, other matters might have come to our attention that would have been reported.

Reforms needed to restore accountability

Private sector financing of infrastructure developments has led to significant erosions of accountability arrangements. Controls over levels of state borrowings through the Loan Council have, for all intents and purposes, been abandoned, along with the practice of public disclosure of the scale of these financing arrangements. First, in 1992 the Loan Council gave up deciding whether financing arrangements should be regarded as 'borrowings', in favour of a new scheme of reporting to financial markets about governments' off-budget financing arrangements. Then in 1995, even the disclosures were terminated. It is ironic that these steps to reduce public disclosure about off-budget borrowings were undertaken at the same time that political leaders were bemoaning the 'problems' of government debt.

The reforms required to restore public sector accountability start at the Loan Council and extend to government budget papers and audited government financial statements. There is a strong case to implement key elements of the reporting framework promised by the Loan Council in 1992. That would require the Loan Council to resume its role as an adjudicator of whether financing arrangements are, in substance, borrowings. There may be a good case to replace the old-style 'global limits' approach with a regime which relates aggregate liabilities and annual deficits to Gross State Product— similar to the fiscal measures introduced by the European Community. Meantime, governments should be required to disclose their involvement in financial arrangements whereby they alienate revenue streams, guarantee returns to private sector investors, or assume responsibility for the repayment of debt incurred by others.

The accounting profession and Auditors-General have a part to play in ensuring fuller disclosure about these arrangements. To date the accounting profession's involvement has been to indicate that its 'preliminary views' are that components of these arrangements should be separately disclosed as assets or liabilities (*Australian Accounting Research Foundation, 1997*). These 'preliminary views' (expressed by a committee on which state Treasuries or agencies involved in infrastructure financing projects were well-represented) emphasise 'form' rather than 'substance'. They are also inconsistent with approaches adopted by other accounting authorities, notably the US Governmental Accounting Standards Board. But even these limited proposals from the local accounting profession have not been fully implemented by Australian governments.

In any event, these proposals for public disclosure of financing arrangements would only apply *after* contractual arrangements have been completed.

There are a number of serious concerns about the use of off-budget financing arrangements (such as BOOT schemes) to privatise infrastructure development.

As the Canadian Institute of Accountants observed, 'a system that requires the prior approval of the legislature of all expenditure will be effective only to the degree that it is not bypassed' (*CICA, 1980*). Current arrangements for private sector financing of public infrastructure are outside the budget process and bypass the scrutiny of parliament. The limited amount of available documentation suggests that some deals have been very lucrative to private sector participants —and unacceptably so, having regard to the distribution of risks.

Private sector involvement in *designing* or *constructing* infrastructure is desirable, and probably inevitable. But the private sector need not necessarily be involved in infrastructure *financing*. In some instances, these deals provide private sector participants with tax deductions (for depreciation or operating costs) that would not be available to state governments, which are exempt from Commonwealth taxation. Hence the deals involve elements of 'cost-shifting', whereby the Commonwealth (for which read, 'taxpayers') bear some of the costs of state-based projects. Even so the effective cost to state governments of financing capital projects through BOOT schemes is far greater than the interest costs which would have been incurred had governments borrowed in their own right.

The main factor inhibiting states engaging in direct financing of tollways or other projects has been political. Some politicians would be seen to be inconsistent: having argued (in opposition) that there was a 'need to reduce debt', they would have difficulty if, when in government, they borrowed to fund capital works. Instead, they prefer back-door (and more expensive) finance, through BOOT schemes.

There can be situations where BOOT schemes are good deals for both government and the private sector.

There are also situations where they are patently bad deals. NSW Auditor-General Tony Harris pointed to a series of 'process' issues which may mitigate against such outcomes. For example, governments tend to announce projects and then be reluctant to abandon them if tendered costs appear to exceed project benefits. Public sector negotiators are often locked in to in-principle commitments which are only optional to the private sector until specifications are finalised and contracts are signed. Governments have been known to change specifications without re-opening the tender process, requiring far greater expenditure from the public side than originally proposed. Government employees have been known to switch sides during or shortly after the tender process. 'At one point of time these employees represented the government; at another they represented the private sector firm with which they were originally dealing.' Summarising, the Auditor-General observed that 'political benefits do not always equate with sound financial outcomes' (*Harris*, 1998).

The remedy? Let the case for such deals be presented openly, and be subjected to the fullest of scrutiny. As the NSW Public Accounts Committee observed in 1994

> If the government proceeds with a project involving private participation, it should demonstrate publicly that it was more beneficial for the project to have been undertaken with private finance than without (*NSW PAC*, 1994).

The Commonwealth government's Productivity Commission echoed these sentiments, albeit by advocating publication of the case for these schemes *after* rather than *before* the event:

> There would be greater community understanding of the benefits of BOOT schemes if the results of the comparative assessment leading to the choice of funding arrangements are made transparent (*Productivity Commission*, 1997).

What is plain is that, unless there is more disclosure and more open debate about these arrangements, our society will be exposed to some basic risks.

There was a time when the concept of corruption in the public sector was commonly associated with the transfer of brown paper bags containing used bank notes. It would be unfortunate if the perception in the next century was that corruption was associated with company boards which managed to get government approval for lucrative BOOT schemes.

Government, and business, both deserve better.

8

Australia's Worst Privatisations

THERE HAVE BEEN so many privatisations in Australia that it is likely that some may have turned out to be bad deals. However, some deals seem to have been very, very bad. The task of examining each and every privatisation would be a major project in itself, particularly since publicly available information about trade sales and contracting arrangements is scanty. This chapter looks at some of the worst deals.

There are many ways to assess the success or failure of privatisations. The obvious tests are whether sales were made too cheaply, or whether they have led to a discernible loss of services (to the community as a whole, or to elements of the community).

Let's start with some of those cases, before looking at some deals which might claim awards as 'bad' privatisations in terms of other criteria.

Finally, let's consider which of these deals deserves the Wooden Spoon Award as *Australia's worst privatisation*.

Loss of value to the public sector

Nominations for this award could include virtually all public floats of government-owned businesses (with the possible exception of GIO, though even then it appears that GIO's 1999 losses from reinsurance may have resulted from decisions made after the business was privatised in 1992).

CSL Ltd

On a percentage basis, the sale of shares in *CSL* (the former Commonwealth Serum Laboratories) would probably be the winner. Shares were sold for $2.30 in 1994, and were trading close to $23 in late 1999.

Telstra

However, on the basis of the gross transfer of wealth from the public sector to the private sector, the standout winner must be the sale of the first tranche of shares in *Telstra*.

Telstra Corporation Ltd had started life as part of a Commonwealth government department—the Postmaster General's Department. Later it became a statutory authority (and known as Telecom), then as a renamed corporation, Telstra became Australia's principal telecommunications carrier.

> Its fixed telecommunications network carries over 90 per cent of calls and serves the vast majority of Australian homes and a substantial majority of Australian businesses. Telstra is also the largest mobile communications provider in Australia (*Commonwealth Auditor-General*, 1998).

The Keating government's decision to establish competition in telecommunications by allowing Optus access to Telecom's network could be viewed as stripping billions of dollars from the value of Telstra. While that decision certainly did introduce competition, one can only speculate whether the same result could have been achieved by splitting Telstra into competing Commonwealth-owned businesses. Further competition was introduced through steps to allow resellers to buy bulk time on existing networks. Indeed, in quest for market share, both Optus and Telstra encouraged the marketing of mobile telephone services through competing service providers.

Many would argue that the community has benefited from this competition, through the availability of new products and services, and (in some instances) lower prices for telephone calls. Arguably, new products and services arose from worldwide technological innovation, and would have continued anyway. Similarly changes in technology had led to reductions in real prices before the introduction of competition. On the other hand, when one recalls that the Commonwealth government had bowed to community pressure to resist the introduction of timed local calls, carriers are now achieving much the same result through the wider use of mobile services.

When Telstra was wholly owned by the Commonwealth, it seemed intent on reducing its reported profits. Possibly this was designed to resist demands for dividends from Treasury, so that funds could be retained within the organisation for re-investment.

In 1997 Telstra established a provision for staff redundancies of $1,126 million, on the assumption that a large proportion of its maintenance staff would be retrenched. This so-called 'provision' was not a liability, in terms of the accounting profession's definitions, since although Telstra was actively shedding jobs in its maintenance divisions, it had not announced plans to undertake retrenchments on that scale.

Another extremely conservative accounting practice adopted by Telstra was that of 'expensing' indirect overheads and all costs associated with the development of software for internal use, and interest incurred during the construction of new infrastructure. It is hard to be too critical of such a conservative accounting practice, since many listed companies (with less secure businesses) tend to err in the opposite direction, and the valuation of software is a difficult issue.

However, from 1997, a newly commercial Telstra board began behaving like other listed companies, and took steps to produce more optimistic profit figures. It reversed these accounting policies retrospectively to 1996. The impact was to increase Telstra's reported profit for 1999 by $606 million.

These are big numbers, but still relatively insignificant in terms of the profits and cash flows now generated by Telstra. Even in its last full year in total government ownership—1996–7—Telstra's operating revenue totalled $16 billion, an increase of 26 per cent on 1992–93. Over the period 1992–97, Telstra had paid the government dividends totalling $7.8 billion (including a special dividend of $3 billion on 30 June 1997).

The price of Telstra shares in the initial public offering in 1997 turned out to be less than half market value. That meant a loss of billions of dollars of proceeds from the public purse. Shareholders can rejoice. Taxpayers can lament.

The Commonwealth government's Office of Asset Sales and IT Outsourcing has stated:

> The Telstra share offer was the largest share offer in Australian corporate history and one of the largest share offers worldwide in 1997 (*OASITO Internet Website*, 2/6/99).

The Office also cheekily claimed that the sale achieved the government's objectives including 'an optimum financial return from the sale'. Optimum return? The facts speak for themselves.

Management of the initial public offer of one-third of Telstra's issued share capital of 12,866,600,200 ordinary shares was contracted out. The three firms chosen to handle the sale were ABN AMRO Rothschild, Credit Suisse First Boston, and JB Were & Son. They were given the title of Joint Global Coordinators.

The sale offer was completed on 17 November 1997, and had the following features:

- 1.8 million investors bought just under 4.29 million shares;
- the shares were purchased in two instalments: the first, payable on application, was $2.00 per share (discounted to $1.95 for retail investors); the second $1.40 (or $1.35 for retail investors) payable 17 November 1998;
- gross proceeds were $14.2 billion;
- the Commonwealth's direct costs of the sale were around $260 million or 1.8 per cent of the proceeds. Telstra also incurred costs estimated at $15 million;
- according to the offer document, the proceeds were to be used to fund the Natural Heritage Trust ($1.15 billion) and the Regional Telecommunications Infrastructure Fund ($250 million), with the balance to be applied to reducing Commonwealth public debt (*Telstra Australian public offer document*, 29/9/97).

Telstra's financial performance continued to improve in 1997–98. On 26 August 1998, Telstra announced a 1997–98 net profit of $3 billion (after tax and abnormals) which was over 7 per cent better than the prospectus forecast of $2.81 billion. Dividends of 14 cents per share were paid, 8 per cent higher than forecast. This meant that even after its one-third sale, Telstra returned to the government over $1.2 billion on its remaining two-thirds interest—not to mention revenues from corporate taxation.

Listing share price of Telstra

The government sought the best advice that money can buy in setting the price for Telstra shares. The prices suggested by its advisers were as follows:

	Suggested Prices for Telstra
Global Coordinators	
ABN AMRO Rothschild	$2.75 – $3.25
Credit Suisse First Boston	$3.30 – $3.45
JB Were & Son	$3.10 – $3.40
Sale Business Adviser	$2.65 – $2.90

Source: Commonwealth Auditor-General, *Sale of One-third of Telstra*, October 1998.

The Global Coordinators finally suggested a valuation of $2.80 to $3.30 per share. This meant gross proceeds of $12.0 billion to

$14.2 billion for the one-third to be sold. Apparently, the Global Coordinators considered a ceiling for the indicative price range of $3.30 to $3.50. However, they recommended the lower value because 'they held reservations about the capacity to attract adequate institutional demand at the higher range' (*Commonwealth Auditor-General*, 1998).

Based on this advice, the Minister for Finance and Administration set the range at $2.80 to $3.30 per share. Perhaps remembering his previous experience in selling government assets, the Minister apparently asked the Global Coordinators to reconsider whether the upper end of the range might be increased to $3.40. The Office of Asset Sales advised a Senate committee on 8 May 1998 that:

> ... the Minister asked the Global Coordinators to reconsider whether the upper end of the range might be increased to $3.40. This was the subject of a further debate among the advisers over several hours. In the end they confirmed their advice, but indicated that a later increase to $3.40 would be feasible if later stages revealed adequate support at higher prices. However, at that stage, the advisers were expressing serious reservations about the capacity to set the price towards the upper end of this range and still attract adequate institutional demand to fill the international component offer. There was then some concern that the 5 per cent fall in the Nikkei Index over the preceding month might foreshadow a more widespread downward rating in the world's stockmarkets (*Commonwealth Auditor-General*, 1998).

The government subsequently increased the top of the indicative range to $3.40. But that was not nearly high enough.

Share price of Telstra after listing

The price of $3.40 per instalment receipt on listing increased by 73 per cent to $5.87 per instalment receipt on 8 October 1998. This means that on that day, the market valued Telstra at $79 billion, or $26 billion for the one-third sold. It compares with the issue price valuation of $44 billion, or around $14 billion for the one-third sold.

As the Commonwealth Auditor-General concluded, 'the size of the initial listing premium and ongoing strong secondary market trading performance indicate that the issue was not fully priced':

> Compared to the expected aftermarket premium of 5 per cent to 10 per cent, Telstra instalment receipts traded at an initial 34 per cent premium over the issue price of instalment receipts and a 20 per cent premium on a fully paid basis. On a fully paid basis, over the eleven

months since listing, the trading price of Telstra instalment receipts has risen more than 160 times the increase in the Australian Stock Exchange (ASX) All Ordinaries Index and more than 20 times the increase in the ASX All Industrials Index (*Commonwealth Auditor-General*, 1998).

As one commentator put it as early as February 1998 when shares had only reached $3.87:

> The ones who are really laughing are the gaggle of investment bankers who got paid $32 million for their expert advice on the pricing (*SMH*, 26/2/98).

By 30 June 1999, Telstra shares reached $8.66. This placed the value of Telstra at $111 billion, and the one-third already sold at $37 billion. Compared to proceeds of $14 billion, that suggests an initial loss of value of $23 billion.

As a footnote to this tale, the government engaged the same 'experts' for the sale of the next tranche of Telstra shares.

Loss of services to the community

There is a range of potential nominations in this category.

Commonwealth Bank

Possibly the sale of the *Commonwealth Bank of Australia* is one. While others have piggy banks, to millions of Australians, a little tin money box in the shape of an art deco bank building once symbolised the virtues of saving, and introduced children to the industry of banking.

Take a money box to a bank today, and more than likely you'll be charged to have your coins counted—when the hard-pressed counter staff have time. In the 1980s, banks focused on the 'products' which returned the greatest financial return. Managing small savings accounts and small loans was far less attractive than servicing major corporations and a few high net worth customers. By the 1990s, banks were looking at the profitability of alternative electronic 'channels' for conducting bank business. Along the way, staff were cut, branches were closed, queues lengthened, and many country towns lost access to banking services altogether. At the same time, fees and charges were increased or invented.

The sale of the Commonwealth Bank was followed by a reduction in service to many traditional customers. But the CBA after privatisation, was only doing what its competitors were doing, in harnessing information technology to speed up transaction processing and closing labour-intensive branches. Indeed, its share price would not be where it is today unless it had kept pace with its competitors.

Housing Loans Insurance Corporation

Another potential nominee is the *Housing Loans Insurance Corporation*. Established in 1965 by a Coalition government, the HLIC operated as a mortgage insurer to overcome the 'deposit gap' which was preventing many from buying a home. Low income earners or those with only a small deposit could arrange housing loans from lenders on condition they took out mortgage insurance. A single premium was paid up front, and this insured lenders (such as banks, building societies, co-operative societies or credit unions) against losses on these housing loans.

Most insurable losses emerged within the second or third years of a mortgage loan, when borrowers irretrievably fell into arrears on their repayments, and then found that the small equity in their house had been eroded by a fall in property values. The HLIC paid out when a mortgagor sale realised less than the sum owing on the loans.

The HLAC had a policy of insuring mortgages 'regardless of postcode', whereas its competitors were not prepared to offer mortgage insurance in high-risk areas of Australia (notably small country towns). The ease of arranging mortgage insurance with the Corporation meant that it dominated the market in its dealings with credit unions and other lenders—gaining about 80 per cent of building society business, and an overall market share of around 60 per cent, despite private operators entering the industry. Significantly, more than one-third of building society loans insured by HLIC were non-metropolitan borrowers (*AFR*, 7/9/80).

The HLIC became a good earner, generating fairly consistent profits despite its conservative accounting policies. Its balance sheet at 30 June 1989 showed a net equity of $19.9 million, after the Commonwealth had stripped the business of $10 million as a special dividend in 1987, on top of ordinary dividends which totalled $2.7 million in 1989. That reported equity of $19.9 million was after a provision of $60.2 million had been established for 'unearned income'. It appears from the published accounts that the single premium insurance policies were brought to account over a period approaching the term of outstanding mortgages, notwithstanding that risks to the Corporation were negligible once a home buyer had established a material equity in their properties.

Treasurer John Howard announced the Commonwealth government's intention to sell the Housing Loans Insurance Corporation in July 1979—but it was later revealed that there was strong industry opposition from building societies, from trustee companies and other financial institutions (AFR, 25/3/80, 2/6/80). Within months, the Fraser government scrapped the plan (AFR, 2/6/80). Soon, the private-sector Mortgage Insurers Association (whose members wanted to buy the HLIC) were calling on the government to reaffirm its opposition to 'wasteful government intervention in areas better left to private enterprise' (AFR, 20/8/80). At the same time, the Master Builders Association was demanding retention (AFR, 7/9/80). The issue was deferred until after a forthcoming election.

In June 1981 a re-elected Coalition government revived the sale of the HLIC, with advertisements seeking expressions of interest (AFR, 5/6/81). Then in 1983 the new Labor government announced the Corporation was not for sale, after all (AFR, 29/3/83). Six months later, a bill was introduced to broaden the HLIC's charter to encompass loans for non-residential buildings (AFR, 8/9/83). Later, a bill was introduced to enable HLIC to insure 'pools' of mortgage loans, a step which was said to pave the way for the trading of mortgage-backed securities in a new secondary mortgage market (AFR, 18/4/85).

But, in 1989, the sale of HLIC was back on the agenda. The Task Force on Asset Sales within the Commonwealth Department of Finance produced an 'Invitation to register interest in the purchase of the business of the Housing Loans Insurance Corporation', foreshadowing that prospective purchasers will be shortlisted with agreement on the detailed terms and conditions 'being finalised by early April 1990, if possible'. In the event, HLIC was not sold by April 1990—indeed, it was not sold for another eight years.

By July 1990 six prospective purchasers (mainly insurance companies) had dropped out of the contest 'due to what was considered an excessive price tag of at least $50 million and sale conditions which included a requirement that any successful bidder indemnify the government against the HLIC's continued government guarantee' (AFR, 6/7/90). In response to this development, the Asset Sales Task Force was thought to have dropped the price in an effort to revive the sale.

Soon afterwards, media reports indicated that actuarial advice was that the HLIC's had overstated its provisions. Instead of being interpreted as indicating that the HLIC was a more profitable asset than its owner may have realised, this was taken as justification for the Commonwealth increasing the sale price above $50 million. A few weeks later, Labor Minister Ralph Willis announced sale of the HLIC to CIC Insurance Limited for '$80 million in net present value terms' (*AFR*, 31/10/90). Later it was explained that CIC was only to purchase the HLIC 'goodwill', and that the balance of the $80 million was to be 'drawn from HLIC's reserves' (*AFR*, 15/8/91). Whatever the likely proceeds, Willis's announcement that HLIC had been sold was premature—seven years' premature. In December 1993, it was announced that the sale to CIC Insurance had fallen through (*AFR*, 7/12/93).

Next year, there was speculation that a potential buyer for HLIC was the AIDC Limited, another government-owned business enterprise which had also been slated for privatisation for 15 years (*AFR*, 9/9/94). However, AIDC's bid was considered inadequate, and five other contenders had dropped out during the year. Finance Minister Beazley announced that HLIC (which had just produced a record profit of $16.6 million) would be withdrawn from sale, and would be restructured as a corporation under the Corporations Law, and would have a capital structure conforming to the prudential requirements of the Insurance and Superannuation Commission. In the process it was planned to re-describe part of HLIC's $124 million unearned premium reserve as shareholders' equity (*AFR*, 22/12/94 and 23/12/94).

The restructure proceeded in October 1995, with the new corporation paying dividends that year of $7.12 million and a further $25 million in fees (for 'reinsurance', effectively a loan guarantee fee) (*AFR*, 20/12/95).

Eventually HLIC was sold in 1997, not for the originally-slated $50 million, or the later estimate of $100 million, but for a modest $8 million. The buyer was a US company, GE Capital, described as the 'finance arm of the US industrial giant General Electric' (*AFR*, 24/12/97).

Standard & Poors maintained HLIC's AAA rating, but Moody's issued a modest downgrade from Aaa to Aa1 (*AFR*, 22/12/97).

Within months, the new owners announced a 30 per cent hike in premiums for mortgage insurance, supposedly to cover risks that 'became apparent during the due diligence process' (*AFR*, 26/3/98). The nature of those risks was not apparent, given that the Federal government had assumed responsibility for mortgage insurance policies written before the sale.

The new owners then split the business of the company, with HLIC focussing on providing services to the top end of the market, principally insuring investments in 'securitised' mortgages which needed AAA rating, while a second company would provide lower-rated mortgage insurance at a lower price (but which was still 'substantially more expensive than the current pricing on the AAA-rated insurance') (*AFR*, 28/3/98).

The sale process had taken from 1979 to 1997, and it is difficult to avoid the conclusion that governments of successive persuasions felt they had to continue pushing the sale of HLIC, to save face.

This was a government enterprise which had been successful, largely because it was a *government* enterprise. It had provided services in a situation where there had been market failure—where the private sector had not provided adequate services. The HLIC provided access to those services to all Australians, not just those living in metropolitan areas. Indeed, because of this, it actually reduced its own exposures. Since the timing of cycles in regional property markets differs across the continent. Moreover, precisely because as a government-owned business it offered services to Australians 'regardless of postcode', building societies and credit unions knew they could get set with the HLIC, with minimum fuss and without having to shop around. Hence the operations of the HLIC lowered the costs of both lenders, and those requiring mortgage insurance.

Privatisation turned a *win-win* into a *lose-lose* situation, for government and the community.

Loss of commercial and social opportunities

Economists often refer to opportunity costs—the costs incurred when one passes up an opportunity to do something. Opportunity costs can take the form of loss of profits, or loss of opportunities to shape the direction of service delivery within the community. Privatisations through the sale of GTEs often involve opportunity costs, though it is often hard to assess their significance—let alone assign monetary values to them.

Consider, for example, the opportunity costs which arise when government owned businesses are transferred to private owners who give higher priority to private than to community interests.

The gaming industry is a case in point. It is difficult to see how any government could consider that it had a core responsibility to operate casinos or betting shops. Governments may well have become involved in gaming to secure a revenue stream which otherwise would have been enjoyed by SP bookies or unlicensed clubs. But if there are other ways to protect those revenues, governments don't have to run gaming businesses like the NSW TAB or Queensland TAB.

Yet governments may consider they have a responsibility to *control* gaming activity, partly to ensure that horse racing or poker machines are operated fairly, and partly to minimise the adverse effects of gambling on the young, or the addicted, and their families.

An inquiry conducted by the Productivity Commission into the gambling industry found, amongst other things, that:

- around 330,000 Australians have significant gambling problems, with 140,000 experiencing severe problems;
- the regulatory environment is deficient and regulations are complex, fragmented and often inconsistent arising from 'inconsistent policy-making processes and strong incentives for governments to derive revenue from the gambling industries' (*Productivity Commission*, July 1999).

This suggests that government ownership has not controlled problems associated with gambling and may even have established a conflict of interest.

Telstra

The partial sale of *Telstra* can be seen as having significant opportunity costs, since it has removed the opportunities for government to be a full participant in the development of electronic communications in Australia.

The 1990s have seen enormous growth in the IT&T industry, and the securities market reflects expectations about the potential of future growth. Indeed, the pricing of Internet and e-commerce stocks (often, despite a track record of losses) signifies the value being placed on any form of 'market share' in this industry.

Telstra management, for its part, appears to be acting commercially and seeking to develop Telstra's presence in the industry. A government majority shareholding will preserve an interest in those businesses. Debate on the future of the federal government's remaining stake in Telstra will continue. But already, the debate shifted in predictable fashion. To reassure the community before the first and second sale, it was emphasised that 'the government will retain a majority interest'. After the event, it is being claimed that 'being partly privatised is like being partly pregnant'. Expect more of that style of sloganeering in coming years.

CSL Ltd

All things considered, the main award in this category must go to the sale of *CSL Limited*.

The Commonwealth Serum Laboratories was established in

1916 to meet the pharmaceutical needs of a nation isolated by war (*The Age*, 3/3/92). CSL was initially a unit of the Commonwealth Department of Health; it was given a separate identity as the Commonwealth Serum Laboratories Commission in 1961, and in 1991 it was converted to a public company in terms of the Corporations Law.

By that time, CSL had a monopoly on the supply of blood plasma products to the Red Cross and Australian hospitals. It also sold human vaccines (including infant triple antigen), veterinary vaccines, antibiotics and diagnostic services (*SMH*, 20/8/92). To quote from one of CSL's annual reports, the company 'develops, manufactures and markets pharmaceutical products of biological origin'.

Early in 1992, CSL was described by David Williams, executive director of Hambros Australia as 'the jewel in the crown' of privatisation candidates because it was already making a profit, had significant potential to expand and the present management had done '90% of the cost trimming needed to bring the company to market' (*The Age*, 3/3/92). CSL had just reported a profit before interest and tax of $21.4 million (in a year of adverse trading conditions), giving a gross return on shareholders funds of around 14 per cent per annum.

The case for privatisation was actively supported by CSL's managing director, Dr Brian McNamee. According to McNamee, there were significant disadvantages for CSL if it remained government owned. Mark the words 'disadvantages for CSL'—not the community. McNamee explained that privatisation was necessary because of CSL's need for additional capital which could not be readily provided by the government:

> We have a lot of requirements for investment in plant upgrades, and to commercialise new 'R and D' projects properly.
>
> We may need to go back to the shareholder and say we need an extra $50 or $100 million. When you're owned by the Commonwealth you don't have the confidence that you'll be supported when you need the funds (*The Age*, 3/3/92).

McNamee went on to suggest that a private-sector corporation could raise funds from a rights issue in four to six weeks whereas a government-owned business could spend four to six years in dealing with bureaucracy for the same result. The latter observation seemed to ignore CSL's recent success in securing government financial support. CSL's 1994 annual report indicated that the Commonwealth had just chipped in $32 million for capital works and other projects, and had financed a facility at Broadmeadows which was then on-sold to CSL. Press reports indicated that the Commonwealth transferred 'full ownership of the new $209 million Broadmeadows processing plant to CSL for shares worth $150 million'. McNamee announced that 'full ownership will underpin CSL's long-term positioning as a leading manufacture of plasma products throughout the region and provide CSL with a secure cash flow well into the future' (*The Age*, 12/2/94).

In the event, the sale of shares in CSL did not inject a single dollar into CSL's coffers. Nor (except for minor sums raised from employee options) was any extra capital raised from the market in the next four years—CSL managed to finance future developments from a combination of government support for investment in the pharmaceutical industry, and internally-generated cash flows. But in 1992, the suggestion that the government should sell a business because it 'needed new capital' was a classic example of pro-privatisation rhetoric.

Within months of this advocacy of the privatisation of CSL, it was predicted that the sale would be announced in the next Commonwealth budget, and that the business 'could be worth between $90–100 million' (*SMH*, 20/8/1992). The government had ruled out the possibility of selling the group to a single foreign company, and proposed to restrict foreign ownership to a maximum 5 per cent stake for individual foreign groups.

A sidelight of the CSL privatisation was the way estimates of sale proceeds steadily escalated. The likely proceeds were reported in August 1992 to be around $90–$100 million; by October 1993, mention was made of a planned $250 million float (*AFR*, 22/10/93); by February 1994 the float was expected to raise $300 million (*The Age*, 12/2/94); and in May 1994 (after the market faltered) it was claimed that 'at least three major broking houses [had been] after several months of painstaking due-diligence investigations, prepared to sign-off on an agreement that would have virtually guaranteed the Federal government proceeds of around $350 million' (*AFR*, 5/5/94). When the float actually took place, the Commonwealth was reported to have collected around $292 million.

How to explain this steep increase in estimated (and later, actual) proceeds? One possibility is that either those responsible for the sale (and for briefing journalists), or the journalists reporting the story, did not really have a good idea of the value of a business which derived strong cash flows from a virtually monopolistic position as a seller of blood products in domestic markets (where the major purchaser, indirectly, was the Commonwealth government, as a major funder of the Australian health system).

Another possibility is that there were major changes in the nature of the risks of investment in the business which was being sold. For example, as the producer of pharmaceutical products, one of the key factors in assessing the market value of an organisation like CSL involves the risks of product liability. Investors in pharmaceutical companies recognise the risk of litigation and damages flowing from the release and sale of products which are later found defective, contaminated, or to have been released on the basis of skimpy or flawed research, or despite mounting evidence of adverse effects. In the event, responsibility for such claims arising from the pre-privatisation sale of products was assumed by the Commonwealth. The indemnity covered AIDS and hepatitis related claims for blood products derived from Australian blood, CJD claims for human pituitary hormones (manufacture of which ceased in 1985), and claims for pertussis vaccines manufactured prior to 3 June 1994.

In effect, this indemnity increased the headline sale price (and so enabled the Commonwealth to enhance its cash-based budget results). At the same time, the Commonwealth retained exposure to claims for product liability—an exposure which could have been divested to private shareholders.

In the 1994 public float, CSL shares were sold for $2.30, generating around $292 million for the Commonwealth government. After listing, the price of those shares steadily increased.

By late 1999, CSL shares were trading at $23, an increase of 900 per cent in less than five years. The market was saying that CSL shares had been sold at a bargain price, or around 1/10 of their value. That is why this float could easily fit into the 'loss of value' category of worst sales. Shareholders who bought in at the ground floor a few years earlier could rejoice. But no one would have grounds to rejoice more than CSL's managing director, Dr Brian McNamee.

One consequence of the corporation's newly privatised status was a steep increase in benefits payable to directors. McNamee's remuneration after privatisation was to increase by almost 25 per cent in a few years, to more than $510,000 per annum in 1997. But that was only part of his rewards. In August 1994, CSL put a proposal to shareholders to establish a retirement scheme for directors—a proposal described by representatives of the Australian Shareholders' Association as being both unrelated to performance, and significantly higher than industry standards—'so much higher that they border on being indecent' (*AFR*, 12/8/94). The proposals (which were only carried after an acrimonious poll) also included the issue of options to managing director McNamee.

CSL's audited financial statements reveal that McNamee was given an interest free loan of $1.4 million to take up options to acquire 600,000 CSL shares at $2.40. On the basis of late 1999 CSL prices of $23, that action would have delivered to this most vocal advocate of CSL's privatisation, an entitlement worth $13.8 million. A handy bonus.

Soon after CSL's privatisation, the Australia Institute claimed that the $292 million in proceeds which the government received from the sale of CSL will be lost soon after the first six years of the sale, and each year thereafter taxpayers will be $45 million worse off:

> That figure is calculated by subtracting $50 million a year in additional blood processing fees which the Commonwealth will pay CSL from $5 million in tax payments. CSL's $20 million to $30 million in expected profits will go to CSL rather than the Commonwealth. Professor Quiggin and Dr. Hamilton then discount that $45 million at 5 per cent (real government bond rate) to estimate the loss to taxpayers at $607 million (*SMH*, 9/8/95).

There is some merit in this argument (though the calculations may be contestable).

Certainly, a core component of CSL's earnings came from processing plasma and other products for use within the Australian health system. Curiously, while the company's up-beat reports to shareholders highlighted revenue growth for each of its divisions, CSL refused to disclose profit results by segments, coyly justifying this stance by claiming that it operated a single business—it was 'primarily in the pharmaceutical industry'. Yet media reports indicated that CSL 'made 40 per cent of its money from processing plasma domestically—blood supplied for free by the Red Cross—and selling it to the Commonwealth government at guaranteed prices' (*SMH*, 6/6/94). The Australia Institute observed:

> Since there is no commercial market for blood in Australia and the Government is virtually the monopoly purchaser of blood products, CSL's profits are heavily dependent on the regulatory and purchasing decisions of government (*SMH*, 6/6/94).

The existence of that economic dependency should have been disclosed to the public in terms of the requirements of Schedule 5 of the Corporations Law which requires an explanation of such relationships. The scale of that dependency should also have been disclosed in the 1994 annual report in terms of requirements for detailed disclosure of related party transactions (since the Commonwealth was 100 per cent shareholder before privatisation). Instead, the 1994 CSL annual report used a less emotive term, 'Significant purchaser', and stated:

Significant volumes of the chief entity's sales of human pharmaceutical and plasma products are to the Australian Government.

No attempt was made to quantify those sales. The 1994 report only disclosed the following:

> Sales to and purchases from the Australian Government were impracticable to quantify because of the complexity of the healthcare industry and the difficulty in defining entities controlled by the Australian Government.

In response to the Australia Institute's analysis, CSL's managing director Dr McNamee observed that 'the figures do not take into account the tremendous investment they have had to make in the facility, and continue to make' (*SMH*, 9/8/95). Given that in October 1993, McNamee had said that CSL wanted to complete construction before the float, so investors did not bear construction risks (*AFR*, 22/10/93), this seemed a strange observation. The construction of CSL's plant and equipment had been undertaken by the Commonwealth, just before the sale. The Commonwealth then sold out of CSL, at what history records was a bargain price, without enjoying any of the returns from its earlier investment.

So CSL is now in private hands, is operating commercially, and is enjoying profits from the sale of products which are effectively paid for by its former owner, the Commonwealth.

Moreover, the Commonwealth continues to support CSL in other ways. To quote from CSL's 1997 annual report:

> Your Company welcomed the Federal Government's decision to continue to compensate pharmaceutical companies (on a selective basis) for the effects of low prices for pharmaceuticals supplied under the Pharmaceutical Benefits Scheme and other Government price suppression policies.
>
> The Pharmaceutical Industry Investment Program has created an environment conducive to further investment at this time.
>
> The Company will be applying for ongoing price compensation under the PIIP . . .

However, the impact of the CSL sale may become evident in coming decades—not through the sale of a monopoly, and not through the extent of economic dependence on its former public sector owner. CSL was in the business of providing basic services to promote public health—and to meet the specialist needs of the Australian population (and smaller countries in the region—CSL has been providing blood and plasma products to New Zealand and Papua New Guinea).

CSL was formed to meet the needs of a nation at war. Perhaps those needs may not arise again. Perhaps a privately-owned business can meet the community needs for blood products and vaccinations and flu shots—albeit at a price. In the short term, CSL can exploit the findings from years of taxpayer-funded research. It may even spend more on research and development, with the aim of developing high-volume high-priced vaccines. But the sale process has probably meant that CSL will not regard serving the localised needs of the Australian community as a commercial priority.

Certainly CSL operates in a competitive industry (with a reputed 1100 pharmaceutical companies operating in the USA, alone). But how many US companies would bother investing in vaccines to deal with indigenous Australian snakes or spiders?

As Dr Struan Sutherland observed when the sale of CSL was first mooted, privatisation 'placed the future of venom and antivenom research in Australia in doubt' as

> researching and refining treatments for snake and spider bites was often unprofitable, and would have little appeal compared with products such as influenza vaccine ... (*The Age*, 14/12/92).

Badly handled privatisations

There are a host of potential nominations in this category, for varying reasons. A selection follows.

Intimidation to prevent public debate: HLIC

The saga of the sale of the Housing Loans Insurance Corporation, stretching over almost two decades (1979 to 1997) is a good example of how privatisation decisions can be made without a full understanding of either what the government might lose in earnings, or the social ramifications of the sale. The decision to put the Corporation on the market seemed to have been made on the basis of blatant political lobbying by an industry which was unhappy about a government-owned business making profits in an area that private firms had previously avoided. But the highlight of the HLIC privatisation was the reaction of politicians and the public service when pertinent facts about the proposed sale came to light.

As outlined above, HLIC had been adopting highly conservative accounting policies, reporting profits on its single-premium mortgage insurance business even after it only treated receipts of insurance premiums as revenues over an extended period of time—the balance being treated as a liability provision for unearned income. Back of the envelope calculations undertaken by one of the authors in 1989 suggested that this provision was overstated in HLIC's books, since the risk of default diminished rapidly after the early years of a mortgage. In effect, HLIC was understating its reported income.

Apparently the Commonwealth government's Asset Sales Task Force commissioned a firm of actuaries to examine HLIC's provisioning, and in time-honoured fashion, the substance of the report was leaked to the media. The response was startling. Federal Police raided the offices of *The Australian Financial Review*, armed with search warrants, to go through the desk of the journalist who had written the story about HLIC's profitability. The warrant referred to 'reasonable grounds' for believing that a Commonwealth officer had disclosed information: an offence under section 70(1) of the Crimes Act 1914 which carried a maximum penalty of two years in jail (*AFR*, 6/7/90).

Peter Robinson, then editor in chief of the offending newspaper, was amazed that the Hawke government had sought to intimidate journalists in this fashion, and observed that 'Ministers, the most senior bureaucrats, advisers and consultants all leak like sieves when its suits their purposes.'

> But why this particular matter should have been chosen to teach the media a lesson is rather difficult to understand.
>
> So far as can be gauged from the published stories, its disclosure or non-disclosure has not the slightest bearing on any threat to the national interest—at the most, there is a narrow coterie of bureaucrats and business interests who may prefer not to see the information more widely disseminated (*Sun-Herald*, 8/7/90).

Amen to that. But this response seemed to accept that the material which was leaked to the journalist (after it had already been provided in confidence to six insurance companies and a firm of accountants) had some commercial sensitivity. A leader in the *Sydney Morning Herald* noted that, given the prior distribution of the actuary's report to short-listed potential buyers, there was no question that anyone 'stood to make a significant economic gain from the publication of the details of the report'. Further

> The Government likes to talk about open and transparent economic debate. If it really wants this, it should see that the Department of Finance calls off the witch hunt (*SMH*, 7/7/90).

The media (and later, the Australian Press Council, and a ginger group, the Free Speech Committee) focused on unprecedented efforts to intimidate journalists and claimed there had been a misuse of State power. But the really significant issue was that the community was being denied information about the real profitability of a business that the government had been trying to sell. Surely this information should have been made available, and adequately explained, not just to potential bidders, but to the parliament.

One of the authors had a special interest in this incident. The day of the Police raid on the Fairfax press, a telephone caller conveyed whispered advice about this event, and the suggestion any papers on the HLIC be immediately burnt. It was assumed by the caller that some earlier comments made about the over-provisioning at HLIC had been based on access to leaked documents. They weren't. They were based on reading published reports and data, and some calculations (literally) on the back of an envelope.

Undermining value: ANL

Another possible candidate for the 'worst handled privatisation' award is the way a Labor government in Canberra set about the sale of the Australian National Line. The sale of ANL might have been regarded as inevitable. If the Keating government hadn't sold it, the incoming Howard government would have done so anyway.

An Australian government owned shipping line was always going to have trouble competing with flag-of-convenience vessels operating with low-paid crews. In one sense, the continuation of the operations of ANL was a symbolic gesture of independence. The island continent of Australia would have its own supply lines for heavy cargoes. The retention of ANL was a contribution to national security. A country with its own fleet of ships was in a better position than one without those resources to provide logistical support to defence forces or to maintain supplies of goods to its population.

In other industries or in other circumstances, the contribution of particular forms of infrastructure to national security seems to be given some weight, though without ever being openly acknowledged. The now-defunct Prices Justification Tribunal and Prices Surveillance Authority made determinations which had the effect of ensuring that inefficient but geographically dispersed petroleum refineries were still able to operate. From a defence point of view, that makes good sense: it would be foolish to concentrate refining capacity in one or two sites. Similarly, the Commonwealth Grants Commission, in the guise of ensuring that members of communities in all states and territories have access to a comparable standard of services, has funded roadworks in the Northern Territory to a standard far beyond the needs of the existing population. Yet those near-empty highways may be of value some day, in a defence context.

ANL was virtually bankrupt in 1983, with accumulated looses of $41 million, debt of more than $600 million, 'and a fleet of ships which were old and fuel inefficient. The average age of the fleet was more than twenty years' while unprofitable services—particularly the passenger trade across Bass Strait and coastal trade routes to North Queensland and Darwin—were adding to ANL's difficulties (*Dempster*, 1997). Rather than close down ANL at that time, and crystallising ANL's debts, the Commonwealth government chose to attempt to 'trade out' of the situation. Commonwealth loans of $110 million were converted to equity, and industry reform began.

The industrial history of the Australian waterfront has been characterised by conflict and distrust. The Maritime Union of Australia has been a tough negotiator and has long been in a position of strength: if industrial disagreements meant that the workforce did not unload a cargo, the cost of delays to the shipper and the owners of those cargoes would often be more than the cost of acceding to demands.

At the same time, few unions can boast of such cohesion within their ranks, or have such a record of generosity to others. That solidarity stems from a history of adversity—though in recent years the take-home pay of some maritime workers would probably be the envy of even some members of the medical or legal professions. A union ticket to work on the wharves could be valuable, and has been 'kept in the family'.

Technological change has substantially reduced the need for the numbers of stevedoring workers required in the hard and risky days when many cargoes were loaded and unloaded manually. By 1994, when the sale of ANL was under consideration, the Commonwealth government had invested around $300–$400 million in 'waterfront reform'—mainly on redundancy payments aimed at reducing the size of the workforce and in creating incentives for improved efficiencies.

One outcome of these investments was that the government found itself the owner of 25 per cent of a stevedoring company—Australian Stevedores—through ANL. Moreover, its equity interest in Australian Stevedores was subject to a Monte Carlo option: if one shareholder wanted out, then the other shareholders could either sell as well, or be a buyer. (The other interests were held 25 per cent by Howard Smith, and 50 per cent by Jamieson Equities.)

ANL could have picked up an additional 25 per cent in Australian Stevedores for around $28 million, but statements by the then Minister for Transport, Laurie Brereton in August 1994 (described below) made that, or any other moves, impossible. Hence, taxpayers lost the chance to enjoy direct returns from their earlier investment in waterfront reform, through ANL upping its stake in a business poised to gain from a recovery in the economy.

Make no mistake, the stevedoring industry was potentially very profitable—even though Australian Stevedores' financial statements had written-up depreciable assets (by $19.3 million in 1993) so as to increase reported depreciation charges and hence reduce reported profits. The use of these accounting tricks—virtually unprecedented by private sector firms—might have seemed like good strategy for a company planning to retrench more of its workforce. But it doesn't follow that a government, as owner of 25 per cent of the company's shares, should have taken those accounting results at face value.

However, in 1991 the Commonwealth government had proposed to sell up to 49 per cent of ANL, and ANL's board chaired by Captain Bill Bolitho proposed a merger with Howard Smith Limited prior to a later float of the government's share in the merged enterprise. Instead the government's Task Force on Asset Sales invited eight merchant banks to express interest in handling the sale. Captain Bolitho—whose later public expressions of concern about the process were documented in Quentin Dempster's account of Australian whistleblowers—complained to the then Minister for Transport Bob Collins that this 'was bound to establish a fire sale mentality ... in which the true value of ANL would not be realised' (*Dempster*, 1997).

And so it came to pass—and along the way, the Government quietly decided to sell not just a minority interest but all of ANL.

The 1993 accounts of Australian National Line showed total shareholders' funds of $157.6 million. On 28 October 1993, the Auditor-General's office gave those accounts an unqualified report. Most of the audit work was carried out by Ernst & Young. Yet in August 1994, a new Transport Minister, Laurie Brereton announced that, according to Price Waterhouse and Salomon Bros, ANL had a value of *negative* $75 million to $118 million. The national shipping line, he said, *couldn't be given away*.

Taxpayers might have contemplated how ANL's $158 million shareholders' equity could turn into negative $118 million in just ten months. Some press stories suggested the turnaround cast doubt on the quality of scrutiny by the Commonwealth Auditor-General. It didn't, for the simple reason that there's a difference between a balance sheet prepared on a 'going concern' basis, and one prepared on a forced sale basis. Both the Australian National Audit Office and Ernst & Young concluded in October 1993 that ANL was a going concern. Arthur Andersen & Co took over the ANL contract, and press reports suggested that the ANAO (presumably, with Andersen's advice) concluded that ANL was still a going concern as late as April 1994.

Plainly, the report from Price Waterhouse and Salomon Bros, which had been commissioned by the Assets Sales Task Force B, valued ANL's assets and liabilities on the basis of a forced sale. A very forced sale.

The question has to be asked, why? And what were the consultants asked to do?

Only a 30 page 'executive summary' of what is reputed to be a 600-page report was released. Of that, most of the interesting bits were blacked out. Left untouched were passages claiming that ANL was unprofitable at the EBIT (earnings before interest and taxes) level—that is, before financing costs. This claim arose from unexplained adjustments to the audited figures.

It appears from what was published at the time that the consultants chose not to analyse ANL's track record on the basis of net cash flows to the Commonwealth. They claimed that in recent years, ANL had been a poor investment (the Commonwealth's major 'investment' was a $130 million debt for equity swap in the early 1980s). There was no reference to the overall cash flows provided to the Commonwealth by ANL through dividends, company taxes, or maritime fuel taxes. Nor was there any assessment of the long-run economic impact of ANL activities on shipping costs to Australia's local and international trade.

On the other hand, the consultants' discussion of ANL's prospects emphasised bad news. Projections of gross cash flows referred to the need to buy or charter new vessels—though without making clear whether cash flows from the sale of old vessels have been deducted. Again, the projected cash flows focused on ANL, rather than the overall cash flows from ANL's activities to the Commonwealth.

Plainly ANL had not been a good earner. It did not have a guaranteed trade, except in coastal shipping. It paid its crews Australian rates of pay, had a relatively modern fleet and maintained ships to local safety standards.

On the other hand, ANL did not appear to have been a big loser. Indeed, a surprising feature of the consultants' report was the projection that ANL would record a loss from operations (before finance costs) in 1993–94 of around $12 million—when the company had apparently projected at least a break-even result. Again, information published at the time did not explain what adjustments to accounting data had been made by the consultants.

From what *was* published of the consultants' report, it can be ascertained that:

- ANL's 14 ships, containers and other equipment had been written down below 1993 audited book values. The consultants said they used 'estimated asset realisation values'. These estimates of the value of ships were an arbitrary 70 per cent of the figures provided by expert valuers, Drewry Shipping Consultants Limited. The values of containers and equipment were reduced even more. All up, these write-downs contributed almost half of the $276 million adjustments made to ANL's 1993 audited balance sheet figures for net assets;
- no value was assigned to shares in conference agreements—the basis on which ANL was entitled to a share of the shipping trade to Europe and Asian ports. Arguably, they would be ANL's most sought-after assets;
- reported liabilities included sums payable on termination of operating leases, and on cancellation of financing facilities for two vessels. Inclusion of these items was only valid if the business was closing down, or if ANL was in liquidation or receivership;
- reported liabilities also included $69.4 million for redundancy and other liabilities—apparently on the assumption that the entire workforce would be retrenched.

Soon after Brereton's announcement, the media disclosed that ANL had been suffering from cut-throat competition in the Asian trade, from rival fleets of low-value ships manned by cut-price foreign crews, whose owners (notably the Peoples Republic of China) were reputedly interested in earning hard currency rather than seeking a commercial rate of return.

However, if ANL stood to produce a 1993–94 profit result which was either break-even or better, that was hardly cause for the consultants to adopt fire-sale valuations. Indeed, the pessimistic Price Waterhouse and Salomon Bros report recommended further study to explore the likely financial outcome of a reconstruction, a rationalisation-driven trade sale of part of the business (presumably with priority given to divestiture of the European trade) or a 'managed trade down'.

In the end, Brereton just sacked the ANL Board and installed a new team. But then the Minister went on to tell the world that ANL was not just worthless, it had a negative value.

Kenneth Davidson of Melbourne's *Age* newspaper described Brereton's announcement as 'an act of economic vandalism':

> Before [last] Tuesday, I could not have imagined that any vendor, from a curbside stall up, let alone a Minister of the Crown responsible for a strategic community asset, and who hopes to sell that asset, would

say about that asset: 'You couldn't give it away, that is the reality ... it's a pretty dismal picture' (*The Age*, 27/8/94).

Davidson might have added that the Minister had even ignored his consultants' advice to proceed cautiously with a 'managed trade-down' of ANL's business. Top priority would probably have been closure of the European route, which had been the main loser.

Yet there's some irony in the fact that the executive summary of the consultants' report had passages blacked out to avoid *commercial damage* to ANL. One has to wonder what potential for commercial damage could remain after the Minister actively publicised the worst-case scenario:

You couldn't give it away ...

Those five words are a wonderful example of how not to do business, let alone explain to the community why a national asset should be sold.[1]

High transaction costs: GIO

The NSW Coalition government's handling of the float of the Government Insurance Office (GIO) warrants nomination as one of Australia's worst privatisations—though not because of low price. Nor could many quibble with the idea of a government selling off an insurance company: in the 1990s, insurance can hardly be viewed as a core, public sector activity.

Some might argue that government involvement in the insurance industry is justified as a means of maintaining competition and keeping premium costs down for ordinary consumers. However, it is not clear that GIO really operated as a price leader. Moreover, GIO's activities raised questions about the role of a government-owned insurer. Pressured to produce a stream of dividends for the NSW government, GIO had become involved in the high-risk international reinsurance business. No one seems to have asked the question publicly, but some watchers wondered what a state-owned

---

1 ANL later 'turned a small profit following the disposal of loss-making operations' and it was reported that its main international division was to be sold to the French company Compagnie Generale Maritime, while an Australian-Canadian joint venture AUSCAN Self Unloading was the preferred bidder for ANL's domestic bulk trades business. Other components of ANL were to be sold separately (*SMH*, 31/7/98). The Commonwealth's Office of Asset Sales and IT Outsourcing later reported through its website www.oasito.gov.au that the Commonwealth had realised $21 million during 1998-99 from the sale of various shipping interests of Australian River Co. Limited (formerly ANL Limited).

business was doing, punting taxpayers' funds on the outcome of Indian satellite launches.

As for price, shares in GIO bounced a bit on listing in July 1992, but soon slipped below the issue price, and took some time to recover. By 1998, GIO was subject to a hostile takeover bid from AMP and AMP gained control but not enough shares to compulsorily acquire minorities. The incoming management of GIO reported reduced profits in 1999 as GIO's provisioning was reassessed in the wake of reinsurance losses initially thought to be around $300 million (an unwelcome surprise to those shareholders who believed that a new board had been pursuing a less risky course). Losses had also been incurred from a Sydney hailstorm—claimed to be the most expensive natural disaster in Australia's history. Reinsurance losses were found to be worse that first thought, and GIO's share price languished, before AMP announced proposals to buy out minorities in September 1999, and later lowered its suggested offer to around half of what it had paid a year earlier during its takeover bid. GIO has since been fully absorbed by AMP.

But to return to earlier times: GIO warrants nomination as one of Australia's worst privatisation.

The transaction costs (advisers, preparation of the prospectus, marketing and underwriting) were among the highest ever experienced in a privatisation. From the perspective of some privatisation enthusiasts, the transaction costs were truly world-class. Not that the costs were disclosed openly (see Box 8.1). Calculations required a careful reading of state Budget Papers. The Coalition government may have been mindful of its extravagance, since it seemed intent on keeping the costs secret, and issuing inflated estimates of the sale proceeds.

The costs of privatising GIO amounted to some $71 million—or around 6 per cent of the $1,200 million raised from the public issue.

That was significantly more than average spending on private sector capital raisings. A survey of 472 capital raisings during 1981–90 showed there were considerable economies of scale: costs of around 6 per cent of proceeds were only incurred by prospectuses seeking $10 million or less, while the costs of five offerings above $100 million averaged only 3.7 per cent (*Woo & Lange*, 1992).

The $71 million spent on the GIO float was spread around accounting and legal firms, stockbrokers and advertising agencies, mainly in the Sydney region. Given that the GIO privatisation was one of the first GTE sales in Australia, the exercise may well have drawn the attention of these firms to the 'attractions' of privatisation.

Australia's Worst Privatisations

Box 8.1
TRACKING DOWN THE COST OF THE GIO FLOAT

Prospectus disclosures: The GIO prospectus, issued in June 1992, provided the following list of payments to 'experts' for the formation or promotion of GIO Holdings or in property proposed to be acquired by GIO:

Investigating accountants to GIO Australia	$4.26m
Investigating actuaries—reinsurance	0.17m
Investigating accountants on behalf of NSW govt	3.71m
Investigating actuaries—life insurance	1.65m
Investigating accountants—general insurance	1.21m
Financial adviser to the government	1.01m
Joint underwriters	1.22m
Solicitors to GIO Holdings	1.76m
Solicitors to the underwriters	0.41m
Solicitors to the NSW government	0.59m

This list of expenses totalled $15.99 million. Some of the expenses listed (plus advertising and associated expenses) were borne by the NSW government, not GIO. The prospectus revealed that 'the costs of privatisation to be borne by GIO Holdings are estimated to be $10 million'. However, both this figure and the list totalling $15.99 million were understated since they did not include expenses such as printing and advertising.

Disclosures in Budget Papers and Ministerial Press Statements: *1992–93 NSW Budget Paper No. 2* claimed that the GIO privatisation was estimated to realise gross proceeds of $1.8 billion, comprising:

- Sale proceeds of $1,200 million which will be applied to reduce State debt;
- Commonwealth tax compensation of $430 million which will be reflected in an equivalent reduction in debt owing to the Commonwealth;
- Payment of the equivalent of Commonwealth income and sales tax of an estimated $65.6 million;
- Deferred tax owing, paid in the form of a transfer of property of $115.8 million. The intention will be to realise this property at an appropriate opportunity and use the proceeds to reduce debt.

Note that the relevant sales proceeds figure was actually $1.2 billion, representing the net proceeds raised by the prospectus. The Commonwealth tax compensation reflected a deal negotiated between the two governments (in the wake of a similar arrangement which provided financial support to the Victorian government after the sale of the State Bank of Victoria to the Commonwealth Bank). That transaction had nothing to do with privatisation *per se*. Likewise, other items listed represented funds and resources effectively stripped from the GIO before it was privatised.

A *News Release* issued by the Premier of NSW on 14 August 1992 revealed that net proceeds of the GIO privatisation on the same basis were $1.75 billion.

Hence the cost of the float can be estimated as follows:

Gross proceeds (per *1992–93 Budget Paper No. 2*)	$1,811.3m
Less Net proceeds (per *News Release* 14 August 1992)	1,750.0m
Costs incurred by NSW government	61.3m
Add Costs incurred by GIO Holdings (per Prospectus)	10.0m
Total cost of float	$ 71.3m

Privatisation

This estimate was largely confirmed by other figures contained in the *1992–93 NSW Budget Papers*, notably the following disclosures about the GIO privatisation:

	1991–92 Actual $000	1992–93 Estimate $000
Logistics and marketing	4,213	8,000
Consultancies	6,261	3,250
Advertising	6,286	7,300
Travelling and other expenses	112	1,450
Underwriting	3,708	20,000
	20,580	40,000

More directly, when the above estimate of $71.3 million in transaction costs were initially published (*Walker and Howard*, 1992) the then NSW Assistant Treasurer George Souris claimed that these estimates were false and overstated, and that the paper was a 'grubby little document'. However a few hours later, on the ABC's *7.30 Report*, Souris told interviewer Quentin Dempster, 'the figures are not disputed'.

The transaction costs of $71.3 million represented 5.94 per cent of the proceeds of the float.

This was almost double the $37.8 million incurred in 1991 by the Commonwealth and the Commonwealth Bank for a share issue, which raised more ($1,292.22 million) (*Walker and Howard*, 1992).

Small wonder that members of the same occupational groups have been among the most fervent advocates of privatisation.

The aggregate fees payable on the GIO sale were later eclipsed by other deals. For example, the Commonwealth's direct costs in arranging the sale of the first tranche of Telstra shares were some $260 million, while Telstra estimated is own costs at $15 million. But that was still around 1.8 per cent of the proceeds.

The GIO transaction stands as an Australian record for the level of fees (as a proportion of sale proceeds) paid to private sector advisers in privatisations. Arguably the overall (world) record for a sizeable float is held by those responsible for the floats of British Telecom (6.8 per cent) and British Gas (6.4 per cent). The following Table details the costs of some notable UK privatisation floats.

To some extent the high costs of the British Telecom float is understandable. That float was a landmark in the globalisation of securities markets. Because of its scale, the offering was made simultaneously in both the UK and the USA—an exercise which involved extensive negotiations with regulators in the two jurisdictions because of differences in securities laws. The resultant issue-documents contained a British-style prospectus with a 'wrap around' prospectus to meet the requirements of the USA's Securities and Exchange Commission.

Table 8.1
COSTS OF SOME UK PRIVATISATION FLOATS

Company (year of float)	Expenses £m	Gross proceeds £m	Expenses/ Gross proceeds %
Cable & Wireless (1981)	7	224	3.1
British Aerospace (1981)	6	149	3.8
Amersham (1982)	3	63	4.6
Britoil (1982)	17	548	3.2
Assoc. British Ports (1983)	2	22	11.2
Enterprise Oil (1984)	11	393	2.8
British Telecom (1984)	263	3,916	6.8
British Gas (1986)	360	5,603	6.4
British Airways (1987)	42	900	4.7
12 regional electricity companies	191	5,181	3.7

Source: *Vickers & Yarrow* (1988); (UK) *National Audit Office* (1992).

Eroding investor protections: GIO

The GIO sale was also an Australian landmark in the history of securities market regulation, and deserves nomination on that ground as well. The GIO sale was a remarkable exercise in the erosion of traditional investor protections. It was also significant as a demonstration of how public moneys could be used for political purposes—in this instance, to promote an ideological position about privatisation.

The GIO float was preceded by an expensive marketing campaign (see Box 8.2).

The Australian Securities Commission had already eroded a fundamental building block of investor protection: the prohibition on pre-prospectus advertising. Indeed, the earlier Commonwealth Bank float could also have been nominated as one of Australia's 'worst privatisations' on that basis. The ASC allowed the bank to mount an expensive advertising campaign (reputedly costing $4.3 million) to promote the share issue before a prospectus was available. Moreover, the Commonwealth Bank prospectus was the first significant prospectus to be issued in terms of the new Commonwealth Corporations Law. That legislation saw the abandonment of an earlier regime of pre-vetting of prospectus documents in favour of a de-regulatory approach which established broad guidelines for the content of prospectuses, and provided for near automatic registration of offer documents with

BOX 8.2
MARKETING SHARES IN GIO

The GIO privatisation account was won by advertising agency NMB&B/Weekes Morris Osborn in what was described as 'one of the top account pitches of 1991', and estimated to be worth up to $10 million . . . (*SMH*, 21/12/91). The extensive electronic and print media campaign which followed proceeded in stages.

The initial advertisements in January 1992—later described as a $2.1 million educational campaign (*SMH*, 9/7/92)—promoted the benefits of 'privatisation', without any direct reference to GIO:

> Privatisation is for everyone. Not just for big investors, but for small investors too. Throughout the world, in over 80 different countries, privatisation of government business is providing opportunities for large and small investors alike . . . (*Sunday Telegraph*, 26/1/92).

Other advertisements promoted the message that the funds produced by privatisation would be diverted to develop infrastructure and improve community services:

> Privatisation is for everyone.
> It means more money for hospitals.
> We all want better hospitals and more medical staff. With the money raised by privatising certain government businesses we can reduce the burden of state debt and make more funds available for important community needs such as hospitals, roads, schools and the police (*Sunday Telegraph*, 26/1/92).

> Privatisation is for everyone.
> It means more money for the Police Service.
> Essential community services such as the police will benefit as a result of the Government's privatisation programme—because the money raised by privatisation reduces the burden of state debt and frees more funds for important community needs such as the police, roads, schools and hospitals (*Sunday Telegraph*, 9/2/92).

The next phase of the GIO advertising campaign was directly aimed at promoting interest in the GIO float:

> Soon everyone can own a piece of GIO Australia. The prospectus for the GIO Australia Public Share Offer will soon be available (*Sun-Herald*, 21/5/92).

A mail-out campaign distributed brochures which included a series of Questions and Answers—including the following:

> 3. Why should I reserve a prospectus?
> As the offer will be open for a limited time only, early receipt of the prospectus will give you more time to consider the information about the share offer in the prospectus.

The paid campaign thus deliberately emphasised the notion that the GIO offering would only be open 'for a limited time' and that shareholders should be quick to lodge their applications. Advertisements, appearing one day before the issue opened, urged shareholders to rush to invest.

the Australian Securities Commission. This approach relied on private shareholders to seek civil remedies if they had been misled. Section 1022 of the Corporations Law asserts that a prospectus should contain 'all such information as investors and their professional advisers would reasonably require and reasonably expect to find in [a] prospectus' for the purpose of making 'informed assessments' about such matters as the financial position, profits and prospects of the corporation.

To many observers, the Commonwealth Bank's prospectus established a disappointing benchmark in terms of the new requirements, since it did not contain a profit forecast—and hence did not provide information about the 'prospects of the corporation'. To others, the omission was defensible provided the prospectus contained sufficient information to enable potential investors to make their own judgements about the extent to which past profit or cash flow streams were sustainable, and the potential impact of changes in activities on reported performance. The Commonwealth Bank presented a lengthy prospectus, leaving it to investors to make up their own minds before subscribing.

After the Commonwealth Bank float, prospectuses issued under the new regulatory regime have steadily provided less and less information. The much vaunted test of 'all such information as investors and their professional advisers would reasonably require and reasonably expect to find' in a prospectus became less significant, as prospectuses registered by the Australian Securities Commission progressively contained less substantive information, and fewer reports from experts on critical issues. Moreover, the high cost of commercial litigation deterred aggrieved investors from seeking compensation for losses incurred from their reliance on offer documents which were misleading or incomplete.

But in 1992 the GIO float marked a serious attack on the prospectus rules. Again, the Australian Securities Commission issued a class order approving a request from the NSW government to approve pre-prospectus advertising (*ASC Memo* 11/92). The promoters then launched an extensive marketing campaign (see Box 8.2).

The high expenditure on advertising the float was justified by NSW Minister George Souris in the following terms:

> We would like to see maximum public participation in this important privatisation project and to this end, the NSW Government will be conducting a public information program to ensure that everyone has the opportunity to consider the issues first hand (*SMH*, 21/12/91).

In the event, Souris and Premier Nick Greiner were soon creating the impression that investors had little time to 'consider issues first hand' if they were not to miss out.

The Australian Securities Commission was very cooperative in granting relief from the prospectus rules. It responded positively to a succession of requests for relief from the Corporations Law to also allow documents to be sent to existing staff or customers, announcements to journalists and displays at offices, information to be sent to advisers, the issue of questionnaires to prospective investors regarding the privatisation, and 'notification' forms to be sent to persons who had requested a copy of the prospectus (*ASC Instruments 92/362, 92/363, 92/364, 92/365, & 92/275*).

No party was provided with an exemption from section 1026(3) of the Corporations Law, which states that a person who is aware that a prospectus for the issue of securities was in preparation or had been issued

> shall not publish a report that is reasonably likely to induce persons to apply for those securities.

The aim of that provision was to protect investors, by avoiding a climate in which unsophisticated individuals are placed under pressure to subscribe for securities. Similar rules prohibit the hawking of shares by door-to-door salesman or direct mail campaigns.

Yet, aided by the print media, the NSW government proceeded to issue a series of 'reports' in which government ministers actively encouraged small investors to rush their applications. The *Sunday Telegraph* (24/5/92) headline was: 'Govt prepares rush on GIO float':

> The State Government will take the first step towards privatisation of the GIO today amid signs of a rush by 'mums and dads' to secure shares in the company.
>
> The Minister responsible for the sale, George Souris, yesterday revealed shares would be sold on a 'first come first served' basis in what was shaping up to be one of the largest floats in Australia's history.
>
> 'It's going to be first in, best dressed and small investors will get 100 per cent of what they want,' he said.

Souris also offered statements which make interesting reading in the context of section 1026(3) of the Commonwealth Corporations Law:

> 'Since the offer is open for a limited time, early receipt of a prospectus ensures the maximum time for people to consider information about the share offer,' Mr. Souris said.
>
> 'What we are going to do is have a first in, best dressed situation.
>
> 'However, reserving a prospectus does not oblige anyone to take up shares.'

He said the response from GIO's one million policy-holders had far exceeded expectations.

'We have been astounded that even before the advertising campaign has started, the flow of coupons to reserve a prospectus was 32,000 on day one, and has continued unabated,' he said.

'It was pandemonium on day one' (*Sunday Telegraph*, 24/5/92).

Such statements were not isolated events. On 15 June 1992 it was reiterated that the GIO float would be on a 'first come first served' basis, and Souris announced that 375,000 people had already applied for copies of the prospectus, while the press indicated that institutional investors were 'already bidding strongly for stock' (*SMH*, 15/6/92). A week later Premier Greiner contributed to the excitement, by revealing that 'more than 420,000 people had reserved prospectuses' (*Telegraph Mirror*, 23/6/92). In the event, more than 425,000 people rang GIO offices to reserve a prospectus by the due date of 22 June 1992 (*AFR*, 23/6/92).

The last advertisements issued to promote the GIO float deserve to be read carefully in the context of section 1026(3) of the Corporations Law. Recall that a person who is aware that a prospectus for the issue of securities was in preparation or had been issued

> shall not publish a report that is reasonably likely to induce persons to apply for those securities

Full-page advertisements published by the NSW government were blatantly inconsistent with the notion that prospective investors should only invest after studying a prospectus. Readers can assess for themselves whether the text was likely to induce persons to apply for GIO shares, and to so do in a hurry:

> The GIO Australia public share offer opens 9 am tomorrow. Get a piece before someone beats you to it.
>
> The opportunity to own a piece of one of Australia's top 100 companies may only be available for a very short time.
>
> This historic offer may close shortly.
>
> Applications are more likely to be successful if lodged early (*Sun-Herald*, 28/6/92).

The issue opened at 9 a.m. on Monday 29 June 1992. The Assistant Treasurer George Souris 'was reported on radio [on 29 June 1992] as saying that it could close as early as tomorrow' (*AFR*, 30/6/92). In the event the share issue closed oversubscribed at 5 p.m. on 30 June 1992, 'just 32 hours after opening' (*AFR*, 1/6/92). There were reports that 'thousands of small investors [had] missed out on the $1.2 billion share issue, many of whom had borrowed money to buy the shares' (*AFR*, 7/7/92). One estimate was that 20,000—

30,000 applications were to be returned (*Sun-Herald*, 5/7/92).

Whatever the legal position, some commentators were in no doubt that the campaign induced a 'stampede' (*Sun-Herald*, 5/7/92) or a 'mad scramble' to buy shares (*Business Review Weekly*, 28/8/92). Robert Gottliebsen, editor of *BRW*, wrote:

> In the scramble to get shares, few people tried to read the prospectus. Even if they made the attempt, their chances of gaining an understanding of the company were not good: it was one of the most confusing documents ever presented to Australian investors.

The broad aim of the prospectus requirements in the Corporations Law were to ensure that prospective investors are afforded the opportunity to make informed judgements in a calm and reasoned way. In those terms, the GIO privatisation was a classic illustration of the kind of practices the Corporations Law set out to prevent.

Arguably the worst feature of this episode was the way that, having observed a pattern of public statements and advertisements which induced a 'stampede', Australia's securities market regulator, the ASC, chose not to intervene. The most it could do was express some misgivings about the conduct of the GIO float—well after the event:

> ASC member Bill Robinson criticised the GIO ads for taking advantage of a relaxation of the ban on advertising because it was a government body.
>
> An ASC spokesman said yesterday: the concern with the GIO float ads was that the GIO was suggesting if you did not get in quickly you might miss out.
>
> The spokesman said the GIO ads ... were not illegal but were cause for concern (*Sun-Herald*, 13/9/92).

Not illegal? Perhaps a better explanation was provided by staff of the ASC. One of the authors invited the Australian Securities Commission to consider whether there had been breaches of subsection 1026(3) of the Corporations Law. At a later meeting of an ASC liaison committee, ASC staff were quizzed about progress with their investigations into this matter. The public response was that the individuals concerned were protected by 'the shield of the Crown'.

That might leave two former NSW Ministers off the hook, but it still raised questions about the responsibilities of advertising agents and others who had endorsed advertisements which stampeded investors by urging them to subscribe for shares in GIO 'before someone beats you to it'. The privatisation tainted the record of the newly-established Australian Securities Commission—and thus marked the decline of an agency in which many had invested high hopes. Whatever the 'concern' and tut-tutting of the regulators, practices have not improved.

The recent sale of the second tranche of Telstra shares saw a repetition of 'stampeding'-style advertisements, and a countdown: 'only 3 days left', 'only 2 days left'. What made the Telstra issue worse was that the Federal government only provided a stripped-down 'public offer document' to investors who had previously registered interest in receiving prospectus information. The public offer document was not a full prospectus, and contained minimal financial information. Potential investors had to read the fine print to discover that if they wanted to examine the detail of Telstra's performance and prospects they had to ask for a detailed 'appendix'. Delivery of this took another 10–14 days, by which time, for many applicants, count-down advertisements were already appearing, and government spokesmen were telling the press about a late rush of applications, and there was speculation that the government might have to scale-down entitlements to individual investors (thus encouraging subscribers to over-bid).

Poorly designed sale arrangements: Pipeline Authority

Mention of the Commonwealth-owned Pipeline Authority brings back memories of the vision of Whitlam government minister Rex Connor—and his grand visions of a national network to distribute natural gas, and his naive view of how to get capital to fund such ventures through contacts with self-styled international financiers. Those memories are reminders that politicians can be catapulted into positions where they are responsible for investment and financing decisions involving billions of dollars, without having prior qualifications or experience in financial matters.

Nevertheless, Connor's vision was grand, and far-sighted. The Pipeline Authority was established in 1973 to construct pipelines for the conveyance of natural gas and other hydrocarbons to centres of population and point of export, with a view to the establishment of a national integrated system, and the maintenance and operation of those pipelines. Initially, it assumed responsibility for constructing a pipeline from Moomba to Sydney, which had already been proposed by the Australian Gaslight Company (AGL).

> The original concept ... took account of long-term issues such as defence, decentralisation, population growth, national development, inter-connected supplies, emergency situations, exhaustion of particular regional energy resources and possible future export of liquefied natural gas (*Sixteenth Annual Report*, 1988–89).

A pipeline system, owned by the Commonwealth government, could be a powerful instrument in promoting economic development, supporting the development of competitive industries, and in ensuring that private sector consumers had access to basic services. Indeed, without government intervention and support, the private sector could not readily obtain rights to establish easements for the construction of pipelines across privately-owned lands. The original 1973 vision was for a national grid:

> The first step involved construction of a pipeline linking the city of Sydney with the natural gas fields in the Cooper Basin in South Australia, with early extension through Wagga Wagga to Albury and Wodonga, and with ultimate extension to Melbourne and the Bass Strait reserves. It was envisaged that the pipeline from the Cooper Basin would later be extended to the Palm Valley field in the Amadeus Basin of the Northern Territory. From there it was to continue to Dampier on the north-west coast of Australia where the resources of the Northwest shelf would be available, and to traverse and serve the Pilbara region of Western Australia. Also a spur line was to serve the Northern Territory (*Sixteenth Annual Report*, 1988–89).

Construction commenced in 1974, and the first 1,300 kilometre pipeline from Moomba to Sydney was commissioned in 1976. Off-takes served regional centres. Lateral pipelines were added in the following years: Young–Wagga Wagga (130 km, 1981), Dalton–Canberra (58 km, 1981) and Young–Orange–Bathurst–Oberon–Lithgow (270 km, 1987).

When the Pipeline Authority was put up for sale in 1989, it marked a remarkable change of policy by a new government. It was announced that the government had decided to sell the existing pipeline system 'in the national interest'—though the basis of that claim was not fully articulated. Possibly the government was suggesting that the original concept of a national grid was overly ambitious, and the remaining components would not be a good investment. Alternatively, it might have been thought that the private sector could develop pipeline systems without the assistance of government—so that the government could stand back, and simply regulate an emerging natural monopoly.

Whatever the supposed rationale, the process whereby the Pipeline Authority was put up for sale can be viewed as a case study of how public sector advisers may lack skills to provide governments with financial advice. If the sale of the Pipeline was intended to maximise financial returns to the Commonwealth, then the arrangements were poorly designed.

The sale was subject to 'an acceptable price being achieved', and satisfactory conditions terms for the future operation of the system being negotiated with the prospective purchaser.

The Authority had estimated that its existing infrastructure had a replacement value of $1.2 billion (which was much higher than its historical cost of $305 million). Advertisements inviting expressions of interest explained that the pipeline system represented a strategic asset with considerable scope for further development. If a national gas pipeline grid was to be established in Australia, 'it is likely to form an integral part'.

In those more innocent days, when media commentators focused almost exclusively on cash-based budget results, the government explained that 'for budget reasons' it planned to finalise the sale in 1990–91 and to receive the sale proceeds before 30 June 1991.

There was one major snag: the Pipeline Authority had only one major customer, the Australian Gas Light Company Ltd (AGL). The Authority carried gas purchased by AGL from various gas producers in the Cooper basin. Gas was hauled from a central collection point at Moomba in South Australia to Wilton, on the outskirts of Sydney, where it was distributed by AGL to industrial, commercial and domestic users in the Sydney metropolitan area. Gas was also distributed to Newcastle, Wollongong, the ACT and regional centres along the pipeline routes in NSW.

Pricing arrangements had been established in a 1974 Haulage Agreement, and renegotiated in 1985. However, the latter agreement in principle had not been formalised in new contractual arrangements, though the parties were operating in accordance with the basic terms of the 1985 agreement when the Pipeline Authority was put up for sale. The arrangements protected the Authority against losses, but allowed it to charge AGL 'no more than sufficient to recover costs' (*Sixteenth Annual Report*, 1988–89).

The sale value of the Pipeline Authority was thus directly linked to the price the Authority could charge AGL for the carriage of gas—and under existing arrangements, that was not a commercial rate. The Commonwealth's Asset Sales Task Force acknowledged that these arrangements did not permit a 'fair and reasonable return to be earned on total Pipeline Authority assets, valued at their current worth'. A new owner would 'probably wish to renegotiate the existing haulage tariff arrangements'.

The Pipeline Authority ran an essentially simple, but capital intensive, business. The Authority was wholly owned by the Commonwealth, but its capital structure comprised a mixture of 'shares' and 'borrowings', mainly from the Commonwealth. This meant that moneys were paid to the Commonwealth as interest, reducing reported profit. However, the Pipeline Authority's strong

Privatisation

and consistent cash flows enabled it to repay its debt at an accelerating rate.

The Authority's 1992 results were as follows:

	$m
Haulage and sales revenue	91.00
Less Natural gas purchased	8.95
	82.05
Less operating expenses (excluding depreciation and interest)	15.36
Cash flows from operations	66.69
Net interest expense	30.45
Net cash flows	36.24
Assets (cost less depreciation)	223.00
Debt	215.00
Equity	8.00

(The gas purchases related to supply arrangements with the Canberra district.)

On an accrual accounting basis, the operating results were less impressive because the pipeline infrastructure was being depreciated over 30 years. But the reported profits of the agency were largely irrelevant to any valuation of the business (and to decisions to sell or retain it), since the pricing arrangements expired in 2006.

In any event, depreciation charges may have been excessive. It was widely accepted that the life of a pipeline could be far greater than 30 years, provided the infrastructure was provided with adequate cathodic protection, and was properly maintained or refurbished. Moreover, the volume of gas carried by the pipeline could be increased by raising operating pressures. In 1989, it was operating at less than 50 per cent of technical capacity.

AGL's massive investment in upgrading Sydney's gas distribution system through inserting plastic sleeves inside the original steel pipes provides an illustration of how new technologies can extend the life (and enhance the functionality) of ageing infrastructure.

However, in the case of the pipeline, interval surveys had confirmed that the pipeline was, 'for practical purposes, free from corrosion' (*Sixteenth Annual Report*, 1988–89). Essentially, the main determinant of the life of the pipeline was the size of the reserves in the fields from which supplies were drawn.

The main determinants of the *value* of the pipeline system to a private sector purchaser would have been the cash flows which could be derived from the assets, the extent to which operating results would be subject to taxation, and the cost of funding the purchase.

The business of the Pipeline Authority did not offer great potential for major operating efficiencies in the hands of a new owner. The pipelines were monitored and controlled by a computer-based supervisory control and data acquisition system (SCADA). In 1989 it was claimed that the newly upgraded SCADA master station placed the Authority in the forefront of pipeline supervision and control technology. The Authority only employed around 140 staff (including part-timers). It seems likely that a private owner would have been hard-pressed to reduce these numbers, given the need to employ maintenance crews and to run compressors and man monitoring stations 24 hours a day, seven days a week. Even a massive cut in manning levels (such as by outsourcing maintenance functions) would hardly have had a great impact on the rates of return potentially earned on the claimed $1.2 billion worth of infrastructure.

When the Commonwealth's Asset Sales Task Force published an 'Invitation to register interest in acquiring the Moomba-Sydney Gas Pipeline System' in 1989, potential bidders were asked to suggest a range of possible prices they would be prepared to pay. These estimates would be based on their own assumptions about operating costs and revenues, projected future demand for gas, scope for increasing haulage fees and 'above all, [the] strategic significance' of the pipeline assets, both before and after the year 2006—when the existing 'cost recovery' haulage agreement with AGL expired (*Department of Finance*, 1989).

All of this suggested that those responsible for selling the assets were anxious to receive industry intelligence about what the sale might produce. And, if this did not sound desperate enough, the documents explained:

- no impediments are placed in the way of international investors, who may participate freely in this industry in Australia;
- there was no need to demonstrate economic benefits or to provide for Australian equity participation;
- the new owners would be able to avail themselves of the normal taxation provisions relating to depreciation. Those provisions generally allow deductions for depreciation based on amounts actually paid for depreciable assets where the relevant parties are dealing with each other at arm's length;
- depending on the country of origin of the purchaser, and the tax laws to which they are subject, any goodwill component in the purchase price may also be able to be deducted for tax purposes in that country of origin (*Department of Finance*, 1989).

This dry language was saying, in effect, that the Commonwealth was only concerned about the 'headline' price, and in receiving a cash payment which could be included as a receipt in the 1990 budget results. It did *not* care what tax minimisation measures were adopted by a purchaser.

A prospective purchaser could revalue assets upwards, and record tax-deductible depreciation on the revalued amounts. It could finance the purchase through borrowings from off-shore entities, enabling profits to be siphoned out of the country in the guise of interest payments, which would be subject to lower tax rates than those imposed on Australian companies.

The 'expression of interest' documents were so clumsily composed that one of the authors felt moved to telephone a senior official in the Department of Finance to point out that the Assets Sales Task Force seemed to have little comprehension of how, left to their own devices, prospective purchasers could establish arrangements which would materially reduce post-privatisation tax payments to the Commonwealth. The response was hardly reassuring:

> You're probably right. We had to lend them some accountants because they didn't know how to read a balance sheet.

In the event, the pipeline assets were not sold, as planned, before 30 June 1990. The Senate refused to pass sale legislation, while AGL took legal action in relation to the status of its contractual relationships with the Commonwealth, blocking the sale.

Again this suggests that those handling the privatisation had not sought high-level legal advice. Documents inviting parties to express interest in buying the pipeline system had acknowledged that the AGL had a first right of refusal to buy out the Pipeline Authority if the Commonwealth was a seller. The same documents pointed out that the Commonwealth was just selling the assets of its statutory authority, not the authority itself. That kind of argument works when company liquidators are trying to pay creditors, and want to avoid preparing a prospectus for the sale of shares. But it didn't wash with the NSW Court of Appeal, and eventually the High Court even rejected an application from the Commonwealth to appeal the decision.

Having won in the courts, AGL continued to negotiate with the government from a position of strength. It emerged as the prospective owner of 51 per cent of the Moomba-Sydney Pipeline in November 1993. Minister for Finance Ralph Willis announced that the government proposed a trade sale to AGL of a 51 per cent interest in the Moomba-Sydney Pipeline, subject to a satisfactory competitive tender for the remaining 49 per cent. The proposed ownership structure was also to be subject to the approval of the Trade Practices Commission. An Interstate Gas

Pipelines Act was to establish a framework encouraging competition. The sale plans were also conditional on new agreements for the haulage of gas.

The criticisms of the failure of the proposed sale arrangements to consider future tax revenues payable to the Commonwealth had apparently been addressed. Key assets were to be transferred to a subsidiary of the Pipeline Authority, so that the level of depreciation deductions available to AGL and a prospective minority purchaser would be fixed.

A new advertising program for the sale of the 49 per cent interest commenced soon afterwards, while meantime the Trade Practices Commission sought undertakings regarding third party access to the pipeline system. It was reported that the Federal government was 'keen to get the sale bedded down by June 30, to add several hundred million dollars to budget revenue' (*BRW*, 21/3/94).

Particulars of the sale proceeds were announced in June 1994. Purchasers of the minority interest were Canada's Novacorp International (25 per cent) and Malaysia's State-owned Petronas (24 per cent). Net proceeds would be 'marginally less than $500 million', with the government assuming debt of $190 million. AGL was to receive $30 million compensation for surrendering long-standing haulage rights, while six Cooper Basin producers were to receive compensation of $20 million (*AFR*, 1/6/94).

Given that the Commonwealth government had been promoting asset sales to reduce debt, it is of interest to note that AGL planned to fund its 51 per cent purchase by borrowing. As AGL's managing director Len Bleasel explained, 'the robust cashflow meant the impact on the group's now low gearing ratio should be short-lived' (*SMH*, 1/6/94).

The sale was duly completed on 30 June 1994:

> Yesterday afternoon, department of Finance officials headed straight to the bank from the signing ceremony and banked the cheques in time to boost the 1993–94 Budget outcome before the books closed on the year (*AFR*, 1/7/94).

Finance Minister Beazley had earlier said that 'the successful completion of the sale will mark the start of a new, more competitive environment for gas transmission in Australia' (*AFR*, 1/6/94). On the other hand, chairman of the Trade Practices Commission Allan Fels seemed less confident. He observed that AGL's purchase was unlikely to present a difficulty:

> It probably won't constitute a problem [as long as it] provides an access regime allowing upstream competitors to receive gas from central Australia (*AFR*, 22/6/94).

Media commentators also stressed the prospects of greater competition:

> Greater competition is not unreservedly welcomed by gas monopolies and oligopolies. But the combination of more competition, new pipelines and access by third parties to existing lines should make it possible for consumers to have a choice in gas supply (*AFR*, 30/6/94).

Announcements of new pipelines were soon forthcoming, notably completion of a $50 million link between Wagga Wagga in NSW and Barnawatha in Victoria, which joined the gas markets in the two states. It was 'believed' that the pipeline would be subject to a third party access regime, and, as a natural monopoly, would be subject to price regulation (*The Age*, 13/8/98).

However, the extent to which sale of the Pipeline Authority heralded a new era of competition and open access was soon looking shaky. Some proposals for new pipelines were being floated simply because AGL was allegedly demanding excessive prices for access to the system.

BHP argued that 'the terms under which AGL suggested access to its pipeline system should be provided did not remove monopoly rents from the NSW gas market' (*SMH*, 22/4/97). The response from the NSW Independent Pricing and Regulatory Tribunal was to order only a staged reduction in access charges. One commentator suggested that AGL would 'lose its monopoly landlord status in such a way that shareholders may never notice the difference' (*AFR*, 29/5/97).

BHP had earlier proposed a new pipeline along the eastern seaboard of Australia, and later in 1997 there were suggestions that this might be abandoned following promises that AGL could meet BHP's needs at commercially competitive rates (*AFR*, 22/10/97).

But by 1999, BHP Petroleum's chief executive Phil Aiken was scathingly critical of the high prices set for access to the NSW gas pipeline system:

> 'Tariff prices for access to the existing AGL pipeline system in NSW are much greater than we, and indeed other potential pipeline users, think is reasonable' ...
>
> Mr. Aiken said the high tariffs had forced Duke Energy to extend the proposed Eastern Gas Pipeline beyond its original end point of Wilton in NSW to Horsley Park.
>
> That would duplicate part of the AGL pipeline system, which delivers gas to the Smithfield power station under a BHP contract signed in 1996.

BHP argued that 'building a new pipeline will cost only a fraction of what would be paid in tariff arrangements', and that this was 'hardly a ringing endorsement of providing access on fair and reasonable terms and conditions' (AFR, 3/6/99). The extent to which a competitive market can be established in gas distribution depends on the charges levied for the carriage of gas by the owners of a natural monopoly.

The extent to which governments can establish an effective regulatory regime over gas distribution remains to be demonstrated, and is likely to impose considerable costs on Commonwealth and state governments in coming years.

Arguably, retention of public sector ownership could have enabled the taxpayer to enjoy the benefit of what AGL later boasted was a 'robust cashflow'. Retention of public ownership would also have placed governments in the position of being able to ensure greater competition in the energy market, rather than having to rely on the top end of town to strike deals which would produce those outcomes.

Sale at any price: State Bank of New South Wales

In his 1993 Budget speech, the then NSW Treasurer Peter Collins stated:

> It is the Government's intention to sell the State Bank at the appropriate time for the best price in the best interests of the people of NSW. For anyone to suggest a fire sale is to fly in the face of the facts (*1993–94 NSW Budget Paper No 1*, 1993).

Fire sales are hasty affairs, and the way the State Bank of NSW was sold was not exactly hasty. It took another 14 months. As to whether the people of NSW got a good price—let the facts speak for themselves.

The financial disasters experienced by state-owned banks in Victoria and South Australia have often been cited as an argument against any public sector involvement in banking. The argument is exaggerated and overstated, since much depends on the risks that a bank's directors accept (consciously or unconsciously) in running their business. Some banks have been run cautiously and judiciously, with strong internal controls over lending, and careful analyses of Treasury risks. Others have been operated with little direction. There have been suggestions some banks have allowed dealers to speculate on foreign currency transactions. The Victorian and South Australian state-owned banks incurred losses because funds had been punted on high risk loans. As one banker observed over lunch: 'It's easy to be wise after the event, but in the 1980s, the imperative was to push money.'

The experience of the State Bank of NSW is not usually grouped

Privatisation

> **Box 8.3**
> **HOW STATE BANK OF NSW WROTE OFF BAD DEBTS
> —BUT NOT AGAINST PROFITS**
>
> When businesses prepare their financial statements, it is accepted accounting practice that amounts owing by debtors be valued at a sum approximating their estimated realisable value—by making allowances for bad and doubtful debts. The amount of this adjustment is treated as an expense, regardless of whether the write-down relates to claims which are known to be 'bad debts', or whether they only represent estimates of the sum likely to be lost in relation to 'doubtful debts'.
>
> The bookkeeping entries giving effect to these estimation procedures usually involve establishing a 'provision for doubtful debts' which is deducted from the aggregate of amounts owing by debtors to give the figure recorded in balance sheets. The value of this provision is adjusted at the end of each accounting period, and these adjustments when combined with sums expensed as bad debts, represent the overall bad and doubtful debts expense to be charged against profits for that year.
>
> The State Bank used a variety of alternative bookkeeping devices, with the effect that for a series of years the profit and loss account was not charged with the full amount of bad and doubtful debts expense which had been incurred by the Bank:
>
> - Doubtful debts were charged against 'contingency reserves', rather than being treated as an expense.
> - Sums were transferred from a 'Special Reserve' into a 'General Provision for Doubtful Debts', and then transferred from that 'General Provision' into a 'Specific Provision for Doubtful Debts'—thus avoiding charging all bad debts against the Profit and Loss Statement.
> - Sums were transferred from the 'General Provision' to the Profit and Loss statement—implying that the provision had been overestimated (though later charges against the specific provision—then described as Specific Provision for Loan Losses—belied this interpretation.)
> - An increase in the Specific Provision was described as an 'increment on corporatisation'.
>
> The overall effect of these (and other) entries, combined with information available about claims arising from indemnity agreements between the NSW government and the eventual purchaser of the Bank, suggest that during 1989–94 the State Bank reported operating *profits* of around $215 million. If that record was adjusted to conform to conventional accounting treatments of bad and doubtful debts, the operating results would show *losses* totalling $365 million over five years. That suggests that during 1989–94 the Bank's profits had been *overstated* by $580 million.

with these other state-owned banks, for the simple reason that it reported a stream of profits while other state-owned banks were foundering. It was also sold before the full scale of its losses became apparent.

Yet the Bank used highly unusual accounting policies to ensure that it usually reported profits when, in substance, it was actually incurring operating losses. These accounting policies were disclosed, though not with great clarity. However, to see the whole story a reader needed to analyse the Bank's annual reports as a series (see Box 8.3).

When the State Bank was put up for sale in November 1993, Premier Fahey suggested that the Bank 'ought to be congratulated' for not recording losses as great as those incurred in Victoria and South Australia. The Bank had recently reported a 1993 loss of $74.6 million (after a 'tax credit' of $10.2 million) which the Bank's chief executive had sought to regard as a positive: 'It's a credit to the bank that it has survived the recession' (*SMH*, 26/11/93).

The bank was to be sold through a trade sale rather than a public float, with Treasurer Collins indicating that the industry would prefer a sale to one of the four large existing banking networks, or sale to a regional or offshore bank (*SMH*, 13/11/93). Within weeks, Fahey had excluded the big four domestic banks from bidding, on the basis that this would mean radical restructuring, job cuts and loss of the Bank's identity. Opposition Leader Bob Carr argued that the government should delay the sale until the Bank showed stronger performance—a sentiment rejected by the leader writer of the *Sydney Morning Herald*:

> Its bad loans are not likely to turn good overnight. And what the bank really needs is the capital injection its public owners cannot afford while State finances are so weak (*SMH*, 30/11/93).

Meantime Mathew Horton and Frank Zeller of the *Telegraph Mirror* (26/11/93) put the range of the sale proceeds at $400 million to almost $1 billion, NSW Treasury estimated $900 million in 1993 Budget Papers, but in a later study leaked by the Opposition, only up to $700 million (*The Australian*, 26/11/93). Most sanguine was Glenn Burge of the *Sydney Morning Herald* with an estimate of $800 million to $1 billion, though an earlier anonymous forecast in the *Telegraph Mirror* had suggested between $800 million and $1200 million (3/9/93). All would (or should) be embarrassed by the final outcome.

Expressions of interest were formally invited in December 1993. Two key bidders were said to have dropped out in February (*Telegraph Mirror*, 26/2/94). In March, the NSW government was believed to be talking to five prospective trade purchasers (*AFR*, 22/3/94).

The prospective purchasers undertook due diligence enquiries, and were invited to inspect documentation under conditions of confidentiality. Bidding teams of staff and advisers would go to a floor where they were assigned their own private office.

The teams began to notice that one or other of the offices on the floor had fallen into disuse, as bidders dropped out. It became clear that there were only three remaining bidders, then two. And then there was only one. The press explained:

> For the past four months the Government has refused to even confirm the fact that Colonial is the only bidder for the bank. Nevertheless Colonial has had a team of advisers inside the SBNSW headquarters in Sydney since May conducting a due diligence examination (*AFR*, 19/9/94).

It was later suggested that 'secrecy clauses signed by all parties have prevented the government from identifying Colonial [Mutual Life] as the sole bidder for the bank' (*AFR*, 22/9/94). A deal was struck for a headline price of $576 million, but with conditions under which the government provided indemnities in relation to the value of outstanding loans.

Opposition and Independent MPs in the NSW parliament demanded that the terms be reviewed by the Auditor-General. Opposition Leader Carr and Shadow Treasurer Egan both argued that the sale should be delayed until bank profitability had improved. The proposed sale price, they argued, was inadequate. A resolution passed unanimously by the NSW legislative assembly sought advice as to whether the proposed deal would provide a 'fair and reasonable economic return of the sale of the Bank'. This was a remarkable opportunity for a privatisation proposal to be formally reviewed by parliament, before it was concluded. But contracts already signed established a $7 million penalty clause if the sale was not consummated by 24 November 1994.

With that short timetable, the Auditor-General Tony Harris had around 22 business days to report. With limited specialist resources within his own office, Harris contracted-out the assignment to CS First Boston and Coopers & Lybrand (hereafter 'CS First Boston'). Harris had invited 11 firms or persons to bid for the work, and noted 'considerable reluctance on the part of many eligible merchant banks to tender', some citing time pressures and others noting 'sensitivities associated with the task' (*Auditor-General*, 1994).

Their report, and Harris's comments and letter of transmittal, were delivered on schedule three days before the 24 November deadline. The report supported the sale. The Coalition government needed the support of only one independent MP in the legislative assembly to get the legislation through, and on distribution of the Auditor-General's report, one independent immediately announced he would support the Bill. The legislation duly passed the lower house on 21 November 1994, and the upper house soon afterwards.

For their fee of $985,000, the consultants received around

$20,000 per published page. Yet the report provided to parliament was incomplete. Whole sections had been excluded from publication on the ground that they were 'commercially confidential'. The omitted sections included an analysis of the Bank's profit record and projected earnings, the justification of the controversially high discount rate used to arrive at a 'valuation' of the Bank. Harris's preamble noted that 'deciding to make exclusions to the advisers' report and to exclude certain data from the report was made only after careful thought'.

> The exclusions made were seen to be necessary in order to preserve the competitive position of the State Bank, whether or not the sale goes ahead (*Auditor-General*, 1994).

The fact remains that the information provided to parliament was inadequate to enable MPs, or their advisers, to make an informed assessment of the sale and retention value of the Bank.

The analysis in the report was fundamentally flawed (see Box 8.4)—and was described as such at the time (*Walker*, 22/11/94). Subsequent events have confirmed the validity of this assessment.

Several years later, Auditor-General Harris, a straight shooter, became a strong critic of the practice of withholding documents from public view on the ground that they were 'commercial in confidence', and later during his seven year term, began expressing those views regularly in the media. Noting this, one of the authors wrote to Harris in January 1999, reminding him of his November 1994 decision to withhold sections of the report on the State Bank sale, just prior to a 1995 election. Would he now publish the full CS First Boston/Coopers & Lybrand report, having regard to his changed views about the inappropriateness of withholding information on the ground that it was supposedly 'commercial in confidence'?

Harris (to his credit—and, no doubt, to the bemusement of his readers) published the full text of the 1994 consultants' report as an appendix in his last annual report to parliament (*NSW Auditor-General*, 1999). Less than 60 of the 266 pages had previously been provided to parliament.

One of the sections of the CS First Boston report which was thus made public was its analysis of the Bank's treatment of bad and doubtful debts. Sad to relate, this did not note the way that the Bank had managed to avoid writing off bad debts against profits (as outlined in Box 8.3)—a matter which could have been identified from published annual reports. Instead, it referred to a four-year analysis of specific and general provisions, sourced from papers provided by Bank staff to the Bank's Audit Committee.

Privatisation

> **Box 8.4**
> **FLAWS IN ANALYSIS OF NSW STATE BANK SALE**
>
> **The process:** The short time frame for delivery of the report meant that the Auditor-General 'had to accept a contract environment and contract conditions which were neither typical of [his] approach not desirable' (*Correspondence*, Harris to Walker, 27/1/99).
>
> The Auditor-General's report to parliament was delivered on 18 November 1994, just before a scheduled debate on 21 November 1994. This time frame placed considerable pressure on independent members who had delayed passage of the sale legislation. The report was highly technical, but politicians had no time (or resources) to seek advice on those technical issues.
>
> **Failure to address terms of reference:** The parliament sought advice on whether the proposed consideration for the sale of the Bank provided a 'fair and reasonable' return to the State of NSW. The report considered a different issue: whether the proposed price was a 'fair and reasonable' price for CML to pay.
>
> The words 'fair and reasonable' were widely used in the securities markets in the context of expert assessments of the merits of takeover bids, and the words had an established technical meaning. According to the Australian Securities Commission, 'fairness' concerns whether the price offered is equal to or greater than the value of the securities. 'Reasonableness' requires an assessment of the circumstances. Bank directors had already expressed the view that CML's offer was 'not fair but reasonable'. Yet the report treated 'fair and reasonable' as a single test.
>
> Parliament sought estimates of the *range* of sale and retention values. This material was not provided to Parliament since it was claimed to be 'commercially confidential'.
>
> **Estimates of future profits:** The consultants used only 'after tax' estimates of future profits. As a government-owned business, the Bank only paid pseudo taxes to the state's consolidated fund (not the Commonwealth). Hence, to the state, these cash flows were the same as other earnings. Their exclusion reduced the valuation by 33c in the dollar.
>
> The claimed rationale for this was the assertion that retention value 'must be the same as fair market value to the private sector'. Yet the basis of all commercial transactions is that vendors and purchasers have different assessments of 'value'— hence one is prepared to sell, and one is prepared to buy.
>
> The valuation was based on the Bank board's 'aspiration forecasts' of earnings, which the consultants claimed were 'more likely to be under achieved than exceeded'. But use of these forecasts without adjustment ignored the fact that the sale agreement provided for the state of NSW to meet 90 per cent of the cost of bad debts.
>
> **Choice of discount rate to calculate 'present values':** CS First Boston selected the extraordinarily high discount rate of 18.9 per cent *after tax*, on the basis of two flawed assumptions. First, that retention value to the state was the same as what was fair for CML to pay. Second, that CML should have used a discount rate that reflected the return demanded by private sector investors who were investing in high-risk banking. The former was wrong in logic, and the latter was wrong in the context of the transaction.

CS First Boston did, however, reveal that from an analysis of published financial statements of Australian banks, the State Bank of NSW 'had the highest proportion of non-performing loans in the banking sector in both 1992 and 1993'. On the other hand, the Bank's levels of provisions and write-offs were 'at the lower end of the scale'. This material would have been political dynamite if published just before the March 1995 election.

Another recently-published section of the CS First Boston report was an appendix containing a subsidiary report from Neville Hathaway & Associates Pty Ltd. This provided the rationale for the choice of the Bankcard-style 18.9 per cent discount rate, used by CS First Boston to arrive at their valuation.

Remarkably, nothing in this previously-withheld material could be construed as 'commercial in confidence'. There was not a single line referring to the circumstances of a single company. Why, then, was it withheld? By accident? Or design? Embarrassment? Or shame?

One thing can be said. Publication in November 1994 would have embroiled the government, the Auditor-General and the consultants in controversy, and cast doubt on the validity of the recommendations. For it highlighted some major internal inconsistencies. The Hathaway report accepted that the public sector's cost of capital should indeed be regarded as *lower* than that of private sector firms. In substance, the CS First Boston report had assumed they should be the same. (The Auditor-General explained that the 18.9 per cent discount rate had been chosen 'for the reason outlined in the Appendix to the advisers' reports'—the same Appendix that had been withheld as 'commercial in confidence'.)

The Hathaway report explained that 'the cost of capital to private and government enterprises differs so that capitalised asset values are the same regardless of whether governments or the private sector owns the asset'. By assuming that the *value of a government-owned business was to be the same, regardless of ownership*, Hathaway had assumed away the very issue on which the NSW parliament had sought advice.

Hathaway, the academic, would later argue the opposite: that it is wrong to suggest that the public sector cost of capital was less than the public sector, because otherwise 'instead of privatising their assets governments should buy all the shares listed on the public stock exchanges' (*Hathaway*, 1997). This seemed to be a case of adopting different arguments (or assumptions) in different situations. Hathaway was a great supporter of privatisation. On the basis of the Auditor-General's acceptance of the general thrust of the consultants' report that retention value was $100 million less than the $576 million that CML was paying, the sale was duly completed.

A condition of the deal finally struck with CML was that the government would assume 90 per cent of the risks of bad debts on a $13 billion loan book. After the first $60 million in bad debts, CML would be reimbursed by the State of NSW.

CML was not assuming the normal risks of banking, since the state of NSW was indemnifying it for virtually all of the risks associated with the Bank's $13 billion loan book. It was a low-risk purchase for CML—as the profits earned by CML on its new subsidiary, and the payouts made by the NSW government, would soon demonstrate.

The terms of these guarantees were summarised by the Auditor-General of NSW as follows:

> Loan Losses
> The arrangements provide that the State indemnifies the purchaser against actual losses (ie loans less special provisions) in respect of loans that exist at Completion Date. However, the first $60m loss not provided for is to be met by the new owner and thereafter only 90% of the actual loss is subject to indemnity (*NSW Auditor-General*, 1995).

It is not clear whether other bidders knew such generous sweeteners were on offer—or if these terms were agreed after other bidders had dropped out.

Under the arrangements, the $576 million headline price paid to the state from Colonial Mutual has been eroded by indemnity payouts.

Between the sale date in 1994 to March 1998, the state of NSW paid out $200.6 million for bad loans. Further outlays for 1998-99 and 1999-2000 were forecast at $104.2 million and $45.7 million respectively, with possibly more to come until the warranties expire in 2006. According to Budget Papers, after offsetting receipts from the lease of the Bank's former head office building, the net proceeds from the sale were only $213.8 million (*1998-99 NSW Budget Paper No 2*).

In its last year in public ownership, the State Bank reported a pre-tax profit to 30 September 1994 of $70.5 million (after writing off $91 million for doubtful debts). In its first year of Colonial's ownership, with a new financial year ending 31 December 1995, the Bank reported a pre-tax profit of $149.6 million, or $100.2 million after tax. This means that the State Bank with its guaranteed loan book was sold for around 1–1.25 times annual earnings.

In comparison, the average price-earnings ratio of Australian banks (the share price divided by current year's earnings—a crude indicator of pricing on the stock market) has long been around 13, and recently has moved closer to the PE ratios of industrial stocks of 17 to 18. At 30 June 1994, the 'average' earnings multiples for banks (excluding Westpac) was 16.6.[2]

The lesson is that, even if there are good reasons for privatisation, governments should pick their timing, and hold their nerve. In 1994 the banking industry was still reeling from loan losses arising from bad deals entered into during the turbulent 1980s. 1994 was not a good year to sell a bank.

But there is never a good time for a government to sell 'at any price'.

If SBNSW had managed to produce maintainable earnings of around $100 million after tax (its 1995 result), then its value on a trade sale would have been more than $1,500 million—considerably greater than the net sale price in 1994 of $213.8 million.[3]

Against this background, it is of interest to re-read the Governor's speech at the opening of parliament in March 1994 in which it was claimed that the sale of the State Bank of NSW would

> reduce the State's debt by $18.4 billion [and] remove a potential financial exposure ...

The reference to 'state debt' in this speech (prepared by the government of the day) was false and misleading. The Bank's liabilities to depositors have never been counted as part of state 'debt', and the way the Bank was ultimately sold actually retained rather than removed financial exposures.

It is also of interest to re-read an undated letter sent by Premier Fahey to State Bank customers, shortly after the sale:

---

[2] Westpac's PE was 245:1, after it had 'taken a bath' by massive write-downs of bad loans, and had only managed to report a modest operating profit after some controversial accounting treatments relating to an 'over-funded' employees' superannuation scheme. These price earnings multiples need to be interpreted in light of the extent to which dividends were fully or partly franked. The *Australian Financial Review*, 1 July 1994, recorded that four banks (Advance, Metway, NAB, and St George) were paying franked dividends, while two others (ANZ and Westpac) were not.

[3] In December 1998 Nathan Vass of *The Sunday Telegraph* estimated that the State Bank 'once valued at $900 million in public ownership, had returned a meagre $240 million to the public coffers' (13/12/98). This estimate of prospective returns were based on prior reports in state Budget Papers, while the estimate of net proceeds was incomplete, so that the resultant estimate of a loss of $660 million was understated. Even so, Vass pointed out that $660 million could buy four public hospitals with 300 beds each; the Olympic stadium; the Eastern Distributor; or 42 high schools.

> My government has been careful to negotiate a contract which is good for both you the customer and the taxpayer of New South Wales. It is also good for the bank and its employees.
>
> I sincerely believe that the sale is good for New South Wales and good for the bank.

Fahey got it badly wrong. The deal was only good for CML.

Wooden spoon award: Australia's worst privatisation

There's a story, perhaps apocryphal, that after selling the Nine Network to the luckless shareholders of Bond Corporation Holdings, Kerry Packer observed that one could only expect to meet 'one Alan Bond in a lifetime'. For thousands of individual investors, there's only one John Fahey.

Fahey has handled a series of high-profile, high-value privatisations, starting when he was Premier of NSW, and continuing when he switched to federal politics and became Minister for Finance.

The Wooden Spoon Award for Australia's Worst Privatisations must be shared by two of Fahey's achievements: the sale of

- the State Bank of New South Wales; and
- the first tranche of Telstra.

The State Bank of NSW—for a range of reasons. The 'sale at any price' approach encouraged potential buyers to bid low. The Fahey government's decision to rule out a trade sale to one of the Big Four Banks ultimately cost the state of NSW millions of dollars. The sale process was managed so ineptly that bidders knew when one or other had dropped out, until there was only one bidder remaining—not a way to ensure a good price. The information provided to parliament about the deal was so inadequate that it provoked a request for an audit review by the Auditor-General—but in circumstances where that report had to be provided under pressure, within weeks. Ultimately that report was incomplete, of limited usefulness, and in many respects, defective. Finally, the terms and conditions of the deal were astonishingly naive. The NSW government claimed to be selling because it was inappropriate for governments to accept the risks of banking—but then did exactly that, guaranteeing the recoverability of most of the Bank's $13 billion loan book. After claiming that the sale was successful, with a headline price of $576 million, the Fahey government only produced net sale proceeds for the Bank (after payments on those infamous loan-book guarantees) amounting to less than one and a half years' earnings.

Telstra—because of the loss of value to the public sector, and the extraordinary strategy of selling off Australia's key communications carrier at a time when the rest of the world seems to be saying that we are all poised on the verge of an 'information revolution', which is likely to have a greater impact on society and world economies than the nineteenth century's industrial revolution.

May all governments learn the lessons of history.

9

A Better Way

Debate about the role of government

The process of privatisation by the Australian public sector has been radical, far ranging, and, it would appear, increasingly unpopular with the electorate.

As explained in earlier chapters, these radical changes have been promoted by politicians from both sides of politics, supposedly because of financial imperatives. Demonstrably, many of those arguments have been distorted and deceptive. Our political leaders have failed to articulate a clear vision for the role of government. Such a vision should encompass what governments should do, and what governments should avoid.

There has been far greater discussion of *how a government should deliver services rather than what should governments be doing*.

Gary Sturgess, who was an adviser to former NSW Premier Nick Greiner, has argued that the role of the public sector is changing:

> I have suggested the term 'virtual government' to describe the networked nature of the state in the decades ahead. This does not necessarily mean smaller government, and it does not mean less effective government. To the contrary, it is about concentrating government on those activities where it adds the most value in society (*Sturgess*, 1996).

The idea of 'virtual government' presupposes that privatising and outsourcing is the optimal policy. The idea is that the public sector should be stripped down to the extent needed to arrange for the private sector to provide services. The respected management writer Henry Mintzberg, noted the popularity of virtual government in the United Kingdom, the United States and New Zealand, and caustically described the 'virtual government model' as 'the great experiment of economists who have never had to manage anything'

A Better Way

(*Mintzberg*, 1996). But ideas, however extreme, at least raise questions about how government can 'add the most value in society'.

Successful and effectively run corporations would not sell off profitable businesses or divisions on the basis of loose ideas about 'reducing debt' or having a 'smaller corporation'. They might (and commonly do) establish a strategy and then decide to move out of one business in order to concentrate on another. Respected corporations undertake careful analyses of proposed courses of action and explain their vision and strategy to their shareholders.

On the other hand, politicians and bureaucrats, who pride themselves for their economic and financial rationality, show no reluctance in selling off huge chunks of the public sector without having articulated their vision about the role of government, and without describing their overall strategy. Nor do they appear to systematically analyse both the financial implications of alternative courses of action, and the impact of those options on the delivery and availability of services to the community (but more on this below).

There may be a good, solid economic case for privatising some government enterprises. One need only look around the world at the kind of enterprises that some governments found themselves owning. Countries in the former Soviet Union operated in an environment where most businesses were nationalised—the Internet periodically invites expressions of interest from firms interested in acquiring everything from wineries to chicken slaughterhouses. From the Australian perspective, there appears to be no need for governments to be involved in those activities. Private firms can produce wine or chicken meat, and the role of government might be satisfied by ensuring that these consumable items are prepared hygienically, and do not incorporate harmful ingredients or additives.

Yet let us reflect on this a little longer. One Canadian province owns bottle shops, many of which are housed almost anonymously in underground arcades. Presumably the rationale is to regulate the consumption of alcohol. It seems a short step from this practice for a government to control the production of alcoholic beverages, including wine. France once held a government monopoly on cigarettes and matches. The British colonial government in India, in Ghandi's time, controlled the production of salt. The government of Thailand produced playing cards.

Different governments have taken differing stances, reflecting the cultural or religious values of their population—or prospects for raising revenues. Canada's national government owned uranium mines, and steelworks. Britain found itself owning car and truck manufacturers, coalmines, steelworks, oil refineries, express coach services and nuclear power stations. In most instances, the Canadian and British governments did not deliberately set out to enter these industries. A common feature of many of these business acquisitions was a desire to protect jobs, in the face of possible business failures or closures.

To understand why government became involved in certain activities, one needs to examine the history of these initiatives: why, over many decades, the Australian people have invested in a wide portfolio of public assets providing services in telecommunications, postal services, roads, ports, shipping, electricity supply, water supply, airports, and so forth. A significant factor in many cases is that the private sector couldn't see a dollar in it, and that the government of the day saw a need to provide services to more members of the community. For example, governments established electricity distribution businesses to service regional areas. Another reason is that governments intervened for strategic reasons. Water and sewerage businesses owe their existence to public health considerations, particularly after Sydney's experience with the 'great plague' in the late nineteenth century.

Australian governments have now got out of running many activities. Often this was because there was no need to continue doing things itself where privately-owned, competing businesses were also serving consumers well.

Other activities have been seen as more difficult to privatise. In some cases, there would be community resistance to granting private firms the coercive powers of government (e.g. privately-run police or quarantine services). In other cases, highly-subsidised activities would not be profitable if new owners were required to maintain existing standards of service. In these circumstances, resistance to privatisation has more to do with political realities than a theoretical analysis of the role of government.

Yet that debate is worth having.

Traditional statements about the role of government have referred to the need to ensure the defence of the community, the maintenance of law and order, and preservation of public health. Another traditional view is that there is a case for government involvement to regulate the pricing practices of monopolies, to regulate externalities (such as industrial pollution) and to intervene to ensure that markets work properly since, otherwise, market mechanisms will not allocate resources efficiently within the community.

One of the few Australian political leaders to have ventured to describe his ideas about core government functions was Prime Minister John Howard, who wrote:

A Better Way

> I believe there will always be an irreducible minimum of public service functions. Defence, justice, a social security safety net, the monitoring of outcomes of, and alternatives to, existing policies—all these will require public service input. And there will always be a need for high-quality economic, constitutional and other policy advice ...

This short list hardly represented a clear view of the role of the public sector in a changing society. Indeed, the Prime Minister seemed conscious of this, adding

> And lest there be any misunderstanding, the examples cited are just that: they are illustrative, not exclusive. They highlight the key discrete public service functions that are distinct from the private sector (*Howard*, 1998).

But so long as political leaders avoid articulating their vision about the role of government in Australia, or are not challenged to do so, it would seem that we will continue debating the merits or otherwise of privatising the latest potential target.

Many potential targets are now profitable enterprises providing reliable services, and a good revenue stream to the government. Others are attractive sale prospects simply because governments have had difficulty in reducing existing levels of service when they are in public hands. The gains to government take the form of costs which can be avoided. It would be nice to see political leaders enter this debate.

The authors' views, in outline, are that the primary activities of government are to promote national security, public health and public safety; to ensure the maintenance of law and order, and the equitable treatment of citizens; to provide support for those unable to look after themselves; to provide basic infrastructure (for water, waste water, energy distribution, and transport); to ensure equitable access to education; to ensure that markets work effectively and fairly (and to ensure that the community is not exploited by monopolies); and, in order to maintain and develop our democratic institutions, to ensure that information and diversity of opinion can be freely disseminated within the community.

There are higher priorities for government investment than ownership of banks, providers of venture capital, and gaming businesses. Historically government intervention in these areas may have been justified. But times have changed. Those businesses have been sold, and good riddance to them. Some projects might not have got started without seed money from the government but are now well able to stand on their own feet, and provide roughly equivalent services in private hands. Indeed, there are higher priorities for government than running airlines, though the public sector has an important and continuing role in regulating air safety and pricing practices. Arguably more important than ownership of airlines is the continued retention of the airport infrastructure to enable genuine competition among potential suppliers of airline services. To date government policies have singularly failed to ensure that potential new entrants have fair access to public-owned infrastructure (because landing slots have been pre-allocated, and good terminal sites have been subject to long-term leases). The sale of many airports has seen some improvement in catering and shopping services, but not in the access of the core business of airports to competitors.

But one should draw the line at selling off public utilities. Water is basic to life, and waste water facilities are basic to public health. They should be retained in public hands, grimly. Similarly, retention of electricity distribution facilities seems as fundamental as the sale of gas pipeline infrastructure seems to have been foolish. Both provide fundamental services to consumers and to industry. The loss of public ownership of these resources dooms government to an ongoing and expensive regime of monitoring and regulatory oversight—which is likely to be periodically subject to regulatory capture, at the expense of consumers.

Without a national grid for electricity distribution it is not possible to have a truly competitive market for electricity generation, except at the margin. Clumsy attempts to introduce competition into the energy market have proved embarrassing to a number of operators (and arch-proponents of competition). The earlier, bargain-priced privatisation of Victorian base-load generators, on terms which virtually guaranteed their new owners an attractive rate of return, left these entities in a strong position to pursue market share by price-cutting when bidding for additional business. NSW broke up its electricity businesses into smaller units, in the name of promoting 'competition'—but these proved no match for larger players. Nor did competitive trading work well. The Queensland Power Trading Corporation was said to have lost all of its shareholders' funds through losses of up to $575 million on contracts. NSW's Pacific Power was reported to have engaged in 'hedging' activities which its board may not have fully understood or effectively controlled: the result was that Pacific Power contracted to supply more electricity than it could actually generate, at a price lower than its own costs (*The Australian*, 20/11/99).

Some re-aggregation of Victorian electricity businesses has already occurred through acquisitions, more are mooted following overseas takeovers (*AFR*, 1/12/99), while proposals are now being heard for the re-aggregation of NSW-owned corporations to establish units which could compete more effectively (*SMH*, 30/11/99). It may be too late to unscramble the eggs, but retention of the remaining coal-fired generators in public hands at least provides governments with the opportunity to take direct responsibility for reducing greenhouse emissions as required by the Kyoto agreements.

As for road infrastructure, governments should resist the temptation to allow private firms to control major arterial roads, partly because the public sector (through control of public transport, the planning apparatus and ancillary road works) are better able to manage developments of this nature. Moreover, there is little justification for allowing private interests to enjoy most of the profits of such ventures when governments are assuming most of the risks. Private firms have considerable expertise in design and construction work which could be harnessed just as effectively through the tender process.

Governments have a key role in establishing the conditions under which markets work efficiently and our democratic institutions are sustained. For those reasons, there is cause to reflect on some anomalies created by recent events.

The 1990s have seen the growth of what has been described as the information super-highway. The Internet is likely to prove vital to the way governments communicate, businesses enter into transactions, and individuals seek information or express opinions.

Yet during that period, the Commonwealth has been actively selling off its major asset in information technology and telephony, Telstra. The loss of value to the community might seem a catastrophe, but it may pale into insignificance if the full sale of Telstra (and its associated basic infrastructure) leads to losses of commercial opportunities for the Australian community to exploit these new technologies.

So too would the loss of an opportunity to maintain or extend diversity in the mass media. Telstra has a role in providing more channels for the dissemination of news and opinion. So too has the national broadcaster, the ABC; the integrity of the ABC's Internet businesses is already under threat because they are saleable or capable of commercial exploitation. According to the Commonwealth Auditor-General:

> Although not endorsed by the ABC Board, it has been suggested that the sale of 49 per cent of ABC Online may generate around $250 million ... It should be noted that this estimate has not been tested (*Commonwealth Auditor-General*, September 1999).

Technologies are changing fast, and predictions about the ways IT is being harnessed tend to look silly within a few years or even months. Arguably the greatest challenges facing governments in the new millennium are in the areas of communications and information technology. One challenge is to preserve equality of access and opportunity to the new technologies. A second is to ensure the survival of independent and non-commercial media outlets, since the maintenance of independent voices in the media is fundamental to the preservation of free and open debate about our institutions.

More careful and skilful analysis

One should never underestimate the power of ideas to transform and inspire. Equally, one should not underestimate the power of *poorly developed* ideas to waste resources, damage institutions, and impose hardship on stakeholders.

One of the factors which have contributed to gross waste of taxpayers' funds has been the way that government policies have been based on crude slogans, rather than careful and skilful analysis. For example, claims that we need 'smaller government' either assume that the community demands fewer or poorer services than before, or that it would cost less to replace existing government services through outsourcing. Neither may be the case.

Changes in government often see radical changes of policy direction, the closure or expensive restructuring of some agencies, the dismantling of programs, and the establishment of new ones. No one could complain if changes of government saw fresh initiatives to provide better services to the community and if evidence was published about these outputs and impacts of these efforts to improve services.

But sadly, changes of government often lead to reversals of policies on the basis of ideological prejudice without evidence about whether the previous policies were producing socially desirable outcomes.

One of the themes of this book has been that the uncritical promotion of 'smaller government' or the virtues of 'competition', or the merits of 'virtual government' through the sale of government businesses and wholesale contracting, can have damaging and wasteful consequences. As noted above, proponents of privatisation have studiously avoided presenting projections of the loss of long-run cash flows arising from the sale of government trading enterprises (GTEs) and the investment of proceeds into facilities which would not only earn no income, but would actually cost a lot to run in future years.

There's nothing wrong with putting money into schools, hospitals or public transport. But one might expect that among all our politicians, expert commentators and self-styled reformers—all of whom claim to have the public interest at heart—at least some would have explored (or even acknowledged) that the implications of privatisation on future revenue streams are deserving of respectful attention. After all, privatisation revenue has a one-off only effect compared with the continuing loss of interest, dividend revenue and other revenue. Despite the lack of attention to this issue in policy statements or media reports or academic papers, it certainly leads to a lot of headshaking in business circles.

The closest that pro-privatisation advocates come to exploring future financial implications of privatisation is to claim that selling GTEs can reduce debt which will reduce interest costs. The interest savings which get bandied about ignore when existing borrowings (at different interest rates) are due to be repaid, and often use simple averages of interest costs (ignoring the fact that in a time of falling interest rates, outstanding loans can't be repaid prematurely without penalty payments to compensate lenders for loss of income).

But usually privatisation proponents want to repay some debt and put the rest into electorally appealing infrastructure projects in marginal seats. It costs money to run schools and hospitals and national parks. Where will the money come from? State budgets have been supported by dividends from GTEs—and the level of those dividends increased sharply in the late 1980s, as various governments established rate of return and dividend targets, and in some cases sought 'special dividends' from GTEs. Not surprisingly, after an extended period of dividend stripping, the capacity of GTEs to pay dividends has been reduced. For that reason, it is all the more important to look beyond dividend streams to the cash flows earned by GTEs from their operations. The suggestion that GTEs should be sold because their value is declining because they are paying less and less in dividends—a proposition seriously advanced in one recent political tract—just reflects a very poor understanding of state finances.

GTE dividends may have declined from the dividend-stripping days of the mid 1990s, but they still represent a substantial source of revenue to state governments. The demand for water and electricity services in urban communities is largely inelastic. While industry demand for energy usage is associated with economic activity, residential demand is likely to be little changed during an economic cycle. On the other hand, other major components of the revenues of major states (such as stamp duties on property and stock exchange transactions) are extremely volatile. If GTEs are sold, state governments lose a relatively stable source of earnings and become more dependent on other sources of revenue.

The combination of loss of stable revenues, and an increasing requirement to maintain infrastructure, seems likely to place government budgets under new pressures. The Commonwealth's proposals for GST revenues to be distributed to the states may make state government revenues even more volatile as spending levels change during an economic cycle. Time will tell.

But the general point remains. There may well be a case for privatising some GTEs if initial public sector investment has served its purpose in establishing services where the private sector had failed to deliver—and if now the private sector is willing to buy those businesses (because they are now less risky). The strength of that case depends on

- whether controls can be established to ensure the continued delivery of services to the community without new entrants exploiting monopoly power; and
- whether there are more attractive ways in which the government can invest the proceeds of privatisation.

Analysis of the real returns earned by many GTEs—particularly those in the water or electricity industries—suggests that privatisation is not an attractive option if the proceeds are to be applied to debt reduction. There may be other, more attractive options. But advocates of privatisation have yet to articulate them.

In the same way as the sale of government businesses, governments which have resolved, in principle, to 'contract out' services without first knowing about the current costs of service provision and the quality of services currently provided, are pursuing economically irrational policies. Similarly governments which insist on putting services 'out to tender'—every service, even those for which there are no private sector equivalents—are just groping in the dark. Even if a government monopoly is grossly inefficient, that may be easier to rectify internally than the task of controlling the prices charged by the private sector monopoly that replaces it.

Currently, some agencies in the public sector are being forced into compulsory competitive tendering. At the same time, private sector firms are learning to establish special partnerships with other firms to develop new products or services, or to share in productivity savings if they can drive down production costs. In contrast to these win-win arrangements, public sector agencies are often unable or unwilling to develop special relationships with suppliers because of concerns about probity and the risks of corruption.

There may be merit in some outsourcing arrangements while others may be disasters. In either case, it is just commonsense to drive internal efficiencies before contracting out an activity, because otherwise bidders will be in a position to charge more anyway.

Improved accountability for the use of public resources

Accountability involves a relationship between two parties, whereby one is held responsible to the other for their conduct in some sphere of activity—and if their performance has not been satisfactory, they may be subject to some form of sanctions. A host of formal and informal accountability relationships have been established by parliaments and governments, and they are continuously evolving over time. But privatisation has exposed some glaring loopholes and anomalies in the way governments (and bureaucracies) are accountable to parliament and the community. Most privatisation decisions undertaken in Australia have been pushed through without the opportunity for a thorough and detailed scrutiny. There have been attempts to analyse and debate a number of the privatisation deals—though in retrospect it is clear that the information made available to parliament and the community has been inadequate. Existing arrangements for parliamentary approval and review of budgeted expenditure are outdated and inadequate.

There is a need to redesign accountability arrangements in the public sector, in recognition of the fact that things have changed since the Westminster system evolved in the mid nineteenth century:

- Governments no longer raise monies from taxes alone—these days, government-owned public trading enterprises raise monies by charges for services. The monies held and invested by these enterprises are just as much 'public' as monies provided to government departments—yet GTEs are subject to far lesser standards of accountability.
- Matters which warrant parliamentary oversight are no longer solely concerned with spending. Experience with BOOT schemes suggests that parliaments should be just as concerned about arrangements whereby revenues derived from government assets (such as road corridors) can be exploited by private firms.
- Just when parliamentary committees and Auditors-General were developing ways of holding agencies accountable for the efficiency and effectiveness of service delivery, governments have started putting those activities out of reach through contracting out.

That is not to say that traditional, Westminster-style accountability arrangements do not need refinement. Under current arrangements, parliamentary approval is required for budgeted expenditure by individual government departments, generally in terms of programs and broad categories of 'line items'. The result is that members of parliament and the community can only readily access information about the aggregate budgets and spending of those departments, or major programs.

However, departments are frequently restructured, while 'programs' are regularly redefined. The end result is that the information published in budget papers or departmental annual reports does not provide a meaningful indication of overall trends in public sector expenditure.

Moreover, there is little opportunity for a parliament or the community to consider trends in *components* of expenditure by general government agencies. First, published information is highly aggregated—referring only to a few categories of spending, such as

Employee related expenditure
Other operating expenditure
Depreciation and amortisation
Maintenance
Grants and subsidies

without indicating how much of that expenditure went on administrative staff and other overheads, as opposed to the salaries and materials used by teachers, nurses, ambulance officers, social workers, police, firemen and others who are actively engaged in delivering services to the community.

Another anomaly is the lack of data about spending in regions. While information can be obtained about the aggregate spending of government departments, some actually consume fewer resources than Sydney's Kings Cross police station, and certainly far less than that spent by individual hospitals. On the other hand, spending by the largest Commonwealth, state or territory departments is not reported in budget papers in any detail: budget papers may simply report aggregate appropriations running into billions of dollars, without details about how that spending has been distributed between urban, suburban and country areas.

Unfortunately, it is highly likely that senior public sector managers are themselves unaware of the cost structure of their own agencies. Little has been written about such problems. The NSW Council on the Cost of Government found in 1995 that public sector accounting systems did not routinely track spending on functional activities, or even on major line items—so information about spending on corporate services could only be compiled by distributing questionnaires. Other states and the Commonwealth have the same inadequate accounting systems and financial management processes. The

Commonwealth government has acknowledged that financial management is treated 'as a low priority at best, and an irrelevant one at worst, in many parts of the [Commonwealth] public sector'.

> Less than 50% of core Commonwealth agencies know their full product/service costs. In contrast, 100% of New Zealand agencies and Australian local government agencies and private sector agencies surveyed have that information (*Commonwealth Management Advisory Board*, 1997).

Yet without fuller reporting about expenditure on line items, programs and functional activities, public sector managers can't manage effectively, and executive government cannot be fully held accountable for the way it spends taxpayers' funds. Better, and standardised, recording and reporting arrangements are a necessary component for higher standards of public sector accountability.

It is emphasised that these changes in reporting practices are *necessary*, but not *sufficient* to achieve a higher standard of accountability. They need to be matched by better-designed requirements for the disclosure of information about operational performance. That information should include performance indicators relating to the quantity and quality of services provided to the community. A number of governments have requirements for the production of performance information 'where practicable', but experience suggests that reliance on information that is volunteered by agencies will tend to produce reports which only contain 'good news'.

The Council of Australian Governments has directed the compilation of information about the performance of government-provided services, though the focus to date has been on joint Commonwealth-state programs, and the exercise has only covered around 26 per cent of government expenditure (*Steering Committee for the Review of State Service Provision*, 1999). In NSW, the Council on the Cost of Government has prepared a more comprehensive series of reports on 'service efforts and accomplishments' of the NSW state sector, broadly arranged by 'policy areas' rather than by agency, covering around 96 per cent of expenditure. The involvement and intervention of an independent agency in the compilation of performance information has led to balanced reporting, with a greater focus on the relationship between government activities and community outcomes (*Walker*, 1999).

In short, parliamentary oversight of government activities needs improvement. Currently the focus is on what is to be 'spent' by governments from funds obtained in the current year from taxes, fees and fines. A more intelligent approach would be for parliament to look at how efficiently and effectively governments propose to utilise resources—not just the financial resources to be raised in a coming year, but the physical and human resources currently available to governments.

There are some practical, low-cost steps that could be undertaken to start re-focusing parliamentary accountability on the big picture:

- **Budget coverage:** All governments should present budgets in terms of the Australian Bureau of Statistics definition of 'general government', without leaving any scope for localised interpretations. Currently the formal processes for prior parliamentary approval of budgets only cover spending by whatever agencies the government of the day chooses to identify as part of its 'budget' or 'general government' sector. That means that governments can choose to regard some agencies as 'public trading enterprises' and exclude them from the budget, and hence, avoid formal parliamentary scrutiny through the workings of Estimates Committees.
- **Budget summary:** In addition, governments should also present a *summary* of their budgets and financial results on a 'whole of government' basis—encompassing public trading enterprises and central borrowing authorities. The current restriction of budgets to the 'general government' or 'budget' sector is artificial.

  The budget summary should be in a format consistent with that used in statements of cash flows prepared by listed public companies: it should summarise projected cash flows for operating, investing and financing activities. If nothing else, this would reduce the incentives facing governments to sell off profitable businesses in order to improve reported budget results. It would also prevent governments from claiming budget surpluses while their public trading enterprises were being forced to borrow to pay 'special dividends'.
- **Role of the Auditor-General:** Legislation establishing the powers and functions of Auditors-General should not limit the role of that office to reporting on the affairs of 'budget sector' or 'general government' agencies. It is not acceptable that the Australian National Audit Office should have to explain that its mandate did not allow it to investigate government business enterprises such as ANL (*Dempster*, 1997). Nor is it acceptable that governments should constrain the role of an Auditor-General by requiring public sector audits to be subject to competitive tendering.

  (For that matter, the role of an Auditor-General in reporting on the internal controls governing expenditures by the parliament

itself might also be clarified. In some jurisdictions, the Auditor-General is only *invited* to perform a limited 'financial statement' audit.)
- **Proposals to sell GTEs:** Whenever a government proposes to sell a business, full details of that proposal should be presented to parliament for consideration—and adequate time and funding should be made available for that review. It is not acceptable for governments to force proposals through without giving all members (government, opposition or crossbench) the opportunity to review the case for sale or retention in a professional and systematic way.

    This proposal would merely bring public sector requirements for the disclosure and prior approval of proposals closer to the standards already established in the private sector. Usually, public sector requirements are the more demanding, because of higher expectations about accountability for the use of taxpayers' funds. Yet, in this area, the private sector has more rigorous requirements. Australian Stock Exchange listing requirements have long prescribed that public companies should formally provide explanations and seek shareholder approval before they can dispose of a company's major undertaking, or change the scale of its activities. Currently, Chapter 11 of the Listing Rules provides

    > If an entity proposed to make a significant change, either directly or indirectly, to the nature or scale of its activities, it must provide full details to the ASX as soon as practicable. It must do so in any event before making the change (*Australian Stock Exchange*, 1999).

    The Listing Rules specify that the entity must give the ASX (and hence 'the market') information regarding the change and its effect on future potential earnings, 'and any information ASX asks for'. If the ASX requires, the entity must get the formal approval of shareholders by calling a special meeting.

    As a minimum, proposals for the sale of public trading enterprises should include 5–10 year forecasts of the earnings likely to be lost on sale, together with the cash flows associated with the investment of the proceeds (be it interest saved from debt reduction, or the costs of maintaining non-revenue producing infrastructure).
- **Government liabilities:** Governments should be required to provide parliament in a timely way, with full information about public sector aggregate 'liabilities' (not just debt).

    Most Australian governments now produce audited public sector consolidated statements, which provide a 'whole of government' view of public sector finances. These reports are only given limited circulation, and are not tabled in parliament. Often they are issued quietly, when parliament is not sitting, thus ensuring limited scrutiny and even more limited media coverage. Indeed, if the Commonwealth parliamentary press gallery had read and understood these reports, the community would have been laughing every time a federal politician claimed that the full privatisation of Telstra would lead to the 'elimination' of Commonwealth debt.

Moreover, these reports have not been produced in a timely way. Whereas listed public companies are required to provide annual reports or concise reports to security holders within 17 weeks after the end of a financial year (*ASX Listing Rule 4.6*), governments tend to take eight months or so to produce public sector consolidated statements.

- **Information on government infrastructure:** Governments should be required to provide parliament with better information about actions being undertaken to maintain and upgrade publicly-owned infrastructure. A common claim about the need for privatisation has been that without much-needed funds, governments would soon be unable to afford much-needed infrastructure. Yet, currently, there are no formal requirements for Commonwealth or state governments to report on how they have managed infrastructure, and what resources may be needed to maintain or upgrade those assets. An improved reporting regime could ensure that debate about emerging needs for capital investment was better informed.

A lead can be taken from the innovative (and, apparently, unique) reporting requirements introduced in 1993 for NSW local governments. Local councils are required to provide summary reports on the condition of infrastructure assets (including roads, bridges, water treatment and reticulation infrastructure, and drainage and waste water systems), and on what it was expected to cost to bring those assets to a satisfactory condition. There is no requirement for reports on these matters to go to the community, or even to councillors—they are to be provided to the Minister, but are available for public scrutiny. While the design of these requirements needs refinement, and many local governments are still using crude and preliminary figures, some startling estimates of the cost of upgrading local infrastructure have emerged from councils' first attempts to report on all of their infrastructure. 177 NSW councils, managing infrastructure with a reported value of $26 billion, estimated in 1996 that the cost of bringing those assets to a satisfactory condition would be around $6 billion. The annual cost of maintaining assets in a satisfactory condition was estimated to be around

$825 million per annum—as opposed to the funding actually provided for that purpose in current annual budgets of only $585 million (*Walker, Clarke & Dean*, 1999).

The extension of similar requirements to the Commonwealth and state sectors would enable far closer scrutiny of the maintenance of infrastructure. The kind of information currently provided in published annual reports avoids these issues. Often many types of infrastructure are extremely durable, so that irresponsible management of those assets does not become apparent until there is some catastrophic failure of the system. All the more reason why greater attention should be devoted to holding governments (and bureaucracies) accountable before, not after, such events.

- **Information on BOOT schemes, etc.:** Requirements for parliamentary oversight of spending should be formally widened to encompass BOOT schemes, take-or-pay contracts, and similar exercises in financial engineering. The drafting of rules to ensure this outcome would be difficult, but might be expressed as covering proposals to transfer to third parties any rights to revenues to be earned on government assets, or any proposals to grant options to third parties to acquire or use public sector assets.

The current arrangements in NSW for a review of 'contract summaries' by the Auditor-General do not go far enough. Such scrutiny should be undertaken before the deals are signed, not after. The content of the analyses submitted to review (and the Auditor-General's terms of reference) should be established not by ministers but by the Auditor-General's employer, the parliament. Such reviews should not be confined to the terms of the contract but should also encompass the full scale of the government's contributions to a project, and should provide assessments of the extent to which the parties to the proposed contract will share or bear risks. The documents submitted for scrutiny should include an independent analysis of the likely financial outcomes of a project, and of the manner in which the parties would receive financial rewards, under different scenarios. Above all, the analysis should encompass estimates of the effective cost of finance incurred by taxpayers as a consequence of involvement in those schemes.

- **Operational information on contracts:** Parliamentary committees, Auditors-General and public sector managers should be provided (through a mix of statutory amendments and standard contract conditions) with access to operational information held by contractors providing services to the community on behalf of the Government.

Public sector agencies cannot effectively monitor the quality of service being provided by contractors if the latter do not record complaints—or, if they do, refuse to provide access to complaints registers to the agency paying for those services. Auditors-General are not able to represent the interest of parliament properly if private firms doing audit work under contract seek to deny access to their working papers on grounds of client confidentiality. Concern about the effect of contracting out on public accountability have been expressed by the Commonwealth Auditor-General and Commonwealth parliamentary committees (*Barrett*, 1999; *Commonwealth Auditor-General*, October 1999; *Senate Finance and Public Administration Committee*, 1997), but have yet to be adequately addressed in the Commonwealth, or elsewhere.

This package of reforms could contribute to a cultural change within both governments and the public service. Public sector managers and executive government have a tendency to regard parliamentary processes and enquiries as a bit of a nuisance—as a constraint within which they are required to operate, rather than as a fundamental and valued component of democracy. Opposition to such reforms must be expected. But, in the face of such resistance, it may be useful to recall the observation of US writer Bernard Rosen:

> In a democracy the object is to keep the government subordinated to the people (*Rosen*, 1989).

Fostering the values of public service

Also, in a democracy, there is an expectation that the public service exists to carry out the wishes of the government of the day—subject, of course, to some formal checks and balances. There is a view that, in times past, the public service was fiercely neutral and independent, and gave advice to the government of the day, without fear or favour. Whether this was true is beside the point. It is not true today, and there is little hope of reversing history. The current situation is probably closer to the *Yes Minister* portrayal of the English civil service as a network of self-interested players, who in the interests of maintaining their own quality of life, frequently manage to deflect the good intentions of their ministers. As a former Ministerial staffer once suggested, 'It's *Yes Minister* without the jokes.'

Even so, some people point out the myth of an independent public service and lament the alleged 'politicisation' of the Westminster system. 'Permanent secretaries' are no longer permanent but short-term appointments. Similarly senior staff—those termed 'senior executives', and above, are likewise given short-term appointments. This is alleged to make agreeing with (or supporting) a minister's proposals necessary for survival. The fact is senior administrators in the public service are largely political appointments. Politicians may deny this, but this has been the situation for at least a decade.

There are exceptions: some are appointed to senior positions because they are cautious. They adopt the principle that, if you don't do anything, you don't make mistakes. Their main contribution is as 'yes men' (or women), providing comforting support to their superiors, and never challenging existing practices. Deference to the myth of an 'independent' and 'apolitical' public service can waste a lot of time. Incoming governments often struggle to work with chief executives who were trusted appointees of a predecessor government. Some of these executives have as keen an idea of the state of opinion polls and the timing of elections as politicians. Many set out to survive the current government and await the return of their own team. Others make themselves inconspicuous, but are ready to drop from the trees when a government changes. Within the ranks of executives are those who can be very good at frustrating the wishes of an incoming government often by simply slowing down correspondence, raising questions about the potential impacts of changes, seeking legal advice, seeking the views of other agencies, or proposing the formation of inter-departmental committees. There is a formidable repertoire of devices available to the public servant who is committed to delaying change. Ministers, in turn, are often reluctant to engage in battles with their departments, for fear that they will not be protected from the complaints of aggrieved constituents, and be left exposed without briefings when a political issue crops up. Ministers have a difficult time if their department leaves them stranded.

It takes time (and, sometimes, a lot of resources) to get rid of uncooperative chief executives. Keeping CEOs who are frustrating the implementation of government policies wastes time, particularly when governments have only a small window of opportunity (just after elections) to implement major changes.

One way of ensuring that public sector employees actually implement government policies is to recognise the reality of an already-politicised public service. The US approach involves wholesale change in senior appointments of executive government when there is a change in the presidency. Some Australian governments have been reluctant to take similar steps in the name of preserving the Westminster tradition.

Adoption of that approach in Australia could involve formalising two streams of contractual arrangements within the public service (as at present), but with the senior stream on short-term contracts which are aligned to the electoral cycle. That would allow an incoming government, if it wished to do so, to have a clean sweep of chief executives, without having to maintain the fiction that the public service is not 'political'.

At the same time, career members of the public service need protection from the discriminatory actions of politicians or of political appointees—since there are plenty of ways that individuals may be given a hard time just because they may dare to provide independent advice, which runs counter to what their superiors want to hear.

Approaches used in Australia have involved public service 'boards' or 'commissioners', and appeal mechanisms, to protect the careers of individuals who fall out of favour for such reasons. None really work satisfactorily.

An alternative would be to borrow another US practice: the idea that independent regulatory agencies should have governance arrangements which recognise political realities. Teddy Roosevelt's term as US president introduced the practice of establishing commissions with a formal composition of three members of the party in office, and two registered party members from the opposition. This acknowledged the politicised nature of such appointments[1], while both introducing checks and balances into the system and virtually ensuring the ventilation of any contentious issues in the treatment of specific cases. Such an approach could be used to operate a new-style 'public service commission': a central agency which would play a role in all but chief executive appointments, and generally nurture (and defend) the public service. Such an agency could ensure that individuals who have fallen out of favour in one bureaucracy have a chance of recommencing a career in another. It could foster mobility within the public sector, and between the public and private sectors.

An independent public service commission of this type could be responsible for recruitment, continuing education and professional development of the career public service. Certainly the latter role

---

1 It has been suggested that US political appointments in the 1990s were proportionately three times more common than they were in the 1930s. 'Each new administration simply replaces the top layers of the departmental hierarchies'—'it is time that this was recognized for exactly what much of it is: political corruption; not technically illegal but nevertheless corrupting of dedicated and experienced public service' (*Mintzberg*, 1996). The approach suggested here is aimed at securing what Mintzberg describes as 'political control without resorting to political administration'.

does not seem to be performed satisfactorily at present, with reliance placed on seminars conducted by commercial organisations. There have been some telling reports of shortcomings in the training of public servants. Former NSW Auditor-General Tony Harris devoted much of his retirement speech to state that many public servants have a limited understanding of their statutory responsibilities regarding fiscal matters.

The same model of direct representation of a balance of political interests could be applied not only to regulatory authorities but also to a range of agencies within the general government and public trading enterprise sectors. Such an approach could be expected to moderate the volatility of policy changes affecting bodies which are performing essentially administrative functions. It would also establish the basis on which talented individuals could be retained on government boards, regardless of perceptions about their political preferences—thus moderating the influence of political extremists from either side of politics.

Better-qualified people

Parliaments can change the rules, and governments can adopt new policies, but at the end of the day all this is meaningless unless there is both the will to make fundamental change, and the talent to implement it. There are many talented, skilful, and hardworking people in the public service. (There are also a lot of sycophantic drones.)

This review of experience with privatisation, in its various forms, suggests that mistakes have been made by politicians—either because they were ideologically blinkered, or because they were not adequately informed. Either way, they have let us down.

Sociologist Michael Pusey has described how the Commonwealth public service has become increasingly populated by 'technocrats' with a narrow background in economics, commerce and business administration—54 per cent of senior executive officers from 13 key departments had these qualifications. Pusey argued that 'economic rationalism' had come to dominate policy making in Canberra, that what was once a 'national building state' was now pursuing policies aimed at smaller government and a reduction of 'public policy' to 'business policy' (*Pusey*, 1991). Many may find such observations disturbing.

Yet despite this apparent domination by economic technocrats, the evidence presented here suggests that the public sector suffers badly from a lack of high-level financial talent. There are few staff capable of matching the highly-paid merchant bankers and advisers from the Big Six accounting firms, when the need arises to analyse complex financial transactions. Many agencies lack staff with the skills to analyse patterns of expenditure within their own departments, or to assess the merits of proposed outsourcing or other privatisation arrangements.

This situation is not new. An academic economist, noted both for his scholarship and his knowledge of public finance, suggested that public investments have been undertaken in Australia because of 'political expediency' or 'technical incompetence' (*Groenewegen*, 1984). Government publications have acknowledged skill shortages in this area: a 1990 NSW publication setting out guidelines on ways that the private sector might be involved in developing public sector infrastructure cautioned that

> Use of consultants may be especially necessary with respect to project financing which requires specialist skills not always found in Departments or agencies (*NSW Department of State Development*, 1990).

Much of the Australian public sector is light on talent in the area of financial analysis and financial management. A Commonwealth survey showed that less than 10 per cent of finance staff operating in Commonwealth agencies hold professional accounting qualifications (CPA, ACA or equivalent)' (*Commonwealth Management Advisory Board*, 1997).

Some jurisdictions have entire 'departments' or 'offices' of finance or financial management which are mainly staffed by persons without basic training in those disciplines. Those who have received basic qualifications have often not kept up to date with developments in their disciplines. Worse, they don't recognise their lack of skills. Even worse, nor do many of their superiors. And even worse again, the chief financial officers of some major agencies are often reluctant to recruit subordinates who are better qualified than themselves.

One consequence is that agencies spending a billion dollars or more per annum of taxpayers' funds may not be analysing their cost structure, establishing systems whereby managers are responsible for effective use of resources, or keeping track of trends in items of expenditure—from salary costs and overtime, to travel and entertainment. Nor do central agencies (such as Departments of Treasury or Finance) have the capacity to drill down into agencies' accounting records to examine the information for themselves—a standard capability in the information systems installed by well-run large corporations in the private sector. Instead, if they have the inclination and will to do so, they must engage in bureaucratic warfare to seek explanations of material variations in spending patterns.

Another consequence is that the chief executives of agencies—

and their ministers—may be provided with financial information which is of such poor quality that it is an unreliable basis for monitoring performance. Even more alarming, internal reporting practices often fail to interpret data concerning year-to-date results to alert management to emerging problems—by raising red flags, and pointing to the need for resources to be shifted from one activity to another if the agency is not to experience financial difficulties or be unable to fund core activities.

Because they lack the management capability to analyse their cost structures, to identify emerging problems, and to deal with them in a timely fashion, there is a tendency for some public sector agencies to lurch from one financial crisis to another.

A by-product of the employment of poorly qualified (or even unqualified) financial staff in senior positions is the chronic inability of some agencies to produce annual financial statements which meet the requirements of Australian accounting standards.

In its *Fifth Report* to the NSW parliament, the Council on the Cost of Government stated:

> The Council noted with concern the practice of some agencies in advertising for accountants or financial managers, without establishing appropriate criteria for appointment to those positions. In some advertisements (even for recruits to the Senior Executive Service) the stated criteria identified the possession of tertiary or professional qualifications as not being 'essential', only 'desirable'.
>
> The Auditor-General has expressed concern about recruitment practices whereby staff responsible for the preparation of financial statements did not hold current professional qualifications—a situation which adds to the cost and delay in the preparation of financial reports. The Council's concerns relate to the knowledge, skill and experience of staff responsible for such matters as the preparation of internal reports for management, the analysis of trends in spending, the provision of advice to senior managers and through them to the Government (*Council on the Cost of Government*, June 1998).

Subsequently, the NSW Premier Bob Carr issued a memorandum indicating that in future, chief financial officers and those responsible for the preparation of financial reports should have relevant tertiary qualifications and be full members of one of the two major accounting bodies in Australia (the Institute of Chartered Accountants in Australia and the Australian Society of Certified Practising Accountants). The memorandum incorporated a grandfather clause to enable existing staff without those qualifications to be re-appointed. It encouraged existing staff to upgrade their qualifications and pursue programs of professional development. This was a pioneering initiative, even if it was benign. The

Commonwealth and other states have yet to follow suit.

But the remarkable aspect of the exercise was that there was any need for such a directive. The public sector claims to make appointments on the basis of merit. No self-respecting agency would contemplate appointing a person to act as an actuary, architect, dentist, engineer, solicitor, medical officer, or veterinary surgeon unless they had relevant and high-level qualifications. A host of agencies insist that applicants be university graduates (in some discipline) when they advertise middle management positions. Yet the same standards are not required for more senior appointments requiring specialist skills. The public sector (and the taxpayer) deserves to attract the best talent—and certainly should not accept lesser standards than those applying in the private sector. No large corporation of any size (let alone one with an annual expenditure budget of billions of dollars) would appoint a chief financial officer who only had TAFE qualifications.

Until the public sector recruits suitably qualified, experienced and energetic financial staff, it cannot expect to get quality financial advice. Without high quality information and high quality advice, governments can also expect to continue to make flawed financial decisions—particularly concerning asset sales, outsourcing, or BOOT schemes involving private sector firms.

Separating players from scorekeepers

Finally, a structural reform which could assist in securing better quality financial information would be to separate the role of *advising* on resource allocation from the role of *monitoring* the performance of the agencies receiving those resources. Bundling the roles of adviser and scorekeeper just creates conflicts of interest.

There is a strong case to separate these roles, along the lines of the Commonwealth's use of separate Treasury and Finance departments, while expanding the role of the 'finance' department to include the job of providing reports on both the financial and the operational performance of agencies, on a 'whole of government' basis. This should lead to information being made routinely available about the efforts and accomplishments of agencies in providing services to the community.

Final comment

The Australian experience with privatisation is mixed. In some cases, it can be seen as a sensible and rational change in the activities of government, in response to changes in society. In other cases, it can be seen as a crude response to defective public administration and laxity in parliamentary oversight. Opinions may differ as to how these problems are addressed. But there has to be a better way.

Appendix to Chapter 5
A Note on the Concept of 'Cost of Capital'

A KEY ELEMENT of any formal analysis of privatisation proposals is the choice of assumptions about the interest rate to be used to discount future cash flows in order to estimate 'sale' or 'retention' value.

A high discount rate gives greater weight to cash flows that a project is expected to earn in the near future. A low discount rate gives greater weight to cash flows that a project is expected to earn in the long term.

Moreover, as illustrated earlier in this chapter, if a stable stream of cash flows is discounted at different interest rates, a high discount rate will produce a *lower net present value* than calculations using a low discount rate. That translates into a low estimate of the retention value of a government enterprise.

If one is a true believer in the privatisation of public trading - enterprises, or just think that privatisation would be good for business (yours), then it makes sense to argue that the cost of capital for the public sector should be the same as the rates identified for private sector firms. High discount rates will reduce estimates of retention values, and hence produce results which are biased towards privatisation.

The claim that the cost of capital 'should be the same' for public sector and private sector firms is not based on empirical evidence. The concept of 'cost of capital' is a theoretical construct, and the cost of capital of individual firms or governments cannot be measured directly. The processes undertaken by financial analysts to quantify the cost of capital involve a series of arbitrary assumptions, several of which are just not relevant to the public sector.

Appendix to Chapter 5

To explain: one can observe the prices at which debt securities are traded, and from these prices and information about redemption dates, calculate the yields that will be earned on those securities to maturity. Hence estimates of yields being earned by investors in government debt securities (and the effective interest rates being paid by government on those securities) can be independently calculated and verified. But one cannot observe and measure the 'cost of equity capital' at any time, despite the closest of studies of market prices and of the rights associated with those securities.

When reference is made to the 'cost of capital' of private sector firms, it is usually taken to mean the 'weighted average cost of capital'—a combination of estimates of the cost of debt finance and the cost of equity finance. Governments issue debt instruments, but don't raise new equity capital.

The calculation of 'cost of equity capital' is a bit like the calculation of accounting profit. In accounting, independent observers can check the calculations used by a firm to value inventories or depreciable assets. But since there are many other ways those calculations could have been made in terms of accepted accounting practices, it is highly likely that no two independent observers would arrive at exactly the same result. So it is with estimates of the cost of capital for private sector firms. Different observers will make different choices of data to be used in those estimates. Moreover, the calculations involve guesses about what will be the future cost of capital—since estimates of the retention value of businesses should be based on discounting future cash flows using interest rates which reflect not the historical but the projected cost of capital in the same future years.

History of the idea of 'cost of capital'

The concept of the 'cost of capital' was introduced into the literature of business finance in conjunction with discussions about the ranking of alternative investment proposals using discounted cash flow analysis. The techniques of discounted cash flow analysis were well understood and popularised by the 1920s (see, e.g. *Fisher*, 1906; *Sprague & Perrine*, 1919), but mainly in relation to the calculation of yields on bonds, annuities and other financial instruments.

It was not until the 1950s that serious attention was given in the business literature to the application of discounted cash flow analysis to 'capital budgeting', corporate planning and project evaluation (see, e.g. *Dean*, 1951). Even then, it was recognised that while discounted cash flow analysis was a useful tool, there were a number of unresolved questions about how to apply that form of analysis in practical circumstances.

Privatisation

The history of some key ideas about project evaluation and the significance of the use of the cost of capital as the choice of discount rate, can be explained through illustrations. Suppose that two projects each required a initial investment of $1,000 at time zero, but produced different patterns of positive cash flows as set out below. Which project should be preferred?

Case 1:

Year:	0	1	2	3	4	5
Project A	-$1000	+$100	+$200	+$300	+$400	+$700
Project B	-$1000	+$500	+$400	+$300	+$200	+$100

Interest rate: 10% pa

Project A promises a higher aggregate return (gross returns of $1,700 over five years) than Project B (gross returns of $1,500), but Project A produces greater returns in the earlier years. The calculation of 'present values' provides a basis for choosing between the projects.

The *present value* of a series of future cash flows can be considered as equivalent to the sum that would have to be invested in an interest bearing deposit in order that an investor could withdraw those specified cash flows over time, until finally the amount originally invested together with interest earned were both exhausted.

In the case of Project A, the present value of the cash receipts in years 1, 2, 3, 4 and 5 is $1,189. That is to say, the sum of $1,189 invested at 10 per cent per annum (with interest payable in a single instalment at the end of each year) would enable an investor to withdraw the sums of $100 at the end of the first year, $200 after the second year, $300 after the third, $400 after the fourth, before a final withdrawal of the remaining balance of $700 at the end of the fifth year.

In the case of Project A, there is also an initial investment of $1,000 at the beginning of the first year. The present value of the outlays is $1,000. The *net present value* (NPV) of the project is ($1,189 less $1,000), or $189.

Similarly, the NPV of the cash flows from Project B is $209.

If an investor was only concerned with financial returns, then he should prefer Project B, which (despite lower gross returns) has a higher NPV ($209) than Project A ($189).

But if an investor had more than $1,000 to invest, then he might decide to invest in *both* Project A and Project B. Both have a positive NPV, indicating that each will generate an 'internal rate of return' in excess of 10 per cent per annum.

Sometimes reference is made to a 'hurdle rate'. In this illustration,

Appendix to Chapter 5

if an investor decided to invest in projects which exceeded the 'hurdle rate' of 10 per cent per annum, then both projects would be attractive. If the hurdle rate was set higher—say 16 per cent—then only Project B would be attractive.

Complications arise when an investor is trying to evaluate projects which involve different levels of investment, or which will produce cash flows over different periods of time. To rank competing projects in that situation, assumptions have to be made about how the proceeds might be reinvested once received. Most times those assumptions are implicit: it is assumed that funds can be reinvested at the discount rate.

Indeed, if a five year project promised a rate of return of 15 per cent, and a ten year project a rate of return of 12 per cent, then an investor might prefer the ten year project with the lower rate (because he may not be confident that the returns from the first project in years five to ten would produce an overall return of 12 per cent over the longer period).

Case 1 assumes that we have certain knowledge about future cash flows. But that is rare. Textbook illustrations of discounted cash flow analysis frequently explore cases where alternative investments are of differing risk. Consider the following:

Case 2
The cash flows for Project C are 'locked in' through contractual arrangements with a major bank. There is thus virtual certainty that the cash flows set out for Project C will eventuate in the pattern indicated. However the returns for Project D are expected to be somewhere in the range $100 to $1,200 per annum, but the best estimate is $400 per annum (as in Project C).

Year:	0	1	2	3	4	5
Project C	-$1000	+$400	+$400	+$400	+$300	+$300
Project D (Pessimistic scenario)	-$1000	-$500 +$100	-$500 +$100	-$500 +$100	+$100	+$100
or—most likely scenario:	-$1000	+$400	+$400	+$400	+$400	+$400
or—optimistic scenario	-$1000	+$900	+$900	+$900	+$900	+$900
or—very optimistic scenario	-$1000	+$1200	+$1200	+$1200	+$1200	+$1200

Because of the uncertainty surrounding future cash flows, Project D is riskier than Project C. So, if Project C is to be evaluated using a 10 per cent discount rate, should Project D be examined using a higher rate—say 12 per cent? Or 15 per cent?

The commonly accepted view is that adjusting the discount rate to reflect risk is fundamentally wrong.

> Should an investment with more uncertainty have a higher rate of discount than an investment with less uncertainty? The answer tentatively suggested is negative. Uncertainty recognized in computing the cash flows is more effective than using a higher discount factor for increased risk (*Bierman & Smidt*, 1960).
>
> The most common mistake in trying to cope with the uncertainties of the benefits and costs of a project is to argue that in the face of risk [one] ... should use a higher rate of discount.
>
> To use a higher discount rate confuses the evaluation of income at different dates with the evaluation of risk: these are two separate issues (*Stiglitz*, 1986).

Rather, texts argued that exactly the same discount rate should be used for alternative projects, and to apply this to a 'best estimate' of future cash flows, or a 'certainty equivalent' (the dollar sum which the analysis would regard as equivalent to the range of cash inflows).

Another, and possibly more popular, approach is to use the same discount rate to work out the presented values of projected cash flows under a range of scenarios, corresponding to outcomes of differing probability. This produces a range of net present values and thus highlights the inherent uncertainty of the outcomes of proposed investments.

Note also that one of the risks facing firms arises from inflation. One way to incorporate expected inflation in the analysis is to use market discount rates and projected cash flows in terms of dollars of the day—and that is the way most analyses of privatisation proposals are evaluated.

Selection of a discount rate to evaluate projects in the private sector

Several approaches have been advocated in the theoretical literature to identify discount rates to be used by private sector firms in evaluating alternative projects:

- selection of a rate which reflects *the rates of return available from other investments* available to a firm;

Appendix to Chapter 5

- calculation of a firm's *expected cost of capital* based on the expected rate-of-return 'demanded' by existing and new investors in both debt and equity securities.

For simplicity, the following discussion generally refers to rates of return *before tax*.

Proponents of the idea that discount rates should reflect the opportunity cost of capital were quick to emphasise that the rate selected should be of projects of *equivalent risk*. In other words, higher discount rates should be used when evaluating projects of high risk than would be used for projects of lower risk. Advocates of this approach did not seem at all troubled by the inconsistency with earlier conclusions that it was wrong to adjust discount rates because of differences in risk. Indeed, in many cases that literature has just been ignored.

In practice, firms typically use rough and ready methods. It has been noted that firms used arbitrary cut-off rates (*Solomon*, 1956), or estimates of what they considered to be their own good past performance, or the performance of competitors or other firms in the same industry (*NAA*, 1967).

Standard texts on business finance continuing to advise either the use of an 'opportunity cost of capital', or the use of estimates of a firm's cost of capital, the issue of how to actually estimate that rate remains problematic. In the 1960s, texts acknowledged that the subject was an 'unresolved area' (*NAA*, 1967) and a topic on which there was 'no universal agreement' (*Bennett, Grant & Parker*, 1964). In the late 1970s it was still acknowledged that '... no one has yet specified an analytical method for quantifying the risk in terms of increased discount rates' (*Weil*, 1978).

Since the late 1950s, a series of academic contributions have sought to develop ways of estimating the cost of capital. It was considered that the rate of interest payable on borrowed funds by a private sector firm was not the appropriate rate to use for discounted cash flow analysis, since a corporation's funds came partly from borrowings and partly from money provided by shareholders. If lenders were receiving a rate of return of around 10 per cent on their money, then equity holders *deserved to be provided with a higher rate of return*, since they were bearing more risk. So theorists referred to a firm's *weighted average cost of capital* (assigning a value to the 'cost' of both debt and equity). To illustrate: suppose that a corporation had a capital structure[1] which was

---

[1] *Bierman & Smidt* (1960) defined the weights to be used in calculating the weighted average cost of capital in a different manner: 'as the ratio of the market value of

Privatisation

50 per cent debt (costing 8 per cent per annum) and 50 per cent shareholders funds (for which an earning rate of 12 per cent was considered appropriate). In this instance, the weighted average cost of capital would be 10 per cent per annum.

But if a firm had 80 per cent debt and 20 per cent equity then its weighted average cost of capital would be only 8.8 per cent.

This led to questions being raised about whether one should use a cost of capital figure based on the current capital structure of a firm, or on some alternative if the current capital structure was not optimal. But, if so, what was a firm's optimum capital structure? Should new projects be financed by debt, equity, or some combination of debt and equity. Since interest on debt was tax deductible, how much should be borrowed? (No author ever suggested that private sector firms should have zero debt.)

It was recognised that high levels of debt (or high 'gearing') would be regarded by lenders as risky, and that lenders would require higher and higher returns as gearing increased, to compensate them for that additional risk. One author (*Lewellen, 1969*) argued that firms should borrow up to their 'debt limit'—the point at which additional borrowings would be reflected in reduced stock prices. But the only difficulty in applying this notion was how to identify, in advance, what a firm's 'debt limit' might be?

Decades later, the issue of what constitutes the optimum capital structure of a private sector firm remains unresolved. However, in the marketplace, it is accepted that some businesses (such as banks) can maintain a more highly geared capital structure than others (such as manufacturers or retailers). Correspondingly, high gearing is seen as positively risky in businesses like property development. The current conventional wisdom is that firms with strong and regular cash flows from operations (for example, breweries) can more readily support higher levels of debt than firms with irregular cash flows (such as firms engaged in tourism or property development).

But that still leaves the question, what is the 'cost' of equity? Granted it must be higher than the cost of loan finance—but how could that rate be estimated?

Theoretical discussions about ways of calculating a private firm's cost of equity capital then started adopting a key assumption. It was *assumed that managers were seeking to maximise the value of the firm* (or, more crudely, increase its share prices). On that basis, all other things being equal, a firm would have to select new

---

the securities representing that source of capital to the market value of all securities issued by the company'.

Appendix to Chapter 5

projects that would be *as* or *more profitable* than those the firm was already undertaking (give or take some allowance for differences in risk).

The following illustrate ways that this assumption was expressed in the technical literature:

> [The theory of capital rationing] assumes, as usual in economic theory, that the objective of the enterprise is to maximise profits in a narrow and calculable sense of the world. But narrow profit maximization is not the only, or, in fact, the usual, goal of large corporate enterprise (*Dean*, 1951).
>
> Implicit in any definition of a cost of capital to guide investment policy is a judgment as to the goals toward which the firm is or should be striving (*Bierman & Smidt*, 1960).
>
> The cost of capital can be defined as ... the rate of return for new investment projects such that, if all projects undertaken by the firm yield that rate, then the market value of the firm's shares will remain unchanged (*Weil*, 1978).
>
> The basic rationale for using the weighted average cost of capital is that by accepting only projects expected to yield returns greater than that cost, the firm will increase the market price of its stock in the long run and thereby increase shareholder wealth (*Rappaport*, 1978).

So, on the basis if this assumption about managers were seeking to increase the value of the firm, as assessed by the stock market, the task became one of assessing what discount rates were implicitly used by the market to value a firm's streams of future cash flows.

Bierman & Smidt (1960) were happy to claim that cost of equity capital was the rate of discount that equated future dividends for perpetuity to the current market price of shares—but that involved predicting whether current levels of dividends would be increased in future.

Academic researchers had been exploring ways of modelling share prices and in constructing portfolios of securities which promised different levels of return, commensurate with risk. The 'Capital Asset Pricing Model' was a way of estimating likely changes in the prices of individual securities—given knowledge of changes in interest rates, general market movements, and of the manner in which individual share prices had changed in association with market-wide movements. The model was expressed in algebraic form and required a computer to run multiple regression calculations. But essentially the Capital Asset Pricing model indicated that the financial returns earned by holding assets could be approximated by a formula combining movements in risk-free interest rates, market-wide movements in asset prices (as evidence of the returns on a 'market portfolio' and the variance of those returns), and the co-variance of the returns earned on an individual asset and market wide returns (commonly known as the Beta factor). Hence it was proposed that this model enabled estimates to be made of the returns likely to be earned from investment in risky assets.

Calculations based on this model (and its variants) were commonly used to examine the rates of return which had been earned by shareholders in particular companies. Mark that the 'returns' earned by shareholders in this context were a combination of capital gains (from increases in share prices) and dividends, and made adjustments for rights or bonus issues.

A range of academics and practitioners then re-interpreted this data in a strange way: they claimed that the historic 'rates of return' earned by investors in shares represented the rates of return *demanded* by equity investors. This was truly a remarkable piece of sophistry. Shareholders might wish that their investments will all be winners. They may dream of making stunning profits. But when they buy shares, they are not in a position to *demand* that the market price of those shares will increase (let alone increase to 18.36 per cent or some other figure worked out to the second decimal place).

'Hope?'—yes. '*Expect?*'—perhaps. '*Demand?*'—no.

The next step taken by these academics and practitioners was to look at the rates of return 'earned' for different stocks in different industries, and use those figures as representing the returns 'demanded' by equity investors. Presto: a calculation of a firm's cost of equity capital. Mix in data regarding the cost of debt finance, and we have a figure for a firm's before tax weighted average cost of capital.

Now this process and the fruits of these calculations involve a lot of assumptions. The first and major assumption is that the exercise is aimed at identifying a discount rate to be used in screening new investment proposals in order to identify those, which (if things work out) will increase the value of the firm. Others are more technical. There is an implicit assumption that business risk has been stable in the recent past and will not change as a result of planned investment. Another is that the firm will continue to raise capital in the same proportions as its present capital structure. Then there is an assumption that the Capital Asset Pricing Model is the right choice to estimate the cost of equity capital (even though academic researchers have since presented a number of alternative models of asset pricing).

For all these reasons, the apparent precision of the calculations of a weighted average cost of capital is illusory.

But use of the Capital Asset Pricing Model produces some

dramatically high estimates of the cost of equity capital for some industries. Those cost of capital estimates figures have been used to support claims for increased prices before price regulatory authorities (because of the need for increased investment in inventories or productive facilities). They have also been used in 'experts' reports' commissioned by warring parties during takeover battles (to justify or contest valuations placed on a company's shares).

In short, there is now an extensive literature on calculating the weighted average cost of capital for private sector firms, and the techniques set out in standard textbooks are widely used in commerce. The calculations are complicated but at the end of the day are based on subjective estimates of what firms are engaged in industries of 'equivalent risk', and heroic assumptions to the effect that past market assessments of a company's risk and returns will remain unchanged in the future. It is essentially a normative literature. It is *based on the assumption that managers are always seeking to increase the value of a firm* (as reflected in increased share prices). Hence the calculations are designed to establish hurdle rates for new investments which (if the predictions of future profits and cash flows come true) would achieve that objective.

However, recall that the starting point of the theoretical arguments for the use of these techniques is an *assumption that managers seek to increase the value of the firm*. This assumption is just not relevant to the public sector. Australian governments are not elected to maximise the value of government assets. They are elected to provide services and benefits to the community.

Selection of a discount rate to evaluate public sector investments

At roughly the same time that discounted cash flow (DCF) analysis was popularised in the business literature, it was also used in the public sector to assist in the process of allocating resources to competing projects, particularly for capital works. In that context, the term 'cost-benefit analysis' was more widely used, since the focus of the analysis were often not cash inflows or cash outflows but economic or 'social' benefits (which needed to be assigned some monetary value).

The assignment of dollar values to benefits such as environmental protection, noise abatement, or the time saved from speedier transport systems, is obviously a fairly rough and ready (and at times, contentious) process.

Similarly, the choice of discount rates has often been a rough and ready process. If politicians are determined to construct capital works, which will benefit their constituencies or influence voters in marginal electorates, then they will hope that any cost-benefit analysis undertaken by the public service supports their proposals. Anecdotal evidence suggests that low discount rates are often selected for projects which a government is determined to undertake—because a low rate may make capital intensive projects 'look good'.

The theoretical literature on public finance suggests there is widespread disagreement about what discount rate is appropriate—reflecting disagreement about the underlying rationale for selecting one rate rather than another in different situations.

At one extreme is the suggestion that cost-benefit analysis should use a *social discount rate*, based on a social rate of time preference—which measures the value society places on foregoing present consumption (e.g. when governments provide facilities which will benefit both current generations and future generations.) The underlying idea is that communities (or paternalistic governments, acting on behalf of those communities) are prepared to leave legacies to future generations, in the form of social and physical infrastructure. If one assumes that communities undertaken a notional form of cost-benefit analysis using discount cash flow techniques, then (at least some) economists can assert that the social rate of time preference is revealed in those decisions, as communities prefer future benefits to present consumption.

It may be easier to describe the social rate of time preference than to measure it. However, it is clear that the use of a 'social discount rate' would generally involve use of a lower rate than the private sector cost of debt. Investors in the public and private sectors display differing time preferences. Private sector investors generally want some kind of pay-off within their own lifetime. Governments represent the interests of several generations, and so can accept lower rates of return than private investors.

At another extreme in debates about the choice of a discount rate to evaluate public sector investments is the claim that the rate selected should be a private market rate. That is generally interpreted in the public finance literature as meaning either the marginal projected returns currently expected or achievable on private sector investment, or the rate at which private firms can borrow funds for investment. The latter rate would be far lower than the rates calculated by the Capital Asset Pricing Model as representing the returns supposedly 'demanded' by private sector investors.

When arguments for the use of a 'private market rate' for the evaluation of public sector projects are inspected in detail, it becomes clear that some are the product of theoretical analyses on the basis of simplifying assumptions: for example, that choices are to be made in an economy in which there is perfect competition, and perfect knowledge about the future profits of all investments:

> The social discount rate will be the marginal return on private investment in an idealized economy that satisfies the conditions of perfect competition in a world of certainty (*Lind*, 1982).

Other arguments of this genre have been highly qualified. For example, economist Kenneth Arrow argued that 'there is a strong case for equating the rate of discount in the public sector to that in the private sector *to the extent that public investment is financed by taxes on profits*' (emphasis added) (*Arrow*, 1982). That qualification has been seen as restricting this analysis to only those government investments intended to increase private income (*Feldstein*, 1982), rather than the wider class of public sector expenditures that produce services to the community directly.

A possible variant of the Arrow argument is that private sector rates should be used to evaluate public sector projects when those who 'pay' for public sector projects are also those who 'use' them. One example of a project where this would apply might be where government charges in the form of boat licences are used to construct new boating facilities; another might be charges levied on users of accommodation facilities in national parks. Other examples are hard to find. Further, there is usually a mis-match between the periods in which infrastructure assets are constructed and the benefits from that infrastructure are received. Moreover, those in society who pay most for projects do always not receive benefits in proportion to their payments. For example, those who pay fuel or road taxes may not be the sole beneficiaries of access to transport infrastructure. Those who pay most in income taxes may receive lesser benefits from the education or health systems than others on lower incomes. Indeed, cross-subsidisation arrangements (between elements of a community, or between generations) are a common feature of civilised societies. Cross-subsidisation underpins the funding of health and education services, social welfare payments, the provision of services to rural communities, or the maintenance of cultural, artistic and scientific collections.

Another argument for the use of the rate at which private sector firms can obtain finance was based on the concern that otherwise, government investment would displace or 'crowd out' private projects.

A rejoinder to this argument is that even when it may apply, it would be inappropriate for governments to use the rate of interest facing private-sector firms unless there is an active government policy to redistribute income across generations. And even then 'there is considerable controversy over whether these special cases provide much guidance for policy purposes' (*Stiglitz*, 1986).

In any case, there are likely to be few clear-cut situations where public investment 'crowds out' private sector investment. Private-sector health care may be profitable. But private sector firms do not rush to build neo-natal wards in hospitals to treat premature babies, or nursing homes to cater for persons with profound disabilities, or respite facilities to provide short-term care for the intellectually disabled when their families are ill or exhausted. Those expensive and loss-making ventures are commonly left to the public sector.

When one moves from a world of theoretical modelling under restrictive conditions to the real world of policy making, there appears to be some consensus that the public sector 'should compute cost, benefits, and discount rates differently than the private sector' (*Rosen*, 1995).

In other words, instead of choosing a discount rate which reflects the rate of return available on alternative investments, or which will lead to maximisation of the value of the firm, the public sector approach should have regard to:

- a wider range of factors than financial costs and benefits;
- issues such as whether those who pay for projects are also the beneficiaries;
- society's preferences in relation to immediate consumption or investment to benefit future generations.

The bottom line is that while economists and public finance specialists disagree about how to choose a discount rate, they still propose the use of discount rates which are significantly lower than those which would be selected in the private sector. At the same time, there is no real agreement about the exact basis for choosing a public sector discount rate. The following have been suggested:

> the government bond rate [if public investment is financed by bonds] (*Arrow & Kurz*, 1970).
> the private market rate (as reflected in the rate of long term, debentures or the long-term bond rate) (*Groenewegen*, 1984).
> any public rate of discount in a range between the before- and after-tax rates of return in the private sector (*Rosen*, 1995).
> somewhat above the real bond rate, but below the average cost of capital to private firms (*Quiggin*, 1997).

In practical terms: economists might argue over whether the relevant discount rate should be between 6 per cent and 9 per cent, when the weighted average cost of capital for private firms engaged

Appendix to Chapter 5

in comparable activities might be 15 per cent or higher.

In the face of this debate, it seems that economic practitioners accept that even though the choice of discount rates is debatable, cost-benefit analysis is still worth doing, to evaluate new projects. And while they can't agree on what rate to use, they generally agree that it should be lower than the rates used by private sector investors.

Finally, they defend the use of cost-benefit analysis using uncertain estimates of costs, benefits and discount rates, on the basis that

> one does not need pin-point accuracy, usually ballpark accuracy is sufficient (*Lind*, 1982).

Use of discounted cash flow analysis in 'valuing' businesses

While the concept of 'net present value' and the techniques of discounting cash flows were initially used to assist in the ranking of competing investment proposals, they also came to be used in the valuation of private sector businesses.

Traditional methods of business valuation used the 'profit capitalisation' method (see, e.g. *Sidey*, 1950). Suppose that a business was earning $100,000 per annum, and current interest rates were 5 per cent. In essence, the 'profit capitalisation' method valued a business as being equivalent to the amount that would have to be invested at 5 per cent per annum to produce an income of $100,000 in perpetuity i.e. $2 million per annum.

Another rough-and-ready method of valuing companies whose shares were publicly traded on the stock exchange was to use price-earnings multiples. The shares of other companies in the same industry may have traded at a price, which represents a certain multiple of last year's earnings. On that basis, the valuation would involve identifying the earnings of the subject company, and multiplying that by the selected price earnings (P/E) factor.

A more sophisticated approach to business valuation was to suggest that the value of a business represented the present value of projected future net cash inflows—discounted at some selected discount rate.

Over 50 years or more, these methods continue to be used. The Australian Securities and Investments Commission, for example, has stated that it is appropriate that experts' valuation reports should consider a series of methods when valuing businesses—and heading the list was the discounted cash flow method, followed by the application of earnings multiples to the estimated future maintainable earnings or cash flows of a company. 'Other methods included the amount that would be distributed to shareholders on an orderly realisation of assets, and the current market price of listed securities—see *ASC Practice Note 43*, August 1997.) The discounted cash flow method continues to be the most commonly advocated method of valuing businesses.

Cost of capital for government—when examining privatisation

As noted above, the choice of a discount rate is of great significance to evaluations of proposals to privatise government trading enterprises.

It has been argued here that while for the purposes of project evaluation, the relevant discount rate may well be a firm's estimated 'weighted average cost of capital' (assuming that managers are seeking to increase the value of the firm), the same rate should not be used in the public sector (since governments are not seeking to increase their net worth). Governments finance their activities by taxes, fees, fines charges—and borrowings. Hence, for project evaluation purposes, the relevant estimate of the cost of capital for governments is roughly the interest rate expected to be paid on new borrowings—possibly a bit more to cover transaction costs.

However, there is merit in the argument that different discount rates should be used to evaluate proposed investments in different areas of government activity, having regard to alternative opportunities for the use of scarce resources. Managers of a profitable public trading enterprise should use a higher discount rate than that used elsewhere in the public sector to evaluate proposed expenditure on hospitals or ambulances or medical equipment.

We can observe that Australian governments are able to borrow at attractive rates—paying less interest than even the largest, blue-chip corporations. That is because markets view government borrowings as low risk, as there is little chance that Australian governments will default on repayment of interest and principal. If government borrowings were doubled or quadrupled, one might expect markets to become uneasy and for interest rates on borrowings to increase.

A few (mainly Australian) academics have suggested that the cost of capital for governments 'should be the same as for the private sector'. Since the 1980s there has been minimal academic debate about this issue, partly because most academics working in business finance or financial economics have little interest in matters of public policy. Of the few senior academics with a specialist interest in this field, most have been actively engaged in consultancy activities to support proposals for privatisation. Remarkably, these contributors appear to have largely ignored the public finance literature and discussions of the 'social discount rate'.

Not surprisingly, the idea that the cost of capital for governments 'is the same as for the private sector' has been warmly embraced by consulting firms in reports which have supported privatisation proposals (see, e.g. *Coopers & Lybrand and CS First Boston*, 1994). Indeed, one feature of the privatisation debate (particularly in Australia) has been the way that consultants have used extremely simplistic arguments to justify the use of high discount rates to assess specific privatisation proposals.

Observing this phenomenon, if it is of more than passing interest to recall the observations of some economists that 'what is at stake in the choice of a discount rate is not just the acceptance or rejection of specific projects, but also the allocation of resources between the public and private sectors of the economy' (*Brown & Jackson*, 1991).

Claims in support of the idea that *when considering the privatisation of PTEs*, the cost of capital for governments is the same as for the private sector, seem to boil down to the following four propositions.

(i) That if the cost of capital were lower for governments, then governments could buy up all the businesses in an economy

A common theme of contributors has been to use the extreme argument that if the cost of capital for the public sector is lower than that of private sector firms, then governments should 'own everything'. In this tradition, Neville Hathaway, of the Melbourne Business School wrote that if the cost of capital for government was lower than for private sector firms, then

> instead of privatising their assets governments should buy all the shares listed on the public stock exchanges. They should also undertake to invest in many of the risky new ventures that the private sector considers too marginal for investment (*Hathaway*, 1997).

On the other side of the debate has been the economist John Quiggin, who has actively contested claims that the cost of capital for the public sector should approximate that of private firms.[2]

---

2 *Quiggin* (1997) argues that the cost of capital to government will 'in general be somewhat above the real bond rate, but below the average cost of capital to private firms'.

Quiggin dignified Hathaway's claims as the 'comprehensive socialisation argument', and pointed out that use of the present value approach to assessing privatisation actually

> implies support for a mixed economy, with public ownership concentrated in areas of high capital intensity, and private ownership in areas where capital intensity is low (*Quiggin*, 1997).

As Quiggin has pointed out, few economists these days would be brave enough to base an argument on a debating device of *reductio ad absurdem*. The *reductio ad absurdem* device is a popular form of fallacious reasoning among political extremists and assorted ideologues.

Such an argument also amounts to a crude misrepresentation of the view of critics of the pro-privatisation brigade—by hinting that critics are ardent socialists intend on massive programs of nationalisation, or by suggesting that those who argue that the public sector cost of capital is lower than in the private sector are suggesting that such a relationship is invariant.

Note that the analysis of privatisation proposals set out earlier in Chapter 5 explicitly acknowledges that the cost to governments of obtaining new finance could change as debt levels rise and the market re-evaluates the risk of loss from investment in government debt securities. Moreover, the analysis is presented in the context of the low to moderate debt levels of Australian governments. Since finance academics have yet to develop models for predicting the degree of change in the cost of debt finance under those circumstances, the analysis presented earlier in this chapter suggested that interest rates under different levels of debt were likely to lie within indicative 'bands'.

(ii) That governments should use discount rates equivalent to those used by the private sector because otherwise governments would 'crowd out' private sector investment in profitable investments

Recall the economic argument concerning discount rates 'crowding out'. That is, if a government is considering a new venture which otherwise would be undertaken by private firms, then the government should only proceed if it can earn a higher rate of return than potential investors from the private sector (presumably, without resorting to monopolistic pricing). This line of argument proposes that proposals for public sector spending should be evaluated on the same basis as would be used by a private firm when considering investment in a similar venture. Otherwise, governments risk

Appendix to Chapter 5

'crowding out' private sector investment in productive ventures.

As noted above, this argument is, in itself, highly contestable.

Yet privatisation proposals are the converse of the context in which the 'crowding out' argument is advanced. Governments have *already invested* in those ventures (usually because the private sector did not find them attractive. and governments acted to remedy this market failure). The sale of PTEs will draw funds from the pool of available investment capital, thus crowding out private sector investment in new ventures in favour of already established ventures. In that sense, if 'crowding out' is undesirable for new public sector investment, then it may also be undesirable for the public sector to sell established businesses, since that would divert private capital away from other, potential profitable, start-up ventures.

(iii) That because governments are investing on behalf of individuals in society, they should use discount rates equivalent to those used by the private sector

In one sense, this argument is wonderfully inconsistent with argument (ii) above. Argument (ii) is concerned that the public sector might hog profitable investments. Argument (iii) reflects a concern that the public sector might undertake investments which are not profitable enough.

The proposition that the cost of capital for the public sector should be the same as for the private sector is sometimes 'justified' as follows:

> The government is acting for the community. Hence the government's cost of capital should be the same as for the community. Hence the cost of capital for the government should be the same as for private sector investors in the same type of project.

A difficulty with this argument is that it fails to nominate whose financial circumstances shall be taken as 'representative' of the community? Or should one look at cohorts of the community? The average shareholder? The average salary and wage-earner? Or the average member of the population—including the aged, the unemployed and children? Most of those in the latter groups could not afford to invest in the securities market or other ventures.

Or perhaps one should include the average corporation? How would one weight corporations as against individuals? Then one has to ask, 'average' in what sense? After all, highly geared firms would face a higher weighted average cost of capital than lowly-geared firms, because lending to a highly geared firm is much riskier. Should one look at the capital structure of firms already in a given industry? Or should one make assumptions about which of those firms are untypical, and exclude certain cases?

Questions like this could be multiplied. Those who advance this argument (rarely if at all in print) don't seem to be able to answer.

While reviewing these arguments, it is tempting to produce a counter *reductio ad absurdem* argument:

> Since governments can obtain debt finance more cheaply than the private sector, and it is claimed that the (weighted average) cost of capital for government is the same as for the private sector, then that means that the cost of equity finance (in the weighted average calculation) must actually be *higher* for the public sector than for the private sector.

Why? Why should the cost of equity finance for governments be higher than for private sector firms when governments can spread risks across the whole population? Well, it was only a debating point. Governments don't have an equity capital which is publicly traded.

For that reason, the main point is that governments should not mindlessly adopt a management tool which was designed for listed corporations seeking to increase the value of their shares.

(iv) *That a project should be evaluated on the basis of its risks and future cash flows, regardless of the identity of the owner (or prospective owner)*

Some proponents of privatisation, and some commentators (eg *Harris*, 1998) have argued that governments should use private sector discount rates simply because the projects (or investment alternatives) they are contemplating have the same risk as equivalent projects undertaken in the private sector. They argue that risk is a feature of projects, and is (or should be) unaffected by the identity of the 'owner'.

There are a few responses to that argument.

First, it overlooks the key and basic assumption underlying the theoretical case for the use of the weighted average cost of capital in project evaluation: the assumption that managers want to maximise the value of the firm. That assumption just does not apply in the public sector.

Second, there is the technical point that when evaluating alternative projects, interest rates should not be adjusted to cope with risk. Rather, one should hold interest rates constant and perform discounted cash flow analysis on a range of possible outcomes (i.e. a form of 'sensitivity analysis'). (One might, of course, properly use higher discount rates when trying to rank a set of relatively high risk projects than when examining low risk projects—but in this case, all within the set would be assessed on the same basis.)

Third, while private firms often set high hurdle rates for new investments, they also often then fail to achieve the returns predicted. As Alan Castleman of the Institution of Engineers observed in 1994, 'in the private sector firms say they want 15 per cent but never achieve it' (*Howe*, 1994). On that basis alone, use of inflated private sector rates to assess government-owned businesses will lead to understatement of retention values.

And fourth, these arguments ignore the existence of a longstanding public finance literature which, while disagreeing on details, reflects a consensus that the social discount rate should be lower than private sector borrowing or lending rates (let alone inflated estimates of a private sector weighted average cost of capital).

Finally, there is a respectable economic argument—known as the Arrow Lind theorem, which has been summarised as follows:

> for most cases the government can ignore risk when evaluating projects if the benefits and costs of the project are spread over a very large population and if the returns to a public sector project are distributed independently of national income. In these circumstances the value of a project can be measured by its expected value. Thus the government reduces the overall cost of bearing risk to zero in the limit. Risk aversion arises because of the diminishing marginal utility of income. As the scale of a risky project (gamble) increases, the difference between the utility of the potential income gain and the loss increases also. In other words, the average cost of the risk will (assuming risk aversion) rise with the scale of the gamble. The scale effect of risk costs provides the advantages of risk spreading. Therefore, because the public sector enjoys the advantages of diversification and risk pooling, the risk premium on government investments is lower than that on market rates of interest (*Brown & Jackson*, 1991).

What happens in practice?

The above discussion highlights the broad support in the economics literature for the proposition that public sector investment (or disinvestment) proposals should be evaluated using discount rates reflecting a lower cost of capital than that which might be used in the private sector. The few economists who have argued differently have done so in relation to highly restricted contexts (for example, where a government was contemplating investments which would increase private sector incomes) or in terms of entirely hypothetical restrictive assumptions (an economy characterised by perfect competition, in which all have perfect knowledge of the future).

On the other hand, a small group (mainly finance academics and private sector consultants) have been quite forthright in arguing that privatisation proposals should be examined by assessing the retention value of government-owned businesses with estimates of the private sector cost of capital.

These advocates of privatisation have overlooked a foundation assumption of the theoretical arguments about the private sector cost of capital: that managers of a firm are seeking to engage in projects *which will increase the value of the firm* (or its share price). Plainly such an assumption does not apply to governments, which are not in the business of trying to maximise the value of the government's net assets. Governments are elected to provide services to the community.

But what happens outside textbooks and academic articles?

Many Australian businessmen regard the proposition that 'the cost of capital to the public sector is the same as for the private sector' as nonsense:

> Generally speaking, the private sector, in terms of weighted average cost of capital, is somewhat different from weighted cost of capital for the public sector (David Lennon, Schroders Australia, in *Howe*, 1994).
>
> The cost of capital to public infrastructure providers is typically much lower than to a private provider because the public sector benefits from the pooling of its investment projects and its access to taxation to service debt (Richard Kirwin, in *Howe*, 1994).

It seems ironic that while some advocates of privatisation have insisted that government should use the *before tax* private sector cost of capital to assess retention values of privatisation targets, businessmen have been lobbying for tax breaks to reduce their finance costs for new infrastructure projects.

In any event, Treasury departments do not use estimates of the private sector cost of capital when they undertake day-to-day project evaluation. A few Treasuries or line agencies pay lip-service to what they regard as 'current thinking' by referring to the weighted average cost of capital—a concept which arguably has no relevance to the private sector. But in practice, they then assume that their sources of finance are 100 per cent debt—and use government borrowing rates. Most Treasuries simply publish the discount rates which are to be used for cost-benefit analysis, or

Appendix to Chapter 5

related purposes. Again, those rates appear to approximate the current rate at which governments can borrow.

However when a privatisation proposal is in the offing, several governments have engaged 'experts' to produce reports justifying the sale of those businesses. Rather than use the conservative discount rates routinely recommended by Treasury departments when assessing capital works proposals, the outside experts have invariably selected much higher discount rates. This leads to far lower estimates of retention values—thus tipping the analysis in favour of sale.

Ultimately, the proof of the pudding is in the eating.

Evidence is now available about the validity of some past estimates of sale and retention values for privatisation targets.

Take the advice of CS First Boston regarding discount rates to evaluate the sale or retention by the NSW Government of its poorly performing State Bank of NSW. The discount rate selected was equivalent to a rate of return of 18.9 per cent per annum *after tax*—equivalent to 29.5 per cent per annum before tax (using the 1995–96 corporate tax rate of 36 cents in the dollar). Selection of this extravagantly high discount rate substantially reduced the 'retention value' calculated for the Bank, and lent support for its privatisation. Subsequent events showed that the State Bank of NSW was sold for a fraction of its value—and at great loss to taxpayers (see Chapter 8).

References

Accounting Standards Committee (UK), Exposure draft ED42, 'Accounting for special purpose transactions', March 1988.
——, Financial Reporting Standard FRS 5, 'Reporting the substance of transactions', 1994.
Allen Consulting Group, J.B. Cox & Centre of Policy Studies, *The Economic Impact of Melbourne City Link—Transurban Project*, May 1996.
ANZ McCaughan, *The Australian Water Industry—Future Ownership Options*, 1993.
Arrow, K.J., 'The rate of discount on public investments with imperfect capital markets', in R.C. Lind (ed.), *Discounting for Time and Risk in Energy Policy*, Resources for the Future, Inc. & John Hopkins University Press, 1982.
Arrow, K.J. & M. Kurz, *Public Investment, the Rate of Return, and Optimal Fiscal Policy*, Resources for the Future, Inc. & John Hopkins Press, 1970.
Australian Accounting Research Foundation, *Private Sector Provision of Public Infrastructure*, 1997.
Australian Bureau of Statistics (ABS), *Wage and Salary Earners*, December Quarter 1998, Cat. 6248.0, April 1999.
Australian Securities Commission, *ASC Instruments*, 92/362, 92/363, 92/364, 92/365, & 92/275.
——, *ASC Memo* 11/92.
——, *ASC Practice Note 43*, August 1997.
Australian Society of Certified Practising Accountants & The Institute of Chartered Accountants in Australia (1991), Statement of Accounting Standards AAS 10, 'Accounting for the revaluation of non-current assets', 1981; revised 1991.
——, Statement of Accounting Standards AAS23, 'Set-off and extinguishment of debt', 1988; revised 1990.
——, SAP 1, 'Statement of accounting practice—current cost

References

accounting', 1976; revised 1978, 1983 and 1989.

———, Urgent Issues Group, 'Accounting for contributions of, or contributions for, the acquisition of non-current assets', 1996.

Australian Stock Exchange, *The Stock Exchange Financial and Profitability Study*, 1992.

———, *1994 Australian Shareownership Survey*.

———, *October 1998 Australian Shareownership Update*.

———, *Listing Rules*, 1999.

Australian Water Resources Council, *Interagency Performance Review*, Department of Primary Industries and Energy, Canberra, 1990.

Barrett, P., 'Wither accountability—the wisdom of Solomon', paper presented to Australian Defence College, 13 September 1999.

Bennett J.W., J. McB. Grant & R.H. Parker, *Topics in Business Finance and Accounting*, Cheshire, 1964.

Bierman H. Jr. & S. Smidt, *The Capital Budgeting Decision*, Macmillan, 1960.

Brown C.V. & P.M. Jackson, *Public Sector Economics*, Basil Blackwell, 4th edition, 1991.

Canadian Institute of Accountants (CICA), *Financial Reporting by Governments*, 1980.

Commonwealth Auditor-General, *Sale of One-third of Telstra*, 1998.

———, *Management of Contracted Business Support Processes*, October 1999.

———, *Financial Aspects of the Conversion to Digital Broadcasting: Australian Broadcasting Corporation*, September 1999.

Commonwealth Department of Finance, 'Invitation to register interest in acquiring the Moomba-Sydney gas pipeline system', 1989.

Commonwealth Department of Finance & Administration, *Competitive Tendering and Contracting—Guidance for Managers*, exposure draft, 1997.

———, *Competitive Tendering and Contracting*, 1998.

Commonwealth Department of Treasury, *Financial Monitoring of the Government Business Enterprises—an Economic Framework*, 1990.

Commonwealth Government, *One Nation*, 1992.

———, *Working Nation*, 1994.

———, Management Advisory Board, *Beyond Bean Counting*, 1997.

Coopers & Lybrand & CS First Boston, 'Report to the Auditor-General: proposed sale of State Bank NSW', in Auditor-General of NSW, *Special Audit Report: Proposed Sale of the State Bank of New South Wales*, November 1994; complete version in Auditor-General of NSW, *Report to Parliament for 1999*, Vol. 1, 1999.

Curran Committee of Inquiry into Prospect County Council, *Challenges in Prospect*, NSW Government, 1992.

Dean, J, *Capital Budgeting*, Columbia University Press, 1951.

Dempster, Q., *Whistleblowers*, ABC Books, 1997.

Domberger, S., 'Public sector contracting: does it work?', *Australian Economic Review*, 3rd quarter, 1994.

——, *The Contracting Organization*, Oxford, 1998.

Domberger, S. & J. Piggott, 'Privatisation policies and public enterprise: a survey', *Economic Record*, June 1986.

Domberger, S., S.A. Meadowcroft & D.J. Thompson, 'Competitive tendering and efficiency: the case of refuse collection', *Fiscal Studies*, Vol. 7, 1986.

——, 'Competition and efficiency in refuse collection: a reply', *Fiscal Studies*, Vol. 9, 1988.

Economic Planning Advisory Council (EPAC), *The Size and Efficiency of the Public Sector*, October 1990.

——, *Profitability and Productivity of Government Business Enterprises*, Research Paper No. 2, prepared by R. Clare & K. Johnston, August 1992.

——, *Private Infrastructure Task Force Interim Report*, May 1995.

——, *Private Infrastructure Task Force Report*, September 1995.

Egan, M., *A plan for a secure New South Wales*, May 1997.

Federal Liberal Party/National Party, *Fightback! Taxation and Expenditure Reform for Jobs and Growth*, 1991.

Feldstein, M.S., 'Comment', in R.C. Lind (ed.), *Discounting for Time and Risk in Energy Policy*, Resources for the Future, Inc. & John Hopkins University Press, 1982.

Financial Accounting Standards Board, Statement of Financial Accounting Standards FAS 48, 'Revenue recognition when right of return exists', June 1981.

Fisher, I., *The Nature of Capital and Income*, 1906; reprinted Augustus M. Kelly, 1965.

Fitzgerald, V. W., J. Carmichael, D.D. Mcdonough & B. Thornton, *Report of the Queensland Commission of Audit*, June 1996.

Ganley, J. & J. Grahl, 'Competition and efficiency in refuse collection: a critical comment', *Fiscal Studies*, Vol. 8, 1987.

Groenewegen, P., *Public Finance in Australia*, 2nd edition, Prentice-Hall Australia, 1984.

Harris, A. C., 'Credulity and credibility in infrastructure funding', paper presented at the 'BOOT—in the public interest?' conference, University of Technology, Sydney, 1998.

Hathaway, N., 'Privatisation and the government cost of capital', *Agenda*, Vol. 4, No. 2, 1997.

Hayward, D. & M. Salvaris, 'Rating the states: credit rating

References

agencies and the Australian state governments', *Journal of Australian Political Economy*, December 1994.

Hilmer, F.G., *Strictly Boardroom*, Information Australia & The Sydney Institute, 1993.

Hodge, G., *Contracting Out Government Services: A Review of International Evidence*, Montech, 1996.

Howard, J., 'A healthy public service is a vital part of Australia's democratic system of government', *Australian Journal of Public Administration*, March 1998.

Howe, B. (convenor), *Investing in Infrastructure*, proceedings of a seminar convened by Brian Howe MP, Deputy Prime Minister, August 1994.

Independent Commission Against Corruption [NSW], *Private Contractors' Perceptions of Working for the NSW Public Sector*, January 1999.

Independent Commission to Review State Finances [WA], *Agenda for Reform*, June 1993.

Independent Commission to Review Tasmania's Public Sector Finances, *Tasmania in the Nineties*, April 1992.

Independent Review of Victoria's Public Sector Finances (Nicholl's Report), *State Finance Victoria*, September 1992.

Industry Commission, *Measuring the Performance of Selected Government Business Enterprises*, August 1990.

——, *Water Resources and Waste Water Disposal*, Draft Report, 1992.

Laffin M. & M. Painter (eds.), *Reform and Reversal—Lessons from the Coalition Government in New South Wales 1988–1995*, Macmillan, 1995.

Lewellen, W.G., *The Cost of Capital*, Wadsworth, 1969.

Lind. R.C., 'A primer on the major issues relating to the discount rate for evaluating national energy options', in R.C. Lind (ed.), *Discounting for Time and Risk in Energy Policy*, Resources for the Future, Inc. & John Hopkins University Press, 1982.

Loan Council of Australia, *Guide to the Global Limits*, May 1991.

——, *Future Arrangements for Loan Council Monitoring and Reporting*, July 1993.

Megginson W.L., R.C. Nash & M. Van Randenborgh, 'The financial and operating performance of newly privatised firms: an international empirical analysis', *Journal of Finance*, June 1994.

Mintzberg, H., 'Managing government—governing management', *Harvard Business Review*, May–June 1996.

Morkel, A., *Company Directors' Handbook*, Australian Institute of Company Directors, 1990.

National Association of Accountants (NAA), *Financial Analysis to Guide Capital Expenditure Decisions*, 1967.

National Audit Office (UK), *Report by the Comptroller and Auditor General on Sale of the Twelve Regional Electricity Companies*, HMSO, 1992.
National Commission of Audit, *Report to the Commonwealth Government*, June 1996.
Nicholls, D., *How the Government has Performed 1988–91*, NSW Government, November 1991.
NSW Auditor-General, *Report to Parliament for 1994*, Vol. 2, 1994.
——, *Private Participation in the Provision of Public Infrastructure*, Vol. 1, October 1994.
——, *Special Audit Report: Proposed Sale of the State Bank of New South Wales*, January 1995.
——, *Report to Parliament for 1998*, Vol. 2, 1998.
——, *Report to Parliament for 1999*, Vol. 1, 1999.
NSW Commission of Audit, *Focus on Reform*, 1988.
NSW Council on the Cost of Government (COCOG), *First Report*, June 1996.
——, *Service Competition Guidelines*, 1997.
——, *Fifth Report*, June 1998.
——, *Sixth Report*, December 1998.
——, *Seventh Report*, June 1999.
NSW Department of State Development, *Guidelines for Private Sector Participation in Infrastructure Provision*, nd, circa 1988.
——, *Guidelines for Private Sector Participation in Infrastructure Provision*, July 1990.
NSW Government, *Microeconomic Reform: The NSW Government's Achievements*, June 1990.
NSW Joint Parliamentary Inquiry by the Public Bodies Review Committee and the Standing Committee on Public Works, *Report on Competitive Tendering and Contracting in the NSW Public Sector*, December 1998.
NSW Liberal Party/National Party of Australia, *Investing in Our Future: Coalition Energy Reform Plan*, February 1999.
NSW Public Accounts Committee, *Report on Superannuation Liabilities of Statutory Authorities*, August 1984.
——, *Infrastructure Management and Financing in New South Wales*—Vol. 2, 'Public-private partnerships—risk and return in infrastructure financing', February 1994.
NSW Premier's Department, *Competitive Tendering and Contracting Out—Guidelines*, 1991.
——, *Competitive Tendering and Contracting Out—Costing Guidelines*, 1992.
NSW Treasury, *Guidelines for Private Sector Participation in Infrastructure Provision*, July 1990.

References

——, 'Public authority pricing in New South Wales', *Research Paper*, January 1992.

——, Circular G1992/3, 'Accounting for contributions', February 1992.

——, *Competitive Tendering and Contracting in the NSW Budget Sector—1994 Survey Findings*, 1994.

——, *Guidelines for Private Sector Participation in the Provision of Public Infrastructure*, September 1995.

——, *Contracting of Services in the NSW Public Sector—1995 Survey Findings*, May 1996.

——, *Implementing Contracting Policy in New South Wales—Lessons from Initial Experience*, September 1996.

——, *Contracting for Services in the NSW Public Sector—1996 Survey Findings*, February 1997.

Organisation for Economic Co-operation and Development, *OECD Economic Outlook 64*, December 1998.

Osborne D. & T. Gaebler, *Reinventing Government*, Addison-Wesley, 1992.

Paddon, M., 'The real costs of contracting out: re-assessing the Australian debate from UK experience', UNSW Public Sector Research Centre, *Discussion Paper*, 1991.

Productivity Commission, *Private Investment in Urban Roads*, 1997.

——, *Performance of Government Trading Enterprises 1991–92 to 1996–97*, 1998.

——, *Australia's Gambling Industries, Draft Report*, July 1999.

Pusey, M., *Economic Rationalism in Canberra*, Cambridge, 1991.

Queensland Treasury, *Output Costing Guidelines*, September 1998.

Quiggin, J., 'Does privatisation pay?', *Australian Economic Review*, 1995.

——, 'The equity premium and the government cost of capital: a response to Neville Hathaway', *Agenda*, Vol. 4, No. 4, 1997.

Quiggin, J., H. Saddler, M. Neutze, C. Hamilton & H. Turton, *The Privatisation of ACTEW*, Australia Institute, Discussion Paper 20, December 1998.

Rappaport, A., 'Divisional cost analysis for decision making and performance evaluation', in S. Davidson & R.L. Weil (eds), *Handbook of Cost Accounting*, McGraw Hill, 1978.

Report of the Committee of Inquiry into Sale of the NSW Electricity Assets ('Hogg Report'), 1997.

Report of the Victorian Commission of Audit, May 1993.

Reserve Bank of Australia, 'Privatisation in Australia', *Bulletin*, December 1997.

——, 'Demutualisation in Australia', *Bulletin*, January 1999.

Robinson, P., 'New tunes for the infrastructure piper', *Decisions*, June 1994.
Rosen, B., *Holding Government Bureaucracies Accountable*, Praeger, 1989.
Rosen, H.S., *Public Finance*, Irwin, 4th edition, 1995.
Saunders, C., 'Government borrowing in Australia', *Melbourne University Law Review*, December 1989.
Self, P, 'Nonsense on stilts', *New Society*, 2 July 1970.
Senate Finance and Public Administration Committee, *Contracting Out of Government Services: First Report—Information Technology*, Parliament of Australia, 1997.
Sidey, R.L., *The Valuation of Shares*, Law Book Company, 1950.
Solomon, E., 'The arithmetic of capital budgeting decisions', *Journal of Business*, April 1956, reprinted in E. Solomon (ed.), *The Management of Corporate Capital*, Free Press, 1959.
South Australian Commission of Audit, *Charting the Way Forward: Improving public sector performance*, April 1994.
South Australia Government, *Competitive Tendering and Contracting—Framework and Guidelines*, July 1995.
Sprague E. & L.L. Perrine, *The Accountancy of Investment*, Ronald, 1919.
Steering Committee for the Review of Commonwealth State Service Provision, *Report on Government Service Provision 1998*, Commonwealth of Australia, 1999.
Steering Committee on National Performance Monitoring of Government Trading Enterprises, *Government Trading Enterprises Performance Indicators 1987–88 to 1991–92*, July 1993.
——, *Guidelines on Accounting Policy for the Valuation of Assets of Government Trading Enterprises*, October 1994.
——, *Government Trading Enterprises Performance Indicators 1991–92 to 1995–96*, May 1997.
Stephanopoulos, G., *All Too Human*, Little Brown, 1999.
Stewart, M., 'Should we concern ourselves with foreign debt?', *Economic Papers*, March 1994.
Stiglitz, J.E., *Economics of the Public Sector*, W.W. Norton, 2nd edition, 1986.
Sturgess, G., 'Virtual government: what will remain inside the public sector?', *The Australian Journal of Public Administration*, September 1996.
Temple-Heald, S., 'The importance of asset valuation and implications for performance monitoring of GTEs', Industry Commission, *Research Unit Working Paper*, 1991.
United Nations, *A System of National Accounts*, New York, 1968.
——, *Revised System of National Accounts: Draft Chapters and Annexes, New York*, nd, circa 1993.

References

Vickers I. & G. Yarrow, *Privatization: Economic Analysis*, MIT Press, 1988.

Victorian Department of Treasury & Finance, *Outsourcing and Contract Management Guidelines*, 1995.

Victorian Government, 'Public authority pricing and rate of return reporting', *Information Paper*, No. 1, 1986.

Walker, R.G., 'Losing the tax in the trees', *Australian Business*, 9 March 1988.

——, 'When options are called to account', *New Accountant*, 23 March 1989.

——, 'NSW Water Board pumps up its value', *New Accountant*, 13 December 1990.

——, 'How NSW managed to hide a $1.2 billion deficit', *New Accountant*, 2 May 1991.

——, 'The SEC's ban on upward asset revaluations and the disclosure of current values', *Abacus*, No. 1, 1992.

——, *The Curran Report—a Response*, report prepared for Prospect County Council, January 1993.

——, 'How a water board became a milch cow', *The Sydney Morning Herald*, 23 February 1993.

—— 'Evaluating the financial performance of Australian water authorities', in M. Johnston & S. Rix (eds), *Water in Australia*, Pluto Press, 1993.

——, 'Sydney's airport link: anatomy of a deal—a case study of private sector involvement in a public infrastructure project', *Working Paper*, Public Sector Research Centre, University of New South Wales, 1994.

——, 'Privatisation—a reassessment', University of NSW School of Accounting, *Working Paper Series*, November 1994.

——, 'Why Parlt must scrutinise projects with private sector', *The Sydney Morning Herald*, 18 October 1994.

——, 'One-sided scrutiny of the State Bank sale just not good enough', *The Sydney Morning Herald*, 22 November 1994.

——, 'Privatisation—a reassessment', *Journal of Australian Political Economy*, October 1995.

——, *Reporting on Service Efforts and Accomplishments in the NSW Public Sector*, NSW Council on the Cost of Government, 1999.

Walker, R.G., F.L. Clarke & G.W. Dean, 'The use of replacement price accounting to shape perceptions and "control" the public sector', *UNSW School of Accounting Working Paper*, 1997.

——, 'Reporting on the state of infrastructure by local government', *Accounting, Auditing and Accountability Journal*, Vol. 12, No 4, 1999.

——, 'Use of CCA in the public sector: lessons from Australia's experience', *Financial Accountability and Management*, 2000.

Walker R.G. & M. Howard, 'Implementing privatisation: the case of the GIO float', *UNSW Public Sector Research Centre Working Paper*, September 1992.

Webb, E.J., D.T. Campbell, R.D. Schwartz & L. Sechrest, *Unobtrusive Measures: Non-reactive Research in the Social Sciences*, Rand McNally, 1966.

Weil, R.L., 'Capital budgeting', in S. Davidson & R.L. Weil (eds), *Handbook of Cost Accounting*, McGraw Hill, 1978.

Western Australia Public Sector Management Office & State Supply Commission, *Competitive Tendering and Contracting—Framework and Guidelines*, July 1995.

Western Australia Treasury, 'Costing guidelines for use by agencies', 2nd edition, July 1995, in W.A. Public Sector Management Office & State Supply Commission, *Competitive Tendering and Contracting—Framework and Guidelines*, July 1995.

Woo, L. & H.P. Lange, 'Equity raising by Australian small business: a study of success and survival', *Small Enterprise Research Journal*, Winter 1992.

Index

ABC 281
ABN AMRO
  Rothschild 140, 226–7
Accounting standards 52, 98–101, 165, 189n, 192, 222
ACTEW 140–1
AGL Ltd 257, 259–65, 262–3
AIDC Ltd 232
Aiken, P. 264
Airlines 279–80
Airport Link, Sydney
  Airlink 204–7
Airports 1, 4, 18, 20, 85
Air safety 280
Allan, P. 59, 81
Alston, R. 27, 32, 67–8, 77–9
AMP 248
ANL Ltd 242–7
ANZ McCaughan 110–1
Arrow, K. 311
Arrow, K.J. & M. Kurz 312
Arthur Andersen 81, 244–5
Asset Sales Task Force 231, 241, 245, 261–2
Auditors-General 10, 30, 45, 46n, 67–8, 103, 105, 154, 186–7, 205, 218, 222, 228, 285, 288–9, 291
Austin, P. 30

Australia Institute 141, 238–9
Australia Post 32
Australian Accounting
  Research Foundation 96, 110, 222
Australian Airlines 11
Australian Bureau of
  Statistics 5n, 14, 43, 45, 49, 54, 181, 288
Australian Communications
  Authority 27
Australian Council for
  Infrastructure
  Development 70, 75, 80
Australian National Audit
  Office 244, 288
Australian National
  Line 242–7
Australian National Railways
  Corporation 18
Australian Resources
  Council 104
Australian River Co. 247n
Australian Securities &
  Investments
  Commission 313
Australian Securities
  Commission 251–3, 256, 270, 314

Australian Shareholders' Association 16, 237
Australian Society of Certified Practising Accountants 297
Australian Stevedores 243–4
Australian Stock Exchange 11, 84, 105–6, 229, 289–90
Avoidable costs 171, 173, 176
AWA Ltd 74

Baird, B. 206, 216–8
Banks 4, 26
BankWest 24
Barrett, P. 292
Beazley, K. 232, 263
Bennett, J.W., J.McB. Grant & R.H.Parker 305
BHP 264
Bierman, H. Jr & S. Smidt 304, 305n, 307
Bleasel, L. 263
Blount, F. 77
Bolitho, B. 244
Bond, A., Bond Corporation 190, 274
BOOT schemes 10, 29, 32, 33, 193, 196, 202–23, 285, 291, 298
Borbidge government 29
Brereton, L. 243–4, 246–7
British Airways 19
British Gas 250
British Telecom 250
Brown, C.V. & P.M. Jackson 315, 319
BT Investment Bank 203
Budget 'black holes' 42, 44–7
Budget results 14, 42, 44, 46, 83, 139, 262, 288
Burge, G. 267

Cable & Wireless Optus 84, 225
Cain government 12
Capital charges 175
Capital structure 116–7, 124, 129–32, 137
Carr, B., Carr government 29–30, 50, 53, 175, 267–8, 297
Chikarovski, K. 53
Clinton, B., Clinton Administration 75, 150
CML Ltd 84, 268, 270, 272, 274
Collins, B. 244
Collins, P. 50, 59, 155, 205, 265, 267
Commonwealth Auditor-General 174, 228, 244, 281, 292
Commonwealth Bank of Australia 11, 18, 20, 24, 84, 229–30, 251–3
Commonwealth Department of Finance 91, 165, 231, 261
Commonwealth Grants Commission 242
Commonwealth Management Advisory Board 287, 296
Community service obligations 71
Community services 33
Compulsory competitive tendering 172
Connor, R. 257
Contract summaries 218–221, 291
Contracting out 15, 34, 38, 144–88
Coopers & Lybrand 47, 268–71, 315
Corruption 75–6, 223
Cost of capital 126–7, 131,

Index

137, 143, 210–211, 271, 300–21
Costello, P. 27, 51–5, 78–9, 201
Council on the Cost of Government 156, 159, 163–4, 168, 170–2, 175, 286–7, 297
Court, R., Court government 49
Creative accounting 119–20
Credit ratings 16, 59–63, 126
CS First Boston 226–7, 268–71, 315, 321
Crowding out 312, 316–7
CSL Ltd 24, 84, 224–5, 234–40
Curran Committee 94–5
Curran Commission of Audit 39, 40
Current cost accounting 89–90, 96, 100–1, 110, 112–5

Davidson, K. 246–7
Dean, J. 301, 307
Debt, public sector (government) 2, 37, 54, 56–7, 196, 201
Debt, national 54–5
Debt, net 50, 52–4, 56, 65
Debt reduction 2, 3, 14, 48–9, 51, 58–9, 136, 222, 263, 283, 289–90
Debt versus liabilities 53, 56, 289–90
Deloitte Consulting 29
Dempster, Q. 102–3, 243–4, 250, 288
Deprival value 96, 101, 113
Deutsche Morgan Grenfell 29, 81

'Different costs for different purposes' 192
Domberger, S. 155–61
Domberger, S., S.A. Meadowcraft & D.J. Thompson 156–7
Domberger, S. & J. Piggott 136, 155
Drewry Shipping Consultants 246

Eastern Creek Raceway 12
Eastern Distributor 211, 273n
Economic vandalism 4
Education 15, 34, 35
Efficiency 2, 3, 125, 134, 149, 184, 288
Egan, M. 29, 81, 268
Elcom 45, 90–1
Electricity 4, 9, 18–19, 21, 29–30, 52, 68, 72–3, 80–82, 85, 93–5, 111, 119, 142, 148, 278, 280–1
Employment 9, 14
Environmental damage 9–10
EPAC 105–7, 108–9, 218
Ernst & Young 244
European Community 57

Fahey, J. 27, 50, 60, 72, 155, 267, 273–4
Fels, A. 263
Feldstein, M.S. 311
Ferguson, A. 203
Financial engineering 189–90
Financial qualifications 5, 7, 295–8
Fisher, I. 301
Franchising 31–33, 35
Fraser government 231
Freedom of Information 6, 216

Funder/provider model 151–3

Gaming 1, 233–4
Ganley, J. & J. Grahl 156–7
Gas 4, 9, 18–9, 21, 111, 257–65
GE Capital 232
GIO 11, 65, 84, 127, 224, 247–56
Global limits 191–5, 221
'Good idea' budgeting 162
Gottliebsen, R. 256
Government finance statistics 43
Greiner, N., Greiner government 39, 47, 76–7, 93–4, 146, 155, 181, 206, 247, 253, 255, 276
Griffiths, A. 29
Groenewegen, P. 296, 312
Guidelines on costing 7, 173, 175
Guidelines on outsourcing 169, 172–6, 179

Hambros Australia 235
Hamilton, C. 238
Harris, T. 155, 178, 186, 212–3, 217, 223, 268–72, 274, 295, 318
Hathaway, N. 271, 315–6
Hawke government 186, 241
Hayward, D. & M. Salvaris 60
Health services 15, 31, 33
Hill, R. 67
Hills Motorway 217–8
Hilmer, F. 71–4, 81, 102–3
Hodge, G. 156, 158, 177
Hogg Report 80–1
Hooker Corporation 52

Horton, M. 267
Housing Loans Insurance Corporation 21, 140, 230–3, 240–2
Howard, J., Howard government 26–7, 35, 67, 181, 231, 242, 278–9
Howard Smith 243–4
Howe, B. 319–20
Human services 34
Hungarian TAB 12

Independent Commission Against Corruption 76
Independent Commission to Review State Finances (WA) 48n, 69
Independent Commission to Review Tasmania's Public Sector Finances 48n
Industry Commission 92, 95–7, 104–5, 107–9, 118
Inefficiency 38
Information technology 86, 281
Infrastructure 10, 15, 27, 29, 31, 32, 86, 108, 142, 199, 202–3, 222. 280–1, 290–1, 311
Institute of Chartered Accountants in Australia 297
Insurance companies 26

Jails 1, 4, 33, 177, 182
Jamieson Equities 243
J B Were & Son 226–7
Joss, B. 77

Keating, P., Keating government 218, 225, 242
Kennett, J., Kennett

government 14, 28–9, 32, 40–1, 47, 60, 112, 186–7, 216
Kirner government 41

Lambert, M. 81
Lewellen, W.G. 306
Liabilities 289
Lind, R.C. 311, 313
Loan Council 8, 190–202, 221
Loan Council allocations 196–8, 200–1
Local government 290–1
Low balling 178
Loy Yang B. 19

M2, M4 & M5 Tollways 208, 211, 213, 217–8
Maastricht Treaty 56–8
Mackay, H. 183
Macquarie Bank 211, 217
McCrann, T. 61
McNamee, B. 235–9
Management information systems 156, 161–5, 170, 286–7, 296–8
Maritime Services Board 147
Maritime Union of Australia 243
Market failure 11–2, 64
Master Builders Association 231
Medibank Private 31
Megginson, W.L., R.C. Nash & M. Van Randenborgh 136
Melbourne Electricity 105
Melbourne Water 28
Mintzberg, H. 276–7, 294n

Moodys 59, 61, 232
Moomba–Sydney Gas Pipeline System 261
Morkel, A. 92
Morris, D. 75

National Audit Office (UK) 127, 251
National Association of Accountants 305
National competition policy 30, 70, 72, 124
Nicholls, D. 41, 45, 62
NMB&B/Weekes Morris Osborn 252
NSW Commission of Audit 48n
NSW Department of State Development 216, 296
NSW Equity Trust 195
NSW Independent Pricing and Regulatory Tribunal 264
NSW Public Accounts Committee 180, 206, 214, 218, 223
NSW TAB 24, 233
NSW Treasury 96, 105, 107, 158–60, 216
NSW Treasury Corporation 62

OECD 17, 56–7, 79
Office of Asset Sales and IT Outsourcing 226, 228, 247n
Osborne, D. & T. Gaebler 150
Outsourcing (also see contracting out) 31, 144ff, 298

Pacific Power   45, 71–4, 81,
   98–9, 102–3, 280
Paddon, M.   156–7
Parliamentary scrutiny   6, 7–8,
   15, 86, 268, 285, 288–9,
   299
Perry, M.   214
Perth Southern Suburbs
   Railway   194
Phillips, R.   81
Piggott, J.   155
Pipeline Authority   140,
   257–65
Police services   33
Porter, M.   34
Powercor Australia   74
Pre-prospectus
   advertising   10, 252–7
Price Waterhouse   244–6
Productivity
   Commission   118–9, 223,
   234
Prospect Electricity   98–9,
   102, 107–8
Prices Justification
   Tribunal   242
Prices Surveillance
   Authority   242
Public safety   33
Pusey, M.   60, 295

Qantas   11, 18, 19, 24
Queensland Commission of
   Audit   29
Queensland Power Trading
   Corporation   280
Queensland TAB   233
Quiggin, J.   140, 238, 312,
   315–6
Quiggin, J., H. Saddler, M.
   Neutze, C. Hamilton & M.
   Turton   141

Rappaport, A.   307
Reagan, R.   3
Reagan-Bush
   administration   3
Recoverable amount
   test   101–2 113–5
Removals Australia   186
Reserve Bank   19, 23
Retention value   69, 129,
   137–8, 143, 271, 300, 321
Roads & Traffic Authority
   (NSW)   76, 217–8
Robinson, P.   139
Robinson, Peter   241
Robson, K.   98
Role of government   1, 4, 26,
   276–82
Roosevelt, T.   294
Rosen, B.   292, 312

SA Commission of Audit   48n
SA Water   28
Salomon Bros   244–6
Saunders, C.   190
SCADA   261
Schroders Australia   320
Securities and Exchange
   Commission   88, 250
Senate Finance and Public
   Administration
   Committee   292
Self, P.   219
Service levels   9, 11, 152, 284
Service quality   151, 154,
   173–4, 177, 179, 184–5,
   187, 291–2
Share ownership   10–11
Shortland Electricity   108
Sidey, R.L.   313
Smaller government   2, 3, 14
Snowdon, W.   27
Solomon, E.   305
Souris, G.   81, 250, 253–5

Index

Special Premiers' Conference   91
Sprague, E. & L.L. Perrine   301
Standard & Poors   59, 232
State Bank of NSW   11, 21, 60, 65, 84, 139, 265–74, 321
State Bank of Victoria   18, 127, 249
State Rail Authority (NSW)   76, 146–7, 205
State Transit Authority (NSW)   76, 147
Statewide Roads   208
Steering Committee for the Review of Commonwealth State Service Provision   287
Steering Committee on National Performance Monitoring of GTEs   92, 95–7, 118
Steering not rowing   150–1, 153, 186
Stephanopolous, G.   75
Stiglitz, J.E.   304, 312
Sturgess, G.   39, 276
Substance over form   41, 189, 203
Superannuation   119, 156, 180–2
Sutherland, S.   240
Sydney Electricity   108
Sydney Institute   74
Sydney Water   45, 71, 91, 98–9, 105, 107, 111
System of National Accounts   43

Tabcorp   24
Take or pay contracts   193
Talbot, J.   70, 75, 80
Tasman Institute   34
Telecom   116, 225

Telecommunications   4, 26–8, 278
Telstra   11, 18, 19, 24, 26–8, 49, 51, 53, 56, 67, 72, 77–8, 84, 225–9, 234, 257, 274, 281, 290
Temple-Heald, S.   97
Thatcher, M., Thatcher government   3, 157
Thomson Financial Securities   18
Time horizons   63–4, 171, 174
Toll roads, tollways   4, 15, 30, 70
Trade Practices Commission   263
Transaction costs   127, 137
Transport   12, 18, 30–1, 70, 111, 281
Transurban tollroad   209–11, 216

United Water   28
United Nations   43
User pays   13, 35

Vass, N.   273n
Vickers, I. & G. Yarrow   127, 251
Victorian Commission of Audit   40–1, 47, 48n
Victorian Equity Trust   194
Virtual government   276–7
Voluntarism   33

Walker, R.G., F.L. Clarke & G.W. Dean   103, 107, 291
Walker, R.G. & M. Howard   127, 250
Warby, M.   26
Water, waste water   4, 28–9,

32, 69, 86, 110–1, 142, 212, 278, 280
Water Watch 28
Webb, E.J., D.T. Campbell, R.D. Schwartz & L. Sechrest 159
Wealth transfers 9, 24–5
Weil, R.L. 305, 307
Westminster system, tradition 6–8, 214–5, 285, 292–3

Whitlam government 180, 257
Willis, R. 55, 200, 232, 262
Woo, L. & H.P. Lange 127, 248
Wran government 191

Zeller, F. 267